The French Film Musical

The French Film Musical

Phil Powrie and Marie Cadalanu

BLOOMSBURY ACADEMIC
LONDON • NEW YORK • OXFORD • NEW DELHI • SYDNEY

BLOOMSBURY ACADEMIC
Bloomsbury Publishing Inc
50 Bedford Square, London, WC1B 3DP, UK
1385 Broadway, New York, NY 10018, USA
29 Earlsfort Terrace, Dublin 2, Ireland

BLOOMSBURY, BLOOMSBURY ACADEMIC and the Diana logo are trademarks of Bloomsbury Publishing Plc

First published in the United States of America 2020
Paperback edition published in 2023

Copyright © Phil Powrie and Marie Cadalanu, 2020

For legal purposes the Acknowledgements on p. xii constitute an extension of this copyright page.

Cover design by Eleanor Rose
Cover image: Still from La crise est finie (The Crisis Is Over, 1934, dir. Robert Siodmak © ArenaPAL

All rights reserved. No part of this publication may be reproduced or transmitted in any form or by any means, electronic or mechanical, including photocopying, recording, or any information storage or retrieval system, without prior permission in writing from the publishers.

Bloomsbury Publishing Inc does not have any control over, or responsibility for, any third-party websites referred to or in this book. All internet addresses given in this book were correct at the time of going to press. The author and publisher regret any inconvenience caused if addresses have changed or sites have ceased to exist, but can accept no responsibility for any such changes.

Library of Congress Cataloging-in-Publication Data

Names: Powrie, Phil, author. | Cadalanu, Marie, author.
Title: The French film musical / Phil Powrie and Marie Cadalanu.
Description: New York: Bloomsbury Academic, 2020. | Includes bibliographical references, fimography, and index.
Identifiers: LCCN 2020009512 | ISBN 9781501329807 (hardback) | ISBN 9781501329777 (pdf) | ISBN 9781501329784 (ebook)
Subjects: LCSH: Musical films–France–History and criticism.
Classification: LCC PN1995.9.M86 P96 2020 | DDC 791.43/6–dc23
LC record available at https://lccn.loc.gov/2020009512

ISBN: HB: 978-1-5013-2980-7
PB: 978-1-5013-7387-9
ePDF: 978-1-5013-2977-7
eBook: 978-1-5013-2978-4

Typeset by Deanta Global Publishing Services, Chennai, India

To find out more about our authors and books visit www.bloomsbury.com and sign up for our newsletters.

In memory of Danielle Darrieux (1917–2017), Michel Legrand (1932–2019), Michel Piccoli (1925–2020) and Agnès Varda (1928–2019), who passed away while we were writing this book

Contents

List of illustrations		viii
Note on the text		xi
Acknowledgements		xii
1	Introduction	1
2	Multi-language versions	13
3	The French operetta film	29
4	Pills and Tabet and the Marseille operetta	43
5	Fréhel and Édith Piaf	57
6	Josephine Baker and Charles Trenet	67
7	The classical music film	79
8	The big-band film	89
9	The musical sketch film	103
10	Tino Rossi	113
11	Georges Guétary and Luis Mariano	129
12	The transition to the modern musical	145
13	Jacques Demy	159
14	Around Demy	175
15	The opera film and the modern classical music film	191
16	The modern auteur musical	205
17	The fairy-tale musical and the documentary musical	223
18	Conclusion: The musical and nostalgia	233
Filmography		247
References		262
Index		280

Illustrations

Figures

1.1	The Opéra-Lyrique sequence in *Le Million*	4
1.2	The main periods of activity for the French film musical	11
2.1	Modernity in *Le Chemin du paradis*	16
2.2	The final number in *Le Chemin du paradis*	18
2.3	The arrival of the Tsar in *Le congrès s'amuse*	20
2.4	Henri Garat as Mack the Knife in *L'Opéra de quat' sous*	25
2.5	The opening ball sequence in Grémillon's *Valse royale*	27
3.1	Georges Milton sings 'La Fille du Bédouin' in *Le Comte Obligado*	30
3.2	The first shots of *Ciboulette*	31
3.3	A portrait sings in *Il est charmant*	35
3.4	A comparison of the first sequence of *Gold Diggers of 1933* and the final sequence of *La crise est finie*	38
3.5	The start of the final sequence of *La crise est finie*	38
3.6	Marcel and his piano at the top of the fantasy tropical island in *La crise est finie*	40
4.1	Jungle drums in *Toi c'est moi*	46
4.2	Jacques and Maricousa in paradise in *Toi c'est moi*	49
4.3	The title song in *Prends la route*	50
4.4	Nine sings to her miniature lover Jean in *Les Gangsters du château d'If*	54
4.5	Busby Berkeley-style overhead shots in *Titin des Martigues*	54
4.6	Alibert singing 'J'aime la mer comme une femme' in *Un de la Canebière*	55
5.1	Piaf singing 'Mariage' in *Étoile sans lumière* (Courtesy M6 Vidéo)	63
5.2	Piaf sings 'Hymne à l'amour' in *Paris chante toujours*	64
5.3	Piaf plays the *chanteuse réaliste* Eugénie Buffet in *French Cancan*	66
6.1	The opening sequence of *Zouzou*	70
6.2	The spiral motif in the first part of the party in *Princesse Tam-Tam*	72
6.3	Aouïna on stage in *Princesse Tam-Tam*	73
6.4	'Quand un facteur s'envole' from *Adieu Léonard*	76
7.1	Beethoven realizes he is going deaf in *Un grand amour de Beethoven*	83
7.2	The storm in *Un grand amour de Beethoven*	83
7.3	The storm in *Louise*	86
7.4	The storm in *La Symphonie fantastique*	88
8.1	'Comme tout le monde' in *Feux de joie*	95
8.2	Christine paints half her face black in *Mademoiselle s'amuse*	97

8.3	Different communities and nationalities come together in *Nous irons à Monte-Carlo*	99
8.4	'À la mi-août' in *Nous irons à Paris*	100
9.1	Paris locations in *Paris chante toujours*	105
9.2	The uncle records a TV message in *Paris chante toujours*	107
9.3	The inside of the TV studio in the Georges Guétary sketch in *Paris chante toujours*	107
9.4	Charles Aznavour sings 'Viens pleurer au coin de mon épaule' ('Come and Cry on my Shoulder') in *C'est arrivé à 36 chandelles*	108
10.1	Renée compares the two performances on disc and on radio in *Le Chanteur inconnu*	122
10.2	'Tango d'un soir' repeated in *Sérénade aux nuages*	123
10.3	Fred and André in *Destins*	124
10.4	Sylvain and Désiré in *Deux amours*	124
10.5	Désiré in *Deux amours*	125
10.6	'Petit Papa Noël' in *Destins*	127
11.1	'On peut blaguer l'amour' in *Plume au vent*	133
11.2	'C'est tout Paris' in *Plume au vent*	134
11.3	'I'll Build a Stairway to Paradise' in *An American in Paris*	134
11.4	The dream sequence in *Plume au vent*	135
11.5	Mariano's Hispanic and exotic costumes	140
11.6	Mariano sings 'Rossignol' in *Le Chanteur de Mexico*	140
12.1	Jeanmaire's two showcase numbers in *Folies-Bergère*	146
12.2	Echoes of 'Girl Hunt' in *Folies-Bergère*	147
12.3	'La Java' and 'Ça, c'est Paris' in *Folies-Bergère*	148
12.4	Johnny as 'cowboy' in *D'où viens-tu, Johnny?*	153
12.5	Johnny and Django fight in *D'où viens-tu, Johnny?*	156
13.1	Echoes of *Gentlemen Prefer Blondes* in *Les Demoiselles de Rochefort*	163
13.2	References to *Snow White and the Seven Dwarfs* in *Peau d'âne*	167
13.3	'Entre vous deux': the bisexual moment in *Parking*'s recording studio	171
13.4	Versions of the past: 'Lorsqu'on revient' (left) and 'Ciné qui chante' (right) in *Trois places pour le 26*	173
14.1	The two 'musical' numbers in *Une femme est une femme*	176
14.2	The contrast in musical styles in *L'une chante, l'autre pas*	181
14.3	The girls' and boys' choruses in *Golden Eighties*	182
14.4	Sylvie and Jeanne's emotional musical moments in *Golden Eighties*	185
14.5	Parody of Marylin Manson in *Rendez-vous au tas de sable*	187
14.6	Margot and Corinne sidelined in *Paroles et musique*	188
15.1	Anti-realism in *Boris Godounov*	195
15.2	The three strands in the close of Act 1 in *Tosca*	197
15.3	The close-up of father and daughter in *Louise*	198
15.4	Farinelli sings 'Ombra fedele anch'io'	201
16.1	Simon sings 'Vertiges de l'amour' in *On connaît la chanson*	207

16.2 Theatrical staginess in *Pas sur la bouche* — 209
16.3 Direct address to the audience in *Pas sur la bouche* — 210
16.4 The eight songs of *8 femmes* — 213
16.5 Pierrette and Gaby kiss after their catfight in *8 femmes* — 214
16.6 The eight women line up holding hands in the last shot of *8 femmes* — 215
16.7 The musical numbers in *Le Bal des actrices* — 217
16.8 The paper crown worn by Deneuve in *Les Parapluies de Cherbourg* and Mastroianni in *Les Chansons d'amour* — 220
17.1 Choreography by figures dressed in black in *On va s'aimer* — 225
17.2 The first song-and-dance sequence in *Toi, moi, les autres* — 227
17.3 The Romani people in *Latcho Drom* — 230
18.1 Biopics of popular performers — 237

Tables

1.1 Generic Assignation of a Range of Film Musicals — 9
4.1 The Marseille Operetta — 53
9.1 Musical Sketch Films — 104
10.1 The films of the Three Tenors — 114
13.1 Film Musicals by New Wave Directors and Others — 160
13.2 The Six Musicals of Jacques Demy — 173
15.1 Opera Films 1975–2001 — 192
16.1 The Nostalgic Modern Auteur Musical — 206
18.1 Biopics and Pseudo-biopics — 236

Note on the text

- Dates for films are release dates, not production dates.
- Film titles are given in the original with translations in the filmography.
- Song titles are given in the original with our translations in brackets.
- Quotations are in the original French with our translations in footnotes.
- We have normally given time-codes for musical moments or dialogue to which we refer; for example, 0.59 signifies the approximate beginning of the event at the 59th minute of the film.
- Audience figures are given when known, and are rounded up to fractions of millions; for example, 0.2m means approximately 200,000 tickets sold.

Acknowledgements

We are grateful to the following colleagues whose input and support made it possible to write this book: Tim Bergfelder, Kelley Conway, Kevin Donnelly, Richard Dyer, Rémi Fontanel, Claudia Gorbman, Renaud Lagabrielle, Sébastien Layerle, Hannah Lewis, Raphaëlle Moine, Charles O'Brien, Thomas Pillard, Robynn Stilwell and Ginette Vincendeau.

We are grateful to the publishers for allowing us to incorporate modified versions of previously published work:

- 2013. Phil Powrie, 'The French Musical: Swing and Big Bands in the Cinema of the 40s and 50s', *Screen* 54 (2): 152–73.
- 2014. Phil Powrie, 'Luis Mariano et l'exotisme ordinaire', in S. Layerle and R. Moine (eds), *Voyez comment on chante!: films musicaux et cinéphilies populaires en France (1945–1958)*, 19–29, Paris: Presses Sorbonne Nouvelle.
- 2015. Phil Powrie, 'Soundscapes of Loss: Songs in Contemporary French Cinema', *A Companion to Contemporary French Cinema*, edited by A. Fox, M. Marie, R. Moine and H. Radner, 527–46, Chichester: Wiley-Blackwell.
- 2015. Marie Cadalanu, 'De *La Veuve joyeuse* à *La Valse de Paris*: Marcel Achard et le film musical', in Christian Viviani (ed.), *Marcel Achard entre théâtre et cinéma*, *Double jeu* 12: 69–85.
- 2016. Phil Powrie, '*L'une chante, l'autre pas*: Music, Movement and the Utopian Community', in *Agnès Varda Unlimited: Image, Music, Media*, edited by M-C. Barnet, 45–64, Oxford: Legenda.
- 2017. Phil Powrie, 'Mobilising Desire: The Operetta Films of Pills and Tabet in 1930s France', *Historical Journal of Film Radio and Television*, 37 (3): 436–54.
- 2018. Phil Powrie, 'Looking Back at the (French) Opera-Film', *Open Screens*, 1 (1): 1–39.
- 2018. Marie Cadalanu, 'Que reste-t-il de Jacques Demy?', *Positif*, 692: 142–4.
- 2019. Phil Powrie, 'La musique classique et le cinéma: *Un grand amour de Beethoven* (1936) et *Louise* (1938) d'Abel Gance', *Écrans*, 8–9: 41–58.
- 2019. Marie Cadalanu, 'Jean Grémillon à l'épreuve de l'opérette: *Valse royale*', in Y. Calvet and P. Roger (eds), *Jean Grémillon et les quatre éléments*, 133–146, Villeneuve d'Ascq: Presses universitaires du Septentrion.
- 2020. Phil Powrie with Marie Cadalanu, 'Crooning 1936–1956: The Film Musicals of Tino Rossi and Georges Guétary', *French Screen Studies* 20 (3–4): TBC.

1

Introduction

In his brief introduction to the film musical published in 2002 Michel Chion lamented the fact that there existed no history of the French variant (2002: 94). The current book is the first to attempt a critical and cultural history of the French film musical. Provocatively, we will be claiming that the French film musical exists as a major genre of French cinema, and that it has always existed, continuously, since the advent of sound cinema. We will also claim, equally provocatively, that what makes the strength of the French film musical is the reverse side of what has often been seen as its weakness, its inability to consolidate as a genre with recognizable codes in the same way that the Hollywood musical was codified during the 1930s. Our claim is that the strength of the French film musical lies in its refusal to be strictly codified, the variety that it displays as a result, and the difference within the continuity of older musical genres. Within that variety, the echoes of Hollywood, whether mimetic or occasionally parodic, are only one of many ingredients in the genre's history.

If the Hollywood musical's history is one of centripetalism and the gradual consolidation of a solid centre that reached its apogee in the MGM musicals of the 1950s, the French variant in this Hollywood-centric metaphor, while not necessarily centrifugal, is circumferential. There is no solid centre; rather, there are many formulas that ebb and flow as they gesture to a centre, only some of them towards what we might recognize as the Hollywood genre. For that reason we will not be trying to define a 'standard' variant of the French film musical, as that standard does not and could never exist, for a number of reasons. First, the French industrial context is one of an artisanal production environment, rather than a well-developed studio system. Second, the cultural context is one in which popular song prevails rather than song and dance; as Tom Brown points out (2015), French musical films are less spectacular than Hollywood musicals because they are rooted in the popular *café-concert* tradition, and therefore a more realist space. Finally, there is the historical importance of European forms such as opera and operetta (although we should remember that these also influenced the development of the Hollywood musical). None of these reasons mean that the genre does not exist; it means that it is often radically different from the Hollywood genre and is more diverse and often more experimental because of that diversity.

It is also arguably the most nostalgic genre of French cinema, not just because music and nostalgia are often considered as a pair, but because of the genre's roots in other musical forms and the way that these live on as recollected practices, whether they are, as Svetlana Boym terms them, 'restorative' nostalgia or 'reflective' nostalgia. The first is the more conservative gesture that yearns to restore the past as it was, the second 'does not shy away from the contradictions of modernity' (Boym 2001: xviii), and 'points to the future' (Boym 2001: 55); they frequently shade into each other, as we shall see. If we have retained the metaphor of the circle, it is not because we think that the French film musical can only be defined in relation to the Hollywood variant, but because the centre of that circle is not 'Hollywood' but more often than not a return to a range of pasts, only one of which is the Hollywood film musical. The circumference, constituted by a wide range of sub-genres or types, appears to be drawn towards a fantasized and homogenous past, but is immediately referred back to that circumference and the heterogeneity that constitutes it. Paradoxically then, the French film musical un-constitutes itself at the same time that it constitutes itself, often with relatively short-lived sub-genres, such as the chase film, the big-band film, the popular tenor spectacular. In that respect, it demonstrates nostalgia for past forms while also demonstrating a repositioning and evolution of musical forms as they take account of sociocultural and technological developments, such as the rise of television, or industrial developments, such as the increasing hybridization of genres in the contemporary period.

In this introduction, we will consider the transition to sound and the way that musical forms were incorporated in film, the emergence of the film musical genre as a recognizable category, and an indication of what we consider to be the development of the genre's history.

René Clair and the emergence of the film musical

The first French talkie was *Les Trois Masques* (André Hugon), released on 1 November 1929. The first film musical was released only a few weeks later, on 24 January 1930. This was *La route est belle* (Robert Florey, 1930), best known for its title song, sung by the film's star André Baugé, who plays a poor singer substituting for a famous tenor and achieving fame as a result. These two films were made in the UK, as the French studios were not equipped for sound. René Clair's better-known *Sous les toits de Paris* was made in France in the Épinay studios and released three months later on 28 April 1930. In it, Albert Préjean plays a street singer who is in love with the same woman as his friend. These two early film musicals exemplify one of the more interesting tensions in the genre's history, that between performances by singers and performances by actors. Baugé was a well-known singer of opera and, in the later 1920s, operetta; Préjean was a film actor who had begun his film career in the early 1920s. Moreover, whereas Hugon's film is now remembered only for the title song, Clair's film is seen as an auteur film, helped in part by Clair's own perception of his work; he preferred to call himself 'auteur' rather than 'metteur en scène' or director (Clair 1928: 3). Clair's four films of the early 1930s – *Sous les toits de Paris*, *Le Million* (1931), *À nous la liberté* (1931), *Quatorze juillet* (1933) – strike us now as considerably more inventive in their use of sound and music than most films of the period. But as we shall see in the first chapters of this book, in some respects they were not much different from many other musicals of the early 1930s, as filmmakers experimented with the new medium. As John Kobal points out: 'Between 1929 and 1931 European writers and directors went farther in the exploration of sound than did the Americans, who were limited by an enormous public and by producers who wanted to make good their publicity slogan: "A one hundred per cent talking motion picture!"' (1971: 72). Nonetheless, by the 1950s Clair was seen as a major filmmaker, as evidenced by the appearance of what was to be a long list of academic works in both French and English devoted to him.[1] His status as an auteur was consecrated by his admission to the Académie Française in 1960, with the director of the Cinémathèque Henri Langlois pronouncing him the successor of Feydeau and Molière.

Ironically, *Sous les toits de Paris*, now seen as one of the most innovative films of the early sound period, did less well in France than abroad. Clair, like other directors of the time, considered that sound cinema would detract from cinema-as-dream or as enchantment; his attachment to music as a concept that could shape film form led him to make *Sous les toits de Paris* 'as though [he] had orchestrated a silent film' (cited in Fischer 1977: 47); music is present and structures what we see for 23 of the film's 80m minutes (Marie 2000: 162). But French audiences were more attracted to dialogue in the nascent sound film, not least because it was a newer experience than film accompanied by music as had been the case in the silent period (Billard 1998: 165).

In *Le Million*, which is called a 'comédie musicale' in the credits, a range of characters are chasing a lottery ticket. Music replaces dialogue and natural sounds, and structures the shots in many sequences (see Fischer 1977: 43–5), as characters file across the sets in time to it, and occasionally break into exuberant song and dance. Jean Mitry called it a masterpiece, partly because the characters sing more than they talk, partly because of the extraordinary mix of genres: 'Mélange d'opéra-bouffe, de ballet et de vaudeville burlesque où le vaudeville se tourne lui-même en dérision et où l'opéra devient pastiche'[2] (1960: 70). Other critics were divided in trying to identify the film, calling it among other things rhymed fairy-tale vaudeville, sung and spoken comedy-vaudeville, fairy-tale operetta, as well as 'comédie musicale', the French term that was eventually used to denote the film musical (Kermabon 2000: 177). The shock created by the film did not pall over the years, with one reviewer saying of the film's rerun in 1959, after the expiry of the original play's copyright, that *Le Million* was one of the ten most important films ever made (Magnan 1959). By common accord the most remarkable sequence of the film takes place in the Opéra-Lyrique (0.55). The tenor performing is wearing a jacket that has the ticket in a pocket; he removes the jacket as part of the opera's action, causing consternation in the various characters chasing it,

---

[1] Bourgeois (1949), Charensol and Régent (1952), De La Roche (1958), Amengual (1963), Fischer (1977), McGerr (1980), Barrot (1985), Green (1985), Dale (1986), Gorbman (1987), Billard (1998), Herpe (1998), Herpe and Toulet (2000), Herpe (2001), O'Brien (2009), Boillat (2014), Flinn (2017).
[2] 'Mix of opera-bouffe, ballet and burlesque vaudeville in which the vaudeville is self-derisive and the opera a pastiche.'

Figure 1.1 The Opéra-Lyrique sequence in *Le Million* (Courtesy Criterion).

and at one point we see the real lovers, hidden behind the stage set, miming the song sung by the stage lovers (Figure 1.1).³

Clair's films use music to perpetuate a silent film aesthetic to which he was more attached than the 'talkie'; indeed, he frequently uses music to prevent characters from talking, or as an architecture on which the narrative depends (Basile 2000: 145). But for all that, unlike the majority of films using songs, he does not put songs forward as major attractions, preferring, rather, to weave them into the fabric of the film, much as Demy was to do some thirty years later. In the first sequence of *Sous les toits de Paris*, the song matters less than the antics of the characters as pickpockets try to steal from onlookers. Indeed, we see a variety of characters in the apartments singing the title song, the song bringing the community together, to such an extent that at one point a character says that he has had enough of it. This impregnation of the song in the narrative and its circulation across a range of characters and shots is unusual. More usually, film musicals include a number of songs that emerge from the narrative situation rather than the narrative being anchored in the songs and other aspects of the soundtrack. Indeed, one of the specificities of the French context is the all-pervasive

---

³ For an extended analysis of this sequence see Mitry (1960: 74–6), Fischer (1977: 49–50), McGerr (1980: 92–4).

nature of songs; there are some 740 films in the period between 1930 and 1939 (Basile 2000: 141) that contain one or more songs (not counting shorts, especially the filmed song,[4] and documentaries). This raises the issue of how we should differentiate between films with songs and film musicals, that question also being relevant to the terms used to describe musical films.

Defining the French film musical

Genre theory has a long history; it is not our intention to review this here.[5] It is nonetheless useful to recall one of the key theoretical distinctions established by the acknowledged field leader in the study of film musicals, Rick Altman (1987), between the *film musical* in which narrative development is subordinated to song-and-dance performance, and the *musical film* in which song-and-dance performances merely interrupt the narrative. This distinction has been questioned in the only work so far to tackle the film musical as an international genre (Creekmur and Mokdad 2013). The collection demonstrates the extreme variety of musical films across the globe, and a recognition that in many cases they are considered film musicals in their national cultural context. In the concluding chapter of the collection, Altman reminds us that the film musical genre requires the identification of common syntactic structures that tie together the semantic items such as star persona, directorial mannerisms, song type and iconography. Altman associates the semantic with disparity and difference, and therefore the musical film, while the syntactic establishes generic conventions that allow a specific generic form of film musical to emerge, even though it may have local (i.e. national) inflections and comprise, as does the Hollywood musical, sub-genres. But this binary is far too inflexible, as Altman himself recognized: 'Choose the semantic view and you give up *explanatory power*, choose the syntactic approach and you do without *broad applicability*' (Altman 1984: 11). As he points out, 'numerous films innovate by combining the syntax of one genre with the semantics of another' (1984: 12; see also Altman 1999); the two work together (synchronically) and evolve together over time (diachronically), and are embedded in audience expectations and critical practices, leading to what Altman calls an 'accommodation' (1984: 14) as both audiences and industry engage in practices that eventually establish the parameters of the genre. Altman accepts that 'only by providing the appropriate intertextual knowledge can we expect to contextualize, interpret and classify films from another national tradition properly' (Altman 2013: 260). In the same collection Kelley Conway presents an overview of what a French film musical tradition might mean, taking account of local inflections; our book builds on Conway's brief overview. She

---

[4] Radios were to become a standard household item only from 1935 and the gramophone was too expensive for many people; film shows would begin with short overtures comprising well-known songs, this substituting for the street singer that we see at the start of *Sous les toits de Paris* (Jeancolas 1983: 87–8).

[5] For a recent overview of genre theory, see Moine (2002).

emphasizes the heterogeneity of the genre, contrasting it with the relative homogeneity of the Hollywood variant, at least as presented by Altman and others:

> French musicals tend not to possess those elements identified by Altman as essential to the classical Hollywood musical, the 'dual focus' narrative structure and the 'audio dissolve', nor are they easily divided into the three subgenres found in Hollywood: the backstage, the fairytale and the folk musical. Instead, the French film musical is decidedly eclectic, in its choice of music, its plot patterns and its relationship between sound and image. (Conway 2013: 29)

To the extent that generic definitions are determined by a combination of industry labelling and audience preferences, it is clear that one national cinema's 'film musical' is unlikely to be another's. Our working definition of the French film musical is *films in which musical performance is integral to the promotion and subsequent enjoyment of the film*. In other words, the genre is defined as much by what audiences expected from the films as by categorical taxonomies by critics. For that reason in our history of the genre we include films that Altman would normally reject; for example, Altman sees the Hollywood revue film as having only a tenuous 'second cousin' relationship to the film musical as he wishes to establish it in the American context (1987: 102). In the French context, where the focus is much more on the singer than on the actor, at least until the 1960s, the revue film which incorporated musical sketch films (Chapter 9) is more obviously in the same category as other film musicals. Audiences were attracted to revue films because they could see performances by their favourite singers, who were also starring individually in their own operetta-style film musicals; this circulation of singers across sub-genres creates a continuum in which no one sub-genre dominates.

The labelling of genres in a variety of communicative contexts such as critical reviews, event guides, websites and encyclopaedias is a combination of the work of distributors, exhibitors, journalists, academics and, increasingly, personal blogs. As Moine explains, these taxonomies are frequently heterogenous and at odds with each other (2002: 10–20). Given that they shape audience expectations, which themselves then shape industry practice, it is useful to outline how the film musical genre was constituted linguistically at the beginning of the sound period, and, indeed, how current taxonomies function, especially given the resurgence of the film musical in France as elsewhere since the mid-1990s. As Altman explains, the Hollywood musical 'achieves cycle status not just by modifying the silent romance genre with the new musical technology; on the contrary, early musical forays involve modification of every genre in sight' (Altman 1999: 66). The French film musical is no different, as is suggested by a brief overview of the terms used to describe a variety of musical films during the 1930s.[6]

During the 1930s the basic terms were lifted from theatrical genres, the default term being *opérette*, this being frequently modified by critics in an effort to differentiate between different types of films. For example, *Prince de Minuit* (René Guissart, 1934)

---

[6] See Cadalanu (2016: 342–91) for a more detailed account.

is described as 'une opérette, mais combien amusante, mouvementée, vivante'[7] (Derain 1934a: 915); more widely, the term *opérette viennoise* is used to differentiate films based on Viennese stage operettas. The term *opérette* is frequently modified by a range of terms to distinguish films from stage versions: *opérette filmée*, *opérette cinématographique*, *film-opérette* and *film d'opérette*. Similarly, the term *revue* is frequently used, and like *opérette* is modified to indicate the cinematic version (*revue filmée*, *revue cinématographique*), although the term was reserved mainly for American films, as was the case for *film de music-hall*, corresponding to Altman's backstage musical. More properly in the French tradition, the third basic term lifted from theatrical genres is *vaudeville*, for example, in the description of *L'amour chante* (Robert Florey, 1930) as a 'vaudeville d'un genre bien français'[8] (Sannier 1930: 713).

These three basic terms – *opérette*, *revue* and *vaudeville* – are also frequently modified with terms such as *à couplets* ('with couplets'), *à grand spectacle* ('great show', meaning approximately a big-budget spectacular) or, finally, *musical*. This last term was also systematically used to modify the words *comédie* and *film*. The compound *comédie musicale* is today the term used in France to identify a film musical in the Hollywood sense. But in the 1930s, usage oscillated between three meanings. It could indicate a comedy film that happened to have music, as, for example, 'une comédie musicale et variée' for *Le Grand Refrain* (Yves Mirande, 1936) (Frank 1936: 6). It was also a means of differentiating a film from other musical genres, as, for example, in a review of *La Pouponnière* (Jean Boyer, 1932), in which a distinction is drawn between the film and the other two basic genres, operetta and vaudeville: 'Je ne le rangerai pas dans la catégorie des opérettes; on n'y chante point assez. Je le placerai peut-être dans la série des comédies musicales ou, plus simplement, dans le groupe des vaudevilles à couplets'[9] (Barreyre 1933: 4). But it was also used as a blanket term covering *all* film musicals from 1931, as is evidenced by its use as a category in *Cinémonde*'s list of new releases; *Si tu veux* (André Hugon, 1932), for example, is described as belonging to 'une lignée de comédies musicales agréables'[10] (Sorel 1932: 758). By the middle of the decade, the term *comédie musicale* seems to have been more accepted in its current usage, especially when applied to Hollywood films. Where popular cinema magazines are concerned, *Cinémonde* used it as a category as early as 1931, *Pour Vous* adopted it in January 1935 for its new releases, while *Ciné-Miroir* adopted the French term *film musical* in mid-decade. Like *comédie musicale*, however, the term *film musical* could be used to differentiate a film from other musical films; Trenet's *La Route enchantée*, for example, 'n'est pas une opérette, mais un film musical tout bourdonnant de chansons'[11] (Garrigues 1939: 19). But it was, like *comédie musicale*, also used as

---

[7] 'An operetta, but so amusing and lively.'
[8] 'A vaudeville in the very French style.'
[9] 'I would not call this an operetta as there are not enough songs. I would put it in the series of film musicals, or more simply in the group of vaudevilles with couplets.'
[10] 'A series of pleasant film musicals.'
[11] 'Isn't an operetta but a musical film humming with songs.'

broad catch-all category; Claude Bernier wrote a survey piece on film musicals in 1939 that included a wide range of films, justifying the term *film musical* in the following way: 'On nous prépare des films gais dont les principaux attraits seront constitués par le chant et la musique: ce sont des films musicaux. À vrai dire, ce sont des comédies où la parole et le chant se mêlent, où la musique occupe une grande partie du dialogue'[12] (1939: 675).

The semantic hesitation throughout the 1930s is no different from the Hollywood situation as described by Altman (1999). However, the French context with its hesitations around a range of terms emerging from French-specific theatrical practices makes Altman's distinction between 'film musical' and 'musical film' less appropriate, both for the 1930s and in the contemporary context. The latter becomes apparent if we look at the terms currently used to categorize some of the films we will be referring to in this book; these are taken from the website Allociné, a French version of the Internet Movie Database, whose categories we also include in Table 1.1.

Whereas the IMDB is relatively consistent in its use of genre tags, with 'comedy' and 'musical' figuring systematically, Allociné varies, sometimes wildly. The first five films in the list are all light operettas, whatever their differences; whereas this is reflected to some extent in the IMDB with the tag 'musical', Allociné's tags sometimes do not even recognize the musical elements. Both websites give up on the Marseille operetta *Un de la Canebière*, despite the fact that like the first five it is a light film musical in the operetta tradition. The most surprising tag is the one given by Allociné to *Les Parapluies de Cherbourg*, which is not a light film musical; the fact that *Les Chansons d'amour* is a homage to Demy's melancholic musicals makes the disparity even more obvious. Our position is that all of these films are film musicals, whatever generic tags they are given either by Allociné or by the IMDB. To recall the point we made earlier, they are films that attracted audiences with the performance of songs by recognized popular singers or, from Demy onwards, recognized popular stars, either singing the songs themselves or lip-synching them. Either way, the issue here is the popularity of singers and songs, rather than the way that the songs are integrated into the narrative or not.

We now need to consider a further methodological issue, which is quantitative: how many songs are required for a film to be considered a film musical? Jane Feuer begins an article on the international art musical by questioning the nostrum (provided by one of her students) that a film can only be a musical if it has six or more musical numbers. As she points out, this does not take account of 'those borderline cases where a film "feels like" a musical but has only one or two "numbers"' (2010: 54); as she concludes, 'it is misleading to define the film musical as a film with diegetic numbers. This is to mistake a period of musicals for the genre as a whole' (2010: 62). Our choice of films, in line with this view, is broad, and occasionally subjective: we consider *La Belle Équipe* not to be a film musical, despite the fact that we hear

---

[12] 'A range of gay films are currently in production whose main attractions are songs and music; they are musical films. In fact, they are comedies mixing dialogue and songs, in which music occupies a large part of the dialogue.'

Table 1.1 Generic Assignation of a Range of Film Musicals (consulted 17 June 2019)

Title	Date	Director	Allociné	IMDB
Le Chemin du paradis	1930	W. Thiele	comédie, comédie, musicale	comedy, musical, romance
Il est charmant	1932	L. Mercanton	comédie musicale	comedy, musical
La crise est finie	1934	R. Siodmak	comédie dramatique	comedy, musical
La Veuve joyeuse	1935	E. Lubitsch	comédie, comédie, musicale, romance	comedy, musical, romance
Toi, c'est moi	1936	R. Guissart	comédie	comedy
Marinella	1936	P. Caron	musical	comedy, musical
Un grand amour de Beethoven	1937	A. Gance	drame, biopic	biography, drama, musical
Un de la Canebière	1938	R. Pujol	divers	comedy
Montmartre-sur-Seine	1941	G. Lacombe	romance	comedy, romance
Le Cavalier noir	1945	G. Grangier	aventure	adventure
Nous irons à Paris	1951	J. Boyer	musical, comédie	comedy
Paris chante toujours	1952	P. Montazel	musical	comedy, musical
La Belle de Cadix	1953	R. Bernard	comédie musicale, romance	comedy, musical
D'où viens-tu, Johnny?	1963	N. Howard	musical, drame	drama, musical
Les Parapluies de Cherbourg	1964	J. Demy	comédie musicale	drama, musical, romance
Carmen	1984	F. Rosi	drame, musical	drama, musical, romance
Golden Eighties	1986	C. Akerman	comédie dramatique, comédie musicale	comedy, musical
On connaît la chanson	1997	A. Resnais	musical, comédie dramatique, romance	comedy, drama, musical
Les Chansons d'amour	2007	C. Honoré	musical, drame, romance	drama, musical, romance

the well-known signature song, 'Quand on s'promène au bord de l'eau' ('When We Stroll by the River'), on several occasions during the film, and despite the fact that Jean Gabin, who sings it, came from the music hall; but we do consider Josephine Baker's two 1930s films to be film musicals, even though they only have three songs/musical numbers, for reasons that will become apparent when we consider them in more detail (see Chapter 6).

An outline history

In the 1930s the genre absorbed two very different traditions – operetta and French *chanson* – these being inflected by the American jazz that had reached Paris in the 1920s. There are two key points to note. First, the coming of sound meant that established cultural forms such as nineteenth-century middlebrow European operettas and popular songwriters/singers were recycled and reshaped in the new medium. The cinema industry seized on operettas in particular, alongside other existing cultural forms such as plays and opera, as ready-made, successful and easily adaptable subjects. As a result, actors and singers operated across performance spaces: cabarets, theatre, music hall, radio, record and film. Indeed, unlike the modern period, the focus in film musicals between 1930 and 1960 was the singer: Henri Alibert, Josephine Baker, Danielle Darrieux, Fréhel, Henri Garat, René Lefèbvre, Georges Milton, Édith Piaf, Jacques Pills, Albert Préjean in the early period, followed by the 'three tenors', Tino Rossi, whose career in film had started just before the Second World War, Georges Guétary and Luis Mariano.

Second, the new medium of film was particularly international, something that had been inherited from the silent period, leading to the short-lived multi-language vehicles (MLVs) of the early 1930s. Operettas were international in flavour; they developed across Europe during the latter half of the nineteenth century, with considerable artistic exchange across France, Austria and Germany in particular. To take one example, Offenbach's Paris production of *Les Deux Aveugles* (The Two Blind Men, 1855) was staged in Vienna the following year. Johann Strauss began producing operettas following Offenbach's advice; Strauss's *Die Fledermaus* (1874) is a good example of the interchanges between France and Vienna. This started as an adaptation of a farce, *Das Gefängnis* (The Prison) by Julius Roderich Benedix (1851), which was turned into a vaudeville play by Henri Meilhac and Ludovic Halévy, *Le Réveillon* (The Supper Party, 1872); this was translated into German by Karl Haffner and the libretto was completed by Richard Genée who had previously worked with Strauss. The operetta was reworked for the French stage under the title *La Tzigane* (The Gypsy, 1877) by Alfred Delacour and Victor Wilder, but was to find success only in 1904 in a version by Paul Ferrier entitled *La Chauve-Souris* (Traubner 2003: 109–13).

A further characteristic of the internationalism of the genre was its sustained emulation of the Hollywood musical. The major characteristic of the French operetta film is therefore its diversity, leading to a range of aesthetic and formal features that are much broader than those found in Hollywood (see Por 2014: 75–83). Despite the international flavour of operetta, a specifically French type of operetta film slowly emerged from the MLVs of the early 1930s. German or American films made as French-speaking MLVs demonstrate subtle changes in tone; even from the earliest operetta films, there is an unmistakable 'Frenchness', despite the variety of operetta forms. Moreover, local variants of the operetta were developed, such as the Marseille operetta, generally, like other operettas, devised for the stage and adapted subsequently for the screen. What transpires is the genre's inventiveness faced with the opportunities of sound; the operetta film may be diverse, but a common characteristic is the way it pushes the boundaries of cinema in its early-1930s experimental phase with music and image.

By the end of the 1930s, the genre had stabilized; operetta evolved into big-budget spectaculars and revue films with star performers. Revue films were themselves varied, the musical sketch variant often structured loosely around a chase for an object, with popular singers performing at different stages (in both senses) of the narrative. This phase came to an end with the development of youth culture around pop singers at the start of the 1960s.

At this point there was a key shift to a genre focused on the auteur from Jacques Demy onwards, in what could be called its 'revisionist' phase. The film musical changed from being a popular genre to one explored principally by art cinema. This turn is exemplified in the appearance of Johnny Hallyday in *D'où viens-tu, Johnny?* (Noël Howard, 20 October 1963), followed by Jacques Demy's *Les Parapluies de Cherbourg* (19 February 1964). It marks the end of the tradition of the realist singer, symbolized by the death of Édith Piaf on 10 October 1963, three weeks before the screen consecration of the modern pop singer. Films focused on pop singers were few and short-lived, and the genre switched from a focus on the singer to a focus on the director-as-auteur; the few musicals released were either those of Jacques Demy, occasional reflections on the genre by New Wave directors – Jean-Luc Godard, Jacques Rivette – and other auteurs, such as Agnès Varda and Chantal Akerman, or a small handful of popular films. However, during

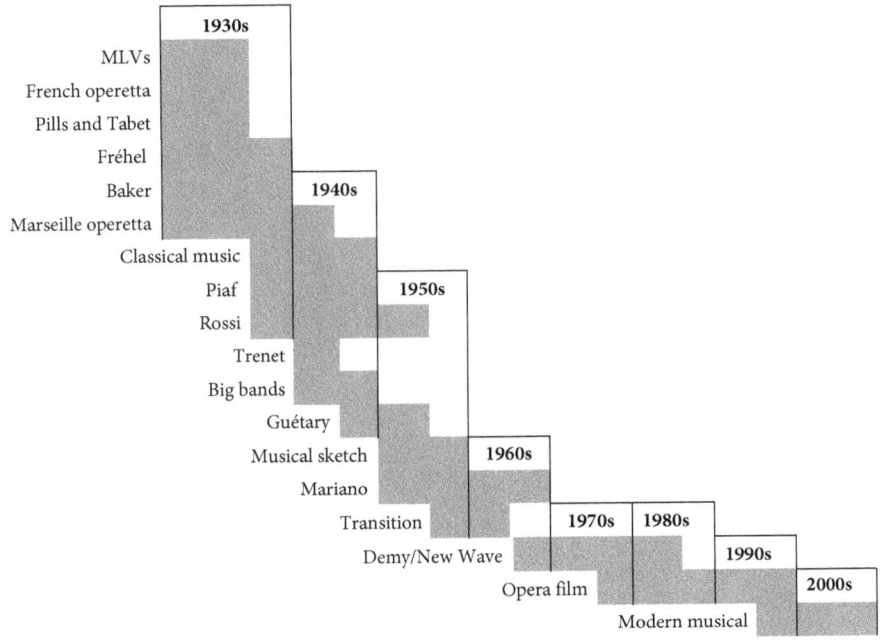

Figure 1.2 The main periods of activity for the French film musical.

this same period, the interest Europe-wide in 'heritage' during the 1980s led to the development of the opera film and films based on classical musical performance, which we also consider to be film musicals, even if they are very different from the light operettas of the 1930s.

Since the mid-1990s, there has been a significant and self-conscious renewal of the film musical with a range of popular film musicals, films by auteurs and a considerable number of singer biopics. The latter should be considered as film musicals in the broader sense, and it is possible to argue that this renewal is the beginning of a new cycle (rather than the end of the genre) that repeats elements of the 'classical' phase (the reliance on major stars in biopics) and auteur musicals indebted to Demy (the 'revisionist' phase). The musical biopic is an example of a broader trend of generic hybridization (not confined to French cinema) in the contemporary film musical, which frequently incorporates other genres, such as the documentary, auto-fiction, rom-coms and teenpics.

Although the film musical has ebbed and flowed in quantitative terms, with a significant number released between 1930 and 1960, followed by a leaner period between 1960 and 1995, and a recent resurgence, as a genre it has, nonetheless, been consistently present. We have tried to suggest this in Figure 1.2, which is a graphic representation of the periods of activity of a range of sub-genres and singers. Our book does not follow this chart chronologically, because many of the periods of activity overlap. However, it should help the reader gain a sense of the genre's presence and its continuity in French cinema since the advent of sound to the present day.

2

Multi-language versions

Multi-language versions (MLVs) developed rapidly with the advent of sound. Where operetta films are concerned the key production companies were UFA (Universum Film AG) for Franco-German versions and Paramount for Franco-American versions. Films made by these studios were influenced by German operetta traditions and, given the many émigré filmmakers fleeing Nazism in the 1930s, they also benefited from German filmmaking practices more generally. As the history of UFA, Franco-American MLVs and émigré filmmakers has been well explored,[1] we will only give a brief account in this chapter before turning to the analysis of a few selected films so as to explore some of the specificities of those influences, and also consider how the versions differ from each other.

This is all the more important given the reciprocal influences between the United States, France and Germany as the sound cinema developed. The Hollywood musical emerged from the Broadway musical, which was itself influenced by French music-hall traditions, such as, for example, the chorus girls found in Busby Berkeley's films with show-stopping choreographed numbers: *42nd Street* (Lloyd Bacon, 1933), *Footlight Parade* (Lloyd Bacon, 1933), *Gold Diggers of 1933* (Mervyn LeRoy, 1933), *Fashions of 1934* (William Dieterle, 1934), *Dames* (Busby Berkeley and Ray Enright, 1934), *Wonder Bar* (Lloyd Bacon, 1934), *Gold Diggers of 1935* (Busby Berkeley, 1935), *Gold Diggers of 1937* (Lloyd Bacon, 1936). Contemporary commentators were very aware of the impact of French traditions on the Hollywood musical as can be seen in Lenauer's 1933 article with its evocative title.

In return, French cinema adopted typically Hollywood musical forms such as the backstage musical, both in MLVs, such as *Le Masque d'Hollywood* (Clarence Badger and Jean Daumery, 1931), the French version of Mervyn LeRoy's *Show Girl in Hollywood* (1930), and for original French films such as *La crise est finie* (Robert Siodmak, 1934). René Clair was heavily influenced by certain Hollywood musicals, remarking of *The Broadway Melody* (Harry Beaumont, 1929) that 'the talking film has for the first time found an appropriate form: it is neither theatre nor cinema, but something altogether new' (quoted in Barrios 1995: 162). But Clair reciprocally influenced Hollywood filmmakers, such as Rouben Mamoulian: in the first sequence of *Love Me Tonight* (1932), based on Paul Armont and Léopold Marchand's 1931 play

---

[1] Kreimeier (1999); Bock and Töteberg (2002); Phillips (2004); Barnier (2004) and (2007).

Le Tailleur au château and starring Maurice Chevalier and Jeanette MacDonald, the music arises from street sounds much as Clair's does in *Sous les toits de Paris*.

American studios also encouraged the fusing of traditions, whether by hiring French personnel in Hollywood, or by implanting themselves in France; of thirty-five MLVs made in Hollywood, thirteen were musicals (Barnier 2004), eight of them starring Maurice Chevalier.

Paramount established studios in Paris at Joinville-le-Pont in Gaumont's former studios, and produced twenty-two films over a three-year period before prohibitive costs forced them to abandon film production, the studios being subsequently used for dubbing American films (Barnier 2002: 120–4). Paramount's decision to locate studios in Paris was an attempt to tap into the French market (Barnier 2002: 120–4), and to exert greater control, as an extraordinary article published in Hollywood's *Film Mercury* in March 1930, and translated *in extenso* in the French *Courrier cinématographique*, made abundantly clear:

> We won't permit ourselves, you say, to grab their theatre circuits! Aren't we doing just that right now in London, in Berlin, and in Paris? The heads of the European film industry moreover hold out their hands to the all powerful American dollar with such greediness that they don't even see opening before them the grave into which they will soon stumble. Another part of our plan consists in luring to Hollywood all European artists of any renown. ... In the theaters of England, Germany, and France will resound national sound tracks made in the USA. What European producer will vie with us when we have captured their greatest actors with our money? (cited in Andrew 1995: 95)

Unlike Paramount, with its studios in Paris, UFA made its MLVs at its German studios in Neubabelsberg (with a French subsidiary, the Alliance Cinématographique Européenne) where about 11 per cent of French films in the 1930s were made (Jeancolas 2005: 317n19). UFA privileged Franco-German MLVs; a 1930 circular, for example, announced that 58 MLVs were being produced, twenty-nine of which were French. The reason for the disproportionately high number of Franco-German MLVs, according to the circular, was that the French language would facilitate access to Central European and Balkan markets, these being France's allies (Icart 1988: 63). Musicals were among the more popular MLVs for technical and economic reasons: they dispensed with the need for dubbing, which was seen as too artificial by audiences (Cornu 2014: 76); and they allowed UFA to compete internationally, especially in the American market: 'Until the advent of the Third Reich, the *Operettenfilm* was UFA's most successful weapon in its fight against Hollywood dominance of the world market' (Claus and Jäckel 2000: 95).

The exchange of personnel across the different national cinemas meant that there was increasing and reciprocal influence in the making of operetta films. Wilhelm Thiele, the director of *Le Chemin du paradis*, worked first in Germany for UFA before fleeing to the United Kingdom in 1933 and then the United States in 1936. Ludwig Berger began making operettas for UFA with the adaptation of Oscar Strauss's *Ein Walzertraum* (1925), then moved to Hollywood to co-direct *Street of Sin* with Mauritz Stiller (1928) and make two more Hollywood films by himself, *The Woman from Moscow* (1928) and *Sins of the Fathers* (1928), followed by the musical *The Vagabond King* with Ernst Lubitsch (1930) and the MLV *Playboy of Paris/Le Petit Café* (1930/1931) starring Maurice Chevalier. He then returned to UFA to make Franco-German MLVs, *À moi le jour, à toi la nuit/Ich bei Tag und du bei Nacht* (1932; the French version with Claude Heymann) and *La Guerre des valses/Waltzerkrieg* (1933; the French version with Raoul Ploquin). Berger's *Les Trois Valses* (1938) was, in fact, not the adaptation of Oscar Straus's 1935 stage operetta *Drei Walzer* (1935), but the adaptation of the 1937 French version of the stage operetta created by Léopold Marchand and Albert Willemetz. This had been adapted for the French market, notably by including a new song for Yvonne Printemps, 'Je ne suis pas ce que l'on pense' ('I'm Not Who You Think'). Moreover, the technical crew demonstrates just how international the film was: a Franco-German scenario, a German director (Berger), French actors (Pierre Fresnay and Yvonne Printemps, among others), a German director of photography (Eugen Schüfftan), a French sound engineer (Joseph de Bretagne), French set designers and decorators (Jean d'Eaubonne, Raymond Gabutti, Jacques Gut), and music by Oscar Straus and Johann Strauss (father and son). The operetta film, then, in its MLV variants, was very much an international affair, making it all the more important for us to tease out its French specificities.

First steps: *Le Chemin du paradis/Die Drei von der Tankstelle* (1930) and *Le congrès s'amuse/Der Kongreß tanzt* (1931)

Le Chemin du paradis is considered by many to be the first and most representative example of the UFA operetta, with extraordinary inventiveness in both the image track and the soundtrack, as an early review of the French version points out, starting with the common view that operetta films just recycled stage operettas, but praising this film for being much more than a filmed operetta: 'C'est une opérette. Quoi! Dira-t-on, encore une! Les producteurs montreront-ils encore longtemps cette veulerie de caractère et cette incroyable débilité d'imagination qui les confinent dans l'éternel recommencement des opéra-comiques ou des opérettes? Calmez-vous ... C'est un vrai film, un film agile, vivant, jeune, un film qui contient du *cinéma*'[2] (Delaprée 1930: 8). It was made both in German (with the title *Die Drei von der Tankstelle*) and in French, with Lilian Harvey as a wealthy woman in both films (Lilian Cossman in the German version, Liliane Bourcart in the French),

---

[2] 'It's an operetta. What! Another one! Are producers going to carry on this craven attitude and incredible feebleness of the imagination which leads them to keep on making opéra-comiques or operettas? Calm down. This is a real film, a nifty, lively, young film that contains *cinema*.'

Figure 2.1 Modernity in *Le Chemin du paradis* (Authors' collection).

but with Henri Garat, René Lefèbvre and Jacques Maury as the three friends in the French version.³ Three penniless friends sell their car and buy a petrol station which is patronized by Liliane with whom each falls in love, unbeknownst to the others. Unlike many of the Viennese operetta adaptations located in a nostalgic nineteenth century, this film was resolutely of its time. As Charles O'Brien says, 'Its updated setting – a contemporary world of high-spirited young men, flirtatious bosses' daughters, sports cars, petrol stations, nightclubs, and bachelor pads – seemed wholly modern' (2005: 74; Figure 2.1). The emphasis on cars anticipates Pills and Tabet's *Prends la route*, which we will consider in Chapter 4, although *Le Chemin du paradis*, while clearly celebrating community (and more particularly male camaraderie and solidarity in the face of unemployment), is also light entertainment aimed at helping the audience forget the worst of the Depression. Spectators were well aware that it may well have been light entertainment – 'ce n'est qu'une bulle de savon qu'emportera le vent de la réalité'⁴ wrote one reviewer poetically (Dumas 1930: 748), and Roger Régent that 'le scénario est gentiment insignifiant'⁵ – but that it was also a parody of the genre based in the nineteenth-century Viennese operetta, as he goes on to comment: 'Une parodie souvent savoureuse de l'opérette et quelquefois aussi du cinéma'⁶ (1930: 5).

---

[3] There was a Franco-German remake as part of the brief resurgence of operettas, particularly the Marseille operetta as we saw in the last chapter, this time directed by two Germans in French with Georges Guétary as the star: *Le Chemin du paradis* (Willi Forst and Hans Wolff, 1956).
[4] 'It's no more than a soap bubble that the wind of reality will blow away.'
[5] 'The scenario is sweetly insignificant.'
[6] 'An often delicious parody of operetta and sometimes of cinema.'

The film's major innovation is the integration of the soundtrack, 'une assimilation intime de la musique à l'action',[7] as one reviewer puts it (Lawrence 1930: 12); and as another writes: 'C'est la première fois qu'une opérette cinématographique ne donne point cette impression de cassure entre les scènes qui est si désagréable'[8] (Marguet 1930: 650). Songs emerge from sound effects, such as the first song in the opening sequence, 'Avoir un bon copain' ('To Have a Good Friend'), introduced during the opening credits by repeated bursts of the car horn, these being taken up by orchestral brass later in the song. The car horn becomes a musical leitmotif, as we hear it each time Liliane arrives in the petrol station, serving as a musical signature for her; it features as a trumpet-like refrain in the film's title song, 'Le Chemin du paradis' ('The Path to Heaven') (0.30). According to one historian, the jingle was so successful that car manufacturers used it for car horns for a decade afterwards (Tournès 2016: 19). As Martin Barnier points out, this repeated motif creates an ambiguous sound space: when we hear the car horn we cannot be sure if it is the signal for a musical intervention or just a car horn (2002: 127–8). Another integrated sound effect occurs later in the film, when Willy dictates a letter to Liliane; the music emerges from the clicking of the typewriter keys echoed by a xylophone (1.17).

The image track is no less inventive: when the three friends become bankrupt at the start of the film and their furniture has to be sold, during the song 'Fauchés comme les blés' ('Broke'), the potential drama of the event is neutralized when the bailiff and then the removal men join in the song, emphasizing a utopian community despite the evident hardships of the Depression that the audience would have been experiencing,[9] and the sequence becomes increasingly fantastical as the furniture flies of its own accord into the waiting van (0.7). The characters frequently dance, but in ironic fashion; in the sequence just mentioned, the three friends weave in an exaggerated walk through the removal men who march in single file as they take away the furniture, in a kind of counter-dance.

Apart from the language and song lyrics modified so as to make sense with the music, there is very little difference between the German and French versions, even if one French reviewer rather predictably privileges the French version because of the supposed superiority of the actors (Vincent-Bréchignac 1931: 6): interiors can be exteriors from one version to the other, and some dialogue is switched from one character to another, but the order of the narrative is the same. There is only one sequence that does not occur in the French version; when the three friends open the petrol station, they repeat 'Bitte sehr! Bitte gleich!'[10] faster and faster until the rhythm blends with the music accompanied by images of the friends serving customers. This kind of montage was familiar in German cinema of the time, such as Walter Ruttman's

---

[7] 'A close association of music and action.'
[8] 'It's the first time that a film operetta does not give the disagreeable impression of gaps between scenes.'
[9] Similar moments of utopian celebration can be found in Thiele's next film, *Dactylo* (1931) in which the typist of the film's title sings 'Voir la vie en rose' ('To See the World Through Rose-Tinted Spectacles') in her apartment and a distance shot shows the other tenants joining in (0.14).
[10] 'Here you go! Straightaway!'

Figure 2.2 The final number in *Le Chemin du paradis* (Authors' collection).

documentary *Die Sinfonie der Grosstadt* (1927), and Barnier suggests that its omission might be due to French spectators' unfamiliarity with the German aesthetic (2002: 126).

The film's irony and self-reflexivity, very different from French operetta films, also makes it very modern in tone, and suggests, moreover, alongside the clumsy dance routines that it might be seen as a parody of stage operetta (Ascheid 2012: 51). The opening song, 'Avoir un bon copain', is repeated several times in the film, but modified according to the situation. Jean (René Lefèbvre) uses the melody to sing about his black eye: 'Avoir l'œil au beurre noir/Voilà c'qu'il y a de pire au monde'[11] (0.43). When Liliane's father picks up on the song and hums it to his mistress, she complains 'Tu ne pourrais pas trouver un autre refrain? Toujours la même chose! Toujours le même refrain!'[12] (0.43), drawing attention to the song's keynote status. The film's finale is even more ironically self-reflexive. We see the two lovers against the backdrop of a theatre curtain; they think they are alone, but then realize that they are, in fact, front of stage in a theatre full of people watching them (1.26). Willy (Henri Garat) asks the public why they are still there, and Liliane answers that they are waiting for the end of the film: 'Le finale, il en faut toujours un dans une grande opérette.'[13] All the actors then come on stage for a chaotic final dance number with cancan-style chorus girls (Figure 2.2) that

---

[11] 'Having a black eye/Is the worst thing in the world.'
[12] 'Can't you find another refrain? It's always the same thing! Always the same refrain!'
[13] 'The finale. A great operetta always needs one.'

reprises 'Avoir un bon copain', introduced, as it was at the start of the film, by the car horn. The film is light, tongue-in-cheek, and endlessly inventive; as Aschied points out, 'Through his unique use of narrative, dance and integrated musical numbers, director Wilhelm Thiele invented the sound musical and anticipated emerging Hollywood forms' (2012: 51).

By contrast, *Le congrès s'amuse* was a much more obviously Viennese operetta film, even if it too was praised as 'une bouffée de jeunesse'[14] (*Cinémagazine* 1931: 78). It again starred Lilian Harvey and Henri Garat for the French version. *Le Chemin du paradis* created a utopian space that allowed spectators to forget the Depression. *Le congrès s'amuse* did the same thing, but trivialized history and to some extent the importance of politics during the early 1930s: as the director commented, and as the title of the film suggests, the point was to allow spectators to forget 'leurs affaires, la crise, la vie ... J'ai voulu que *Le congrès s'amuse* – que nous n'avons pas appelé *Le Congrès de Vienne* pour ne pas faire croire au film historique – entraîne les spectateurs en pleine féerie'[15] (Erik Charell quoted in Régent 1931: 7). The film recounts the Congress of Vienna, to which Metternich invited European heads of state in 1815 to decide the future of Napoleon, held in the Island of Elba. Metternich is presented as a schemer, who wants to ensure that his position – that Napoleon should carry on being imprisoned in Elba – holds sway, and aims to prevent the Tsar of Russia (played by Garat) from attending the Congress. He does so by asking his secretary, Pépi, to keep the Tsar occupied by means of a romance with a pretty glove-seller (Christel, played by Harvey), with whom Pépi is in love. The Tsar falls for her and she becomes his mistress for a day; they spend time together in a tavern singing along to one of the film's two major songs, 'Ville d'amour' ('Town of Love'). To complicate matters, the Tsar has a double (also played by Garat), leading to predictable comic misunderstandings. Not only the Tsar, but also the other heads of state eventually leave the Congress table, attracted by the ballroom with its obligatory waltzes and gaggles of women, allowing Metternich to get his way. The Tsar has to leave, and Christel is forlorn.

Three sequences stand out in the film for their originality, both commented on favourably by reviewers. When the heads of state, distracted by the dancing, leave the Congress table, their chairs all swing in time to the music (1.16) in a 'danse des *fauteuils vides*'[16] (Lehmann 1931b: 9; emphasis in original), when Metternich passes the motion to keep Napoleon imprisoned *nem con* as only he remains in the room. Second, and more stunning for the time is the very mobile camera. When the Tsar arrives, for example, there is a remarkable high-angle tracking shot realized as a result of rails fixed to the ceiling of the studio (0.14; Figure 2.3); and later there is a four-minute tracking sequence as Christel sings the fox-trot 'Serait-ce un rêve' ('Is This a Dream') in the carriage taking her through the city towards the Tsar's countryside villa (0.41). This is comprised of eight left-tracking shots, the longest of which,

---

[14] 'A breath of fresh air.'
[15] 'Things, the crisis, life ... I wanted *Le congrès s'amuse* – which we haven't titled *Le Congrès de Vienne* because we didn't want people to think it was a historical film – transport spectators into fairyland.'
[16] 'Dance of the empty chairs.'

Figure 2.3 The arrival of the Tsar in *Le congrès s'amuse* (Authors' collection).

almost two minutes, occurs as the carriage wends its way through the market square. Throughout the song, the populace sings along with Christel, as had been the case for 'Ville d'amour'; stall-holders, bourgeois, washerwomen, all participate in the song, as Christel celebrates this modern pastoral of the Prince romancing a modern shepherdess:

> Serait-ce un rêve, un joli rêve?
> C'est bien trop beau pour être vrai.
> Ce n'est qu'un songe, un joli songe
> Qui s'évapore et disparaît.
> La belle histoire, je n'ose y croire,
> J'aurai trop de chagrin après.
> Le plus beau songe n'est qu'un mensonge,
> Demain, je me réveillerai.
> C'est un beau rêve, un joli rêve
> Mais bien trop beau je crois, pour être vrai.[17]

---

[17] 'Is this a dream a pretty dream?/It's much too beautiful to be true/It can only be a dream a pretty dream/That evaporates and disappears/A fine tale I don't dare believe in/I'd be too sad afterwards/A fine dream is no more than a lie/Tomorrow I'll wake up/It's a beautiful dream a pretty dream/But much too beautiful to be true.'

As René Lehmann pointed out, the constant sense of crowd movement, whether in the tavern, the market square or the ballroom, imparts a sense of community for spectators of the film: 'On a l'impression ... d'être mêlé brusquement à cette masse et de participer à son enthousiasme'[18] (Lehmann 1931b: 9). The anonymous reviewer of the film's rerun three years later even suggested that this particular sequence should be preserved in a film library:

> On ressent le même enchantement que jadis à voir les fanfreluches et les apprêts de la toilette de Lilian, et le ravissement monte, crescendo, lorsque nous la suivons dans sa calèche triomphale ... Ce joli voyage contrepointé par la chanson immortelle (on la chante encore, on la chantera toujours) est une sorte de 'classique' du cinéma, il mérite d'être conservé dans des archives, dans une 'filmothèque'.[19] (*Cinémonde* 1934a: 589)

As was the case with *Le Chemin du paradis*, apart from the actors – Henri Garat's role is played by Willy Fritsch in the German version – and the language, there are few differences between the French and German versions of *Le congrès s'amuse*. The main difference is in the German version's saucier tone. We see Christel in her petticoats as she dresses before going outside to watch the Tsar's parade, and the petticoats of Christel and her friends as they cavort in her shop; these shots do not occur in the French version. When imprisoned because the bouquet she tossed at him is misconstrued as a bomb, she is condemned to twenty lashes on her naked buttocks. In the French version, we see her waiting to receive them with a head-shot, in 'une piquante amorce de scène de flagellation'[20] (Auriol 1931: 50). In the German version we see her from behind as the lascivious executioner of the punishment begins to lift her dress, the shot being cut before we see her naked.

Although *Le congrès s'amuse* is in many ways a more conventional film operetta than *Le Chemin du paradis*, both updated what had by the 1930s become a moribund stage genre. The frequent comments on the films' cinematic nature, such as the long tracking shots that create a fairy-tale space in *Le congrès s'amuse*, suggest that cinema prolonged the stage genre, often with gentle pastiche if not outright parody. As André Tournès comments, the film 'réussit ... à parodier un genre à bout de souffle tout en nous dispensant un plaisir délicieux'[21] (2016: 19). With Pabst's reworking of Brecht and Weill's *Dreigroschenoper*, the renewal of the genre is considerably more acute; as Lucien Wahl of *Pour Vous* wrote, Pabst's film was 'du neuf absolu'[22] (1931a: 14).

---

[18] 'You feel as though you're suddenly part of the crowd and experiencing their enthusiasm.'
[19] 'You feel the same enchantment as before to see Liliane's finery, and your rapture increases, crescendos, when we follow her into her triumphal carriage. That pretty journey counterpointed by an immortal song (we still sing it, we'll sing it forever) is a sort of cinema classic, it ought to be preserved in archives in a filmothèque.'
[20] 'The racy start of a whipping scene.'
[21] 'Manages to parody a genre that has run out of steam while giving us a delightful pleasure.'
[22] 'Absolutely new.'

Anti-operetta: *L'Opéra de quat'sous/Die Dreigroschenoper* (1931)

Pabst directed both the German and French versions, the production companies being Warner, Tobis and Nero. Bertolt Brecht and Kurt Weill's opera, based on John Gay's *The Beggar's Opera* of 1728, had been staged in Berlin in 1928 and the French version in Paris in 1930. Brecht and Weill's opera is more of an anti-opera, by virtue of the setting (London low-life), its generically unclassifiable nature, the eclectic mix of songs,[23] and Brecht's Marxist inflections. It was immensely successful, with more than 10,000 performances in its first five years, despite being banned by the Nazis in 1933. Brecht drafted an adaptation for the screen, but he and Weill soon came into conflict with Pabst, whose commercial instincts favoured poetic atmosphere over Brecht's social critique. But as Roger Manvell pointed out, the atmospherics of the film were required by the medium: 'Without the self-contained world [the sets] create, a world of dark alleys, hanging rigging and twisting stairways, without their decorative yet realistic values, without the air of finality and completeness which they give, this film operetta would not have been credible' (1973: 295).

The ensuing court case which awarded damages to Weill (for a single inserted trumpet note that he had not composed), but none to Brecht, created considerable coverage, not least because Brecht appears to have used the case to score political points. However, Pabst's film is embedded in the Expressionist aesthetic of Weimar cinema (of little interest to Brecht) and 'the duplicity of representation' (Elsaesser 2000: 316); it is not so much about 'economic or political power directly, but the new category of spectacle power' (326). Pabst's film was released in 1931. The French version was banned after the press show in March 1931, but opened at the Studio des Ursulines in November that year after pressure from cinema professionals.

Mack the Knife marries Polly, the daughter of Peachum, the beggar leader. Peachum disagrees with the marriage and has Mack the Knife arrested; about to be hanged, he is pardoned by Queen Victoria. The film follows the original libretto closely, with some simplifications; Mack escapes once instead of twice, for example. The opera had twenty-one songs, but Pabst reduced them to eight. Lotte Eisner points out the pivotal nature of Weill's songs, and that Pabst's reduction of their number and the use he makes of them runs counter to Brecht's social critique, privileging atmosphere and reducing the songs' impact; they were 'the very pivots of the play, springing up in

---

[23] 'Tous les genres s'y côtoient : la parole, la déclamation, le chant et, à l'intérieur de chacun, toutes les formes où s'élabore l'œuvre. Le chant, par exemple, ce sont tantôt des chorals luthériens, tantôt des romances sentimentales, tantôt des marches militaires, du jazz et Bach, sans oublier la parodie du grand opéra dans la scène finale' (Bernard Dort cited in Rouchouse 1999: 102). ['All genres are mixed together: speech, declamation, song, and within each of these, all the forms that help the work to develop. Where song is concerned, for example, sometimes it's Lutheran chant, sometimes sentimental romances, sometimes military marches, jazz and Bach, not forgetting the parody of grand opera in the final scene.']

the constantly spontaneous dialogue, whereas in Pabst's film they are no more than pleasant embellishments. Their impact is deadened with atmosphere, and though made visual, much of their effect is blurred if not lost altogether' (1973: 318). There is clearly a tension between the critical distance encouraged by Brecht and the imperative to pleasure that the musical genre presupposed.

Spectators of the French film were sensitive to 'atmosphere', however, as the following review by Alexandre Arnoux in a major magazine makes clear:

> L'extrême fertilité de l'intervention cinématographique rebondit, deux heures durant, sans s'essouffler; l'atmosphère d'un Londres de rêve situé aux environs de 1900, y est évoquée par le plus subtil dosage de noirs et de gris; la lancinante complainte de l'orgue de barbarie la traverse et la soutient. Une merveilleuse abondance de types, tantôt croqués au passage, tantôt burinés incisivement, meuble l'écran. Tout cela chante, boit, vole, exploite ses plaies, trahit, aime, suppure, danse, cite la Bible, envahit la rue, se bat avec la police, rôde chez les filles, fonde des banques. Une bigarrure contrastée, une arlequinade sombre, un tissu de folies et de sagesse, de cauchemar et de réalisme, un grouillement rythmé. L'extravagance même, et la vie même, quand nous osons la regarder en face, avec ce désespoir lucide et ce cynisme jovial qui conviennent aux spectateurs d'une telle farce.[24] (1931: 9)

The songs may well lack the incisiveness of Brecht and Weill's social critique, but they accord perfectly with the atmosphere and the songs of French film musicals, such as 'À Paris dans chaque faubourg' ('In Each Quarter of Paris') in René Clair's *Quatorze juillet* (1933).

Moreover, the singers bring with them very particular French film musical styles and connotations; given that there is hardly any change in the filming of the two versions, it is the songs that make a difference, refracted through the lens of the star. Ginette Vincendeau points out that Préjean 'made no mystery of having tried to turn Mackie into a sympathetic character to fulfil his French audience's expectations' (1988: 38), and as the reviewer of *La Revue du cinéma* wrote, Préjean was 'un jeune bandit sympathique plein de laisser-aller et de nonchalance'[25] (Lévi Alvares 1931: 60). Préjean as Mackie had the same bad boy persona as his role in Clair's *Sous les toits de Paris* and in subsequent films with Danielle Darrieux, while Polly was played by Florelle, the well-known music-hall singer and *chanteuse réaliste* who had appeared in a number

---

[24] 'There is extreme inventiveness throughout the two hours: the atmosphere of a dreamlike London around 1900 is evoked by the subtle mix of blacks and greys; the nagging complaint of the street organ runs across it and sustains it. A marvellous gallery of types, sometimes sketched briefly, sometimes incisively chiselled, fill the screen. They sing, drink, steal, exploit their deformities, betray, love, ooze, dance, quote the Bible, swarm in the streets, fight the police, prowl around prostitutes, establish banks. A colourful pattern, a dark farce, a tissue of madness and wisdom, of nightmare and realism, a rhymical swarm. Extravagance itself, life itself, when we dare to look it in the face, with that lucid despair and jovial cynicism that belong to those who look on.'
[25] 'A likeable young bandit, scruffy and lazy.'

of films during the 1920s, and was later to play Valentine in Jean Renoir's *Le Crime de Monsieur Lange* (1936).

Another reviewer from *Pour Vous* emphasized the difference between the two versions. The French version had been censored, but he argued that it was in no way a threat to society, suggesting that it was more comedy than social satire:

> La version française que nous avons vue n'a ni la puissance, ni l'incision de la version originale et n'attente pas au respect de la société ... [Elle] donne d'ailleurs plus l'impression d'une pochade, d'une comédie burlesque et railleuse, que d'une âpre satire des mœurs. Florelle, qui chante mieux encore qu'elle ne joue, est charmante dans le rôle de la pétulante, rêveuse et décidée Polly. Albert Préjean fait de Mackie un rêveur bon garçon et sympathique.[26] (Lehmann 1931a: 9)

The young Henri Langlois, future director of the Cinémathèque française, and an avid cinema-goer, kept notes on the films he saw as a teenager. He compared Pabst's two versions, noting that the French version was 'charmant .... C'est une opérette. Si l'on veut, drôle d'opérette, mais opérette quand-même'[27] (2014: 125), while in the German version, even though the songs were direct translations, they seemed 'plus âpres, plus canailles et plus cyniques', and even though the images were the same, in the German version there was 'plus d'élégance, plus de légèreté ... Finies l'opérette et la poésie élégante, nous voyons un film lourd, âpre, humain' (2014: 125). Nonetheless, more attuned to the French context, he considered the French film 'plus dangereux que la version allemande car son charme morbide est accru par l'apport des qualités françaises qui le rendent plus étrange et plus complexe'[28] (2014: 125). This comment seems to stem from his reaction to Préjean as Mackie (Figure 2.4): 'Préjean est gavroche mais peut-être plus dangereux avec ses airs cyniques. L'Allemand [Rudolf Forster], plus cassant et plus militaire, a l'air d'un hobereau'[29] (2014: 125). Forty-five years later, Claude Beylie also preferred the French version, considering that the German version was too realist and not fairy-tale enough (1976: 6).

This comparison demonstrates that audience expectations and cultural context determined to a large extent the form and tone of the film operetta, accounting for significant differences between the MLV versions.

---

[26] 'The French version we saw does not have the force nor the incisiveness of the original and does not attack society. It gives more the impression of a sketch, a burlesque and derisive comedy, than a bitter social satire. Florelle, who sings even better than she acts, is charming in the role of the petulant, dreamy Polly. Albert Préjean turns Mackie into a sympathetic dreamer.'
[27] 'Charming. It's an operetta. A funny kind of operetta, but an operetta nonetheless.'
[28] 'Harsher, more raffish and cynical/no more elegance, no more lightness. Finished the elegant operetta and poetry, we see a film that is heavy, harsh, human/more dangerous than the German version because its morbid charm is increased by its French qualities that make it more strange and more complex.'
[29] 'Préjean is like a street urchin but perhaps more dangerous with his cynical airs. The German, more abrupt and military, looks like a country squire.'

Figure 2.4 Henri Garat as Mack the Knife in *L'Opéra de quat' sous* (Courtesy BFI).

French inflections: *La Veuve joyeuse* (1935)/*The Merry Widow* (1934) and *Valse royale* (1935)/*Königswalzer* (1936)

Cultural difference can also be seen in a comparison of the English and French dialogues of *La Veuve joyeuse*, the latter written by Marcel Achard, who went on to direct a very Lubitschian operetta, *La Valse de Paris* (1950), which we will consider in Chapter 7.

Lubitsch had been working in Hollywood since 1922, and had turned to musicals with the advent of sound. His first sound film was the MLV musical *The Love Parade* (1929)/*Parade d'amour* (1929), based on a French play, *Le Prince Consort* (Jules Chancel and Léon Xanrof, 1903), which had been turned into a Broadway play in 1905. It starred Maurice Chevalier and Jeanette MacDonald; Chevalier was one of France's most successful music-hall stars, but had gone to make films in Hollywood in 1928, and was to carry on doing so until 1935. *Monte Carlo* (1930) also starred Jeanette MacDonald, while *The Smiling Lieutenant* (1931), based on Oscar Straus's operetta *Ein Walzertraum* (1907), starred Chevalier and Claudette Colbert.

La Veuve joyeuse was based on Franz Léhar's 1905 stage operetta *Die lustige Witwe*, which itself was based on a French play by Henri Meilhac, *L'Attaché d'ambassade* (1861). Chevalier plays Captain Danilo, who is ordered by General Achmet of Marsovie to prevent the wealthy widow Sonia (MacDonald), who pays more than half of the kingdom's taxes, getting married to a Frenchman, and thereby bankrupting the kingdom. The scenario and dialogue for the French version were written by Marcel Achard, who also wrote the scenario and dialogue for Chevalier's next MLV musical, *Folies-Bergère de Paris* (Roy Del Ruth, 1935), the French version being titled *L'Homme des Folies-Bergère* (Roy Del Ruth and Marcel Achard, 1935).

There were minor differences in the two versions of *La Veuve joyeuse*, not least because the French version did not need to conform to the Hays Code; some thirteen cuts were required by the censors for the American version (Bordat 2010: 101). Some differences were required because of cultural transposition: King Achmet becomes a General and Regent of the kingdom in the French version; the women at *Maxim's* have names that would not work in French, so 'Lolo, Dodo, Joujou, Cloclo, Margo, Froufrou' become 'Manon, Ninon, Lison, Franchon, Suson, Toinon'.

But Achard's reworking can be considerably more sophisticated than this, although some spectators did not think much of the dialogue: 'Le dialogue était d'un bête et manquait totalement de finesse',[30] wrote one to *Pour Vous* ('Les Yeux bleus' 1935: 10). On the whole, though, reviewers praised the film, and the dialogue in particular, commenting that it was 'pétillant d'esprit, de douce liberté, d'humeur galante, de grâce'[31] (Marcel-Henry 1935: 95), 'plein de verve, spirituel et tendrement libertin'[32] (Derain 1935: 105). In the American version, the King suggests that it is important to understand the views of the populace on Sonia's departure to Paris, saying: 'The opinion of the shepherd on the street – that's what I want to know', dismissing the oddly New York flavoured 'East Side shepherds' as 'intellectuals'; Achard cleverly transposes this to 'balayeurs de la rive gauche', the *rive gauche* clearly indicating intellectuals to a French audience, and *balayeurs* denoting a lowly urban occupation (road-sweepers) similar to the rural shepherd. In a different register, in Sonia and Danilo's first conversation, she tries to dampen the smooth-talking Danilo's enthusiasm, saying 'You're not terrific. Not even colossal', which Achard converts into suggestive and very French onomatopoeia: 'Vous n'êtes pas oh, oh! Ni même hé, hé!'[33] (0.10). Danilo's English response is to say 'I'm a free man again', which in French becomes the considerably lighter 'Eh bien! Encore un roman de terminé!'[34] Again in comic mode, in the American version Danilo tells the ambassador 'Your Excellency, shut up!', which in French becomes 'Excellence, en bon marsovien, schmudt!'[35] (1.20). When Achmet finds Danilo in his wife's bedroom, he threatens to cut out his tongue, saying that he will deal with him later, to which Danilo responds simply 'yes' in the American version; the French version displays considerably more wit: 'S'il vous plaît mon Général, prenez votre temps, la patience est une des vertus du soldat'[36] (0.27). It is clear that part of the success in adapting the film for a French audience is due to Achard.

---

[30] 'The dialogue was so stupid and lacked any kind of subtlety.'
[31] 'Witty, free-spirited, flirtatious, graceful.'
[32] 'Racy, witty and mildly salacious.'
[33] 'You're not oh, oh! Nor even hey, hey!'
[34] 'Ah well, another novel finished!'
[35] 'Excellency, as they say in good Marsovian language, schmudt!'
[36] 'If it please Your Excellency, do take your time, patience is one of the soldier's virtues.'

Figure 2.5 The opening ball sequence in Grémillon's *Valse royale* (Courtesy René Chateau).

Jean Grémillon was chosen to direct the French version of Herbert Maisch's *Königswalzer*, titled *Valse royale* in France. One of the few brief reviews suggests that the film did not impress: 'La partition est mince … L'ouvrage est soigné, il y faudrait de la drôlerie'[37] (Wahl 1935: 10). If we have chosen this film, despite its failure to impress audiences, it is because Grémillon is considered a major French filmmaker of the 1930s, and this film is usually passed over in accounts of his work, partly no doubt because it was among a number of films he made to order during a fallow period. Geneviève Sellier, for example, includes half a page on it in a chapter significantly entitled 'La traversée du désert'[38] (2012: 114). Contemporaries seemed to think that Grémillon showed no originality; a reader letter in *Pour Vous*, for example, damns the film with faint praise: 'Ce n'est pas très bon, ce n'est pas très mauvais, médiocre

---

[37] 'The score is thin. The work is carefully done, it needs to be funnier.'
[38] 'Time in the wilderness.'

serait un peu sévère, disons passable'[39] ('De Bello Gallico' 1936: 10). Wahl comments that Grémillon 'a mis le film en scène en homme de métier et en ne pouvant pas faire preuve d'initiative'[40] (1935: 10), a view repeated by Henri Agel fifty years later (1984: 36). A more sustained analysis, however, reveals the auteurist aesthetic that makes Grémillon one of the period's great filmmakers.

Interestingly for a 'Viennese' operetta set in 1852 Munich, the film is an upstairs/downstairs operetta with the Emperor Franz-Josef about to marry Sissi, this being paralleled by the romance between Count Michel (Henri Garat) and a humble caterer's daughter, Thérèse (Renée Saint-Cyr). We will concentrate on the central ball sequence, a key topos for operetta films, but also for Grémillon's films, in which it is the occasion for characters to cross the class divide in a privileged if brief musical moment of social inclusion: in *Pattes blanches* (1949) an unremarkable girl is transformed into a princess and in *L'Étrange Madame X* (1951), a rich woman dances with a labourer whom she loves. In Maisch's *Königswalzer* the ball sequence opens with a standard establishing long shot.

Grémillon's version is very different, as he introduces a number of complex shots prior to the same kind of long shot we find in Maisch's version (Figure 2.5):

1. High-angle close up of chandelier
2. Low-angle with right track of dancers through the chandelier
3. Close up of dancers' feet
4. High angle at dancers' shoulder height with the swirling of ball dresses
5. High-angle long shot of the ballroom
6. Long shot from back of ballroom with the door through which Thérèse will enter

The scenario Grémillon worked from (available in the Bibliothèque Nationale de France, Paris) is much simpler than what we find in the finished film; the complexity of the sequence is therefore specific to Grémillon. Compared with Maisch's pedestrian establishing shot, Grémillon's opening shots are part of a recognizable aesthetic, revolving around the familiar motif of the circle as a symbol of harmony in his films. Similarly, in the sequence after the ball when Michel and Thérèse dance together and then each goes home, Grémillon binds their respective spaces together with superimposed shots of Michel singing over shots of Thérèse and her sister in their bedroom. This is not mentioned in the original typescript that Grémillon was given, but the shot corresponds to a notation Grémillon added by hand (shot 153 bis). There is no such superimposed shot or song in Maisch's version (see Cadalanu 2019).

This brief examination of the film suggests very clearly that the French version of the MLV is different, and depends on the small but not insignificant changes wrought by a filmmaker whose interest in music is well attested, and whose attempts to work a kind of musical editing are innovative. Grémillon's changes demonstrate both the considerable freedom given to French filmmakers taking on MLVs, and the fact that MLVs, generally derided as lightweight and insubstantial films, could incorporate innovative auteurist style.

---

[39] 'It's not very good, it's not very bad, mediocre would be too severe, let's say passable.'
[40] 'Has directed the film like a professional, but without initiative.'

3

The French operetta film

The French cinema industry recognized the potential of operetta during the silent period with adaptations of Willemetz's 1918 *Phi-Phi* (Georges Pallu, 1927) and Maxime Boucheron and Edmond Audran's 1890 *Miss Helyett* (Maurice Keroul and Georges Monca, 1928). In the 1930s, there were adaptations of Offenbach (*La Vie parisienne*, Robert Siodmak, 1936), Henri Christiné (*Dédé*, René Guissart, 1934), André Barde and Henri Christiné (*Arthur*, Léonce Perret, 1930), André Barde and Maurice Yvain (*Pas sur la bouche*, Nicolas Rimsky, Nicolas Evreïnoff, 1931; also adapted much later by Alain Resnais in 2003), André Barde again (*Le Comte Obligado*, Léon Mathot, 1935), Reynaldo Hahn (*Ciboulette*, Claude Autant-Lara, 1933) and Albert Willemetz (*Les Trois Valses*, Ludwig Berger, 1938). But there were also many operettas produced specifically for the screen, such as *Chacun sa chance* (Hans Steinhoff, 1930) with a script based on a short story by Bruno Hardt-Warden, and announcing itself in the opening credits as an 'opérette filmée'.[1] Similarly, *Il est charmant* (Louis Mercanton, 1932) was Willemetz's first operetta composed for the screen.

When adapting pre-existing stage operettas, the films tended to be selective for the musical numbers. In the case of *Le Comte Obligado*, for example, which had 400 stage performances in Paris between December 1928 and May 1934, the stage operetta had seven songs, only four of which were retained for the film. Georges Milton plays a lift attendant who comes into money and spends it all in three days pretending to be a member of high society. The songs included the song that Milton had made famous for the stage operetta, the questionably salacious 'La Caravane', also known as 'La Fille du Bédouin' ('The Daughter of the Bedouin'), which tells of a Bedouin girl who sleeps with 6,000 men (0.45). The song, which has nothing to do with the plot, was a favourite of the time and was recorded by fourteen singers between 1928 and 1929.

Despite their frequent homage to the stage origins of the form, operetta films were nonetheless quick to adopt the many possibilities that cinema offered. *Le Comte Obligado*, for example, includes exterior locations that the stage operetta could not, such as Milton losing control of his horse so that it ends up galloping among the cars of the Champs-Elysées, or the lottery results on the stage of the Trocadéro. *Ciboulette*, with dialogue by Jacques Prévert, was Autant-Lara's first feature film. Adapted from the 1923 operetta by Reynaldo Hahn, Francis de Croisset and Robert de Flers, which had 547 performances between 1923 and 1935, it combines vaudeville and fairy tale: its

---

[1] 'Filmed operetta.'

Figure 3.1 Georges Milton sings 'La Fille du Bédouin' in *Le Comte Obligado* (Courtesy BFI).

first shot is of an opening book, a procedure adopted by many films dealing with fairy tales, including Jacques Demy's *Peau d'âne* (1970). The text we see on screen begins 'il était une fois'[2] and speaks of stereotypical fairy-tale characters: a farm girl, a magician-orchestra conductor, animals that speak. An intertitle tells us that this will be a 'féerie cinématographique',[3] insisting on the film's fairy-tale premise: Ciboulette is told in a prophecy that a rich man will fall in love with her and that she will become famous. The rich man, rejected by Zénobie, is Antonin, who falls in love with Ciboulette when she sings in the cabaret of *Le Chien qui fume*.[4]

Autant-Lara greatly admired Méliès and had employed special effects in his silent films; in the short film *Construire un feu* (1930), he experimented with an early version of Cinemascope, the Hypergonar, invented by Henri Chrétien in 1926, which used an anamorphic lens. For *Ciboulette*, in keeping with the fairy-tale atmosphere, the magician fades in transparently, and in the sequence 'À Paris' in which Ciboulette prepares to become a stage character, Conchita Cibulero, a dissolve shows her work clothes being replaced by an Andalusian costume. It is in the use of music, however, that many of the operetta films show their ingenuity and innovation. Before turning to the films of Pills and Tabet, we would like to explore some of the major ways in which music

---

[2] 'Once upon a time.'
[3] 'A cinematographic fairy-tale.'
[4] 'The Smoking Dog.'

Figure 3.2 The first shots of *Ciboulette* (Courtesy Cipar/Pathé).

functions in a range of films, *Ciboulette*, *Il est charmant*, *Dédé* (a 1921 operetta with 643 performances between 1921 and 1928) and *Pas sur la bouche* (a 1925 operetta with 636 performances between 1925 and 1930): theatricalization, fragmentation, continuity and ubiquity.

Principles of the French operetta film: *Il est charmant* (1932), *Pas sur la bouche* (1931), *Ciboulette* (1933), *Dédé* (1934)

Operetta films frequently acknowledge their roots in the theatrical form, even operettas produced specifically for cinema. The opening credits of *Chacun sa chance*

(Hans Steinhoff and René Pujol, 1930) state that it is an 'opérette filmée',[5] but one of the characters stands before a closed theatre curtain and presents the actors and the director (instead of rolling credits) before announcing, 'Et maintenant, place au théâtre.'[6] In similar fashion, *Il est charmant* uses music-hall boards for its credits. The reference to stage origins can be even more sophisticated with the use of self-referentiality in the form of *mise en abîme*, a characteristic shared by other national cinemas, especially Germany and Hollywood. *Pas sur la bouche*, for example, opens on a rehearsal of the operetta, but because of the way that the stage is hidden we realize only later when we see the public performance that this was a stage rehearsal.

Dédé, described by one reviewer as 'typiquement français'[7] (*Cinémonde* 1934b: 1067), is focused on a shoe shop owned by Dédé, who loves Odette, but is loved by the shop girl Denise, who in turn is loved by Leroydet, the manager. The shop is set out to look like a music-hall stage, with two symmetrically placed staircases and a black-and-white checked floor. Four revolving ladders, ostensibly used to bring down boxes of shoes, are in reality more of a prop for dance routines (0.45). On two occasions the shop curtain is used as a stage curtain, the first time at the end of the musical sequence with the shop girls who use the ladders as props (0.40), and more especially at the end of the film during the closing number 'Dans la vie faut pas s'en faire' ('In Life You Shouldn't Stress'), which involves all the characters in an upbeat finale. There is a cut and the camera looks through the shop window from the street outside as the curtain closes and the word 'fin' appears. The performances of song and dance are legitimized by the claim that the salesgirls are part of the Folies-Bergères dance troupe, that the employees write operettas, and that they are all busy rehearsing; but within the conventions of the story it is clear that this claim is ironically self-referential, serving largely to draw attention to the pervasiveness of the musical performance.

Songs are fragmented in three major ways. First, they are sung by more than just the main protagonists. As the presence of a magician who is a conductor might well suggest, *Ciboulette* celebrates music, beginning with the long opening tracking shot sweeping over the roofs of Paris, recalling *Sous les toits de Paris* (Buache 1982: 16), past the Église Saint-Eustache, along the street past a lamplighter among other minor characters, through Les Halles and ending in the cabaret. The chorus is mostly off-screen, so that the distinction between diegetic and non-diegetic is blurred; the music becomes immersive and inclusive rather than attached to the chorus. Indeed, song is not confined to the principal characters, as secondary and minor characters also sing. Unsurprisingly in these circumstances, they are not closed off as singular performance events, but remain open, something that is underlined by the next point.

Second, they are frequently heard in short bursts, often taking the place of dialogue, or emerging from dialogue. Songs are heard in fits and starts, and in snatches, such as *Dédé*'s 'Oh! la drôle de boutique' ('O, What a Strange Shop') sung by the shop girls and serving as an introduction to a sequence in the shop (0.23). They are not self-contained

---

[5] 'Filmed operetta.'
[6] 'And now theatre takes over.'
[7] 'Typically French.'

numbers, but can emerge from conversations between characters, as is the case when Robert and the shop girls discuss the shoe displays (0.45).

And finally, in a different kind of fragmentation, the original stage operetta songs can be adapted so that they correspond to what we see on screen. The most well-known song from the stage operetta *Dédé*, and the first by Robert (Albert Préjean) in the film, 'Dans la vie faut pas s'en faire', has the familiar words from the stage version. Robert stops for a moment when he goes into the lawyer's office and finds two banknotes which he pockets. The song then starts again, referring to what we have just seen: 'Grand merci mon cher notaire/Vous m'tirez d'tracas'[8] (0.5). Similarly, a song by the strikers tells of their concerns: 'Au nom de la fédération/Nous venons en délégation/Faire au patron l'exposition/De toutes nos revendications'[9] (0.56). But after seeing the shop girls employed by Robert and having had a few drinks, they leave empty-handed, but content, raucously singing a modified and comic version: 'Et nous avons sans objection/Obtenu toute satisfaction'[10] (1.00).

As the earlier-mentioned second point suggests, there is a principle of continuity between spoken dialogue and song, which is held in tension with the principle of fragmentation we have explored. Song and dialogue combine seamlessly. A snippet of song can intervene in a spoken conversation, emphasizing its toing and froing, such as Robert's 'Ô Madame je vous trouve exquise/Permettez que je vous le dise'[11] to Odette in *Dédé*.

Moreover, there is a principle of circulation in the use of the music more generally, as can be seen in the cabaret sequence that follows the opening chorus of *Ciboulette*. The men's chorus sings 'Nous sommes les joyeux drilles', with the women's chorus responding 'Nous sommes les jeunes filles'[12] – this alternation supporting and insisting on the relationship between the two lovers more efficiently than dialogue. Later in the same sequence the spoiled young aristocrat Antonin sings 'Je vous aimais, suis-je assez bête'[13] to Zénobie; the song turns into a list of the bills he has to pay her, interrupted by the 'assez, assez'[14] of the cabaret dancers before the assembled clients pick up on Antonin's lyrics. The song does not naturally reach closure, as it mutates into a sung dialogue (*parlé-chanté*) as the characters wish each other goodnight.

Pas sur la bouche is one of the more extraordinary examples of this type of continuity, not just between dialogue and song, but also between sound effects and song; Lucien Wahl's judgement that the film's mise en scène was 'dépourvue d'un style particulier, ne se rehausse d'aucune trouvaille spirituelle'[15] and that the film,

---

[8] 'Many thanks, lawyer, you've saved me a lot of bother.'
[9] 'In the name of the federation we've come as a delegation to explain our demands to the boss.'
[10] 'And we've obtained satisfaction without any objections.'
[11] 'Dear Lady allow me to tell you that I think you're exquisite.'
[12] 'We're jolly fellows/We're the young girls.'
[13] 'I loved you, how stupid could I be.'
[14] 'Enough, enough.'
[15] 'Has no particular style, no witty finds.'

overall, lacked charm seems to be missing the point (1931b: 5).[16] The story is typical of vaudeville: Gilberte's first husband, the American Eric, becomes friends with her second husband, Georges, who does not know about Eric. The title refers to the fact that Gilberte left Eric because he refused to kiss her on the mouth. There are few full musical numbers; rather, song erupts in the middle of dialogue, or else dialogue can be spoken in rhythmical fashion as if it were song. When Georges returns home to find Eric there, presentations are made in song; but this is not a 'musical number', not least because the everydayness of the event does not lend itself to the kind of spectacular performance we might expect; but it is also because the sequence carries on with *parlé-chanté* by the maid inviting them to table – 'Madame est servie'[17] – after which they sing the menu. Rhythmical speech by the maid thus functions as a kind of link between two musical moments (rather than musical numbers). Moreover, music can emerge as much from sound effects as from dialogue, for example the clicking of typewriters or the sound of footsteps. The co-director Nicolas Evreinoff explained that the team was trying to 'transposer, dans le dialogue, le rythme même de la musique ... À huit mesures musicales correspond la valeur de huit mesures verbales', the aim being to avoid 'cette coupure fatale qu'apporte un refrain dans le cours d'une conversation'[18] (quoted in Moustier 1931: 617).

There is therefore no separation between a normal sequence and a sequence featuring a musical number; rather, the film's rhythm is constructed from the interplay between different elements of the soundtrack, whether they be sound effects, spoken dialogue, *parlé-chanté* or full song. Indeed, we may well feel that the narrative functions as a kind of container from which music surges, barely contained, as if, in a reversal of the more usual image–music hierarchy, the music moulds and performs the visual track and the dialogue.

Because songs do not always reach closure, and can be sung by any character, and can also mutate into sung dialogue, they become all-pervasive, circulating through the narrative and irrigating it. In *Ciboulette*, this is exemplified by the sequence in which Ciboulette's fiancés visit her, each one singing a signature song that is intended to characterize them. Ciboulette's father tells her she must choose between them and their dialogue is entirely sung even though its ordinariness does not necessarily justify it. When music is absent, dialogue is nonetheless rhythmed and even rhymed, as, for example, this exchange between Antonin and Zénobie: 'Le cœur parfois a des raisons que la raison partage/Mon cher, pourquoi ce persiflage?'[19]

In *Il est charmant* too, in which Henri Garat plays Jacques, a lazy and fun-loving law student, singing becomes a normal mode of communication. It was the 'première opérette strictement française'[20] according to the director Albert Willemetz, who

---

[16] Other critics were more impressed by the mise en sène. René Jolivet, for example, praises 'les scènes comiques du film, cadres dans des décors vastes, modernes, éblouissants' (1931: 390).
[17] 'Madam is served.'
[18] 'Apply the rhythm of the music to the dialogue. Eight musical beats correspond to eight verbal beats/ the fatal break that a refrain brings during a conversation.'
[19] 'The heart has its reasons that reason shares/My dear, why this persiflage?'
[20] 'The first completely French operetta.'

Figure 3.3 A portrait sings in *Il est charmant* (Courtesy Lobster).

said that he wished to emulate *Le Chemin du paradis* (quoted in Méry 174: 100), and was seen as very original in its use of music, which 'souvent se substitue à l'image'[21] (*Cinémonde* 1932: 146). It was praised as 'une exquise opérette de cinéma, avec des trouvailles sans nombre'[22] (*Cinémagazine* 1932: 73). The film opens with the song 'Nous sommes la milice' ('We Are the Militia') sung by Jacques and his rowdy Folies-Bergère friends in the Paris streets. Their drunkenness and the fact that Jacques's friends are music-hall artists legitimize the use of song; a neighbour tries to get them to quieten down by singing his complaint, naturalizing song as a mode of communication. Later in the film, a clerk in the office belonging to Jacques's uncle suddenly breaks into song (0.43). Song is not just a privileged mode of communication, however. In the reception sequence, the guests sing a welcome to Jacques – 'D'ordinaire un notaire/est un monsieur sévère',[23] and reprise the title song 'Il est charmant' ('He Is Charming'), song becoming contagious as even the portrait of an ancestor begins to sing, a trope reprised in *Prends la route*, as we shall see in Chapter 4 (1.09; Figure 3.6). Song permeates and percolates through all the film's spaces, even when they are not spaces normally characterized by song: the streets, the Jardin du Luxembourg, the Sorbonne, the uncle's law office, in which Moussia practises dance moves from his revue *Le Bifteck aux pommes*[24] (1.16). Moreover, attention is drawn to this procedure when Jacques, who has finally qualified as a lawyer, puts an image of a naked woman in his office to symbolize the Law; the clerk ruefully comments: 'Maître, on ne se croirait plus dans une étude mais dans un dancing'[25] (0.55).

This brief survey of the French operetta film has focused on the integration of musical numbers, and we have seen how some aspects, particularly those of continuity and ubiquity, might suggest something close to the myth of integrated communities explored by Jane Feuer (1995). In the next section we will focus at more length on an operetta from the mid-1930s, namely, Robert Siodmak's *La crise est finie*, and in the next chapter on a pair of films by the male duo Jacques Pills (1906–70) and Georges Tabet (1905–84): *Toi c'est moi* (*You Are Me*) (René Guissart, 1936) and *Prends la route*

---

[21] 'Often takes the place of the image.'
[22] 'An exquisite film operetta with innumerable finds.'
[23] 'Usually a lawyer is a serious man.'
[24] 'Steak with Apple.'
[25] 'Sir, anyone would think we were in a dance hall.'

(*Take to the Road*) (Jean Boyer and Louis Chavance, 1937). The first is an adaptation, and the second a screen original operetta; but their interest for us is the way in which they perform a particular kind of community at a critical political moment, as had Siodmak's film a couple of years earlier.

The Hollywood temptation: *La crise est finie* (1934)

Robert Siodmak fled Germany, where he worked at UFA, to France in 1933 where he made eight films before moving to Hollywood. His first French film was *Le Sexe faible* (1933), based on a 1929 stage farce by Édouard Bourdet. Paul Vecchiali describes *La crise est finie*, his second French film, as a 'comédie musicale à l'américaine quant à l'esprit, française quant aux moyens'[26] (2010, v2: 528). In it a troupe of actors travel to Paris to find work, and create a review called 'La crise est finie'. The film is very clearly influenced by the Hollywood backstage musical, as commentators at the time remarked: Marc Farnèse titles his review '*La crise est finie*, un *42nd Street* français' (1934: 766), and in the same magazine Raymond Berner wrote: 'Et voici un film gai, *La crise est finie*, véritable opérette d'écran visiblement inspirée des modèles américains – *42nd Street* [Lloyd Bacon, 1933], *Prologues* [*Footlight Parade*, Lloyd Bacon, 1933] etc. – somptuosité en moins'[27] (1934: 868). In the then recently established readers' column of *Pour Vous*, the main complaint was precisely the fact that the film was too American, 'une pâle décalcomanie des films américains'[28] ('Monette' 1935: 12). Perhaps because of this, spectators felt that the film was inferior to Clair's *Sous les toits de Paris* or *Le Million*, and that the gags were unoriginal. The following withering critique sums up many of the views expressed by audiences: the film is 'chaotique, heurté sans rythme, avec des longueurs et des puérilités à faire pleurer'[29] ('Jean Godefroy' 1935: 12).

The film was heavily influenced by the Hollywood backstage musical for two reasons: first, it was an upbeat and utopian response to the worldwide financial crisis which took hold in France by 1934. The first Hollywood backstage musicals had been released in 1933, and were also responses to the Depression: 'The backstage musical of 1933 brought a new syntax not only to the backstage subgenre; it also for the first time established the illusionist and happy-go-lucky syntax of the genre as a whole' (Altman 1987: 211). The topos of the preparation of a musical review allowed audiences to accept the realities of the Depression, particularly unemployment and lack of money, while escaping those realities through song and dance, with the added benefit of a parallelism between the on-screen audience and the audience of the film: 'The musical's internal stylistic dichotomy (world/stage, real/ideal) thus corresponds exactly to the audience/image opposition implicit in the cinema viewing situation: the production

---

[26] 'A Hollywood-style film musical in spirit, French in its means.'
[27] 'Here's a gay film … a real screen operetta, visibly inspired by American models … without the sumptuousness.'
[28] 'A pale copy of American films.'
[29] 'Chaotic, jarring rhythms, boring and silly enough to make you weep.'

number on stage compensates for the world's drabness in the same way that the screen image permits the audience momentarily to forget its real situation' (Altman 1987: 75). Second, the Hollywood films had been distributed in France thanks to dubbed versions, in particular *42nd Street* (Cornu 2014: 131), so that audiences would have been familiar with the sub-genre.

Both *La crise est finie* and *Gold Diggers of 1933* focus on a troupe of actors struggling to survive the financial crisis, and hardly surprisingly there are similar scenes in both films: both begin with a cancelled show as a result of the producer's debts, the first sequence functioning as an aborted spectacle whose realization we expect as the apotheosis of the film. Both films have sequences in which the characters look for work. The Depression is directly referred to in *Gold Diggers of 1933*:

Carol: This is the fourth show in two months that I've been in of and out of.
Trixie: They close before they open.
Fay: The Depression, dearie.

And we find a similar exchange when actors from the French troupe pretending to be policemen go in search of a band in Paris, and come across some musicians busking: one of the 'policemen' asks whether the buskers have a permit, to which they respond: 'Monsieur l'agent, nous sommes des pauvres chômeurs ... Il y a la crise.'[30]

More than these fleeting verbal parallels, spectators would have been struck by very similar show sequences, the first sequence of *Gold Diggers of 1933* bearing striking resemblances to the final sequence of *La crise est finie*. Mervyn LeRoy's film opens on a rehearsal of 'We're in the Money', sung by Ginger Rogers surrounded by chorus girls wearing costumes made of giant coins. The chorus girls in Siodmak's film also wear costumes made of giant coins, the largest of which serves as a cache-sexe (Figure 3.4). The song lyrics make the reference explicit: 'À Hollywood c'est un record/On fait des girls en or'.[31] The choreography mimics Busby Berkeley's and the sequence, to use a term employed by Vecchiali (2010, v2: 528), explodes the narrow space of the theatre we encountered at the start of the film to propose a utopian Berkeleyesque space.

The final sequence is seven minutes long, comprising seventy-seven shots. It begins by positing the realist space of the theatre (see Figure 3.5), with the Berkleyesque chorus girls lined up on a rising set of podia, each one with a large letter in front of her, spelling out 'la crise est finie'. Marcel sings the song at a piano in front of a painted backdrop representing the globe, although our sense of diegetic space is undermined when we see six chorus girls magically on top of the globe as the camera pulls back and what we understand as banknotes begin to flutter down (shots 1–17; Figure 3.5). The diegetic space is then 'exploded' as a close-up on a 1000-franc banknote fluttering down functions as a wipe to a series of four micro-scenes: a shot of the Eiffel Tower

---

[30] 'Officer, we're just poor unemployed people. ... There's the crisis.'
[31] 'In Hollywood it's a record/They make girls in gold.'

Figure 3.4 A comparison of the first sequence of *Gold Diggers of 1933* and the final sequence of *La crise est finie* (Courtesy Warner and René Chateau).

Figure 3.5 The start of the final sequence of *La crise est finie* (Courtesy René Chateau).

indicates that we are in Paris, and we see a painter in his garret room. The nude he has been painting comes alive and hands him a banknote, after which he thrusts a butterfly net out of his window to catch more banknotes (shots 18–24). Another banknote wipe, this time of a one-dollar bill, signals the transition to New York whose skyline is superimposed by the sign for 'National Bank of America'; we see gangsters transferring wads of notes into a bank vault as the lyrics of the song explain that they are no longer stealing but saving (shots 25–31). A 500-rouble note fluttering down signals Russia, with shots of Russian church spires, followed by a studio décor as Russian peasants walk past singing, the lyrics again alluding to what we see (shots 32–36). A fluttering £5 note followed by a shot of the Houses of Parliament signals that we are now in the UK; a diner burns a note to light his cigar, and is revealed as a Scotsman wearing a kilt when he leaves, the lyrics telling us that even a Scotsman is prepared literally to burn money because he is rich and has all his pockets full of money (shots 37–42). The diegetic space of the theatre has in this sequence been opened out into an international space of fantasy, echoing the globe that is part of the diegetic décor behind Marcel.

This explosion of the space ushers in a second type of fantasy, that of utopian community, as we return to the theatre audience, the theatre transformed by togetherness and a spirit of generosity: we see the audience singing along to the song, a man placing a ring on the finger of his lover, an older man peeling off banknotes and casting them from the balcony into the crowd (shots 43–51).

The rest of the finale reprises Berkleyesque tropes, this time without the constraint of diegetic space, as the theatre stage appears to be almost boundless. We see five chorus girls stepping out of crates labelled 'Trick Girls', recalling the Hollywood connection, and then a typical Berkeley sequence of kaleidoscopic chorus girls: we face three lines of chorus girls waving multiple arms. As they step away, however, we see that the 'line' which would in a Hollywood film have been made up of real chorus girls is in this case a levered contraption held at each end by two chorus girls, the bodies of the chorus girls between them being cardboard cut-outs (shots 57–60). Arguably, this is what might have led Berner to claim, as we saw earlier, that the film was Berkleyesque but the 'somptuosité en moins' (1934: 868). And yet, the complexity of the contraption suggests that this is more likely to be a knowing ironic dig at the 'Berkleyesque' and its capacity for escapist spectacle; as we shall see, irony is one of the major differences between this film and its supposed Hollywood mimicry.

The explosion of space carries on into the final sequence: Marcel at the piano is now at the top of a 10-metre décor intended to represent a tropical island. Nicole emerges from inside his piano as they sing the love duet 'Sans un mot' (Figure 3.6); Bernoullin, who has blackmailed Nicole into accepting his advances, is released by his wife from the trap beneath the stage where Marcel has put him, and climbs the 'island' to escape, only to fall back in slapstick style (shots 61–77). The show takes place in the Théâtre Élysée-Clichy, which no one recognizes when Nicole's mother arrives in Paris to attend the show, because the theatre has been closed for five years. The name sounds relatively normal in the Parisian context, but its resurrection as a place that everyone in Paris wishes to go to so as to celebrate the end of the crisis – as Nicole's mother seeks help from passers-by, a crowd gathers and they end up chanting '*La crise est finie*, la nouvelle revue', subsequently flocking to the theatre (1.04) – and the emphasis on a tropical paradise in the final sequence, suggests that we should take the Élysée part more symbolically as Elysium, or paradise, the space where the financial crisis really is over. We should not be surprised when the audience all join in to sing along to the title song, as the theatrical space, which is no longer a 'real' space within the diegesis, but a utopian exploded space, becomes a place where the community rises above the crisis through song.

The role of Bernouillin, the nasty piano shop owner who tries to take advantage of Nicole, is not just for comic effect, even if the name is intended to sound comical: not only does he look like Oliver Hardy, but he is also 'berné' ('foolish') like Hardy, imprisoned by the actors in the theatre trap and forced to listen to them noisily rehearsing the show that he wants to prevent at all costs, and then kept in there by his

Figure 3.6 Marcel and his piano at the top of the fantasy tropical island in *La crise est finie* (Courtesy René Chateau).

outraged wife who chases him once she lets him out, so he comes across as 'une nouille', a noodle, a weak character. His fall when he tries to climb up to the paradise island suggests strongly that in this fantasy the devil has been expelled from paradise. And yet, as was the case with the Berkleyesque chorus girls, there is a knowing irony played out with this character: his self-interested loan of the piano is what makes the show possible; and moreover, as the new owner of the theatre, he threatens to turn it into a cinema to prevent the troupe from putting on the show (0.53). But this is precisely what we as spectators have seen: a performance in which cinema makes an exploded utopian space possible in ways that the theatre could not.

The film may well, therefore, appear to be Berkeleyesque in some respects; but its multiple ironies are very European, and commentators were keen to point out its innovative aspects, praising it for its inventiveness relative to its thin and clichéd storyline:

> Mince histoire et pas très neuve depuis les quelque 500 autres qui se passent aussi dans les coulisses avec auteur entreprenant, vedette insupportable, jeune première qui doublera la vedette au pied levé. ... Il semble qu'on l'entend pour la première fois, tant les trouvailles, les enchaînements sonores, les broderies du style ont une marque personnelle. ... Et avec une belle économie de moyens. Pas de luxe, de l'ingéniosité. Trois chansons seulement de Lenoir et Waxman, mais entraînantes, entêtantes, et promises au succès, et si liées à l'action qu'elles semblent n'être plus qu'une paraphrase des couplets.[32] (Vermorel 1934: 7)

There are three ways in which the film is significantly different from the Hollywood films mentioned: aspects of the cinematography, the treatment of the music, and the moral implications of the songs. Money is of no concern, something we will

---

[32] 'A thin and clichéd storyline given the 500 others that take place in the wings with an enterprising author, an insufferable star, a young newcomer who will stand in for the star at the last minute. It feels like we're hearing it for the first time because the creativity, the sound design have a personal stamp. And it's all done economically. No luxury, ingeniousness. Only three songs by Lenoir and Waxman, but they're compelling, exhilarating, bound to be successful, and so integrated into the action that they seem to be no more than a paraphrasing of the couplets.'

return to, as it is somewhat different from the materialist concerns of *Gold Diggers of 1933*. As the review just quoted points out, there are only three songs, but these are frequently repeated, in ways that are typical of the French operetta film as discussed in the previous section, based on the principles of theatricalization, fragmentation, continuity and ubiquity.

As might be expected from a director who had worked in Germany, aspects of the mise en scène and cinematography (by Eugen Schüfftan) are Expressionist, intended to emphasize the class difference between Bernouillin and the troupe. For example, Marcel hides in the wings and whistles one of the film's signature songs, 'On ne voit ça qu'à Paris' ('You Only See This in Paris') so as to trick Bernouillin into stepping onto the trap (0.53). The contrast between the two characters

> is managed by an effective blurring of the French and German inheritances. Marcel is shot from straight on. ... The contours of his white tee shirt ... are brightly illuminated against a background shadow ... . Bernouillin, by contrast, is shot from a prominent high camera angle to emphasize his isolation and malevolent intent. ... The contours of the shopkeeper's body as he moves amongst the pools of diffuse shadow are pitch black. (Phillips 2004: 86)

Second, the organization of the music corresponds to the principles of the French operetta explored in the previous section. There are only three songs: 'On ne voit ça qu'à Paris', 'Sans un mot' ('Without a Word') and the film's title song, 'La crise est finie'. But these are frequently repeated, either because they are being rehearsed or performed, or because the actors burst into song at the slightest opportunity. We hear 'On ne voit ça qu'à Paris' (0.10) and 'Sans un mot' (0.6) at the start of the film as part of the stage review *Mlle Jambes Nues* (Miss Bare Legs). We hear 'La crise est finie' when Marcel proposes it as an additional song for the review he is planning (0.28) and then rehearsed (0.56) and performed in the Élysée-Clichy theatre at the end of the film (1.08), as is 'Sans un mot' (1.14).

But we also hear snippets of these songs. We hear 'Sans un mot' played by the pianist when Bernouillin takes Nicole to the restaurant, and she sings it when she returns to the theatre (0.40). This is ironic because the song is about lovers not needing words to express their love: Nicole has just sold herself to Bernouillin so that they can have the piano, and a jealous Marcel ends up hitting her when she returns to the theatre. Irony is piled upon irony subsequently, as in an ironic echo of the first restaurant scene, we hear the pianist play 'On ne voit ça qu'à Paris' in the restaurant where Nicole stands Bernouillin up (0.46).

Not only are the songs repeated in ironic mode, but they are also used in what might be called epic mode. The most startling example is when the troupe goes to Paris by train. They sing 'On ne voit ça qu'à Paris' exuberantly, looking forward to the jobs they imagine they will easily find on arrival, and the song segues into a series of unsuccessful job-hunting scenes in Paris, the lyrics being adapted to the situation, and sung as much by the potential employers as by the actors (0.17–0.21). The film's title song is given similar treatment: Marcel plays it on the piano in Bernouillin's shop, and adapts the lyrics so that they become a plea to Bernouillin: 'Quand on veut un joli piano/Le marchand vous en fait cadeau'[33] (0.30). The songs are therefore theatricalized by rehearsals and performances, and are fragmented and distributed throughout the film to provide continuity, to emphasize parallel scenes in ironic mode, and to establish the principle of a coherent and supportive community.

Finally, the moral of the film is different from *Gold Diggers of 1933*. 'We're in the Money' is straightforwardly materialist; money allows you to realize your American dream: 'Gone are my blues/And gone are my tears/I've got good news/To shout in your ears/The silver dollar has returned to the fold/With silver you can turn your dreams to gold.' In 'La crise est finie', on the other hand, the dream, as we saw in the final sequence, is of a tropical paradise: 'Je ne peux plus voir tout cet or/Aussi je change de décor/Je serai mieux certes/Sur une île déserte/La crise est finie, la crise est finie/Et je n'aime plus l'or.'[34]

Unlike the Hollywood film with its frankly escapist spectacle, Siodmak's film recognizes the financial crisis but rejects naked materialism – 'je n'aime plus l'or – asking, instead, for a reaffirmation of community, and revelling in the power of community expressed through song. Marcel explains this in the sequence when he is elaborating the title song (0.28), saying that he wants to create

> du nouveau. Des rires, des tempêtes de rire déferlant sur des visages débordants de bonheur, sur des corps secoués par des rythmes nouveaux, explosant de soleil, de vie. Finie la tristesse! Vous là, vous ne comprenez pas? Tenez, exemple. La crise ... est finie! Alors vous voyez bien, vous êtes tous des optimistes, joyeux de vivre, joyeux de monter une revue pleine d'enthousiasme, de couleurs, de lumière![35]

This film was not the only one to contain songs that aimed to make the audience forget the financial crisis. Raymond Berner, in his regular column 'Chansons de films' in *Cinémonde*, mentions 'Tout va bien' ('Everything is Fine') in a film starring Georges Milton, *Nu comme un ver* (Léon Mathot, 1933), with its lines 'Tout va bien, qu'on se le dise/Tout va bien, ne pensons plus à la crise',[36] and 'Un coup d'jambe en l'air' ('Shake a Leg') sung by Albert Préjean in *L'Auberge du Petit Dragon* (Jean de Limur, 1934), 'un fox-trot très gai et facile à retenir'[37] (1934: 868). But Siodmak's film is fascinating for its precarious equilibrium between an American and a Franco-European aesthetic. In the next chapter we focus on two squarely French operetta film sub-genres.

---

[33] 'When you want a nice piano/The dealer gives it to you for free.'
[34] 'I can't stand all this gold/So I'm changing scene/I'd be better off on a desert island/The crisis is over/ And I don't like gold anymore.'
[35] 'Something new. Laughter, waves of laughter breaking over happy faces, over bodies swaying to new rhythms, exploding with light, with life. Finished with sadness. You there, don't you understand? Look, let me give an example. The crisis is over! So you see, you're all optimists, full of life, happy to produce a revue full of enthusiasm, colour, light!'
[36] 'Everything is fine, let's be clear/Everything is fine, let's stop thinking about the crisis.'
[37] 'A gay fox-trot that's easy to remember.'

4

Pills and Tabet and the Marseille operetta

In this chapter we will focus on two very different types of operetta: the films of Jacques Pills and Georges Tabet, which display clear links to the ideology of the Front Populaire, and the local variant of the operetta in Marseille.

The operetta films of Pills and Tabet

In their two films, Jacques Pills plays an upper-class Lothario, who ends up getting his girl, while Georges Tabet plays a middle- or lower-class character who is generally the butt of jokes, in a standard comic duo pairing. These two films have a strong relationship to a key historical moment in 1930s France: the coming to power of the first left-wing government, known as the Front Populaire (Popular Front). This lasted from May 1936 until the autumn of 1938, during which period the two films were released. We will show how the musical numbers in the two films function to create the community and the values associated with the Popular Front.

Toi, c'est moi, their first film, was adapted from a very successful stage operetta. It was performed 265 times from September 1934 to June 1935 at the Théâtre des Bouffes Parisiens. The plot plays on mistaken identities. Like Jacques in *Il est charmant*, Bob (Jacques Pills) parties all the time while pretending to work, thanks in his case to the financial support of a wealthy widowed aunt (Pauline Carton). When she discovers his fecklessness, she sends him to her plantation in the Antilles to learn about the world of work. He is accompanied by his best friend, Pat (Georges Tabet), whom he persuades to take his place, hence the film's title, 'you are me'. However, Bob falls for the wild (White) daughter of the plantation manager; but her father wants her to marry Pat, whom he believes to be the nephew who will inherit. Pat, meanwhile, is the object of a local (Black) woman's attentions, in a typical upstairs–downstairs configuration. Much of the comedy is focused on the two friends' attempts to recover their real identities; a running slapstick gag has Pat dowsed with a bucket of water every time he claims to be Pat rather than the rich nephew. The aunt decides to visit the island in a surprise visit to check up on her nephew. The climate causes all of the characters, including the aunt, to fall in love, so that much of the second half of the film is devoted to the courting of a variety of couples. Pills and Tabet reprise their stage roles, as does Pauline Carton in the role of the aunt.

Audiences and critics appreciated the duo's polished musical performances. One critic writes in extraordinarily eulogistic tones as follows:

> Avec une aisance charmante, leur voix flexibles cheminent parallèlement le long de la chanson, s'écartent, se rejoignent, se séparent, et se croisent en des méandres imprévus et ravissants. Si l'un se tait un instant, on croit que c'est l'autre qui a la plus jolie voix. Mais si celui-ci s'interrompt à son tour, on donne sa langue au chat … Les deux voix, libres, paraissent pourtant soudées l'une à l'autre par un impérieux sentiment musical. Que le mouvement s'accélère ou s'alanguisse en des inflexions caressantes ou ironiques, jamais l'ensemble ne souffre du plus infime décalage. C'est cette perfection qui leur donne un rythme à la fois si précis et si souple et leur permet d'enrouler leurs arabesques vocales avec tant d'infaillible sûreté. La liberté, la fantaisie, la pureté de leur style, fruit d'un long travail de mise au point, ravissent profanes et connaisseurs. Chacune de leur interprétations, chacun de leurs disques est un petit chef-d'œuvre de perfection et d'humour.[1] (Berner 1936: 904–5)

Part of the film's freshness, according to critics, was its clever use of music by the composer Moïse Simons. Its nine musical numbers mix forms that had been around for some time, such as the one-step, the waltz and the foxtrot, with new Latino-American forms such as the rumba, the conga and the samba, congruent with the colonial setting.

Prends la route, which was released two months later, is based entirely in France. It has a dozen songs, and was built on the previous film's success. Unlike *Toi c'est moi*, however, this operetta was written specifically for the screen by the director, Jean Boyer, and was filmed almost entirely in exteriors. This was partly because, as the title suggests, it was a film about the new phenomenon of touring, available to all classes whether on bicycles, motorbikes or cars. Bachelor Jacques (Jacques Pills) tries to shake off his mistress as he travels back to the family home where he is to be married off; his mistress pursues him with her wealthy lover, who is a Touring Club fanatic. Jacques meets Simone (Claude May) on the road; she and her chaperone have run out of petrol. Simone and Jacques elope, little knowing that she is the bride intended by his father. Tabet plays an annoying car insurance salesman, Potopoto, who tags along on his motorbike (hence the moniker, which represents the putt-putt of the motorbike's engine).

While Georges Van Parys's compositions are musically not so inventive as Moïse Simons's music for *Toi c'est moi*, *Prends la route* was, like the previous film, applauded for its freshness, by which was meant the devil-may-care attitude of the younger

---

[1] 'With the most charming ease, their flexible voices follow parallel paths during the song, split apart, come together again, separate and cut across each other in delightfully unforeseen meanderings. If one stops for a moment, you think it is the other one that has the prettiest voice. But if this one stops in his turn, you have to give up trying to decide. The two voices, both free, nonetheless seem welded together by an imperious musical sentiment. When the tempo accelerates or slows down in mellow or ironic inflexions, there is not the slightest change in the overall tone. It is this perfection that gives them a rhythm both precise and supple, and that allows them to twirl their vocal arabesques with such infallible assurance. The freedom, the fantasy, the purity of their style, the fruit of long hours of training, enchant connoisseurs and lay people alike. Each of their songs is a little masterpiece of perfection and humour.'

generation. In the regular readers' column of the popular film magazine *Pour Vous*, a reader wrote that the film 'commence par des chansons: la chanson de la jeunesse, des vacances, de la joie de vivre. C'est un film optimiste qu'il faut voir pour se ragaillardir'[2] (Denain 1937: 10), and a critic wrote in similar terms that 'cette fantaisie musicale est d'une fraîcheur, d'un entrain, d'une jeunesse irrésistibles'[3] (Cambier 1937: 119).

The title song of the film (0.18) is a foxtrot, which urges the French to take to the road. The French Touring Club had been established by cycling enthusiasts in 1890, and had, along with the advent of camping, become a popular although not necessarily populist leisure activity. In the summer of 1936, following the creation of the Popular Front government, the Matignon Agreements gave French workers a range of benefits, among which were the 40-hour working week, and, for the first time, paid holidays. There was a mass exodus to the beaches and the countryside that summer. For many it was the first holiday outside a city, literally constituting a breath of fresh air after the difficult 1920s with their post-war gloom followed by the financial crash of 1929. This is reflected in the song: 'L'air de Paris te donne le teint gris/Mais le grand air te le rendra plus clair/Plus de gouttes pour la toux/Prends la route elle guérit tout/Prends la route et met les bouts!'[4] Moreover, at the end of this number (0.20), which conveys the new freedom felt by ordinary people, we get a taste of the upward mobility that holidays and possible modes of transport have brought. We see a couple walking in the sun, when a tandem overtakes them. The wife asks her husband: 'Dis, chéri, ça coûte cher un tandem?' A motorbike overtakes the tandem; the wife says: 'Dis, chéri, ça coûte cher une moto?' A car overtakes the motorbike; the wife says: 'Dis, chéri, ça coûte cher une petite voiture?' The punchline is delivered when we see the grumpy aunt and her niece stranded in their car because they have run out of petrol, with the aunt saying, 'ça ne coûte peut-être pas très cher, mais ça ne marche pas!'[5] As Philippe Frémeaux points out in his introduction to a CD compilation of songs released at the time of the Popular Front (1996), there may not be an obvious connection between the politics of the period and most of its songs, but what the Popular Front brought was leisure time: 'Le vrai rapprochement entre le Front Populaire et la chanson s'est fait partout où le temps arraché au travail, au patron, dans la grève ou grâce aux cong'pay', a permis aux amoureux de danser, rêver, s'aimer le temps d'une chanson.'[6] As we shall see, this pivotal moment between the old and the new is reflected in the films, particularly *Toi c'est moi*, although less so in *Prends la route*, in values that are organized along generational lines.

Both films depend on geographical displacement: the characters are tourists for whom travel means freedom to express their desires. This is most obvious in *Toi c'est*

---

[2] 'Begins with songs: the songs of youth, of holidays, of joie de vivre. It's an optimistic film that will perk you up.'
[3] 'This musical fantasy has the irresistible freshness and high spirits of youth.'
[4] 'The Paris air has made you go all sallow/The great outdoors will brighten it up/No more drops for your cough/Take to the road, it's a cure-all/Take to the road and get lost.'
[5] 'Is a tandem expensive?/Is a motorbike expensive?/Is a small car expensive?/ It isn't that expensive, but it doesn't work!'
[6] 'The real link between the Popular Front and song can be found wherever the time stolen from work, from the boss, in a strike or thanks to paid holidays allowed lovers to dance, dream, love each other during the time of a song.'

Figure 4.1 Jungle drums in *Toi c'est moi* (Courtesy René Chateau).

moi, where the duo go to the Antilles. The location in the hot and steamy tropics, and the associated music, stimulate the sexual desire of the characters, who all pair up and engage in what Barbara Creed calls the musical's 'mating game' (2009). This is a frequent theme in the dialogue, when the plantation manager apologizes for his daughter's wild ways; Jacques responds that it is due to the climate. Later, local musicians play 'jungle drums' (1.08; Figure 4.1). This appears to prompt a series of passionate declarations by the main characters, who one by one declare their undying love for each other. The younger characters do this in more standard romantic style, while comedy is generated by the older characters who declare their love in farcically excessive style. So, for example, the climate again figures as the reason for sexual desire in a saucy dialogue between Adolphe, the Governor General of the island, and Honorine, the wealthy aunt (1.10), who misinterprets the meaning of 'tam-tam', clearly understanding it to mean sexual intercourse:

> Adolphe: Vous avez les yeux profonds.
> Honorine: J'ai la fièvre.
> Adolphe: C'est le climat.
> Honorine: Allons faire un tour … cette atmosphère!
> Adolphe: Vous aimez le tam-tam?
> Honorine: Je ne sais pas, il y a si longtemps que je suis veuve.

Adolphe: Le tam-tam, c'est une sorte de bal nègre, je vais vous montrez ça.
Honorine: Mais, vous me jurez d'être sage? Gamin …⁷

Unbridled desire leads Honorine to respond to the advances of Pedro, the plantation manager, not long afterwards, in one of the most memorable songs of the 1930s, 'Sous les palétuviers' ('Under the Mangrove Trees'; lyrics by Albert Willemetz; 1.17), covered by many singers in the decades to follow. Its rapid-fire delivery, its comic rhymes and puns are part of the song's pleasure. But the rapid delivery also emphasizes the rush of mounting sexual desire; and the stretching, disintegration and recomposing of words – particularly those in the refrain focusing on the key word 'palétuvier' – underlines the disintegration of propriety. Bodies are shot through with desire, which bubbles through the repeated syllables unanchored from their original words, as if the characters, powerfully moved by lust, can do no more than stammer incoherently:

Pedro:	Ah! Viens sous les pa
Honorine:	Je viens de ce pas
	Mais j´y vais pas à pas!
Pedro:	Ah! Suis-moi veux-tu? …
Honorine:	J'te suis, pas têtu
	Sous les grands palétu
Pedro:	Viens sans sourciller
	Allons gazouiller
	Sous les palétuviers
Honorine:	Ah! Sous les papa papa
	Sous les pa, les létu,
	Sous les palétuviers.
Pedro:	Ah! Je te veux sous les pa
	Je te veux sous les lé,
	Les palétuviers roses
Both:	Aimons-nous sous les palé
	Prends-moi sous les létu
	Aimons-nous sous l´évier!⁸

Sexual desire is rather differently presented by the younger characters, as befits a film that is more interested in modern times than in the more traditional type of

---

⁷ 'You have deep eyes./I've got a temperature./It's the climate./Let's go for a walk … This atmosphere!/Do you like the tam-tam?/I don't know … I've been a widow for so long./The tam-tam is a sort of negro music … let me show you./Do you promise to behave yourself? Naughty boy … .'

⁸ 'Come with me under the ma/I'm coming/But slowly/Ah! Follow me/I'm coming, willingly/under the man/Come without a frown/Let's go and warble/Under the mangrove trees/Ah! Under the man man/Under the ma ng roves/Under the mangrove trees/Ah! I want you under the ma/I want you under the ng/The pink mangroves/Let us make love under the man/Take me under the ngr/Let us make love under the rove! (the final three lines sound like 'under the pallets', 'under the lettuces', 'under the sink' in French).

vaudeville song represented by 'Sous les palétuviers', even if the lyrics are unusually inventive. It is telling that in *Toi c'est moi*, Jacques and Maricousa talk about their love of American films, and decide to act out what happens in them, kissing passionately (0.31):

Jacques:	Est-ce qu'il y a beaucoup de distractions ici?
Maricousa:	Pas énormément ... le cinéma une fois par mois.
Jacques:	Vous aimez le cinéma?
Maricousa:	Les films américains surtout ... Oh! Si on jouait aux films américains! Vous savez?
Jacques:	J'apprendrai!
Maricousa:	C'est simple. Je mettrai mes lèvres sur vos lèvres.[9]

'What happens' is that Maricousa leaps up, to the consternation of Jacques, and starts singing what will become a standard romantic duet. Less standard is the fact that they later swim naked (Claude May's breasts are clearly – and unusually for the period – visible at one point), their clothes are stolen, and they emerge from the seashore in a Botticelli parody clothed only in seaweed, like Adam and Eve (0.43). The Governor of the island tells them without any irony intended: 'Vous êtes très bien comme ça'[10] (Figure 4.2). This is a far cry from the sophisticated verbal duet of 'Sous les palétuviers', but the impetus is the same. It is, as the characters keep on saying, the fault of the climate; and we could say that it is not just the climate of the Antilles, but the social and political climate of the Popular Front with its new-found freedoms focusing on leisure (paid holidays and the forty-hour working week). While these were not sexual freedoms,[11] nonetheless the emphasis on the erotic and the sexual in *Toi c'est moi* suggests freedom of expression, as well as by its very nature a certain kind of mobility.

Geographical displacement is also key to *Prends la route*. In both films, characters come together, but whereas in *Toi c'est moi*, the emphasis is on sexual congress, in *Prends la route* it is more simply congress in the form of community. The film has the format of what came much later to be called the road movie, but which is a well-known literary form, the picaresque novel: as in *Toi c'est moi*, the characters meet other people and form new relationships as they travel. The narratives therefore bring characters together in new formations. There is also a significant shift from the first film to the second. In *Toi c'est moi*, there is still the stereotypical upstairs–downstairs structure

---

[9] Are there many amusements around here?/Not many, the cinema once a month./Do you like the cinema?/American films especially. ... Oh! What if we played at American films? Do you know how?/I'll learn!/It's simple, I put my lips on yours./That's a great idea! Let's try ... we'll see what happens!'

[10] 'You look fine like that.'

[11] The closest the Popular Front got to anything resembling gender reform was the inclusion of three women in the cabinet. French women did not get the vote until 1944, and abortion was not legalized until 1975.

Figure 4.2 Jacques and Maricousa in paradise in *Toi c'est moi* (Courtesy René Chateau).

familiar in French theatre since the seventeenth century. In *Prends la route*, however, the very nature of touring brings the classes together in novel ways; the road is a great leveller.

The staging of the musical numbers is important in suggesting this effect of community. In the films, the singers are often shown to be singing to an audience, to characters who gather round them to listen in rapt attention. This is the case, for example, for the two title songs of the films. In *Toi c'est moi*, Pills and Tabet sing to a group of young women with whom they have been partying (0.6). In *Prends la route*, they sing to the customers in the Touring Club. Moreover, in *Prends la route* the community is mobilized. Pills and Tabet gather the Touring Club customers, high and low alike, around themselves as they sing, and then lead them around the room as they sing, this image being superimposed at the end of the song by a further element of mobility, cars hurtling on the road away from the city (0.18; Figure 4.3). In 'À mon âge' ('At my Age'), again from *Prends la route*, Jacques sings to his male friends; photographs and sculptures in his room are mobilized by the song in an imaginary community, which brings together Jacques's girlfriends, his father and even a bust of Napoleon, who one by one join in the chorus (0.8). Jacques introduces the song by quoting his father who wants him to settle down and work. Later in the song, in a procedure recalling the singing portrait of a forefather in *Il est charmant*, various photographs of (we presume) Jacques's girlfriends come to life and repeat some of these lyrics, adding new ones, followed by Jacques's stern

Figure 4.3 The title song in *Prends la route* (Courtesy René Chateau).

father, and finally, a bust of Napoleon materializes as a shadow with an admonishing finger:

> Girlfriend 1: À son âge on se fout du lendemain
> Girlfriend 2: À son âge l'argent ne vous tient pas aux mains
> Girlfriend 3: On fréquente les bars, on se couche très tard
> Girlfriend 4: On se moque du tiers comme du quart
> Father: À son âge travailler c'est le principal
> Napoleon: À son âge j'étais déjà général[12]

These films therefore depend closely on two types of mobility: the mobility of desire, and the mobility that leads to new communities. These mobilities are intertwined in the desire for community as well as communities of desire.

---

[12] 'At his age you don't care about tomorrow/At his age money trickles through your fingers/You go to bars and you stay up late/You don't care about anything/At his age work is the most important thing/At his age I was already a general.'

The Marseille operetta

A more local community is celebrated and mythified in the Marseille operetta, which forms a substantial part of what is called *cinéma méridional*. Although generally associated with the films of Marcel Pagnol, this regional cinema extends well beyond his work with 150 films in the period between 1929 and 1944, of which only eleven were produced by Pagnol (Peyrusse 1986: 9).

The *cinéma méridional* was seen as a relatively homogenous genre, partly because of its dynamism, and partly because of its counterpoint to an industry based largely in Paris. It was generically diverse:

> À l'intérieur de celle-ci se trouvent des genres traditionnellement répertoriés: vaudevilles militaires, drames paysans, etc. Définition peu claire qui prend en compte des critères hétérogènes: une forme de spectacle (vaudeville); les lieux et milieux qu'ils mettent en scène: une population rurale, des militaires ou des marins; une situation géographique. En fait, il existe des vaudevilles militaires qui sont aussi des opérettes marseillaises (*Trois de la marine, Les Bleus de la marine*).[13] (Peyrusse 1986: 141)

The Marseille operetta, while largely similar in form to the operettas we explored in the previous chapter, has specific characteristics. The most obvious of these, apart from the prevalence of the Midi accent, are the references to local topography, whether Marseille locations or the landscape of Provence more generally, and the use of songs to insist on local colour:

> La plupart des films usent et abusent de la chanson ou du chant conçus comme éléments de couleur locale. Tous les films visionnés consacrés à la Corse résonnent de chants souvent en dialecte; l'opérette marseillaise est d'abord constituée de chansons à la gloire de l'élément local: les pescadous de la Marsiale, la Canebière, le cabanon, la Venise provençale, chez nous en Provence, ce sont les motifs des chansons les plus connues d'*Arènes joyeuses* et d'*Un de la Canebière*.[14] (Peyrusse 1986: 86)

An important aspect of these films is their insistence on a utopian local community in ways that are significantly more obvious than in the films of Pills and Tabet. Criminals

---

[13] 'In "cinema meridional" you could find all the traditional genres: military vaudevilles, peasant dramas, etc. It's not a very clear definition, which includes heterogenous criteria: a type of spectacle (vaudeville); the locations and milieus that they use: a rural population, soldiers or sailors; a specific geography. In fact, some military vaudevilles are also Marseille operettas'.

[14] 'The majority of the films use and abuse song or chant as elements of local colour. All of the films in the corpus based in Corsica have songs, often in dialect; the Marseille operetta is composed of songs sung to the glory of the local: the fishermen of Marseille, La Canebière, the fisherman's cottage, the Venice of the South, chez nous in Provence, these are the motifs of the best-known songs in *Arènes joyeuses* and *Un de la Canebière*.'

and police sing and dance together, and the role of the chorus – usually friends of the principal protagonist – is to cement a sense of togetherness and a somewhat clichéd 'sunny' disposition. Formally, unlike some of the operettas we have already considered, the Marseille operetta's songs are more isolated musical numbers, partly because of the status of the singer – something we will see in the films by the popular tenors of the period such as Tino Rossi and Luis Mariano (Chapters 10 and 11) – and partly because of the influence of other local forms such as the stage revue.

The major star of the Marseille operetta, of stage and screen, was Henri Alibert, known simply as Alibert (1889–1951) who formed a team with his composer father-in-law Vincent Scotto (1874–1952). He shot to fame in 1928 with one of Scotto's songs, 'Mon Paris', and quickly became typecast as a 'méridional', starring in a series of stage operettas most of whose titles reveal their regionalist focus and many of which were very quickly turned into films (Table 4.1), thus spreading his local fame to the national level. The Marseille stage operetta existed before Alibert's contributions, such as *Thérèse* (1920), *Roseline* (1927) and *Mon neveu de Chicago* (1929), but Alibert gave it consistency and longevity, partly by having a repertory company (René Sarvil and Raymond Vincy for the librettos, Scotto for the music and René Pujol as director of three of the films), and partly because he brought so many of his stage operettas to the screen, making it a viable sub-genre. Other Marseille film operettas adapted for the screen in the 1930s include *Au soleil de Marseille* (Pierre-Jean Ducis, 1938) and *Marseille mes amours* (Jacques Daniel-Norman, 1939). Indeed, the Marseille operetta was clearly seen as a success as several of the films were remade in the 1950s, although with considerably less success.

The films are generally faithful to the stage operettas they adapt, with occasional omissions of songs for reasons of length. The songs are readily identifiable musical numbers, and are clearly the high-points of the films, as, for example, in the song that gives its title to *Un de la Canebière*, 'Cane … Cane … Canebière'. The song interrupts narrative continuity as we suddenly and inexplicably cut to its performance on La Canebière, Marseille's famous 'high street', for no other reason than to illustrate the street the song refers to. *Titin des Martigues* exemplifies the foregrounding of musical numbers throughout, partly because it is about the rise of a singer from Marseille to fame in Paris. The first song of the film has Titin singing at Paris's biggest funfair, La Foire du Trône. As he sings 'Je n'ose pas vous le dire, mais je suis fou de vous',[15] the camera cuts from him to the audience who comment on his singing, to the cashier Yvette, who looks on admiringly. The song therefore functions as the natural expression of emotion, but also as the foregrounding of the abilities of the singer. This focus on the singer can be mitigated as we see when he later enrols in a radio talent show leading to two numbers. In the first of these, as he rehearses a song, his assistant steals a camembert by means of a hook while the shop owner complains about people stealing. This kind of comic routine, called 'galéjade' in the Midi, is typical of the Marseille operetta (it is incorporated in the title of one of Alibert's operettas, *Le Roi des galéjeurs*). In the second song, he performs the song he was rehearsing, and

---

[15] 'I don't dare tell you, but I'm mad about you.'

Table 4.1 The Marseille Operetta

Title	Stage	Film	Director	Authors	Music	Lyrics
Elle est à vous	1929				Vincent Scotto	
Au pays du soleil	1932	1934	Robert Péguy	Henri Alibert, René Sarvil	Vincent Scotto	René Sarvil
Trois de la marine	1932	1934	Charles Barrois	Henri Alibert, Arnold Lipp, Raymond Vincy	Vincent Scotto	René Sarvil
Arènes joyeuses	1934	1935	Karl Anton	Henri Alibert, René Pujol, Yves Mirande	Vincent Scotto	René Sarvil
Titin des Martigues		1938	René Pujol	René Pujol	Vincent Scotto	René Sarvil
Un de la Canebière	1935	1938	René Pujol	Henri Alibert, René Pujol	Vincent Scotto	René Sarvil
Les Gangsters du château d'If	1937	1939	René Pujol	Henri Alibert, René Sarvil	Vincent Scotto	René Sarvil
Le Roi des galéjeurs	1938	1940	Fernand Rivers	Henri Alibert	Vincent Scotto	René Sarvil
Ma Belle Marseillaise	1940	–	–	Marc Cab, Émile Audiffred, Charles Tutelier	Georges Sellers	Émile Audiffred
Le Port du soleil	1941	–	–	Raymond Vincy, Marc Cab, Émile Audiffred, Charles Tutelier	Georges Sellers	Émile Audiffred
Les Gauchos de Marseille	1945	–	–	–	Vincent Scotto	René Sarvil

this time, as elsewhere in the film, the camera closes in on his face, with cutaways to an admiring audience, both those in the radio studio and Yvette who is listening to him on the radio. The song and, more particularly, the singer singing the song elide two radically different spaces, transcending them in a musical moment focused on the singer's performance.

The sequences we have just referred to demonstrate what a film can do through editing beyond the stage version of an operetta; and as was the case with the operettas we have already explored, the Marseille operetta is no less spectacular when the occasion demands, the spectacular reinforcing the pause in the narrative created by the musical number. As was the case with *Il est charmant*, there is a shot of a miniature character superimposed on the main shot in *Les Gangsters du château d'If* as Nine sings to a photo of her lover Jean and he leaves the photo frame to sing with her (0.56; see Figure 4.4). A less frequent effect can be found in *Titin des Martigues* with Busby Berkeley-style overhead shots of dancers in geometrical patterns (see Figure 4.5).

Figure 4.4 Nine sings to her miniature lover Jean in *Les Gangsters du château d'If* (Courtesy René Chateau).

Figure 4.5 Busby Berkeley-style overhead shots in *Titin des Martigues* (Courtesy René Chateau).

One of the defining characteristics of the Marseille operetta is the emphasis on local topography. Many of Alibert's films are shot in exteriors, and exterior shots are intercut with shots of the singers singing love songs, accentuating and naturalizing the link between romantic love and love for the region. In the sequences 'Les Pescadous de la Marsiale' ('The Fishermen of Marseille') and 'J'aime la mer comme une femme' ('I Love the Sea Like a Woman') (0.27) from *Un de la Canebière* – the title of the second of these songs reinforcing the link between romantic love and love of the region – shots of Alibert singing are intercut with shots of the sea, the rocky foreshore and the boats (Figure 4.6). In the song 'Si tu veux faire le tour de La Corniche' ('If You Want to Go Around La Corniche') from *Les Gangsters du château d'If*, Jean and Nine, captives in the Château d'If, sing about escaping, shots of the château intercut with shots of them imagining themselves on La Corniche (0.32). That particular song begins 'Chez nous dans notre Marseille', and the visual and lyrical references to Marseille occur throughout the film. The opening credits sequence of *Les Gangsters du château d'If* comprises a vast tracking shot over the port of Marseille as we hear Alibert sing 'Mon cœur vient de prendre un coup de soleil'[16] in voice-over. *Au soleil de Marseille* opens

Figure 4.6 Alibert singing 'J'aime la mer comme une femme' in *Un de la Canebière* (Courtesy René Chateau).

---

[16] 'My heart has just been sunburnt.'

with the title song as we see shots of monuments that are generally seen as typical of the city and often used in Marseille cinema, such as the transporter bridge and the Basilica of Notre-Dame de la Garde.[17] Emphasizing the Marseille community, the song is sung, in turn, by market stall holders, a fisherman and the soap factory workers' chorus. The effect is to embed the narrative in a very specific urban community.

Several of Alibert's operettas were remade during the 1950s, partly because of the rise of star singers such as Tino Rossi, Luis Mariano and Georges Guétary (see Chapters 10 and 11). These remakes were all directed by Maurice de Canonge: *Au pays du soleil* (1951) starred Tino Rossi, while the other remakes had less well-known singers. *Trois de la Canebière* (1955) and *Trois de la marine* (1957) starred Marcel Merkès, for whom these were two of a total of three feature films he made; while *Arènes joyeuses* (1958) starred the rather better-known comic actor Fernand Raynaud. The differences between the originals and the remakes are not substantial, apart, obviously, from the shift to colour film. But the attempt to maintain the sense of community is clear: instead of the one principal protagonist in *Un de la Canebière*, in *Trois de la Canebière*, we have three, as is made obvious in the titles of the films. The opening sequence of the remake is telling. In the original, we see shots of the sea, the rocky foreshore and the boats as Alibert sings. In the remake, there is a reprise of the kind of panoramic shots we see in *Les Gangsters du château d'If* and *Au soleil de Marseille*. The three characters in a boat sing 'Les Pescadous de la Marsiale', as had Alibert in the original; they sing individually and in chorus. This is intercut with shots of the coast, the Château d'If and the port, so that the song comes across not only as a profession of close friendship, but also as a celebration of the community to which they belong. This opening song is interrupted by Toinet singing 'J'aime la mer'[18] in close-up, then returning to 'Les Pescadous de la Marsiale' in chorus as they arrive in the port.

The differences suggest two things. Whereas in the original, the song sung by Alibert was a first sequence after the credits, in the remake two songs that occurred elsewhere in the film have been compressed into the credit sequence. In the original film the credit sequence had a medley of most of the songs of the film; here two well-known songs are used as a nostalgic flag reminding us of the original film. And second, the interruption of a song sung by three of them by a song sung by one of them suggests the shift away from the community musical to the 'film de chanteur' as exemplified by the Three Tenors we will consider in Chapters 10 and 11. In simple terms, community is being eroded by the individual, and is largely shrouded in nostalgia for a regional cinema and the film musical genre associated with it.

---

[17] Similar shots occur at the start of *Marius* (Alexander Korda and Marcel Pagnol, 1931), for example.
[18] 'I love the sea.'

5

Fréhel and Édith Piaf

French cinema of the 1930s is notable for singers known as the *chanteuses réalistes*. While singers from the music-hall tradition included men, such as Jean Gabin, the majority of the singers audiences heard in the films of the 1930s were women. The films in question were rarely the kind of musical in which the singer plays a major role and sings half a dozen songs more or less integrated in the action. Nonetheless, it is difficult to overstate the importance of singing in the films, not least because audiences would have been in part attracted to the cinemas on account of the *chanteuses réalistes*, and the attraction provided by a singer is one of the characteristics of what makes a film a film musical, as we explained in Chapter 1. In this chapter we look at two of the major *chanteuses réalistes*, Fréhel, with clear links to the traditional music hall and who appears in a small number of films, and then Édith Piaf, an icon for French *chanson*, whose *chanson réaliste* style extends into the 1950s and is incorporated in newer film musical genres such as the sketch film. Both have in common their embeddedness in the very particular space of Paris.

Fréhel

The defining characteristics of the *chanteuse réaliste* are authenticity and, as a corollary, nostalgia (Vincendeau 1987): nostalgia for the passage of time but also for song as the manifestation of community. The emblematic scene for this is the opening of *Sous les toits de Paris* with the audience in a street clutching their song sheets while Albert sings accompanied by an accordionist. Work on song has shown the importance of its social function (Calvet 1981; Hirschi 2008; Calvet 2013): song sheets in particular allowed the audience to be more than passive listeners and to become part of a group of singers, affirming their status as a community with shared values.

The opening scene of *Sous les toits de Paris*, however, was already imbued with nostalgia. By the 1920s street song had been overtaken by the development of the music halls and, in particular, spectacular stage shows, and traditional French songs overtaken by the development of jazz forms. But technology also had a significant role: the recording of songs, whether for the radio, on vinyl discs, or in films, changed the active participation of a social group to passive listening. The use of the microphone in live performances was a further significant development, allowing the singer to create a sense of intimacy with the audience by murmuring or whispering into the microphone, this being very different from the kind of vocal projection required without the technology. Ironically, this very intimacy produced by technological means and creating the illusion that the singer was whispering in your ear, masked the fact that the singer was losing the real intimacy and the direct contact with the audience of the street song or similar local environments such as the café or bar known as *bals musette*, popular since the 1880s, in which you could dance to the music of accordions or hurdy-gurdies.

The presence of a *chanteuse réaliste* in so many films of the 1930s is therefore a nostalgic replaying of the status of song some forty to fifty years before, and the films frequently use her to recreate the sense of community that was being eroded by the development of technology as well as more generally by the rise of individualism. We begin with Fréhel because she is one of the clearest examples of this shift. She became well known around 1910, but left France for almost fifteen years after her lover Maurice Chevalier abandoned her for a major star of the music hall, Mistinguett. Ravaged by drugs and alcohol, she returned to the theatre stage in the mid-1920s, presented by Paul Franck, the director of the Olympia, as the 'inoubliable oubliée'.[1] She subsequently appeared in a large number of films from 1931 to 1941, nearly all with a singing role.[2]

Most of Fréhel's performances in films express the nostalgia for her past, in conjunction with nostalgia for a Paris that had long disappeared or was in the process of disappearing. In *Pépé le Moko* (Julien Duvivier, 1937), for example, Fréhel sings 'Où est-il donc?' ('Where is He?') to Jean Gabin's Pépé, expressing, as Ginette Vincendeau points out, a 'double nostalgia' (1998: 24). As Vincendeau, Kelley Conway (2004: 98–101) and Raphaëlle Moine (2015: 42) explain, it is on the one hand nostalgia for the Paris of 1910, far away from the Casbah of Algiers, a Paris that was disappearing: la Scala, originally a café-concert in the mid-nineteenth century before becoming a musical theatre in 1876, had been closed in 1933 and opened as a cinema in 1935 two years before *Pépé le Moko*; the Moulin Rouge was past its prime; the *bals musettes* were disappearing as the large theatres provided more spectacular shows. But the nostalgia is also quite clearly for Fréhel's own past, her youth before drugs and alcohol destroyed her looks:

Où est-il mon moulin de la Place Blanche
Mon tabac, mon bistrot du coin?

[1] 'The unforgettable forgotten.'
[2] *Cœur de Lilas* (Anatole Litvak, 1931), *La Rue sans nom* (Pierre Chenal, 1934), *Amok* (Fedor Ozep, 1934), *Le Roman d'un tricheur* (Sacha Guitry, 1936), *Pépé le Moko* (Julien Duvivier, 1937), *Gigolette* (Yvan Noé, 1937), *Le Puritain* (Jeff Musso, 1938), *L'Innocent* (Maurice Cammage, 1938), *La Rue sans joie* (André Hugon, 1938), *La Maison du Maltais* (Pierre Chenal, 1938), *Une java* (Claude Orval, 1939), *Berlingot et Compagnie* (Fernand Rivers, 1939), *L'Entraîneuse* (Albert Valentin, 1939), and *L'Enfer des Anges* (Christian-Jaque, 1941). Fréhel had a singing role in all of these films with the exception of *Le Puritain* et *Berlingot et Compagnie*. See Conway (2004: 91–117) for a detailed biography and for extensive analyses of Fréhel's performances in *Cœur de Lilas*, *Pépé le Moko* and *L'Entraîneuse*.

Tous les jours pour nous c'était dimanche.
Où sont-ils, les amis, les copains?
Où sont-ils tous mes vieux bals musette
Leurs javas au son de l'accordéon?[3]

The song is, in fact, triply nostalgic, because she had recorded it for the first time a decade before in 1928, and, indeed, in this scene she sings along to a recording of the song, the present grafted indelibly on the past. And the fact that we hear only part of the song in the film serves to reinforce the sense of loss that is its focus: a contemporary audience would have remembered the rest of the song and it is precisely that remembrance in both senses of the word (the remembering of memory and the re-membering of the body of the song) that gives it its affective force. These rich layers of nostalgia, so anchored in specifically French practices, no doubt explains why the American remake of the film, *Algiers* (John Cromwell, 1938), does not include the song, despite the fact that the actress who plays Fréhel's role, Nina Koshetz, was a Russian singer trained in both Russia and France.

The celebration of the past and the acknowledgement that the performance of song was changing is also clear in *Une java* (Claude Orval, 1939) and *Cœur de Lilas* (Anatole Litvak, 1932). In the former film, the director of a show, Mery Cerval, looks for inspiration by attending an evening in a café-concert where the owner, played by Fréhel, sings 'La Java bleue'. In a celebration of popular community, the customers join in the song. Mery reprises the song in her stage show that she calls 'La Java bleue', but the intimacy of popular community communicated by Fréhel's performance is replaced by all the trappings of a spectacular stage show, with sumptuous décor, chorus girls and a clear separation between the star of the show on stage and the seated public. The change is emphasized by the physique of the two singers: on the one hand Fréhel, overweight and 'masculine',[4] ravaged by drugs and alcohol, her lived-in body incarnating the passage of time and loss, and on the other Mireille Perrey as Mery, conforming to the contemporary norms of spectacular femininity. The song therefore signals the transition from café-concert to music hall, from participative song that confirms popular community to the passive individual consumption of song in a theatre, from active singing to passive watching. That nostalgic sense of community can be seen in the second musical number of *Cœur de Lilas* in which Jean Gabin and Fréhel sing 'La Môme caoutchouc' ('The Rubber Girl') in a *bal musette*. There is no key lighting to emphasize their star quality, and Gabin wanders through the crowd as he sings, followed by the camera in long tracking shots, with the crowd joining in the refrain, anchoring Gabin in the community.

---

[3] 'Where is my windmill of Place Blanche/My tobacconist, my corner café?/Every day was a Sunday./Where are my friends, my pals?/Where are all my old *bals musette*/Their javas set to the sound of the accordion?
[4] A term used by commentators at the time; see Conway (2004: 99).

It is true that we find the same nostalgia for community and 'liveness' in the Hollywood musical, as Jane Feuer points out when she explores the paradox of liveness in a recorded medium such as film. Musicals wish

> to capture on celluloid the quality of live entertainment. Yet also from infancy, the dream of immediacy came up against the reality of technological truth: film is not a 'live' medium. Performances on screen are recorded performances. Now the music-hall tradition itself had been founded upon an illusion that the audience really participated in the creation of Jolson's and Chevalier's highly calculated acts. In a sense the Hollywood musical merely compounded an already existing and widely accepted fiction, that of direct and spontaneous performance. (1993: 2)

And like the films we have been exploring, the Hollywood folk musical 'reeks with nostalgia for America's mythical communal past even as the musical itself exemplifies the new, alienated mass art' (Feuer 1993: 16). French cinema differs, however, in the incorporation of the *chanteuse réaliste*, in the etymological sense of the manifestation of her body, a singer who thematizes nostalgia in her song lyrics and in her ruined body, a body signalling the passage of time, and a past filled with suffering and loss.

Édith Piaf

This is just as true of Édith Piaf as it is of Fréhel (or Damia and Florelle, who were other well-known *chanteuses réalistes*). Piaf is an important figure for many reasons, not least the fact that she was the last 'genuine' representative of the *chanson réaliste* (Vincendeau 1987: 107). She appeared in nine films, four of which trade on her persona as a *chanteuse réaliste*: *La Garçonne* (Jean de Limur, 1936), *Montmartre-sur-Seine* (Georges Lacombe, 1941), *Étoile sans lumière* (Marcel Blistène, 1946) and *Neuf garçons, un cœur* (Georges Friedland, 1948).

She appears in only one scene in *La Garçonne*. Based on a novel by Victor Margueritte published in 1922, the film is about a young woman, Monique Lerbier (Marie Bell), who is jilted by a lover and is gradually sucked into the lesbian cabaret subculture. Piaf, who is called by her stage name 'la môme Piaf' in the opening credits, appears in one of these shows singing 'Quand même' ('Still'), a sexually suggestive song that is typical of the *chanteuse réaliste* repertoire: 'Mes sens inapaisés/Cherchent pour se griser/L'aventure des nuits louches/Apportez-moi du nouveau/Le désir crispe ma bouche/La volupté brûle ma peau.'[5] She leans against the mast of a yacht surrounded by women in seductive poses, and eventually comes on to Monique. The second musical

---

[5] 'My unsated senses/Seek the drunken/Adventures of shady nights/Bring me something new/Desire is making me clench my teeth/Pleasure burns my skin.'

number, 'La Vie est un feu de paille' ('Life Is a Flash in the Pan'), is sung by Suzy Solidor, an actress and singer well known for her lesbianism. In this film the *chanteuse réaliste* is therefore associated with a complex and, for the time, dark and dissident sexuality, which was, no doubt, in part why the film was censored (Montagne 2007: 42).

Piaf was the star of *Montmartre-sur-Seine* in which she plays Lily, a flower seller by trade, and amateur singer, who sacrifices love for a vocation as a singer. Piaf sings four songs whose lyrics she composed herself: 'Un coin tout bleu' ('Blue Corner'), 'Tu es partout' ('You Are Everywhere'), 'J'ai dansé avec l'amour' ('I Danced with Love') and 'L'Homme des bars' ('The Man from the Bars'). The film and the songs reprise the tropes familiar in the songs of the 1930s *chanteuses réalistes* and the films in which they appear: disappointment in love, the working-class *faubourgs*, nostalgia for the disappearing contexts of popular song, and the biographical references to the singer's life, real or imagined. The magazine *Vedettes* specifically referred to Damia in its review of Piaf's performance, repeating the term 'tragic' used for Damia: 'Il était une chanteuse qui chantait des tragédies ou si vous préférez, une tragédienne qui jouait des chansons'[6] (cited in Belleret 2013: 164).

The opening sequence shows street urchins and working-class characters, and the arrival of reporters who have come to do a piece on Montmartre. Grafted onto this very specific local context, there is Lily's career which echoes that of Piaf. Lily is employed as a street singer, echoing Piaf's teenage years working with her father's acrobatic troupe and singing with her half-sister Simone. The street-singing recalls Clair's *Sous les toits de Paris* with its emphasis on groups of people singing songs from song sheets; indeed, Lily interrupts her rendition of 'Tu es partout' with advertising for the song sheets – 'Demandez le dernier succès populaire, deux francs. Merci Monsieur. Demandez le dernier refrain à la mode! ... Qui n'a pas son petit format? Demandez le dernier succès du jour!'[7] (0.48) – before urging her public to sing along with her. As her career takes off and she becomes increasingly well known, Lily sings 'J'ai dansé avec l'amour' in a café-concert, recalling Piaf's debut in Louis Leplée's cabaret Le Gerny's in 1935, and at the end of the film she sings 'L'Homme des bars' in a more up-market music hall.

Inextricably entwined with references to Piaf's biography, there is also the nostalgia for the street song and its working-class 'authenticity', an authenticity that had been disappearing since the turn of the century. We find the same development from intimate working-class street-singing to bourgeois music hall as with Fréhel in *Une java*. We hear Lily singing in a domestic setting at Maurice's, where she asks him to accompany her on his accordion; Maurice asks her if the song evokes something for her, which occasions a flashback to the beginning of their relationship. From the beginning, therefore, song is associated with romance and a nostalgic past. Later, when Lily sings in the street, there is an insistence on intimacy, this time not with her man but with her public: ensemble shots show her surrounded by the public holding the song sheets she has sold them so that they can share a musical moment together. The music-

---

[6] 'There was a singer who sang tragedies or if you prefer a tragic actress who sang songs.'
[7] 'Ask for the last popular hit, two francs. Thank you Sir. Ask for the last trendy tune. Who hasn't got a sheet ? Ask for today's hit!'

hall sequence acts as a foil to this intimacy while still insisting on the nostalgic past. We see well-to-do spectators poking fun at the echoes of the working-class *guinguette* recalled by Maurice's accordion, while the mother of one of Lily's friends is shown to be uncomfortable in this unfamiliar and alien space. When Maurice leaves to return to his *quartier* and his working-class roots, Lily becomes isolated from her public; there is no intimacy between her on stage and the customers seated at their tables. As was the case with *Une java* a few years before, *Montmartre-sur-Seine* charts the transition from a nostalgic past that had long disappeared to a consumerist modernism, from working-class authenticity and intimacy, on the one hand, to inauthentic bourgeois spectacle, on the other.

In *Étoile sans lumière*, the French inspiration for *Singin' in the Rain* (Stanley Donen and Gene Kelly, 1952), written specifically for Piaf by Marcel Blistène, Piaf plays Madeleine, a cleaner with a spectacular voice who lends it to a film star whose career is threatened by the arrival of sound. As was the case at the start of *Montmartre-sur-Seine*, there is a clear distinction between Madeleine's world and the world 'outside' her *quartier*; we see Madeleine cleaning the front window of the hotel where she works, while on the pavement side the film star Stella Dora (Mila Parély) and her director lover hear her singing and devise their plan to save Stella Dora's career by having Madeleine dub her voice. But the simple nostalgic isolation of two worlds is considerably more complex in this film; as Moine points out, Madeleine is dissociated from her voice, first by virtue of being Stella Dora's double, and second by the technology of the gramophone and of the cinema screen, both of which turn her into a 'spectatrice muette et admirative de sa propre voix'[8] (2015: 46). The film does not have *Singin' in the Rain*'s happy ending, however, in which Kathy Selden (Debbie Reynolds) has a triumphant career and we hear nothing about what happened to Lina Lamont (Jean Hagen). Piaf's Madeleine, who is Kathy Selden's equivalent, is riddled with guilt after Stella Dora commits suicide in Madeleine's home, as a result of which she shuns both her career and the man she might have loved. Moreover, the type of singing associated with Piaf is directly referenced in a poignantly ironic scene towards the end of the film. We see her singing a typical *chanson réaliste*, 'Mariage' (Figure 5.1):

> une chanson réaliste typique qui raconte un crime passionnel commis par une femme délaissée … avant de se rendre compte, à la faveur d'un contrechamp, que la salle est vide. Il s'agissait d'une répétition, et son unique spectateur est Jules Berry qui dit que 'ça ne marchera pas'. La puissance de Piaf sur scène est donc déliée cette fois de l'interaction avec le public.[9] (Moine 2015: 47)

---

[8] 'Mute and admiring spectator of her own voice.'
[9] 'A typical realist song that tells of a crime of passion committed by a woman scorned, before realizing, thanks to a counter-shot, that the room is empty. It was just a rehearsal, and her only spectator is Jules Berry who tells her that "it won't work". Piaf's charismatic stage presence is thus untied from interaction with the public.'

Figure 5.1 Piaf singing 'Mariage' in *Étoile sans lumière* (Courtesy M6 Vidéo).

In this dystopian parable, authentic street song has been left far behind. As Moine (2015) says, by the 1950s there is no place for the *chanteuse réaliste*; her songs, already nostalgic in the 1930s, no longer have an audience. Conway suggests that the role played by the *chanteuse réaliste* was absorbed by the poetic realist hero par excellence, Jean Gabin, who managed, according to Vincendeau, to combine both masculinity and femininity in his performances (Conway 2004: 181–3).

The authentic performance of a life of suffering has been replaced by something else: the showcasing of performance as performance, a surface spectacle. Nowhere is this clearer than in the musical sketch film, in which singers, including Piaf as we shall see, sing in turn, their collocation reducing each of them literally to a 'show', a brief, fragmented and dislocated appearance among others, a voice – and not a body – of memory signalling a bygone age. We will consider these films in more detail in Chapter 9, and here focus on those in which Piaf appears.

She appeared in *Paris chante toujours* (Pierre Montazel, 1951) in which she sings 'Hymne à l'amour' ('Hymn to Love'; Figure 5.2) and *Boum sur Paris* (Maurice de Canonge, 1953), as well as, curiously, a Mexican film, *Musica de siempre* (Tito Davison, 1958), and in more auteur-focused films such as *Si Versailles m'était conté ...* (Sacha Guitry, 1954) and *French Cancan* (Jean Renoir, 1955). These films trade on Piaf's *chanteuse réaliste* persona, paradoxically at the same time as they undo it. Her performances in these films are no more or less important than those of a plethora of other singers. In *Paris chante toujours*, for example, produced to celebrate the two-thousandth anniversary of Paris, a young couple must collect as many singers' autographs as possible to inherit a substantial fortune. Apart from Piaf, we hear songs from André Dassary, Yves Montand, Line Renaud, Georges Ulmer, Les Compagnons de la chanson, and the 'Three Tenors', Tino Rossi, Georges Guétary and Luis Mariano. *Boum sur Paris* has a similarly flimsy plot involving an explosive hidden in a bottle of perfume; we hear songs by Annie Cordy, Jacqueline François, Juliette Gréco, Mick Micheyl, Charles Trénet, Lucienne Delyle and Mouloudji, as well as Piaf singing 'Je t'ai dans la peau' ('You're Under My Skin') and a duo, 'Pour qu'elle soit jolie ma chanson' ('So That My Song Can Be Pretty'), between her and Jacques Pills, whom we have already come across in the Pills and Tabet operettas.

In *Boum sur Paris* Piaf's persona is used in ways that reveal the transition from what was already a nostalgic and stereotyped authenticity to a more deeply fragmented spectacle. Jacques Pills, who plays her husband (and was her husband in real life) meets

Figure 5.2 Piaf sings 'Hymne à l'amour' in *Paris chante toujours* (Courtesy René Chateau).

with Piaf in their home to ask her to sing with him a song he has composed, 'Pour qu'elle soit jolie ma chanson' (1.06). The song constitutes the conversation that they have. It is lightweight and not at all appropriate to the image of the *chanteuse réaliste*: 'Pour qu'elle soit jolie ma chanson/Il faut bien sûr être deux/Il y a bien sûr un garçon/ Et une fille pour le rendre heureux.'[10] Piaf declines to sing the song, as a result of which Pills sarcastically rolls out a series of clichés that mark her as a *chanteuse réaliste*:

> Je vois bien c'qu'il vous faut
> Un port et un mat'lot
> Des bagarres Dans un bar
> Rien que des trucs sinistres
> Un pauv' type que l'on pend
> Des gens qui parlent haut
> Un Monsieur distingué, un accordéoniste
> J'ai même entendu dire, c'est par trop fantaisiste
> Que vous chantiez un clown
> Eh bien bravo pour le clown.[11]

Piaf, faced with these clichés, agrees to sing Pills's sweetly saccharine song, signalling a transition from her previous repertoire:

> — Alors, à votre avis, cette chanson est pour moi?
> — Mais oui!
> — Eh bien! rechantez-la moi[12]

In the historical fresco *Si Versailles m'était conté ...* and Renoir's homage to the nineteenth-century café-concert, *French Cancan*, Guitry and Renoir also trade on Piaf's *chanteuse réaliste* persona. In *Si Versailles m'était conté ...* Piaf plays a working-class woman who sings the revolutionary anthem composed in 1790, 'Ah, ça ira' ('Ah, It Will Be Better'). Guitry had used the *chanteuse réaliste* Damia in his film *Les Perles de la couronne* (1937) in which she sang the revolutionary song from 1792, 'La Carmagnole'. The mise en scène is exactly the same in both cases: the singers are framed by iron railings and surrounded by *sans-culottes*. Piaf is therefore palimpsestically and doubly grafted onto the image of the *chanteuse réaliste* from the 1930s as well as on an image of revolutionary fervour. This trope is repeated in Renoir's *French Cancan*; Piaf plays the *chanteuse réaliste* Eugénie Buffet, who is discovered by the director of the show played by Jean Gabin, and Piaf briefly sings the refrain from Buffet's 1894 song 'La Sérénade

---

[10] 'So that my song can be pretty/There have to be two of us/There has to be a boy/And a girl to make him happy.'
[11] 'I can see that what you need/Is a port and a sailor/Fights/In a bar/All kinds of bad things/A poor bloke who's hanged/People speaking loud/A distinguished man, un accordionist/I even heard, fanciful though it may sound/That you sang as a clown/Well, bravo for the clown.'
[12] 'So you think this song's for me? / But of course !/Well, sing it again!'

Figure 5.3 Piaf plays the *chanteuse réaliste* Eugénie Buffet in *French Cancan* (Courtesy Gaumont).

du pavé' ('Pavement Serenade') (Figure 5.3). In these two films, as in the musical sketch films previously discussed, Piaf's performance is isolated and minimal, used as a nostalgic gesture within a larger frame. Indeed, the fragmentation and isolation of her performances were intensified over the following years.

Whereas Tino Rossi began his career as part of a film's soundtrack rather than as an actor – he sings 'Du fond du cœur' ('From the Bottom of My Heart') in *La Cinquième Empreinte* (Karl Anton, 1934) – subsequently becoming a major star as we shall see, Piaf's trajectory is the exact opposite, her voice becoming divorced from her screen presence. The key film in this regard is *Les héros sont fatigués* (Yves Ciampi, 1955) in which we hear but do not see Piaf; the song she sings, 'C'est un vagabond' ('He's a Tramp'), is played on a record in the inn where the characters cross paths. Piaf did act in another film, *Les Amants de demain* (Marcel Blistène, 1959), but from the mid-1950s her voice becomes a symbol of Paris, used as a nostalgic trope, whether in Hollywood films, as for example in *La Vie en rose* (Billy Wilder, 1954), or in French auteur cinema, such as *La Maman et la putain* (Jean Eustache, 1973).

6

Josephine Baker and Charles Trenet

Jazz came to France around 1917, brought by American troops fighting in the Great War, and spread among artistic milieus during the 1920s. During the 1930s jazz became more broadly accepted by the public, partly as a result of the development of a French-inflected jazz in which an essentially foreign sound was integrated within more traditional French forms. This gallicization of jazz also occurred because of the economic crisis, during which French bands had to compete with American bands in France (Jackson 2002; Portis 2004). Prominent among these bands were Grégor et ses Grégoriens, Ray Ventura et ses collégiens and Django Reinhardt. Ray Ventura recycled much of the band's material during the 1930s into his big-band films of the 1940s (Chapter 8).

Magazines were created to promote the new music, such as Grégor's *La Revue du jazz*, published in 1929 but which lasted less than a year, and *Jazz-Tango* published from 1930 (Jackson 2002: 162). The Hot Club de France was established in December 1932, in which Reinhardt performed from 1933 to 1934 before forming the Quintette du Hot Club de France, which Portis considers as the 'émergence du jazz français' (2004: 74).

French cinema audiences were aware of jazz in film early on in the sound period through the distribution of Hollywood films. The revue film *King of Jazz* (John Murray Anderson, 1930), for example, focused on Paul Whiteman and his orchestra, and was favourably reviewed in *Cinémonde* with a telling title: 'Vive le jazz' (Labiche 1930). French revue films, often focusing on jazz orchestras, were frequent from the 1930s to the 1950s (Chapters 8 and 9). These films and the big-band films generally have several musical numbers, whether loosely integrated into the narrative in the case of the big-band films, or less so in the case of the revue films. But jazz forms were also found in the films of singers associated with the style, and in whose films there were fewer musical numbers. In this chapter, we deal with two of the more prominent performers: Josephine Baker and Charles Trenet. Baker was very much in the public eye during the 1920s and 1930s, and her status as the first Black film star has, among other reasons, led to the many academic studies devoted to her and specifically to her films.[1] Her films demonstrate the fusion of the Hollywood backstage musical with

---

[1] Coffman (1995), Ezra (2000), Francis (2005), Balcerzak (2006), Raynaud (2007–8), Powrie and Rebillard (2008), Julien (2009), Staszak (2014).

dramatic tropes connected, on the one hand, to the realist singer tradition and, on the other, to Baker's position in between French and American cultures. Trenet, although a popular performer, has had next to no academic work devoted to him, even though his songs can often be heard in contemporary films.

Josephine Baker

Josephine Baker's success was in part due to the 'negrophilia' which had begun in earnest with the international exhibitions and colonial fairs of the late nineteenth century and early twentieth century (Francis 2005); this was reinforced by the arrival of Black performers in Paris during the 1920s (Archer-Straw 2000; Berliner 2002). After the success of the Revue Nègre at the Théâtre des Champs-Elysées in 1925, Josephine Baker developed a music-hall career, first in the Folies-Bergère with the show 'La Folie du jour' ('Today's Fads') (1926), then in the Casino de Paris with 'Paris qui remue' ('Paris Is Stirring') (1930–1). In 1934 Baker performed the main role in Offenbach's operetta *La Créole* in the Théâtre de Marigny as a mixed-race woman seduced and then abandoned by her sailor-lover, but who decides to follow him to France. Acting in films was an adjunct to her stage work in the 1920s; indeed, the Franco-German *Die Frauen von Folies Bergères* (Joe Francis and Max Obal, 1927) appears to have been based on a music-hall revue. In the same year, she played a character who follows a Frenchman back to Paris in *La Sirène des tropiques* (Mario Nalpas and Henri Étiévant, 1927). The songs she sang in the early revues, such as 'J'ai deux amours' ('I Have Two Loves') in the Casino's 'Paris qui remue', as well as the early film roles played on Baker's status in between cultures, in which her characters suffer as a result of their love for men who reject her and who return to the mainland. This topos is also the focus of her two musical films, *Zouzou* (Marc Allégret, 1934) and *Princesse Tam-Tam* (Edmond T. Gréville, 1935), which adopt many of the tropes of the American backstage musical, but reject that genre's happy ending.

In *Zouzou* the eponymous mixed-race heroine and Jean (Jean Gabin) are the adopted children of Papa Mélé. As an adult, Zouzou comes to love Jean, who in turn loves the daughter of the owner of the laundry where Zouzou works. Zouzou, realizing that she will not have Jean, devotes herself to a career as a showgirl. Like Baker, Gabin started in the music hall, and was well known as a singer in his early films, notably for his rendering of 'La Môme Caoutchouc' with Fréhel in *Cœur de lilas*. In *Princesse Tam-Tam*, Albert Préjean plays a writer who seeks inspiration in Tunisia, finds Aouïna (Baker) and decides to use her as his inspiration, taking her back to Paris as a fictitious princess, although we discover at the end of the film that her presence in Paris has been part of the novel Max was writing, and that she has remained in Tunisia.

It is not only the narrative themes, closely aligned with Baker's own trajectory, that allow us to consider these two films as a diptych; both films were produced by Arys Nissoti, both films had Lazare Meerson as decorator and Floyd du Pont as choreographer, both had big Berkleyesque dance numbers. This is particularly the case with *Zouzou* as a backstage musical. Like all backstage musicals, the film is punctuated by rehearsal sequences, which reprise tableaux from *La Folie du jour* (Pessis 2014: 51): Miss Barbara, the show's star (0.26), the showgirls (0.37), and finally the premiere (1.02). Zouzou energetically practises singing ('C'est lui'/'It's Him') and dancing in private, parodying the star, Miss Barbara, whose clothes she launders, cut with a parallel sequence in which Miss Barbara is lifelessly rehearsing for the revue. Zouzou's brother Jean becomes the theatre's electrician, and he lifts the stage curtain just as Zouzou, who has borrowed a showgirl's costume, is dancing the kind of energetic dance associated with Baker. As a result, she becomes a successful revue star, as is shown in the Berkleyesque sequence of the show's premiere, which *Cinémonde*'s reviewer commented on very favourably: 'Cette suite de scènes de Music-hall est certainement le plus gros effort qu'on ait tenté dans un studio français'[2] (Derain 1934b: 1038). The three sequences parallel Baker's own trajectory; in the first sequence where she performs for her friends in the laundry

> [s]he is the poor little black girl defined exclusively by the spectacle of her race ... . Her acrobatic shadow dance at the music hall, directed by Jean, corresponds to her Revue nègre phase, with its emphasis on exoticism and racial otherness. Finally, her star appearance in the music hall revue evokes the 'real' 1930s Baker: the elegant *meneuse de revue* who has conquered Paris. (Conway 2004: 143)

Moreover, as Conway suggests, the development across the three sequences is also spatially critical, taking Baker from the intimate space of the realist singer characterized by authenticity to the world of the revue which is the antithesis of 'Paris *populaire*' (144). Arguably, the biographically motivated and spatial transition parallels the musical transition from the realist song to the jazz-oriented revue of the premiere.

The premiere is almost twenty minutes long and reprises the structure of a revue with a series of tableaux, of which three are shown *in extenso*. The first of these is a typically Berkleyesque number opening with a shot of a line of showgirls waking up on a giant bed before getting up to dance, giant objects (the bed, a telephone and a comb serving as a xylophone) forming part of the surprise of the sequence. In the second major tableau Zouzou sings 'Haïti' suspended in a giant cage. In the third tableau, we hear the song 'Y'a qu'un homme dans Paris' ('There's Only One Man in Paris'), already heard when Zouzou sang it in private. The number is typical of Parisian revues, both in terms of the lyrics that evoke the Paris of realist songs, and in terms of the mise en scène: Zouzou descends an immense white staircase in a sequin dress, surrounded by and contrasted with men in tails, as can be seen in Figure 6.1.

These aspects of the film echo the Hollywood backstage musical, but the film ends dystopically, without the utopian closure typical of Hollywood in which success in the profession coincides with success in love. The final sequence of the film represents the hundredth show, and we see a repeat of Zouzou singing 'Haïti' in her golden

---

[2] 'This sequence of music-hall scenes is certainly the biggest endeavour so far for a French studio.'

Figure 6.1 The opening sequence of *Zouzou* (Courtesy René Chateau).

cage whose metaphorical valence is abundantly clear: Zouzou may have achieved professional success, but it comes with a cost.

Reviewers failed to recognize the specificity of Baker's performances, and the way in which these undermine racial stereotypes. It is true that *Zouzou*'s narrative does nothing to undermine those stereotypes: the very first sequence presents a fantasy of origins with Papa Mélé pointing out that his two adopted twin children, one of whom is visibly white, the other Black, had a Chinese mother and a Red Indian father. Quite apart from the lack of colour logic in this filiation, their origin is a combination of mystery and mystification, turning both of them into freaks (Staszak 2014: 657). But it is the Black Zouzou who is constantly racialized, not the White Jean: on seeing Zouzou dance, Jean's girlfriend comments: 'C'que c'est bath! Ah ils ont la danse dans le sang!'[3] (0.8). The film constantly accentuates racial stereotypes in Zouzou's actions: her love of dancing, her clumsiness (e.g. when she opens a tap by mistake and is drenched), her closeness to animals (the mongrel she adopts). Unsurprisingly, critical comments at the time reproduced these stereotypes: 'Zouzou, la jolie Zouzou, chante, danse, mène l'action avec ce rythme endiablé qui est l'apanage de la race noire, cette sorte de joie explosive qui se communique, se répand, don inné qui explique l'espèce de fascination

---

[3] 'That's really super! They have dancing in the blood!'

d'une telle nature sur le blanc fatigué et pour qui la joie n'est trop souvent qu'un mot'[4] (Escoube 1934: 7).

Critics saw *Princesse Tam-Tam* as a pale reflection of Hollywood musicals, failing to recognize the hybridity and specificity of the French musical, which welded together traditional music hall and jazz: 'Les ballets de la fin, s'ils n'ont pas la richesse et l'ampleur de ceux que nous ont montré tant de films américains, nous présentent néanmoins des costumes attrayants, de jolies filles, et sont montés avec un brio qu'on regrette de ne pas retrouver dans la musique'[5] (Frank 1935: 10). *Princesse Tam-Tam* is predicated on Aouïna's Rousseauist naiveté; her comments on what she sees in France portray her as the innocent abroad; for example, she underlines the absurdity of eating when the bell rings rather than when one is hungry: 'Si j'ai bien compris, il faut avoir faim quand la cloche sonne.'[6] It is true that Aouïna is not the only character to critique the 'blanc fatigué', to reprise Auriol's terms. Tahar, Aouïna's Bedouin friend, tells her that 'si les oiseaux du ciel prennent leur nourriture dans la main de l'homme, ils n'ont plus leur liberté',[7] and another non-white character, the Maharajah de Datane, says to Max's wife: 'Je sais bien que vous nous appelez des sauvages, mais le plus misérable chez nous a une indépendance que vous ne soupçonnez pas.'[8] These comments and the fact that Aouïna's spell in Paris is no more than Max's imagination radically separate the Other from the Parisian 'norm'. As the Maharajah says to Aouïna: 'Il y a dans ma demeure deux sortes de fenêtres. Celles qui donnent sur l'Orient, et celles qui donnent sur l'Occident. Celle-ci donne sur l'Occident. Celle-ci donne vers l'Orient.'[9] Aouïna sees Max through the 'Western' window, and Tahar, whom she asks to wait for her, through the 'Eastern' window. In the final sequence, we see her nursing her baby in Tunisia, surrounded by animals, among which is a donkey eating the novel that Max was writing, *Civilization*. To an admirer who has asked him to sign his novel and commented that it is a pity that Aouïna is not there too, Max says that she is better off where she is.

It is worth asking why the film's closure is predicated on such a radical separation of East and West, particularly at a time when negrophilia was a feature of French culture. Our hypothesis in the light of recent scholarship is that Baker is too 'modern American' and not 'colonial' enough. This can be seen in her signature hairstyle:

> By straightening her hair, Baker represented the modern Black woman. In Baker's era, choosing to process one's hair helped to signify a break with 'country' and older ways, because it involved being serviced by another person, engaging a

---

[4] 'Zouzou, pretty Zouzou, sings, dances, takes the lead with the frenzied rhythm natural to the Black race, a kind of explosive and infectious joy, an innate gift that explains the kind of fascination it holds for the jaded white man whose joy is no more than a word.'
[5] 'The ballets at the end, if they don't have the richness and scale of so many American films, still give us attractive costumes, pretty girls, and are edited with a panache that it would have been nice to find in the music.'
[6] 'So if I've understood rightly, you have to be hungry when the bell rings.'
[7] 'If the birds of the sky take food from the hand of man, they lose their freedom.'
[8] 'I know that you call us savages, but the poorest of us has a freedom that you can't suspect.'
[9] 'In my house there are two sorts of windows. Those that look out onto the Orient and those that look out onto the West. This one looks out on the West. This one looks out onto the Orient.'

chemical process and reconstructing the self in order to play a public role, usually within white society. What was at stake in hairstyle was Baker's public identity as a modernized American woman, which was layered over the Africanist dancing. (Francis 2005: 836)

Her appearance and her dancing – 'vague gestures toward Africa with her personal signature moves such as crossing her knees and eyes' (Francis 2005: 836) – subvert expectations. They are grounded in an imaginary African-ness, but her 'comedic, parodic behaviour' (Coffman 1995: 179) make her performances '"oppositional" because whenever she dances, she seems to disperse and "trouble" the monolithic, or in other words, the "white" tendencies of the cinematic apparatus' (Coffman 1995: 169).

This complex layering is instantiated in the nine-minute Berkleyesque showcase of *Princesse Tam-Tam* (1.00). The number functions as a party intended by Max's jealous wife and her friend to undermine Aouïna, who has captivated Parisian society. As is typical of Berkeley's dance numbers, the sequence focuses on geometric designs, in particular the spiral formed by the showgirls' hoop costumes (Figure 6.2). The sequence begins with a close-up on a spiralling magician's ball from which the showgirls emerge in a face parade typical of Busby Berkeley, a fade revealing the enormous set with its shiny mirror-like black surfaces and white staircases, and a turning platform with

Figure 6.2 The spiral motif in the first part of the party in *Princesse Tam-Tam* (Courtesy René Chateau).

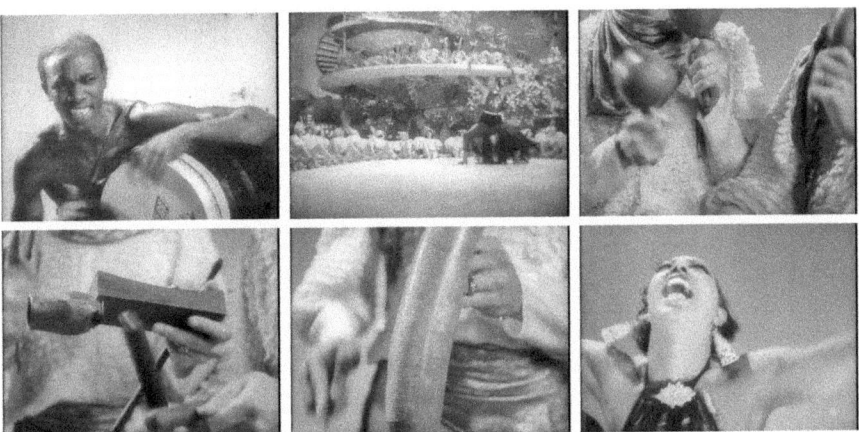

Figure 6.3 Aouïna on stage in *Princesse Tam-Tam* (Courtesy René Chateau).

immobile showgirls. The sequence employs typical Berkeley shots with a face parade and a series of kaleidoscopic overhead designs, including an overhead shot of the girls as pieces on the magician's chequerboard, in which the contrast between black and white is insisted on.

Five and a half minutes into the sequence, there is a significant change of pace (Figure 6.3), as we cut to a close-up of an African drummer, whose drumming leads the music into a conga. Max's wife's friend, in a bid to get Aouïna to make a spectacle of herself, exclaims 'Ah cette musique! Comment pouvez-vous résister, mais dansez voyons!',[10] and plies her with drink, as a result of which Aouïna, visibly excited by the dancing, singing and alcohol, leaps onto the stage and performs an energetic dance for a couple of minutes while the showgirls sit to watch. Whereas in the previous part of the sequence, the showgirls had been dressed in both white and black costumes, in this part they are all in white, while Aouïna strips off her white satin dress to reveal a gauzy black costume underneath. The editing is fast as close-ups of Aouïna are intercut with close-ups of Brazilian instruments one might associate with the conga in what functions as the climax of the sequence. Much to the surprise of Max (who is embarrassed by Aouïna's dance) and his wife (who thought the dance would discredit Aouïna), the assembled company, far from rejecting Aouïna, clap for her furiously.

The sequence constructs racial difference spatially: Aouïna dances in her own Black space on stage, to what is connoted as Black music, and her dancing is very different from the geometrically uniform formations of the White showgirls. But the sequence also demonstrates the combination of attraction and rejection of what the African body represents: Max, his friend, his wife and her friend are embarrassed by Aouïna's impassioned display, while the rest of the audience are excited by it. At stake here is the issue of control: 'The colonist fears that his own inability to control his

---

[10] 'Ah this music! How can you resist it, dance!'

body will resurface in his inability to control the bodies of the colonized; therefore, he repeatedly sets up a supposedly "safe" space for black performance' (Coffman 1995: 198). Baker is kept apart from the showgirls, and ultimately kept apart from the narrative, as we discover a few minutes later that what we have been watching is supposed to be part of Max's novel, and that Aouïna is better off where she is, according to him, in Tunisia, nurturing children and animals. This ideological closure has been carefully prepared by the film: one of the better-known songs sung by Baker is 'Sous le soleil d'Afrique' ('Under the African Sun'), a nostalgic ballad that she sings in a bar where the band and many of the clients are Black, and in which she laments the country she has left behind (0.53).

While we agree with Katherine Groo that 'Baker produced an empty space open to any projection or possibility, neither wholly African nor American, but something or somewhere in-between' (2013: 26), in view of the way that the music functions in the two films, we are more inclined to accept Elizabeth Ezra's view that they 'seem to celebrate a mixing of cultures, but they actually seek to preserve the exotic as such – that is, to keep it literally on the outside' (2000: 99), that is, in a 'safe space'. The safe space was perhaps not safe enough; for all her success during the 1920s and 1930s, the songs Baker sang have not endured in the same way as the often more timid melding of traditional chanson and jazz evidenced by Trenet and the jazz orchestras.

Charles Trenet

Trenet discovered jazz when staying with his mother for several months in Berlin in 1928 at the age of fifteen. He went to Paris in 1930, working for a time in the Pathé Studios as a clapper board assistant, and composed his first songs for a film made by his stepfather, Benno Vigny, *Bariole* (1934). In 1933, taking his cue from Pills and Tabet, he formed the jazz duo Charles et Johnny with his friend Johnny Hess, whom he had met the previous year in the College Inn jazz club. Josephine Baker helped the duo get a permanent contract at Le Palace in Montmartre. The duo broke up in 1936 when Trenet was called up for military service, during which he composed many of his best-known songs.

Trenet wrote and performed the songs as well as playing the starring role in a handful of films over a five-year period. His first film was *La Route enchantée* (Pierre Caron, 1938), in which he sang five songs: 'Vous êtes jolie' ('You're Pretty'), 'Il pleut dans ma chambre' ('It's Raining in My Room'), 'La Route enchantée' ('The Enchanted Road'), 'Je chante' ('I'm Singing'), and 'Boum!', which won the Grand Prix du disque. In the same year, he starred in *Je chante* (Christian Stengel), with four songs: 'Quand j'étais p'tit' ('When I Was Small'), 'Ah dis ah dis ah bonjour' ('Ah Say Ah Say Hello'), 'Les Oiseaux de Paris' ('Birds of Paris') and 'La Vie qui va' ('Life as It Goes'). In *La Romance de Paris* (Jean Boyer, 1941), there were three songs: 'La Romance de Paris', 'Je veux, je veux t'aimer, ma mie' ('I Want to Love You, My Love'), and 'Tout ça c'est pour nous' ('All This Is for Us'). In *Frédérica* (Jean Boyer, 1942), there were once again five songs: 'Frédérica', 'Marie-toi' ('Get Married'), 'C'est bon' ('It's Good'), 'C'est une noce dans un carrosse' ('It's a Wedding in a Carriage'), 'Le Bonheur ne passe qu'une fois' ('Happiness Only Comes Round Once'), and 'Le Bonheur' ('Happiness'). *Adieu Léonard* (Pierre Prévert, 1943) is the last of the films starring Trenet, although the original version was shortened first by the producers and then by the Prévert brothers in the 1950s, as a result of which two of Trenet's songs – 'Quand un facteur s'envole' ('When a Postman Flies Away') and 'Je n'y suis pour personne' ('I'm Not in for Anyone') – were dropped; he subsequently appeared in cameo roles, usually playing himself.[11]

Much as was the case with Josephine Baker, Trenet's films form a coherent body of work. In Baker's case it was largely the rags-to-riches Cinderella narrative that echoed her real-life career. In Trenet's case it was the artistic control he had over the films which imparts a similar feel to them. Unlike most other singers who sang and acted what others had created for them, from his first film onwards Trenet took an active role in shaping the material, writing the script and dialogue for *La Route enchantée*, then writing the lyrics and composing the music for *Je chante*, co-composing the music with Georges Van Parys for *La Romance de Paris*, and co-composing the music with Joseph Kosma for *Adieu Léonard*. His persona across his five films is remarkably consistent, and very different from the *chanteurs de charme* (crooners) such as Tino Rossi, Réda Caire, Jan Kiepura and André Baugé.

The films are comical, surreal fantasy normally overtaking reality, with socially marginal characters whose imagination typically runs away with them. In his first film, Trenet plays a singer, Jacques, who chases after a castle he has seen in his dreams, and the film is structured around the confusion between dream and reality. Jacques's younger brother proposes a treasure hunt to Jacques, and shows him a pretend 'enchanted road' on his map, to which Jacques responds: 'Ça me paraît d'autant plus exact que tout est méticuleusement inventé';[12] and when Jacques has found the castle, and has fallen in love with the Countess's niece, Geneviève, the latter says to Jacques: 'C'est merveilleux. On croirait rêver. Ce serait si terrible de se réveiller.'[13] In *La Romance de Paris* Trenet plays a dutiful son who against his mother's wishes becomes a successful singer with the name Papillon. In *Frédérica*, he plays yet another dreamer who yearns for an ideal woman with that name; his letters to the ideal woman are seen by a real Frédérica, leading to the inevitable comical clashes between reality and the ideal, typical of boulevard comedy (the film adapted Jean de Létraz's stage play, *Épousez-nous, Monsieur*). Surreal fantasy is at its most obvious in *Adieu Léonard*, as might be expected from a script written by the Prévert brothers. Léonard, ruined by his wife and her lover, is caught by Bonenfant as he tries to crack Bonenfant's safe. Bonenfant blackmails Léonard into killing Ludovic, played by Trenet, who is a free spirit and runs a kind of commune in his castle, so as to deprive him of his inheritance.

---

[11] A sketch in *La Cavalcade des heures* (Yvan Noé, 1943), cameos in *Bouquet de joie* (Maurice Cam, 1951), *Boum sur Paris* (Maurice de Canonge, 1954), *Printemps à Paris* (Jean-Claude Roy, 1957), *C'est arrivé à 36 chandelles* (Henri Diamant-Berger, 1957), and as an anonymous singer in *Giovinezza* (Giorgio Pastina, 1952).

[12] 'It seems even more true to me in that everything is meticulously invented.'

[13] 'It's marvellous. It's as though I'm dreaming. It would be terrible to wake up.'

Figure 6.4 'Quand un facteur s'envole' from *Adieu Léonard* (Courtesy René Chateau).

The song 'Quand un facteur s'envole', dropped in later versions of the film, show Trenet as a postman casting the letters he is supposed to be delivering as if they were seeds or confetti, and singing: 'C'est le courier du cœur/Le courier du bonheur',[14] and celebrating freedom and love (Figure 6.4). At the end of the film Léonard and Ludovic go on the road together. The film is a celebration of bohemianism and a condemnation of the grubby materialism of the petite-bourgeoisie.

The dialogue of the films frequently rely on surreal fantasy, as can be seen in the film over which Trenet had the most control, *La Route enchantée*. For example, Jacques says to an old man he meets while travelling 'je ne marche plus. Je fais marcher ma tête, en rêve',[15] to which the old man responds, 'c'est le plus court chemin d'un point à un autre'.[16] The songs contribute to the attraction of the dream life and the rejection of social norms, as can be seen in the refrain of the title song: 'Pars, oublie la terre/Pars, viens avec nous, tu verras/Les joyeux matins et les grands chemins/Où l'on marche à l'aventure/Hiver comme été/Toujours la nature/La route enchantée'.[17] The urgency of this attraction is conveyed not just by the lyrics but also by the syncopated swing

---

[14] 'They're love letters/Letters of happiness.'
[15] 'I'm not walking any more. I'm making my head walk, in a dream.'
[16] 'It's the shortest distance from one point to another.'
[17] 'Leave, forget the earth/Leave and come with us you'll see/Happy mornings and highways/Where you seek adventure/Winter and summer/Always nature/The enchanted road.'

rhythms, and by the mise en scène: Trenet constantly moves around the constrained circular space of the tower, with the stars in the background, and briefly a shot of nothing but the stars, figuring the freedom and the freedom of the imagination that Trenet's songs so frequently address.

Trenet's surreal fantasy is supported by the syncopated jazz rhythms of his songs, emphasized by onomatopoeia, such as the evocation of falling rain in *La Route enchantée*, typical of scat in American jazz: 'Mais la pluie fredonne/Sur un rythme joyeux/Tip et tap et tip et top et tip/Et tip tip et tip/Et tip top et tap/Voilà ce qu'on entend la nuit/ C'est la chanson de la pluie.'[18] *La Romance de Paris* is the most interesting of Trenet's films in that it is in part a reflection on what it means to be a singer in a period of musical transition. Trenet plays Georges Gauthier, a workman who dreams of becoming a singer, and who under the name Papillon achieves success while revolutionizing singing. The film opens on an accordionist whom passers-by ignore. Georges stops to talk with him, and advises him to add lyrics that tell a story, leading to the first musical sequence of the film in which Georges sings the title song with passers-by stopping to listen and joining in the chorus as Georges teaches them how to sing differently. Later, in the kind of opposition familiar in musicals more generally, Georges talks in the wings with the concert tenor Lormel, who asks him what he thinks of Lormel's performance, and Georges responds that he would sing 'avec plus de simplicité, plus de naturel ... J'y mettrais un peu plus d'allant, un peu plus de rythme'.[19] He then sings the song with a jazz rhythm, the sequence, like the opening sequence with the accordionist, constituting a master class on a more modern kind of music. Later, once he has successfully passed his audition, Georges goes to a number of sheet-music shops in search of a new song to add to his repertoire. In the first shop, the shopkeeper recommends a song which Georges rejects, saying that he wants 'quelque chose d'un peu plus moderne, d'un peu plus original. Je voudrais faire quelque chose de nouveau.'[20]

Somewhat like Baker's films whose narratives paralleled her real-life career, so too in the case of this film Georges is calqued on Trenet's own persona, as is made clear by the poster for the premiere of George's music-hall show which lists 'Jean Papillon, le fou chantant', 'le fou chantant' being a term used for Trenet himself. The films themselves emphasize the radical turn represented by Trenet's music, so different from what had preceded it. We will return to jazz in Chapter 8 when we consider the big bands. In the next chapter, however, we focus on a major strand of what we consider to be the French film musical, the classical music film, which, like other musicals of the 1930s, began by exploring the opportunities provided by sound.

---

[18] 'But the rain hums away/With a happy beat/Tip and tap and tip and top and tip/And tip tip and tip/ And tip top and tap/That's what the night can hear/It's the song of the rain.'
[19] 'More simply, more naturally. I'd give it more of a kick, a bit more rhythm.'
[20] 'Something a bit more modern, a bit more original? I want to try something new.'

7

The classical music film

Although films focusing on classical music are not numerous in French cinema, they are significant as they deal with a key issue: How can more sustained musical pieces be integrated as an essential component of a form dominated by dialogue and the visual track? Prior to the advent of sound, music was played separately from the image track,[1] but with sound, new opportunities arose. A key figure for French cinema is Abel Gance who experimented with music in the 1930s; his work influenced the classical music films that followed in the 1930s and 1940s.

Biopics and adaptations of well-known operas (as opposed to the operettas we have already considered) had occurred prior to the 1980s (the heyday of the opera film, which we shall consider in Chapter 15) and the 2000s (which saw a large number of musical biopics, which we shall consider in our Conclusion):

1. Chopin (biopic): *La Chanson de l'adieu* (Géza von Bolváry and Albert Valentin, 1934)
2. Beethoven (biopic): *Un grand amour de Beethoven* (Abel Gance, 1937)
3. Charpentier (opera): *Louise* (Abel Gance, 1939)
4. Schubert (biopic): *Sérénade* (Jean Boyer, 1940)
5. Berlioz (biopic): *La Symphonie fantastique* (Christian-Jaque, 1942)
6. Lizst (biopic): *Rêves d'amour* (Christian Stengel, 1947)
7. Offenbach (biopic): *La Valse de Paris* (Marcel Achard, 1950)

Gance followed his biopic of Beethoven with the adaptation of a well-known opera by Gustave Charpentier (1900), *Louise*. Surprisingly, there were very few opera films – defined as films in which the characters sing – in France in this period. *La Vie de bohème* (Marcel L'Herbier, 1945) is based on the Henri Murger novel (1851)

---

[1] There were many opera films prior to sound, particularly in the first years of commercial cinema; among them *Le Barbier de Séville* (George Méliès, 1904), *La Damnation de Faust* (Georges Méliès, 1904), *Mignon* (Gaumont, 1906), *Cavalleria rusticana* (Émile Chautard, 1909), *Don César de Bazan* (Victorin Jasset, 1909), *Rigoletto* (André Calmettes, 1909), *Carmen* (André Calmettes, 1910), *Faust* (Henri Andréani and Georges Fagot, 1910), *La Fin de Don Juan* (Victorin Jasset, 1911), *Fra Diavolo* (Alice Guy-Blaché, 1912), *Manon Lescaut* (Pathé, 1912), *Mignon* (Alice Guy-Blaché, 1912), *Faust* (Gérard Bourgeois, 1922).

adapted by Puccini, and uses Puccini's music as background,[2] while at the opposite extreme, *Le Barbier de Séville* (Jean Loubignac, 1948) was not an adaptation but the filming of the very successful production of Rossini's opera by the Théâtre national de l'Opéra-Comique; neither of these are film musicals as we have defined them. We will focus on Gance's two films, partly because they are among the first of this type of film, partly because he essayed both genres – biopics and adaptations of well-known operas – and partly because the solutions he found for the incorporation of music into film influenced the films that followed.

Gance is best known for his silent films, in particular the anti-war *J'accuse* (1919), the formally complex *La Roue* (1923), and the epic six-and-half-hour-long *Napoléon* (1927), restored by Kevin Brownlow in 1979. It is hardly surprising, given Gance's formal experimentation in the two latter films in particular, that he should explore a variety of techniques to integrate the music and the visual tracks in his two film musicals. Moreover, given Gance's interest in heroic men, as well as the obvious links between Beethoven and Napoleon – both lived in the same period, Beethoven wrote the Eroica Symphony in praise of Napoleon – a film on Beethoven was a natural choice for Gance.

Un grand amour de Beethoven

Un grand amour de Beethoven, which film historian Jean-Pierre Jeancolas considers Gance's best sound film (1982: 21), is based loosely on Romain Rolland's biography (1903), and focuses on Beethoven's relationship with the mysterious 'immortal beloved'. Gance presumes fictitiously that the 'immortal beloved' gestured at in the title of his film is Juliette Guicciardi.[3] Beethoven pines for her even after her marriage to Count Gallenberg, but eventually accepts the self-sacrificing devotion of Juliette's older sister Thérèse. The major concern of the film, however, is less the sentimental intrigue than the heroic tussle with fate as Beethoven gradually goes deaf. In that respect, the film, as one critic put it, is 'un film musical comme il n'est pas possible de l'être davantage', a 'symphonie héroïque' demonstrating 'un profond amour de la chose musicale'[4] (J.L. 1937: 27). This was not how most critics and audiences reacted to the film, however.

While some spectators lavished praise on the film and its star, Harry Baur, others pointed out the disparity between what they saw on screen and the Beethoven they imagined when listening to his music. Harry Baur simply did not convey the heroic image of the tormented artist: 'Fantoche ivrogne et joueur … qui pas un instant nous émeut car il lui manque cette flamme de la création et de l'improvisation que devait

---

[2] A similar strategy is used for Charles Gounod's *Mireille* (René Gavault and Ernest Servaës, 1953) and *Le Mariage de Figaro* (Jean Meyer, 1959).
[3] See Alion (1978: 6).
[4] 'A musical film that couldn't be more so/heroic symphony/a profound love of music.'

posséder Beethoven quand il composait'[5] ('Boris' 1937: 12); 'la musique souligne avec une impitoyable ironie par sa fougue, son énergie, les attitudes somnolentes clownesques de son acteur'[6] ('Le Junkee' 1937: 11). The music, which appears in fragments throughout the film rather than in sustained performance of individual works, is used not as background score but integrated within the narrative, as emotional moments in Beethoven's life are seen to motivate the compositions. For example, early in the film he walks past his neighbour's house where the mother is grieving the death of her young daughter (0.12); Beethoven sits at the piano and plays the *adagio cantabile* of the Piano Sonata no. 8 in E minor, opus 13, known as the 'Pathétique', a non-diegetic orchestra taking over from the piano. (The musical arrangement echoes the opening sequence in which we see Juliette playing a lied at the piano, 'Ich leibe dich', but we do not hear the voice and instead of piano we, rather oddly, hear the full orchestra.) The intertitle 'Improvisation de la *Pathétique*' signals the sequence's purpose: intense emotion in specific situations leads Beethoven to compose well-known pieces. Later in the film (0.54), rejected by Juliette, Beethoven locks himself in the organ loft of the church where she is getting married to Count Gallenberg and plays what, appalled, she comments on as 'musique de mort',[7] the '*marcia funebre sulla morte d'un eroe*' from Piano Sonata no. 12 in A flat major, opus 26. The crashing organ and Thérèse's fainting led one spectator to say that he had never laughed so much at the absurdly melodramatic nature of the sequence ('A.B.C.D.' 1937: 11).

The criticism of the film's music can be summarized as follows: the transposition of pieces, such as a full orchestra playing a piece that a character plays at the piano, something which incensed the musically oriented critic Émile Vuillermoz;[8] the music's portentous melodrama; and the diminution of the music's power through fragmentation. In relation to these last two points, another musically oriented critic of the time, Henry Malherbe, was particularly exercized that the emphasis on fate recurs throughout the film with the first four notes (G G G A) of the Symphony no. 5 as a convenient but overinflated and false signifier of 'destiny', and further complained that the beauty and force of Beethoven's music cannot be conveyed by the multitude of musical fragments used for the film (Malherbe 1937: 5).[9]

These critiques, whether from critics or spectators, assume that there should be congruence between reality and Gance's melodramatic fantasy. Gance may well have integrated well-known facts about Beethoven's life in the film – such as the raised fist on the deathbed – but the identity of the 'immortal beloved' as Juliette is pure conjecture,

---

[5] 'A drunken and playful puppet who doesn't move us at all because he doesn't have the spark of creativity and improvisation that Beethoven must have had when he was composing.'
[6] 'The music with its fervour and energy emphasizes with merciless irony the somnolent and clown-like attitudes of the actor.'
[7] 'Death music.'
[8] See Roger (2000: 260–1) for an account of Vuillermoz's review.
[9] Richard Will more positively suggests that 'the fragmentary use of the music captures the incoherence of lovers, who can no more maintain the tonal and formal continuities of classical music than they can the syntactic connectivities of normative language. ... Their brevity might then be heard as meaningful in and of itself, a sign of the characters' inability, in the face of love, to articulate anything more than fragments' (2013: 351).

as is the linking of the music to events that allow Beethoven to create fully formed and well-known pieces at the piano. Moreover, these pieces are chronologically out of synch with what we know of their composition history, which would have disappointed those who were familiar with Beethoven's music; and for those who might be less familiar, disappointment was frequently voiced over the fact that we see pieces played on the piano but hear them played by a full orchestra, what Philippe Roger calls Gance's 'tentation symphonique'[10] (2000: 257). Gance is clearly not interested in some kind of biographical truth; he is more interested in creating what one might call a 'tone poem' in which music and narrative combine to generate extreme and heroic emotions, even if, as Richard Will perceptively notes, 'Gance depicts greatness as more passive than active, and in musical terms more sensuous than developmental' (2013: 347). Nowhere is this clearer than in the sequence admired by even the most critical spectators, when Beethoven realizes that he is going deaf, this being followed by the thunderstorm when he realizes that deafness was in this case temporary. The point of the sequence is to demonstrate the hero's overcoming adversity in spectacular fashion (0.33–0.47).

Introduced by an intertitle – 'vint le matin le plus tragique de la vie de Beethoven'[11] – and the dramatic opening chords of *Coriolanus*, Beethoven hears nothing other than distorted clanging. We see shots of him holding his head and close-ups of his face alternating with shots of his help, Pierrot, during which the sounds stop.[12] Then, in a somewhat startling reversal of the trope, when Beethoven hits the piano keys, we hear nothing, but when he asks Pierrot to do the same thing, we hear the sound. Beethoven, distraught, leaves the Heiligenstadt windmill to the sound of the *lento assai, cantata tranquillo* of the String Quartet no. 135 in an arrangement for string orchestra. We see him wandering through the countryside and the village as in silence we see sounds that he cannot hear: a violinist playing, a blacksmith's hammer, water, bells ringing, washerwomen; they can be heard only when he has walked away from their source; this part of the sequence finishes on Beethoven's death mask signalling melodramatically that loss of hearing is like death for him (Figure 7.1). The sounds lead to the *allegro ma non troppo* of the Pastoral Symphony, signalling that Beethoven is imagining music in the place of what he can hear of the outside world. When the storm starts (Figure 7.2), Beethoven exults in the fact that he can hear the thunder, and we see his hands run over the piano keys to the full-orchestra accompaniment of the storm section of the Pastoral Symphony, shots of lightning mickey-mousing with the cross-editing of him playing and the sky illuminated by lightning flashes. When the storm dies down, we see a range of countryside shots with his hands superimposed on the piano.

The sequence is overly melodramatic by modern standards, but Gance's manipulation of the soundtrack works well as an attempt to convey the horror of disability in its most immediate and haptic sense. The editing is integrated with the music – very obviously

---

[10] 'Tempation of the symphonic.'
[11] 'The most tragic morning of Beethoven's life.'
[12] Roger suggests intriguingly that this might represent the struggle between silent cinema and sound cinema for Gance (2000: 255).

The Classical Music Film

Figure 7.1 Beethoven realizes he is going deaf in *Un grand amour de Beethoven* Léonard (Courtesy René Chateau).

Figure 7.2 The storm in *Un grand amour de Beethoven* (Courtesy René Chateau).

for the brief moments of mickey-mousing – and although at least one critic dismissed Gance's use of cinematographic tricks such as blurred images and superimpressions (J.L. 1937: 27), there is a consistent logic in the editing as Beethoven feels cut off from the external world and its sounds and transmutes those sounds into music, separate shots becoming melded together with superimpressions as he rediscovers his hearing. As the same critic points out after dismissing Gance's mannerisms, the film is nonetheless 'une symphonie héroïque'[13] (137: 27). The music is a pretext for a cinematic equivalent of Beethoven's *Storm und Drang*; but it is also essential to it, legitimizing the narrative excesses required by Gance's vision of the hero. The music and the narrative may seem incongruous but fundamentally they are congruent.

Louise

Gance's adaptation of *Louise* is less impressive, both in terms of the problems it tries to solve, and in terms of the music. He was intent on adapting operas for the screen: a 1929 note suggests that it would be possible to 'filmer entièrement un *Boris Godunov*, un *Coq d'or*, ou une *Thaïs*'[14] (cited in Icart 1983: 253; he is referring to operas by Mussorgsky, Rimsky-Korsakov and Massenet). His intention for *Louise* was to create 'un mariage entre le cinéma et l'opéra' (Gance cited in Caumartin 1938: 1068), as well as to privilege music so that it was 'non point plaquée, extérieure, sorte de remplissage, de bruit de fond, d'accessoire sonore, mais la musique devenue objective, baignant tout, devenue importante au même titre qu'un personnage, au même titre qu'une image qui vaut plus encore par ce qu'elle suggère que par ce qu'elle montre'[15] (Gance cited in Doringe 1939: 8–9). This may partly account for the fact that Gance, following Charpentier's recommendation, changed the hero's profession from that of a poet to a *poète-musicien* in the film (Niccolai 2016: 82–3). His problem, as Roger Icart points out, was how to avoid the music becoming secondary to what we see on screen, either by overloading the image track or by going for realism (1984: 288); his solution was to film everything using his invention, the Pictographe (Niccolai 2016: 84 n47) in the studio with decors by Georges Wakhevitch, an aesthetic choice that Benoît Jacquot was to emulate for *Tosca* (2001; Chapter 15). In Icart's view, this gives the image track an unreal character, thereby preserving 'cet allant, cette fluidité, ce charme qui caractérisaient l'œuvre musicale de Charpentier'[16] (288).

One of the key challenges for the opera film is what to do with arias. Focusing on a singer singing, as opposed to the typical Hollywood film musical in which characters sing and dance at the same time, creates a pause in the narrative, a potentially unnatural interlude. This can be minimized in the case of a narrative focusing on the music, such

---

[13] 'A heroic symphony.'
[14] 'To film in their entirety a *Boris Godunov*, a *Coq d'or*, or a *Thaïs*.'
[15] 'A marriage between cinema and opera/Cladding, external, a kind of filler, background sound, but as important as a character or as an image that carries more weight by what it suggests than what by what it shows.'
[16] 'The vigour, the fluidity, the charm characteristic of Charpentier's work.'

as the backstage musical; but in *Louise*, despite the fact that the hero is composing an opera called *Louise*, the musical numbers are not rehearsals. To avoid the image becoming static, especially during musical numbers, Gance used a very mobile camera with frequent travelling shots, pointing out in an interview that 'tous mes plans sont en mouvement'[17] (Caumartin 1938: 1069), an aesthetic choice emulated by Andrzej Żuławski for *Boris Godounov* (1989; Chapter 15).

Henry Malherbe was impressed by the integration of music and dialogue, commenting that 'la partie musicale du film laisse une forte impression et nous prend par des liens mystérieux'[18] (1939: 9). In his view Gance succeeded in creating a new type of film: '*Louise* n'est ni un opéra filmé ... ni une comédie musicale envolée au hasard dans un studio. C'est une œuvre cinégraphique, bien distincte du roman musical d'où elle a été tirée'[19] (9). This was partly achieved by turning recitatives into dialogue, with musical numbers interspersing the action. This solved another key problem for the opera film: what to do about realist ambient sound. But the film as a result is a standard sentimental melodrama with high-point musical numbers, even if this was unusual for the time. The male lead, Georges Thill, explained why he thought that the rearrangement of the score worked well: 'Le chant n'intervient que lorsque les situations sont arrivées à leur paroxysme .... Alors, comme si les mots devenaient incapables d'exprimer ce que ressentent les personnages, le chant s'élève et entraîne le public sur l'aile de la musique'[20] (cited in Caumartin 1938: 1068). We can gauge just how new this might have been for audiences at the time by Thill's evaluation of the procedure: 'Cette façon de *conclure* chaque scène, chaque situation dramatique par une effusion musicale est une trouvaille assez sensationnelle'[21] (1068; emphasis in original).

Thill's comment that the music bursts out when characters cannot contain their emotions is a standard melodramatic device. When compared with *Un grand amour de Beethoven*, however, the film is not melodramatic enough, as a critic writing in the 1980s pointed out: 'On ne fait qu'effleurer le mélodrame, alors que Gance a besoin de s'y vautrer'[22] (Beylie 1987: 65), and appears tame in comparison. This can be seen in *Louise*'s storm sequence (0.40–0.47), clearly an attempt by Gance to capitalize on what had been seen as a very successful piece of filmmaking in *Un grand amour de Beethoven*. Louise has finally agreed to run away with Julien, and he takes her to a safe place. He returns to his apartment when a storm breaks out. Louise, frightened, runs back to him, only to find her friend Lucienne with him. Believing the worst, she runs back out into the rain. We find the same sound effects and lighting effects (thunder and lightning) as in *Un grand amour de Beethoven* (Figure 7.3). But there is no music at all, and Gance uses somewhat hackneyed expressionist techniques (strong lighting effects, chiaroscuro,

---

[17] 'All my shots are mobile.'
[18] 'The musical part of the film leaves a strong impression and captivates us mysteriously.'
[19] '*Louise* is neither a filmed opera nor a film musical. It's a cinematic work, quite distinct from the original musical novel.'
[20] 'Song happens only when situations have reached a climax. ... Then, as if words were incapable of expressing the characters' feelings, song rises up and lifts the audience on the wings of music.'
[21] 'This way of *concluding* each scene, each dramatic situation by musical effusion is quite sensational.'
[22] 'Melodrama is gestured at, but Gance's filmmaking requires him to wallow in it.'

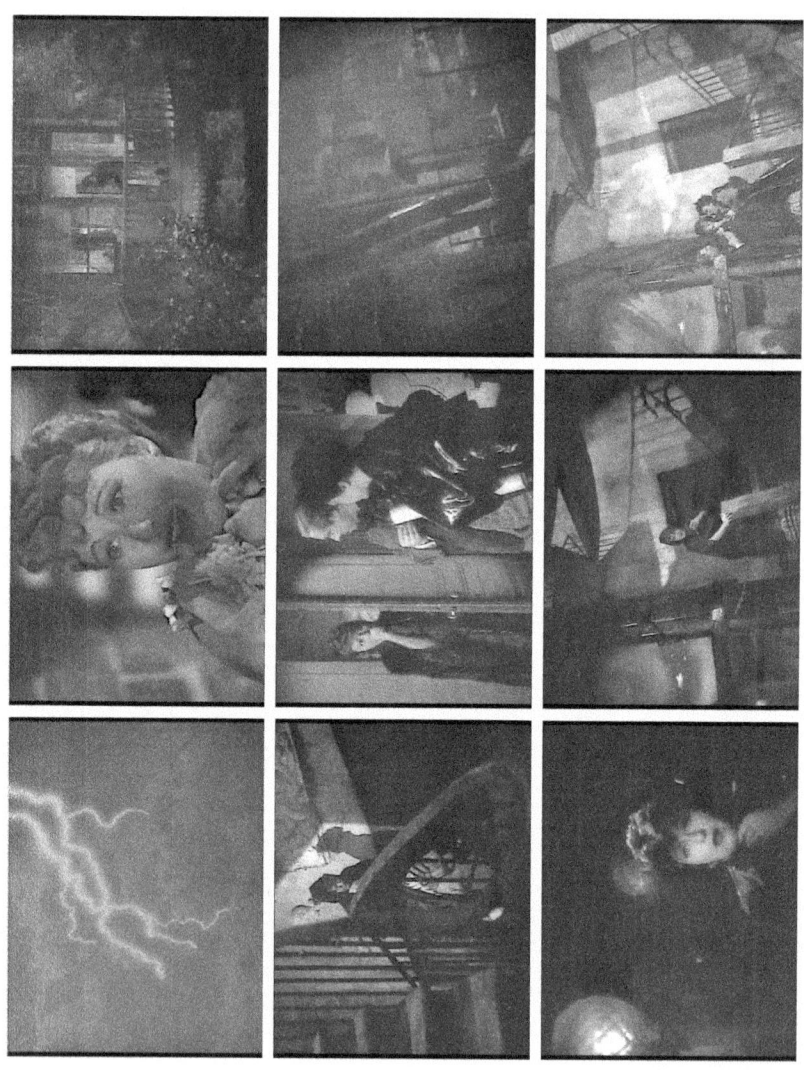

Figure 7.3 The storm in *Louise* (Courtesy René Chateau).

angular décor, canted frames) to mimic the *Storm und Drang* of the previous film. As one of Charpentier's 'mystery-shoppers' reported to him, this sequence and others not in the opera 'font très "cinéma", mais ne peuvent faire tort à *Louise* roman musical'[23] (Niccolai 2016: 94). *Louise* comes across as less creative in its use of the music track; indeed, Claude Beylie dismisses the film as a 'pot-pourri un peu académique'[24] (1987: 65).

Gance's film musicals show the two principal approaches to the integration of classical music in film. First, there is the soundtrack composed of fragments of well-known music. This can illustrate the narrative: we need to know that Beethoven is a sensitive genius, so we see him improvising a well-known piece that fits the occasion. But it can also, less frequently, provide narrative direction. The storm in *Un grand amour de Beethoven* does the latter: the music calls up the storm as metaphor for the act of creation, and the key moments of mickey-mousing, brief though they may be, signal the impossibility of deciding what determines what. Does the stormy music bring forth the images of the storm, or are the images of the storm illustrations of the storm section of Beethoven's *Pastoral*? The latter approach was adopted by Walt Disney's *Fantasia* (1940) four years later, for example, the mickey-mousing of the *The Sorcerer's Apprentice* section. Second, as seen in *Louise*, a whole work is adapted, causing a different type of fragmentation as cuts are made, requiring compensation in the image track (décor, camerawork).

La Symphonie fantastique and *La Valse de Paris*

Subsequent biopics followed the pattern of *Un grand amour de Beethoven*, often reprising some of its tropes (chiaroscuro lighting, canted frames, superimpositions). In *La Symphonie fantastique*, for example, Berlioz (Jean-Louis Barrault) is inspired by a storm and hears what he knows is a completely new type of music inside his head, exclaiming 'c'est la symphonie de ma vie, c'est la symphonie fantastique!' (0.25),[25] furiously writing down notes as we hear the finale, 'Songe d'une nuit de sabbat' ('Dream of a Witches' Sabbath') (0.26) (Figure 7.4). We also hear fragments from the *Messe solennelle*, *Benvenuto Cellini*, 'Reviens' ('Return') from *Nuits d'été*, *La Damnation de Faust* and the *Grande messe des morts*, this last fragment being chronologically out of sequence, as had been the case with the musical fragments used in Gance's film: it is suggested that Berlioz composes it after his wife Marie dies (1862), whereas it had been performed long before (1836).[26]

La Valse de Paris also uses musical fragments to support the narrative, in this case a fictitious account of the relationship between Offenbach and his collaborator, Hortense Schneider, played here by the real-life partners Pierre Fresnay and Yvonne Printemps. The director insisted playfully that apart from Offenbach's myopia, 'tout

---

[23] 'Are very cinematic, but don't detract from *Louise* as a musical romance.'
[24] 'Academic pot-pourri.'
[25] 'It's the symphony of my life, it's the fantastic symphony.'
[26] For more on this film see Bellemare (2018).

Figure 7.4 The storm in *La Symphonie fantastique* (Courtesy René Chateau).

le reste est rigoureusement faux'[27] (cited in Rodrigue 1949: 4). Offenbach's music, in jumbled chronological order (Senelick 2018: 26), is used to illustrate a sentimental and lightweight film, in the tradition of the operetta film and very different from Gance's biopic. There is, however, an astonishing sequence in *La Valse de Paris* in which dialogue is replaced by music (1.19). The Calife de Ramsoun visits Offenbach, who realizing that the Calife does not speak French, exclaims that 'la musique est un langage international, nous nous entendrons très bien'.[28] Offenbach proceeds to ask questions using music rather than words so that the Calife can mimic a response, the first for example being the 'Galop infernal', also known as the cancan, from *Orphée aux enfers*, intended in this case to find out whether the Calife has been enjoying a ribald moment with Hortense. Although formally interesting, the procedure is, like the film itself, lightweight, more akin to operetta films and quite unlike the ponderousness of Gance's two films. Much less ponderous, and considerably more joyous, is one of the major musical sub-genres of the late 1930s through to the early 1960s, the jazz-inflected big-band film, which we consider in the next chapter.

[27] 'Everything else is completely false.'
[28] 'Music is an international language, we will get on very well together.'

8

The big-band film

The big-band films began appearing in the late 1930s, and remained an important part of French film culture during the 1940s and early 1950s. Like Trenet before them, they engage more obviously with American-style jazz, and as a result raise key questions about the relationship between French and US culture in France. Pre-eminent among these films are those of Ray Ventura and his orchestra, known as 'Ray Ventura et ses Collégiens', who played on stage and on radio throughout the 1930s and 1940s, and whose songs were incorporated in their films. Ventura was the most famous band leader of the variety style (Régnier 2009: 54). He and his orchestra performed in the major Paris venues during the 1930s,[1] and were regularly praised for creating a French jazz style, partly because they created jazz versions of well-known traditional French songs, such as 'Sur le pont d'Avignon', and 'Frère Jacques', combining modern jazz with nostalgia (Jackson 2002: 160–1).

This was the period of the big bands more generally. During the 1930s there was Fred Adison and his orchestra (a Frenchman despite his name), then the orchestras of Raymond Legrand and Jacques Hélian during the Second World War, and later of Aimé Barelli. American and British orchestras performed regularly in Paris. Jack Hylton, for example, an Englishman, was proclaimed 'king of jazz' by the French, and awarded the Legion of Honour in 1932 (Mawer 2008). In this chapter we focus mainly on Ventura, not just because he Gallicized jazz, but also because he was a film producer; he established his own production company, Hoche, in 1947, which produced some fifteen films, including the film that launched the screen career of the rock 'n' roll star Johnny Hallyday, *D'où viens-tu, Johnny?* (Noël Howard, 1963; Chapter 12). And unlike other bandleaders, he and his orchestra starred in a substantial number of films. Adison and his orchestra appeared in only one minor film, *À nous deux, Madame la vie* (René Guissart and Yves Mirande, 1937), as did Legrand, in *Mademoiselle Swing* (Richard Pottier, 1942), although this one had a significant impact because it represented a generational shift towards a very specific youth culture, that of the *Zazous*.[2] Hélian and his orchestra appeared in six. One of these, *Pigalle-Saint-Germain-des-Prés* (André Berthomieu, 1950; Chapter 9), was produced by Hoche, and Ventura was one of the co-writers. By contrast Ventura and his orchestra appeared in eight films.

---

[1] For example, Bobino (1932, 1933, 1935, 1936), L'Empire (1931, 1932) and L'Alhambra (1932, 1936).
[2] On the *Zazou* film, see Burch and Sellier (1996: 133–41).

Ventura's first film was a film version of his very popular song 'Tout va très bien Madame la Marquise' ('Everything is Fine, Madame la Marquise'), which had sold 600,000 records in 1935. The orchestra's role was small, as was the case with *Aventure à Paris*, an adaptation of Henry Falk's stage play *Le Rabatteur* (The Beater), with Arletty and Jules Berry; the orchestra did not even feature on the film poster. That changed with *Feux de joie* in 1939; the orchestra became the star of the film, the romantic subplot being relegated to second place as the focus is principally on the role of the musicians. In *Feux de joie* a group of Parisian musicians cycle down to the Côte d'Azur to set up a hotel after their military service. They attract custom, and therefore the wrath of a competitor, with their musical shows. In *Tourbillon de Paris*, the journey is the other way round: the Collégiens improbably play the role of schoolchildren, this being partially legitimated by their orchestra's name. They have come to Paris to sit for their exams, and earn their living by giving shows.

At the outbreak of the Second World War, Ventura, who was Jewish, left for South America with his orchestra, their musical and film career in France taking off once more on their return in 1947, when Ventura changed many of the musicians, in addition to setting up his production company. Christine, in *Mademoiselle s'amuse*, is the spoilt daughter of a rich American. She loves jazz, and manages to persuade her father to pay for Ventura and his orchestra to follow her everywhere she goes; the musicians end up deserting her, and as a result of trying to persuade them to come back, she discovers the realities behind their lives as well as learning a lesson in humility. In 1950 Ventura released the bestselling *Nous irons à Paris*, in which Henri Genès, a former Resistance fighter unhappy with the job he has in state radio, decides to set up a clandestine radio with his friends. They are supported by Ventura and his orchestra. The team, as is indicated by the title, travel from the country to the capital with state radio and police in hot pursuit; but 'Radio X' has become such a popular phenomenon that they are welcomed as celebrities. In the film that tried to repeat the winning formula of *Nous irons à Paris*, *Nous irons à Monte-Carlo*, the journey is once more in the opposite direction. The orchestra goes to Monte Carlo for a festival, with a baby that Honorin (Max Elloy) believes to be his grandson; but the boy is, in fact, the son of warring American film stars, each of whom wants the child. There is considerable confusion as to the child's paternity, Ventura himself being accused at one point of being the child's father. The film starred Audrey Hepburn as the mother of the child, prior to her breakthrough two years later in *Roman Holiday* (William Wyler, 1953); Boyer made an English-language version at the same time as the French version, entitled *Monte Carlo Baby*, and this was released in the United States two months after *Roman Holiday*.

The backstage musicals of Ray Ventura

The central films, on which we will focus, are backstage musicals; they are about the eventual success of Ventura's orchestra on stage. Even when the ostensible narrative goal is establishing a successful hotel, as is the case in *Feux de joie*, success is predicated on a successful show. The formula appears to change in *Nous irons à Monte-Carlo*, but this is only in appearance. The orchestra is in Monte Carlo for the jazz festival, and the events surrounding the baby prevent them from performing as expected. While the majority of the orchestra is in pursuit of the baby and his kidnapper, Ventura and his quintet mime to the music played on a record behind the scenes, with orchestra director Julien (Henri Genès) doing a comic turn as he rushes from one instrument to the next.

While the orchestra is the main protagonist in these films, there are nonetheless several subsidiary protagonists: the young romantic couple, generally formed by the main singer of the orchestra and a woman who is at first external to the orchestra, but is gradually accepted as part of the team by virtue of her affair with the singer. This is the case for Micheline (Micheline Cheirel) in *Feux de joie*, who gets together with Roland (René Lefèbvre), as it is for Christine (Gisèle Pascal) in *Mademoiselle s'amuse*, who separates from Jacques (Bernard Lancret), only to get back together with him at the end of the film. He is not part of the orchestra, but he nonetheless sings.

Alongside the romantic couple are the two comic protagonists: first, a larger-than-life member of the orchestra, and second, the father of the woman, who, like his daughter, is eventually won over by the music and the musicians. In the case of the first internal comic character, it is Coco Aslan in *Feux de joie* and *Tourbillon de Paris*, followed by Henri Genès (*Nous irons à Paris*, *Nous irons à Monte-Carlo*), and Max Elloy (*Mademoiselle s'amuse*, *Nous irons à Paris*, *Nous irons à Monte-Carlo*). In the case of the second, external comic character, it is the director of the college in *Tourbillon de Paris*, but in subsequent films it is always the father of the female romantic character, and in two of the films he is a widower (*Mademoiselle s'amuse*, *Nous irons à Paris*).

Consistency of narrative form and consistency of character formations are paralleled by a second systematic characteristic: consistency in the musical numbers. There are generally no more than six musical numbers in these films. These are systematically distributed across the film. At the beginning of the film during the credits there is always a version without the words of the main song of the film. The final number is a medley of the preceding numbers, and signals the end of the film (with the exception of *Mademoiselle s'amuse*). The reason it is worth dwelling on these characteristics is that they are different in other film musical sub-genres; for example, the number heard at the end of Tino Rossi's equally codified films is rarely a medley.

A third systematic characteristic is the nature and performance of the musical numbers. The music is, as might be expected from a big band, brass heavy, mostly swing, with frequent samba rhythms; the music and lyrics are boisterous. Although there is a front singer, generally the internal comic character or the romantic lead mentioned earlier, the musicians frequently take turns to sing, this occurring more in the film versions than in the recorded versions of the songs. The songs fall broadly into two categories: the song that tells a story, and the song that uses a series of vignettes to illustrate a theme. In both cases, André Hornez's lyrics systematically use puns, bathos and innuendo in inventive ways, and the singers typically use exaggerated and frequently camp singing styles, gestures and facial expressions as part of their performance.

An example of the story song is the samba 'Maria de Bahia' published in 1946 and integrated in *Mademoiselle s'amuse* two years later. It tells the story of Maria, the free and easy belle of the town, who becomes a film actress and returns to Bahia, presumably abused and rejected, where she marries a nerd and remains forever faithful. At the beginning of the song, which describes her coquettish ways, Henri Salvador campily simpers as he mimics her seductions. There is innuendo: 'Quand on l'avait trop embrassée/Elle allait se confesser et puis elle recommençait'.[3] There are witty puns, such as the following play on 'tamtam': 'Le <u>tamtam</u> disait t'as bien raison de <u>t'am t'amuser</u>.'[4]

An example of the sketch song exemplifying a theme is 'Tout mais pas ça' ('Anything but That') from *Nous irons à Monte-Carlo*. The theme is what the future career of the baby at the centre of the story might turn out to be; Henri Genès proposes descriptions of potential career choices, which members of the band try to guess. Verbal dexterity yields by the end of the number to energetic gestures as the musicians illustrate the careers; indeed, towards the end of the number Henri Genès does a rapid sequence of comic charades, almost as if the music and lyrics' energy had caused the number to explode into highly visual acting outs:

Moi je connais un métier magnifique,	I know of a magnificent job,
Je dirais même un apostolat.	Why it's a sacred mission.
En plus de ça, c'est honorifique.	Moreover it's honorary.
J'ai trouvé: marchand de nougat!	I know: nougat merchant!
Mais non, c'est le métier de celui qui protège	No, no, it's the job of he who protects
Les honnêtes gens contre les margoulins,	Honest folk from swindlers,
Et qui de plus, comment dirai-je,	And what's more, how can I put this,
Soutient la veuve et défend l'orphelin.	Stands up for widows and defends orphans.
Eureka! Avocat! Avocat! Pourquoi pas?	Eureka! Lawyer! Lawyer! And why not?
Avocat? Avocat? Non, tout mais pas ça,	Lawyer! Lawyer! Anything but that,
Tout tout tout mais pas ça!	Anything anything anything but that!
Un avocat c'est noir et c'est triste,	A lawyer's black and sad,
Moi je préfèrerais général.	I would prefer a general.
Tout mais pas ça,	Anything but that,
Tout tout tout mais pas ça!	Anything anything anything but that!

[3] 'When she had been kissed too much/She'd go to confession and then start all over again.'
[4] 'The tamtam said you're right to have fun.'

Moi je propose plutôt dentiste, hein	I propose dentist then.
Ah non, ça fait trop mal.	Oh no, it hurts too much.
Il sera médecin. C'est malsain.	He'll be a doctor. It's unhealthy.
Il sera poète. Pas si bête.	He'll be a poet. Not so bad.
Commis voyageur ou plongeur.	Salesman or diver.
Ce serait bien plus battant d'en faire un acrobate.	It would be much better if he were an acrobat.
Non, tout mais pas ça,	No, anything but that,
Tout tout tout mais pas ça!	Anything anything anything but that!
Vous voyez bien que c'est un artiste,	Can't you see that he's an artist?
Il est fait pour chanter l'opéra,	He's made to sing opera,
Il vous épatera en chantant la Tosca.	He'll wow you by singing Tosca.
Tout mais surtout pas ça!	Anything, anything but that!
…	…
L'amour c'est la plus belle des richesses,	Love is one of life's great riches,
Alors il faut en faire un pasha.	So let's make him a pacha.
Il aura comme cela des tas de femmes sur les bras.	He'll have loads of women on his hands.
Tout mais surtout pas sha!	Anything but especially not that!
Cordonnier?	Cobbler?
Tout mais surtout pas!	Anything but that,
Couturier? Cuisinier? Gangster??	Fashion designer? Cook? Gangster?
Eh bien Messieurs, si l'on en faisait tout simplement un musicien?	Well, sirs, what if we made him simply a musician?
Tout mais pas ça,	Anything but that,
Tout tout tout mais pas ça!	Anything anything anything but that!
C'est le dernier métier sur la terre.	It's the worst job on earth.
Mais qu'est-ce qu'il vous a fait ce bébé-là?	Whatever did that poor baby do to you?
C'est les travaux forcés avec Ray Ventura.	It's hard labour with Ray Ventura.
Tout tout tout tout tout, mais surtout mais pas ça!	Anything anything anything anything anything but that!

There are a number of points to note in this song: first, there is bathetic disintegration as respected professions (lawyer, dentist, doctor) give way to considerably less status-driven jobs (salesman, diver); second, the constant rhyming of short statements with comical emphasis (e.g. *médecin/malsain*; *poète/bête*; *voyageur/plongeur*; *riche/fiche*); third, the sly campiness that permeates the number. Genès pretends to be a ballerina at one point, something the band immediately rejects; he falls into Max Elloy's arms as we are told he could be a pasha with 'loads of women' falling into his arms. Finally, the number ends, as several others in these films do, with a self-reflexive dig at Ventura himself.

A third characteristic of the musical numbers in the big-band films is repetition. The musicians rehearse as they prepare for the show, in such a way that we hear extracts of numbers several times over; and the final medley re-repeats those numbers. Repetition occurs not only within the films, but also from one film to another. 'La Marche des copains' ('The March of the Buddies') is heard at the start of *Nous irons à Paris*, and then again at the start of the following film, *Nous irons à Monte-Carlo*. A film is just as likely to repeat numbers from Ventura's general repertoire. 'Maria de Bahia' was published in November 1946, while the film in which it occurs, *Mademoiselle s'amuse*, was released in February 1948. In the same film we hear 'Tout va très bien, madame la marquise' (published in May 1935) and 'Ça vaut mieux que d'attraper la scarlatine' ('It's Better than Catching Scarlet Fever', published October 1936), snatches of these two songs occurring in the medley 35 minutes into the film.

Repetition has several functions. First, given that most of the songs were not new but reprises from the Ventura repertoire, they have a nostalgic function, frequently referring the listener back to the pre-war period; although as we will see later, this function is held in tension with the new, post-war France. Second, the constant crisscrossing of the repertoire in a body of films, combined with the other formal codes discussed earlier, helps to cement the genre.

A final characteristic of these films is the frequent use of the animated sketch (found in *Feux de joie*, *Tourbillon de Paris*, *Nous irons à Paris*, *Nous irons à Monte-Carlo*). This is a number in which the musicians illustrate the words of the song in comic fashion, generally using disguises (rather than just acting it out as in 'Tout mais pas ça'), and often introducing substantial props and decor. This feature creates a space of fantasy that undermines diegetic spatial conventions. The number 'Comme tout le monde' in *Feux de joie* (1.02) is a song that confronts dream and reality – what one does and what one would like to do – so as to affirm the importance of the everyday (doing things, as the title says, just like everybody else).

During the first stanza, a variety of singers sing to the camera; however, in the second stanza Jimmy Gaillard puts a military cap on his head, as he sings 'on rêve d'être général'.[5] Then he takes a cowboy hat and gun as he sings 'ou cowboy dans le Transvaal',[6] and then a boater as he sings, with a Maurice Chevalier accent, 'd'être mondial'.[7] There is nothing particularly odd in the use of these props; a hat appears to illustrate each line. But suddenly, for the fourth line, 'et pour finir on devient rond-de-cuir',[8] we see and hear a chorus of desk clerks with traditional cuffs and bonnets. This introduces a stanza devoted to clothing, where the singers are more and more ridiculed; we see them in pyjamas, long johns, sock suspenders, finishing on 'on se rase chaque matin',[9] the chorus lined up like Busby Berkeley dancers. And in the last stanza, which focuses on the exotic locations where a man might take a woman on a romantic holiday, a number of countries are evoked not only through costumes, but also by extensive decor reminiscent of the music hall. We see a gondola passing across the back of the stage as we hear the words 'on lui parle de Venise',[10] men in top hats and drinking whisky as they sing 'For He's a Jolly Good Fellow' ('ou des bords de la Tamise'),[11] pretend-Chinese

---

[5] 'You dream of being a general.'
[6] 'Or a cowboy in the Transvaal.'
[7] 'Or a worldwide star.'
[8] 'And in the end you're just a pencil pusher.'
[9] 'We shave every morning.'
[10] 'You speak to her of Venice.'
[11] 'Or the banks of the Thames.'

Figure 8.1 'Comme tout le monde' in *Feux de joie* (Courtesy of LCJ Éditions).

('ou encore de Saïgon');[12] but we finish bathetically in a very traditional *bal dansant* (popular dancehall): 'et finalement on l'emmène à Meudon' (Figure 8.1).[13]

Although the more technical aspects of musical numbers might not seem to be as ideologically driven as narrative situations, they convey very specific meanings. The systematic and the repetitive, and any sense of comfort that these might generate, are undermined by the animated sketch. The orchestra's stage set is gradually invaded by fantasy elements of decor that fissure any sense of realist space. And as the details of the narratives and musical numbers may well have suggested, the persistent comic elements involving misunderstandings and cross-dressing, as well as the often extraordinary puns in Hornez's lyrics, which draw us away from narrative to an energetic performance space, all function to destabilize the diegesis.

That destabilization functions as a marker of ideological tensions between the old and the new. Both in their opposition between the young and the old (the latter incarnated by the comical father), and in their opposition between jazz and so-called classical music (the first associated with the United States, and the second with French high culture), these films constantly return to the fundamental opposition between old, pre-war France and post-war France in transition to something new, something

---

[12] 'Or Saigon.'
[13] 'And in the end you take her to Meudon.'

younger and more modern. Two examples of this opposition are the frequent American references, and the contrast between different types of music.

Just as was the case with the *Zazous*, revolt is associated with a respect for all things American, which is flagged positively throughout Ventura's films as a culture to be admired and emulated. The orchestra's success is signalled at the end of *Feux de joie* by an American promoter's enthusiasm for the orchestra's performance and an invitation to go to the United States. In other films, it is achieved by the incorporation, sometimes more miss than hit, of American artists, characters or activities. In *Mademoiselle s'amuse*, for example, the heroine's father is a loud and jokey American businessman, who lets his selfish and strident daughter get away with everything she wants. Her governess reminds us that Christine 'n'est pas américaine à 100%, sa pauvre mère était française' and a cook comments that the mother was 'sérieuse, austère et comme il faut',[14] accentuating the national stereotypes of the film, according to which Americans are impulsive loudmouths, while the French are reasonable and measured. The orchestra finds itself caught between these two extremes. It supports Christine's childish joy in the number 'Bon appétit Mademoiselle', where each dish of her breakfast is described musically. But it also applies French restraint, when, after a series of outrageous and socially disruptive activities by Christine, the musicians desert her. American stereotypes shade into bad taste in a long masked ball sequence (0.45). Christine wants the musicians to be in blackface; her father agrees with the musicians that it is going too far, only to announce that everyone attending should be in blackface. Christine, meanwhile, distracted by the fact that her best friend has stolen her boyfriend, only paints half of her face black (Figure 8.2). This emphasizes her half-French half-American nationality, and signals only too well the way in which the film keeps on returning to questions of national identity, as well as underlining the fracture between the 'real' French world and the fantasy of American culture.

A second example of transition to the new is the opposition between so-called classical music and swing jazz. In *Mademoiselle s'amuse*, as was the case for *Mademoiselle Swing* seven years before, swing music is associated with the United States, and opposed to something more traditional and genteel. The orchestra follows Christine into a tea room at one point, disrupting the string quartet playing there. There is a more extended and complex opposition of this type in *Tourbillon de Paris*, in which the orchestra heckles the provincial premiere of an opera by the fictitious Maître Blanche, *Brunehaut et Frédégonde, ou les deux reines* (*Brunehaut and Frédégonde, or the Two Queens*). It is an ironic reference to the unfinished opera by Ernest Guiraud, *Frédégonde*, which Camille Saint-Saëns completed and which was performed in 1895. The tenor's aria, 'Un amour sans chagrin' ('A Love Without Pain'), is performed by Ventura's orchestra later in the film as part of their routine, but the musicians insist that the tenor should sing it with 'plus de mélodie, et de rythme',[15] reminding us of Trenet

---

[14] 'Isn't a 100% American; her poor mother was French/serious, austere and proper.'
[15] 'More melody, and rhythm.'

Figure 8.2 Christine paints half her face black in *Mademoiselle s'amuse* (Courtesy of LCJ Èditions).

in *La Romance de Paris*, classical music in this case thus being metamorphosed into swing jazz.

It is a commonplace that the film musical constructs the myth of community, where social and class differences disappear in moments of musical *jouissance*. As Richard Dyer points out (1977), the musical film genre engages in displays of energy to counterbalance social and moral exhaustion, and proposes images of utopian community; in the case of the US musicals he explores, he suggests that this is to counterbalance the fragmentation consequent on the Great Depression of 1929. For the French musicals explored here, the exhaustion and fragmentation are arguably those consequent on the Second World War.

Ventura's trajectory could not be more timely. Before the war, he began with two joyful films (as the title of one of them makes clear: 'feux de joie' means bonfires in French, but literally means 'fires of joy'). Ten years later, Ventura and his orchestra returned from their self-imposed exile in South America. His post-war films recalled the 'good old days' before the war, as evidenced in his pre-war films; the constant repetition of previously published songs, many of them dating from before the war, is crucial in this respect. But at the same time, the films engaged with the new, youthful, post-war France, heading towards rapid industrialization, Americanization and consumerism, what the French call the 'thirty glorious years' of 1945–1975. Repetition is key for the effect of community to happen. Music and generic situations are repeated.

Repetition creates the illusion of a distinctive territory, of a social and musical tissue, Benedict Anderson's 'imagined community' (1991).

Iconic images of this imagined community occur at the end of *Nous irons à Monte-Carlo*. Characters separated by generations and nationalities, and separated by the plot revolving around the paternity of the child, are reunited. The orchestra put on a show on TV to find the parents, the show containing sketches of different nationalities that could be ascribed to the child (Scottish, Spanish, Swiss, Russian, Neapolitan), thus bringing nationalities together. Moreover, and closer to home, (French) Philippe holds little Nicolas in his arms on TV as he appeals to the (American) parents to come forward. At the very moment that he sings 'qui se ressemble s'assemble' (1.40),[16] we see the parents, Melissa and Rudy, on the brink of divorce throughout the film, smiling to each other as they recognize their child on the TV screen; and we also see Philippe's future father-in-law, previously critical of his daughter consorting with a mere singer, finally accepting that he has talent and that he is a worthy suitor for her. The final scene of the film emphasizes even more obviously the notion of community: first, it centres on the child, and therefore on the bright new future; second, the scene brings together husband and wife, father-in-law and son-in-law, American and French in a moment of utopian reconciliation; finally, the last shot is a special effect focusing in almost megalomaniac fashion on Ventura himself, sitting at the piano with his orchestra in miniature on the piano lid in front of him (Figure 8.3), reminding us nostalgically of a similar shot in the earlier film *Il est charmant*. Previously accused, falsely as it turned out, of having fathered the child, Ventura becomes metaphorically the father of both the family represented by the orchestra, and of the extended cross-cultural family associated with it.

Nous irons à Paris

Nous irons à Paris was one of the most popular films of its time. When released, it was nineteenth in Paris for both the number of tickets sold and takings. But in the provinces, it was another story entirely, partly, we can assume, because it tells the story of a group of young musicians conquering that magnet for provincial youth, Paris. The film was in first place in Bordeaux, second in Lille, third in Lyon and Marseille and fourth in Toulouse. It broke all local records in Brest, Nantes, Nice, Périgueux, and Reims; in Grenoble, for example, it earned 3.3 million French francs and had 44,728 spectators in the first seven weeks, representing approximately 40 per cent of the total population. It was in the first place for French films in 1950 at 6.7 million, a million of those being in Paris. When Ventura tried to repeat that success the following year by employing a rising American star, Audrey Hepburn, *Nous irons à Monte-Carlo* only managed to achieve 3.4 million spectators, and it was only the tenth French film.

---

[16] 'Birds of a feather flock together.'

Figure 8.3 Different communities and nationalities come together in *Nous irons à Monte-Carlo* (Courtesy TF1 Vidéo).

The film is exemplary in its deployment of the codes we have discussed. We find the standard two pairs of protagonists: the comical father and the comical musician on the one hand, and the romantic couple on the other. The romantic couple is formed by Micheline Grosbois (Francoise Arnoul) and the orchestra's lead singer, Jacques Lambert (Philippe Lemaire). Micheline's father is the choleric Monsieur Grosbois (Fred Pasquali), who is the owner of a business dealing in women's girdles, the brand name being Lotus. The clandestine radio mocks the product to start with: 'La gaine qui écrase le plexus, la gaine qui déforme la femme',[17] and – a play on the homonyms chère (expensive)/chair (flesh) – 'la gaine la plus chère qui boursoufle les chairs'.[18] This naturally arouses Grosbois's anger, but as the free, if negative, publicity leads to higher sales, he designs new lines trading on negative catch lines: 'Plexus endolori', 'Taille meurtrie' and 'Chair boursouflée'.[19] His daughter joins the orchestra persuading them to change tack, and to support the brand. The radio broadcasts a new and positive tagline: 'Toute femme devient Vénus en portant la gaine Lotus.'[20] Grosbois is even more incensed, claiming that they are ruining him by praising his girdles. The other comical

---

[17] 'The girdle that crushes the plexus, the girdle that deforms women.'
[18] 'The priciest girdle that makes your flesh swell.'
[19] 'Sore Plexus/Bruised Waist/Swollen Flesh.'
[20] 'Women become Venus with the Lotus girdle.'

Figure 8.4 'À la mi-août' in *Nous irons à Paris* (Courtesy René Chateau).

character is the one associated with the orchestra. In this case it is Honorin, the dim-witted local plod who rapidly joins the ill-assorted radio team; he is played by Max Elloy, whom audiences would have recognized from his roles in *Mademoiselle Swing* and *Mademoiselle s'amuse*.

The focal musical number of the film is a medley midway through the film (0.42; Figure 8.4) which centres around the main song, 'À la mi-août' ('In Mid-August'), heard both at the start and at the end of the film. Its lyrics play on the sound of a cat mewing ('mi-août' can be pronounced 'miaow' in French). Numbers from previous films are incorporated in the medley, for example, three numbers from Ventura's first important success, *Feux de joie*, fourteen years before. We learn from the dialogue that the reason for them in this film is that they are the musicians' favourites: there is 'Comme tout le monde', here accompanied by an accordion, unlike *Feux de joie*, suggesting the traditional music of the *guinguette* (riverside tavern), 'Sur deux notes' ('On Two Notes'), and 'Qu'est-ce qu'on attend pour être heureux'. The medley continues with 'Le Chef n'aime pas la musique' ('The Conductor Doesn't Like Music') from 1939, but which had not appeared in any of Ventura's previous films, before finally arriving at the main song, 'À la mi-août'. There are references in the song both to *guinguettes* and to a very rural area of France, the Auvergne. 'À la mi-août' segues into a scat performance by the American trio The Peters Sisters, accompanied by a familiar French face, Henri Salvador, the four of them arriving comically by parachute on the farm where all this is taking place.

The various elements of this medley work to create a distinctive set of meanings for the audience. There is the polarity between the old and the new, which is the defining feature of this sub-genre. Where the 'old' is concerned, there are the references to rural France (the farm, village life), and to traditional music, whether the provincial *bourrée*, or the more obviously popular music of the *guinguettes* associated with Paris. Indeed, the references to popular culture are emphasized by the recalling of Ventura's first major film in the song 'Comme tout le monde', with its 1930s-style community spirit, the same spirit found in the Popular Front films such as *La Belle Équipe*. In other words, a major aspect of the medley is its nostalgic appeal to utopian pre-war sensibilities.

But the medley also gestures to the new in distinctive ways. The central song, 'À la mi-août', conveys the chirpy effervescence of the emerging youth culture, with a refrain that manages to combine the romantic and the suggestively saucy, as well as the energy of youth:

À la mi-août
C'est tell'ment plus romantique
À la mi-août
Y a d'la joie pour les matous
À la mi-août
On se sent plus dynamique
À la mi-août
On s'amuse comme des fous[21]

More importantly, the medley moves from the past to a very American-flavoured present in musical terms. The Peters Sisters' scat is the climax of the medley, closing off a series of allusions to musical numbers rooted in the past, either by their allusions or by the fact that they would have been heard by audiences in Ventura's previous films. Remembering that the plot of the film is about a clandestine radio set up by a former Resistance fighter illuminates another aspect of the medley. The fact that The Peters Sisters and Salvador are parachuted into the farm is not just funny; it is also arguably a reference to GIs being parachuted into the French countryside to join forces with the Resistance so as to liberate France from its past.

This theme of liberation is taken up by what follows, as the orchestra heads towards Paris, pursued by the police across the French countryside; once in Paris, the orchestra triumphs, the media are there to applaud them on the Place de la Concorde, a key location associated with the Revolution, and its name referring to unity and reconciliation. The echoes are less of the 1930s, and more obviously of the liberation of Paris five years earlier. The freedom promised by the film in this case, however, is a combination of youth culture and freedom of expression, anchored in a Gallic-flavoured American swing music.

Ventura's films bridge different musical forms; bridge countries and cultures, in this case France and the United States; bridge the generations, the young represented by the romantic couple and the old, represented by the father; and bridge that familiar tension in French culture, between the rural and the urban. In *Feux de joie*, the orchestra went to the provinces and stayed there. In *Nous irons à Paris*, the orchestra

---

[21] 'In mid-August time/It's so much more romantic/In mid-August time/Tomcats get what they want/In mid-August time/You just feel so much more dynamic/In mid-August time/Everyone has a ball.'

goes back to the countryside to find its past and characters from the past – the village policeman, the farmer's wife, the resistance fighter – and reconnect with their roots in order to reshape it for the future. But in so doing it also takes the future back into the past: American swing (epitomized by The Peters Sisters), an American star (a cameo by George Raft), and an Americanized French starlet (a cameo by Martine Carol)[22] into the French countryside. And then, having created a fantasy of community, the orchestra goes back to Paris, ending up in the Place de la Concorde, thus emphasizing the issue of community. The crossover between the past and the future, and between cultures, is neatly characterized by the name of the radio, Radio X; 'x' marks the spot where cultures and time cross.

Ten years later, Hoche Productions tried to renew the successes of the early 1950s with *Nous irons à Deauville* (Francis Rigaud, 1962), this time without Ventura and his orchestra on screen. He was the producer, and the film starred Louis de Funès – the year before the film that made him a top-billing star, *Pouic-Pouic* (Jean Girault, 1963) – Michel Serrault, and, as himself, Ventura's nephew, Sacha Distel. The film had barely 2 million spectators. It would therefore be reasonable to say that *Nous irons à Paris* is the apogee of the pre-Demy musical comedy. A decade after its release, the genre had petered out, to be followed by a new type of film musical, the films of Jacques Demy, after a brief transition which we will explore in Chapter 12. But before this we return in the next chapter to a major musical sub-genre, the musical sketch film, and then to one of the most popular sub-genres, the singer spectacular, with the Three Tenors, as we have called them, Tino Rossi, Georges Guétary and Luis Mariano, all three of whom regularly starred in the musical sketch films.

---

[22] Carol had become 'an increasingly American-style vamp' (Cohen 1986: 38) well before the film that catapulted her to stardom the year after *Nous irons à Paris*, *Caroline chérie* (Richard Pottier, 1951). As was pointed out at the time, 'she brings together the art of the American pin-up girls and a very French refinement' (*Cahiers de la cinéphilie*, supplement of *Film magazine*, quoted in Cohen 1986: 48).

9

The musical sketch film

Musical sketch films began to appear in the 1950s. In Italy Alessandro Blasetti's *Europa di notte* (1959), a compilation of shows from famous nightclubs, spawned a large number of such sketch films, for example *Il mondo di notte* (Luigi Vanzi, 1960) and *America di Notte* (Carlos Alberto de Souza Barros and Giuseppe Maria Scotese, 1961) (Liehm 1984: 187).

Unlike the Italian sketch films, familiarly known as 'night films' because of their titles, the French variety were not comprised of sketches by different directors, nor were they particularly erotic. As we saw in relation to the big-band films, some of these films focused on well-known music-hall names. Apart from Ventura, other examples are Trenet in *Bouquet de joie* (Maurice Cam, 1951), Jacques Hélian and his orchestra in *Pigalle-Saint-Germain-des- Prés* (André Berthomieu, 1950), and *Musique en tête* (Georges Combret and Claude Orval, 1951).

Performances by singers, both real singers in their own roles and fictitious singers, are often anchored in a loose and frenetic chase narrative whose function is to legitimize the performances in a range of usually Parisian locations (see Figure 9.1) much like the Italian variety, as several of the titles in Table 9.1 suggest; this led to their being baptized *comédies-poursuites* or chase comedies by commentators (Layerle and Moine 2014: 76). A few had more rounded narratives, such as *Pigalle-Saint-Germain-des-Prés*. Part of their function, much like the opera films of the 1980s that we consider later in this book, was to give provincial audiences a glimpse of Paris-focused events and locations.

The films were derided by critics, dismissed as 'music-hall filmé' whose narrative was 'de la plus parfaite stupidité',[1] as *L'Humanité*'s review of *Boum sur Paris* commented (cited in Layerle and Moine 2014: 79). They were nonetheless successful, as can be seen in the selection given in Table 9.1, with an average number of 1.8 million tickets sold. While there are outliers, the musical sketch films constitute a recognizable sub-genre of the film musical, as we argued in the Introduction, while also containing very variable narrative types, which we will outline in what follows: chase comedies, radio and TV adaptations, cabaret films and crime films.

The outliers include the two films made by the Branquignols, a troupe of comedians directed by Robert Dhéry specializing in Marx Brothers-style burlesque shows on theatre stages from 1948 through to the end of the 1970s. They were sufficiently

---

[1] 'Filmed music hall/perfectly stupid.'

Table 9.1 Musical Sketch Films

Title	Year	Director	Tickets France
Branquignol	1949	Robert Dhéry	2,191,018
Pigalle-Saint-Germain-des-Prés	1950	André Berthomieu	3,009,638
Boîte de nuit	1951	Alfred Rode	2,050,956
Bouquet de joie	1951	Maurice Cam	549,190
Musique en tête	1951	Georges Combret, Claude Orval	2,491,684
Les Nuits de Paris	1951	Ralph Baum	1,264,483
La Rose Rouge	1951	Marcello Pagliero	557,371
Paris chante toujours	1952	Pierre Montazel	3,144,242
Quitte ou double	1952	Robert Vernay	2,147,966
Femmes de Paris	1953	Jean Boyer	1,606,829
La Tournée des grands-ducs	1953	Norbert Carbonnaux	1,207,255
Ah! Les belles bacchantes	1954	Jean Loubignac	2,629,305
Boum sur Paris	1954	Maurice de Canonge	1,663,858
Crime au concert Mayol	1954	Pierre Mere	828,221
Soirs de Paris	1954	Jean Laviron	Not known
Bonjour sourire!	1956	Claude Sautet	1,256,883
Ce soir les souris dansent	1956	Jean Fortuny	573,840
Printemps à Paris	1956	Jean-Claude Roy	Not known
C'est arrivé aux 36 chandelles	1957	Henri Diamant-Berger	1,371,000
Panique au music-hall	1958	Antonio Santillán	Not known
Énigme aux Folies Bergère	1959	Jean Mitry	Not known

popular to take their show both to the UK (for two years) and to Broadway (for three years). In their first film, *Branquignol*, the troupe sabotage a gala thrown by the marquis de Pressaille, and in the second, *Ah! Les belles bacchantes*, Robert Dhéry, the director of the troupe, is organizing his show which is under investigation by the police for indecency (the police commissioner is played by Louis de Funès): the showgirls engage in striptease, as a result of which the film was banned for under-16s. Both films did well with well over 2 million tickets sold.[2] The films are not just outliers in tone but also in terms of their music; unlike most of the musical sketch films that recycled well-known songs by a variety of performers, these two films depend on the compositions of Gérard Calvi who mixes musical styles, whether 'classical', variety or jazz. *Bonjour sourire!* is in the same burlesque vein, and was directed by Claude Sautet who took over from Robert Dhéry after a disagreement with the producer (Layerle and Moine 2014: 83–4).

Chase comedies and radio/TV adaptations

Many of the musical sketch films are chase comedies, which are particularly interesting for the perception they give us of what a musical Paris might have meant for audiences

---

[2] For more on these films see Meyer-Plantureux 2014.

Figure 9.1 Paris locations in *Paris chante toujours* (Courtesy René Chateau).

in the 1950s. In *Paris chante toujours* the two main characters have to collect autographs from well-known singers as a condition to inheriting their uncle's estate. In so doing they go to a variety of well-known Parisian locations where we watch and hear the singers (see Figure 9.1):

1. André Dassary in the Place de l'Opéra, singing 'Il n'y a qu'un Paris' ('There is Only One Paris')
2. Yves Montand, Pont-neuf, 'À Paris' ('In Paris')
3. Luis Mariano, Eiffel Tower, 'Merci Paris' ('Thank You Paris')

4. Line Renaud, Roger & Gallet shop, 'Sans savoir ni pourquoi ni comment' ('Don't Know Why or How')
5. Georges Ulmer, Place Pigalle, 'Pigalle'
6. Tino Rossi, Sacré-Cœur, 'Sérénade sur Paris' ('Serenade on Paris')
7. Compagnons de la chanson, Tour Saint-Jacques, 'Le Prisonnier de la tour' ('The Prisoner of the Tower')
8. Georges Guétary, ORTF TV studios, 'Journée de Paris' ('A Day in Paris')
9. Jean Sablon, Chez Maxim's, 'Le Fiacre' ('The Carriage')
10. Édith Piaf, Notre-Dame, 'Hymne à l'amour' ('Hymn to Love')

The songs are interspersed with different types of chase: the two main characters are chasing autographs, but they also chase each other because they are in competition, and they are both chased by gangsters after the money as well as the police as they get more desperate and steal different modes of transport. Similarly, in *Boum sur Paris* the object of the chase, as is hinted at in the title, is an explosive mistakenly hidden in a perfume bottle that is the prize to be awarded during Jean Nohain's radio show *La Kermesse aux étoiles*. The main characters visit a range of performance spaces including the Moulin Rouge, the Kermesse aux étoiles, the Théâtre Fontaine where a 'festival du rythme' is taking place with Charles Trenet, among others.

If many of the spaces are real, and showcase musical numbers by real singers in their own roles, some of these films have fictitious spaces, although with real singers in their own roles. In *Boum sur Paris*, for example, among the real and recognizable performance spaces, we also find the fictitious cabaret Le Pingouin in which real singers sing: Mick Micheyl 'Rien, jamais rien' ('Nothing, never nothing') and Juliette Gréco 'Je hais les dimanches' ('I Hate Sundays').

Chase comedies also served to celebrate sites of modernity, whether these are Orly airport where we see Piaf boarding a plane, or in another register, new media. Radio was well established before the Second World War, so it is hardly surprising that these films relay musical performances on radio. More surprising is their insistence on radio as a medium; when the main characters are late for a performance in *Paris chante toujours* they listen to it on someone's radio. Television was introduced in France in the early 1930s, but became widespread only during the 1950s with under 4000 televisions in people's homes in 1950 and still only one million by 1958 (Rozat 2010). Its appearance in *Paris chante toujours* therefore is an example of the novelty of the new medium, the almost miraculous aspect of TV compared to radio being emphasized by the fact that it is used by the uncle to record a statement prior to his death (Figure 9.2). We also see the inside of a TV studio as a presenter introduces a song by Georges Guétary, and one of the songs sung by Jean Sablon, 'Le Fiacre' ('The Carriage'), is a Belle Époque 'reconstitution historique pour leur TV',[3] as we are told, the 'leur' suggesting a disconnection with this new medium (see Figure 9.3).

A number of films are musical sketches based on well-known radio or TV shows. *C'est arrivé à 36 chandelles* reconstitutes the TV show *36 chandelles*, which was shown

---

[3] 'Historical reconstruction for their TV.'

Figure 9.2 The uncle records a TV message in *Paris chante toujours* (Courtesy René Chateau).

Figure 9.3 The inside of the TV studio in the Georges Guétary sketch in *Paris chante toujours* (Courtesy René Chateau).

on French television from 1952 to 1958. It was presented by Jean Nohain whom we see in his own role in the film, and includes performances by Charles Trenet, Charles Aznavour (Figure 9.4), Georges Guétary, Juliette Gréco and The Bluebell Girls, among many others. The film, released less than a year before the final TV episode in July 1958, was therefore an affectionate tribute to the show, as well as giving spectators privileged backstage access to it. Here too the status of TV is foregrounded, not least when the (female) Ministre de la jeunesse et des sports tries to curry favour with Nohain, remarking haughtily that 'je suis intime avec [...] le Ministre des Beaux-Arts'.[4] He points out to her that TV is part of the information ministry, to which she responds 'je pensais que la TV c'était un art'.[5]

---

[4] 'I know the Minister for the Arts very well.'
[5] 'I thought TV was an art.'

Figure 9.4 Charles Aznavour sings 'Viens pleurer au coin de mon épaule' ('Come and Cry on my Shoulder') in *C'est arrivé à 36 chandelles* (Courtesy René Chateau).

However, the majority of these films refer principally to radio shows. *La Famille Duraton* (Christian Stengel, 1939) is based on the popular radio soap opera of the same name which ran from 1937 to 1966, similar in conception to the British show *The Archers* which began in 1950. In the film version, the producer of the show is stranded in a village and after listening to the conversation around the dinner table of the family where he has found a room, sees an opportunity to create a radio show with the ordinary conversations of ordinary people. The conversations alternated with songs including some by Noël-Noël who starred in the show. The show was popular enough for a second film to be made during the heyday of this kind of musical sketch film, *Les Duraton* (André Berthomieu, 1955), in which the eponymous protagonist complains to the producers of the show about the complications that his name has caused, given that it is the same as the radio show; however, there are no songs in this film.

Quitte ou double was also inspired by the radio game show of the same name ('Double or Quits'), which ran from the 1950s through to 2006. It focuses on the adventures of Radio Circus, an improbable combination of circus and radio show. Structured like most of this strand of the musical sketch film as a backstage musical, it alternates sequences of the show with the love affair between its real-life director, Zappy Max (his real name) and Marie (Danielle Godet), a girl he meets in village while the circus is on tour. Unlike *La Famille Duraton*, the songs are fully integrated in the narrative: we see the circus parade, followed by the preparation for the song competition during which Marie is persuaded to sing, the circus show itself with acrobats, a song by the director – 'Si les dames avaient des moustaches' ('If Women Had Moustaches') – the game that gives its title to the show, and the song competition won by Marie who sings an aria from the *Barber of Seville*.

The cabaret film

Some musical sketch films reflect more acutely the changing musical and cultural tastes after the Second World War. The history of musical performances in Paris can be broadly summarized by three emblematic districts in the capital. During the Belle Époque, Montmartre was where the artistic elite gathered, partly because it was one of the few districts of Paris to retain a village atmosphere after Haussmanization, and where the cost of living allowed a bohemian lifestyle. During the 1920s, the centre of gravity shifted to Montparnasse; after the Second World War, Montparnasse was less attractive to artists and the intelligentsia than the crowded basement cellars or *caves* of Saint-Germain-des-Prés with its mix of musicians (Juliette Gréco), writers (Jean Genet, Jacques Prévert, Boris Vian) and the existentialist philosophers Simone de Beauvoir and Jean-Paul Sartre who patronized the café Les Deux Magots in the heart of the district. Existentialism in post-war Paris was not just an intellectual movement, made popular by Jean-Paul Sartre, but also a bohemian and oppositional way of life for students and intellectuals. Focused on the cafes and nightclubs of the Left Bank around Saint-Germain-des-Prés, and analogous to the Beats in the United States, this phenomenon was very much linked to jazz and poetry, as much as to philosophy.[6]

A number of films are located in the *caves*. The very title of *Pigalle-Saint-Germain-des-Prés* demonstrates the cultural and geographical shift, as it contrasts two very different parts of Paris and two different styles of dance music. The film contrasts a large cabaret in the Pigalle area belonging to gangsters, with a *cave* in Saint-Germain, where young people gather together and listen to poetry enthusiastically, or frenetically dance to be-bop and swing. The film treats this cultural shift ironically in a number of ways. It opens with a musical number by The Bluebell Girls in Le Tambourin, a cabaret that is failing to attract customers, to the consternation of some of its employees; but this is evidently ironic, as The Bluebell Girls had been the key act at the Lido cabaret since 1948 after their move from the Folies Bergère. The employees – Jacques Hélian in his own role as director of his jazz orchestra, the barman Gustave (Henri Genès), and the flower girl Pâquerette (Jeanne Moreau) – open their own cabaret in Saint-Germain-des-Prés, La Pivoine écarlate (The Scarlet Poppy), an unambiguous reference to the famous cabaret La Rose Rouge (The Red Rose). Existentialism is consistently mocked in its superficial manifestations. When the new club set up by the friends begins to attract the crowds, Gustave says: 'L'existentialisme n'est pas une cave, c'est une mine d'or.'[7] When the police close the cellar after a battle there with the gangsters, Jean-Pierre complains, saying that 'l'existentialisme a le droit d'exister.'[8] Hornez's lyrics for the main song of the film use contemporary stereotypes to gently mock the existentialist set: 'Tout le monde se ressemble à peu de choses près/Jamais rasés, cheveux mal taillés, air dépenaillé,/C'est vrai! Mais pour nous c'est sacré./On est crasseux mais on le fait

---

[6] For a recent account, see Chapter 6 'The Left Bank' in Wakeman 2009: 241–88.
[7] 'Existentialism isn't a cellar, it's a goldmine.'
[8] 'Existentialism has the right to exist.'

exprès!"⁹ The references to collision and wrestling accompany images of be-bop rock 'n' roll- style dancing, while the references to hair accompany shots of lookalike young men with long hair and beards, smoking long clay pipes. During the same song, a waiter shouts an order for 'deux demis existentialistes',[10] and Genès explains to the camera that this means 'sans col', pointing to his own open-necked shirt, the word 'col' referring both to a shirt collar and a head on a glass of beer. Mockery also includes musical forms associated with the 'existentialist' youth culture: earlier in the film we see the musicians playing a be-bop parody during the rehearsal of a more classic big-band number. Poetry, long hair, and be-bop: these are the accoutrements of a generation in revolt, the inheritors of the *Zazous* and swing music during the early 1940s.

La Rose Rouge is also a gently mocking portrait of the young set as well as a homage to one of the best-known cabarets of the time. It opened in 1947 with Jacques Prévert among its founders, and it soon attracted actors such as Gérard Philipe as well as prominent intellectuals and writers, such as Boris Vian, Louis Aragon and Jean Genet; it was active until the mid-1950s.[11] In the film's headline act of the evening, the vocal quartet Les Frères Jacques, are unable to perform, announcing this just before a film star Évelyne Dorsey (Dora Doll) arrives to find an actor to play the part of Don José in the film adaptation of *Carmen* she is starring in. A variety of characters drift in and out of the action, including Louis de Funès as a glass-eating poet, and a busload of tourists who are visiting Saint-Germain-des-Prés as 'centre de la vie nocturne et quartier général de Jean-Paul Sartre et des existentialistes'.[12] At the end, a film does get made with the director of the real film, Marcello Pagliero, playing himself as the director of the film-within-the-film. A further irony is the fact that the real Rose Rouge to which the film refers had the real Frères Jacques as its headline act, and Yves Robert who plays the director of the cabaret was the real director from 1949 onwards. The film we have been watching is therefore an affectionate homage to the cabaret in mise en abyme.

Crime films

The final group of musical sketch films is what we could loosely call 'music-hall film noir', films that focus on a criminal investigation located in the night time world of Paris's show business. Structured as backstage musicals, they normally alternate police procedural investigations and rehearsals or shows, the two worlds overlapping and occasionally colliding.

Femmes de Paris is one of the films made by Ray Ventura and his jazz orchestra (Chapter 8), but is quite unlike his other films which feature the orchestra's adventures; his orchestra plays only one number. This film seems to have been an attempt by Ventura

---

[9] 'They all look like each other more or less/Unshaven, unkempt hair, altogether scruffy,/It's true! But for us it's sacred./We're filthy, but it's done on purpose!'
[10] 'Two existentialist halves.'
[11] For more details on this cabaret see Vian 1974 and Schlesser 2006.
[12] 'Centre for night life and headquarters of Jean-Paul Sartre and the existentialists.'

to engage with the popular sub-genre of the musical sketch film, and is dubiously erotic, with bare-breasted women (Guido 2015). In *Femmes de Paris* a professor of astronomy played by Michel Simon goes to Le Ruban bleu nightclub after receiving a phone call in which a young woman has threatened to commit suicide there. This is a thin pretext for the performance of a range of acts, including the singer Patachou and a troupe of showgirls with breasts displayed. A similar procedure is followed in *Énigme aux Folies Bergère*, historian and theorist Jean Mitry's only feature film, although the murder investigated is in this case linked more firmly to the location as the Inspector ends up investigating an earlier murder that took place in the Folies Bergère. Nonetheless, the musical numbers are relatively free-standing with a solo dance number and a long sequence comprising several tableaux from the Folies Bergère show only briefly interrupted by the Inspector's investigation. The point is clearly, as it had been for *Femmes de Paris*, for spectators to enjoy the show as if they had been there, and the fact that the numbers are shot front-on without a break and with frequent close-ups of the chorus line's legs merely emphasizes this.

In some crime films the musical moments are better integrated. In *Crime au concert Mayol*, for example, someone tries to poison Mado (Claude Godard), a dancer in the revue, following which Inspector Million (Jean-Pierre Kérien) investigates a number of suspects. The opening sequence of the film shows the first number of the revue and a subsequent tableau in their entirety, but in the remainder of the film we cut between the Inspector's investigations in the wings and snatches of musical tableaux, so that the musical numbers and the investigation are interwoven. Even the criminal's activities are closely linked to the musical moments, as gunshots on stage during an Indian tableau drown out his shooting of another dancer.

The last two films we shall mention are also better integrated, and are interesting because they take place in cities other than Paris. This is partly because they are Franco-Spanish co-productions, both produced by the prolific and little-known producer Marius Lesœur, with over 50 B-movies to his credit between 1952 and 1989.[13] In the whodunnit *Panique au music-hall* the investigation takes place literally in the wings of the theatre whose secretary, Rosario (Claudine Dupuis), has been wrongly imprisoned for theft. On her return to the theatre she confronts the director, who is subsequently murdered. The crime is investigated by her lawyer, who firmly believes she is innocent, and her policeman cousin; they interview potential suspects in the wings, thereby allowing frequent musical moments to be performed on stage. Similarly, in *Ce soir les souris dansent*, which takes place in Barcelona, Inspector Revel (Howard Vernon) investigates the murder of a violin maker, the suspects being a range of performers, principal among whom is the singer Lydia (Mick Micheyl who sings three songs), her ex-husband, Lydia's lover the actor Florencio (Carlos Otero) and a young dancer, announced as 'la délicieuse Lucie et ses girls'.[14] These films are darker and more dystopian than those we have considered in this section. In *Panique au music-hall*,

---

[13] See the article on Marius Lesœur on *Nanarland* (http://www.nanarland.com/acteurs/acteur-mariuslesoeur-marius-lesoeur.html).

[14] 'The delicious Lucie and her girls.'

Rosario leaves the city and the world of show business with their criminal associations to return to the village where she was born, and in *Ce soir, les souris dansent*, the murderer, who turns out to be Lydia's lover Florencio, abducts 'la délicieuse Lucie'. He dies after a police chase, and Lucie, wounded, expresses her disillusion with the world of show business.

The musical sketch films are a good example of how genre functions in relation to Hollywood cinema. They are nearly all structured as backstage musicals, albeit with varying levels of integration of musical numbers. To take the crime films as an example, in some films the integration is almost non-existent with the two worlds of the crime film and the musical operating separately (*Femmes de Paris, Énigme aux Folies Bergère*); in others, the integration is considerably closer (*Panique au music-hall, Ce soir les souris dansent*). The musical sketch films died out by the beginning of the 1960s, partly because radio and TV became increasingly important for the broadcasting of musical performance, in the case of TV by the development of musical variety shows, such as the weekly 'Discorama' (1959– 75) or 'Âge tendre et tête de bois' (1961–5), later renamed 'Tête de bois et tendres années' (1965–9) when it transferred to the State TV channel, ORTF (Looseley 2003: 29), partly also because of the attraction of *yéyé* for younger audiences in the 1960s, as we shall see in Chapter 12. But before that we will explore the films of the Three Tenors.

10

Tino Rossi

Running parallel with both the jazz-oriented big-band films and the musical sketch films were films by three *chanteurs de charme* (crooners) as they were called, a term coined for Tino Rossi (born 1907) at the beginning of his singing career, and then used for crooners more generally. The other two were Georges Guétary (born 1915) and Luis Mariano (born 1914).

All three began their careers as singers, Rossi's breakthrough being in 1934, those of the other two a few years later in 1937. All three included careers in film as adjuncts to their stage, radio and recording activities. Rossi's major films as star lasted from 1936 to 1952; but arguably his last big film was *Le Chanteur inconnu* in 1947, just as the films starring Mariano and Guétary were taking off at the end of the war (Table 10.1). Both of the younger singers' film careers lasted until the end of the 1950s. Their films, that one critic defined as 'des films qu'on voit avec les oreilles'[1] (Minotaure 1946: 3), regularly attracted several million spectators; the average number of tickets sold for their films was 2.8 million per film. Rossi's average was 2.8 million, Guétary's 2.2 million and Mariano's 3.4 million. Table 10.1 also shows the position of films within the top twenty bestsellers for their year of release (the first figure is the absolute position which includes non-French productions, the second figure is the position relative to French productions alone). Rossi and Guétary's films were in the top twenty in the years immediately after the war, while Mariano was considerably more successful than them in the 1950s. A measure of how much they were in the public eye as the major tenors of the period can be seen in the sketch film *Paris chante toujours*, in which they appear alongside Yves Montand and Édith Piaf among others, which with 3.1 million tickets sold was the eleventh bestselling film of 1951.

There are several reasons why we should consider these singers as a group. First, their films are generally constructed to showcase their songs, and there are more of these than was the case with Trenet, Piaf or Baker; most of the films, like the big-band films, comprise around six songs. Second, they shared a composer, Francis Lopez, who scored two of Rossi's films, four of Guétary's, and eleven of Mariano's. Third, all Three Tenors had exotic appeal through their Mediterranean connections: Rossi was Corsican, born Constantin Rossi in Ajaccio; Mariano was Spanish Basque, born Mariano Eusebio González y García close to the French border in the town of Irun;

---

[1] 'Films that you see with your ears.'

Table 10.1 The films of the Three Tenors

Tenor	Date	Title	Director	Composer	France	Paris	Position
Rossi	March 1936	*Marinella*	P. Caron	V. Scotto	Not known		
Rossi	October 1936	*Au son des guitares*	P.-J. Ducis	V. Scotto	Not known		
Rossi	December 1937	*Naples au baiser de feu*	A. Genina	V. Scotto	Not known		
Rossi	October 1938	*Lumières de Paris*	R. Pottier	M. Simons, M. Yvain	Not known		
Rossi	January 1942	*Fièvres*	J. Delannoy	H. Bourtayre	Not known		
Rossi	January 1943	*Le soleil a toujours raison*	P. Billon	J. Kosma	Not known		
Rossi	April 1943	*Le Chant de l'exilé*	A. Hugon	H. Bourtayre	Not known		
Rossi	September 1943	*Mon amour est près de toi*	R. Pottier	F. Lopez, V. Scotto	Not known		
Rossi	May 1944	*L'Ile d'amour*	M. Cam	L. Gasté	3.1	0.5	
Guétary	June 1945	*Le Cavalier noir*	G. Grangier	F. Lopez	3.7	0.5	6 (5)
Guétary	December 1945	*Trente et quarante*	G. Grangier	F. Lopez	2.2	0.4	
Rossi	March 1946	*Sérénade aux nuages*	A. Cayatte	V. Scotto	3.5	0.6	
Rossi	May 1946	*Le Gardian*	J. de Marguenat	L. Gasté	3.5	0.6	19 (11)
Rossi	December 1946	*Destins*	R. Pottier	R. Legrand	4.7	0.8	11 (6)
Guétary	March 1947	*Les Aventures de Casanova*	J. Boyer	R. Sylviano	4.4	0.4	9 (6)
Rossi	April 1947	*Le Chanteur inconnu*	A. Cayatte	R. Legrand	3.6	0.5	14 (10)
Rossi	November 1948	*La Belle Meunière*	M. Pagnol	F. Schubert	1.7	0.4	
Rossi	January 1949	*Deux amours*	R. Pottier	R. Legrand	2.7	0.4	
Guétary	February 1949	*Jo la romance*	G. Grangier	Luiguy	2.3	0.3	
Mariano	February 1949	*Fandango*	E. E. Reinert	F. Lopez	2.6	0.4	20 (10)
Mariano	June 1949	*Je n'aime que toi*	P. Montazel	F. Lopez	2.1	0.3	
Rossi	September 1949	*Marlène*	P. de Hérain	F. Lopez	2.1	0.3	

Singer	Date	Title	Director	Composer			
Guétary	January 1950	Amour et compagnie	G. Grangier	M. Coste	1.9	0.2	
Rossi	May 1950	Envoi de fleurs	J. Stelli	Dorémi	1.8	0.3	
Mariano	September 1950	Pas de week-end pour notre amour	P. Montazel	R. Lucchesi	1.3	0.2	
Mariano	October 1951	Andalousie	R. Vernay	F. Lopez	5.7	0.8	2 (1)
Mariano	November 1951	Rendez-vous à Grenade	R. Pottier	F. Lopez	2.4	0.3	
Rossi	December 1951	Au pays du soleil	M. de Canonge	V. Scotto	Not known		
Guétary	March 1952	Une fille sur la route	J. Stelli	F. Lopez	1.7	0.2	
Mariano	December 1952	Violettes impériales	R. Pottier	F. Lopez	8.1	1.0	2 (2)
Rossi	December 1952	Son dernier Noël	J. Daniel-Norman	R. Legrand	2.4	0.3	
Guétary	February 1953	Plume au vent	L. Cuny	C. Pingault	2.0	0.3	
Mariano	December 1953	La Belle de Cadix	R. Bernard	F. Lopez	4.3	0.5	8 (5)
Rossi	April 1954	Tourments	J. Daniel-Norman	P. Misraki	1.7	0.1	
Mariano	April 1954	L'Aventurier de Séville	L. Vajda	F. Lopez	2.5	0.3	
Guétary	December 1954	Baron Tzigane	A. M. Rabenalt	J. Strauss	2.3	0.3	
Mariano	February 1955	Le Tzarevitch	A. M. Rabenalt	F. Lehár	1.8	0.2	
Mariano	October 1955	Quatre jours à Paris	A. Berthomieu	F. Lopez	3.2	0.5	
Guétary	December 1955	Liebe ist ja nur ein Märchen	A. M. Rabenalt	W. Mattes	1.1	0.04	
Guétary	May 1956	Le Chemin du paradis	H. Wolff, Willi Forst	W. R. Heymann	1.5	0.1	
Mariano	December 1956	Le Chanteur de Mexico	R. Pottier	F. Lopez	4.8	0.6	5 (4)
Mariano	April 1957	À la Jamaïque	A. Berthomieu	F. Lopez	2.7	0.3	
Guétary	May 1957	Une nuit aux Baléares	P. Mesnier	L. Gasté	1.4	0.2	
Mariano	December 1958	Sérénade au Texas	R. Pottier	F. Lopez	2.6	0.3	

[a] The films listed here are the films in which the singers had a starring role. Audience figures were collected only from 1945. Colin Crisp's work on audience figures suggests that *Marinella* was the third most popular French film for exclusive release and the twentieth for general release (2002: 319).

and Guétary was Greek, born Lámbros Vorlóou in Alexandria.² Despite their relatively exotic appeal for audiences, Rossi and Mariano strove in their films to come across as ordinary and approachable, as we shall see. Their films were despised by critics for their sentimentalism, which was deemed to appeal to *midinettes*; this pejorative and now archaic term referred to shop girls, who were stereotyped as overly sentimental and easily swayed by the *chanteurs de charme*, as a rare detractor from this view pointed out, while reaffirming the pejorative connotations: 'Je ne vois pas pourquoi les critiques tiennent absolument à frustrer les midinettes du charme tinorossiste, avec ce que cela comporte d'évasion du réel'³ (Tachella 1947: 4).

Tino Rossi

Rossi was one of the most popular male stars of the late 1930s. In the annual polls of *La Cinématographie française* he figures in the top ten for 1936 and 1937, and is the only singer featured in the list (Crisp 2002: 269), no doubt because of his 'voix chaude, fluide et simple' (Cambier 1936: 248), his 'voix veloutée, pleine de chaudes inflexions [qui] émeut les femmes au plus profond d'elles-mêmes'⁴ (Jean de l'écran 1941: 5). Even in 1960 when he had stopped making films, a brief portrait of him in *Mon Film* commented that he remained 'le roi de la chanson de charme. Sa voix dont la tessiture exceptionnelle couvre deux octaves et demi, est vraisemblablement la plus belle qu'on ait connue, dans le genre, depuis le début du siècle'⁵ (*Mon Film* 1960: 53). He was compared to Valentino, and he introduced 'un nouveau romantisme fait de chansons et de cordes de guitare'⁶ (Jean de l'écran 1941: 5). In his films, Rossi plays a singer. In the early films, the singer is rising to fame; in later films, he is trying to escape from what fame brings in terms of unwanted public adulation.

Although born in Corsica, Rossi began his singing career in the south of France, in the Vaucluse, and then under the aegis of his manager Louis Allione, known as Petit Louis, in major venues in Marseille and Aix-en-Provence.⁷ However, his first records for Columbia in 1933 were of Corsican folk songs and by Easter 1934, he was on a major tour organized by Columbia alongside established singers such as Pills and Tabet and the realist singer Damia. The 'Parade de France' revue later that year – a series of tableaux devoted to the French regions and colonies – made him a

---

² Another well-known tenor of the period, André Dassary, who acted in a few films, one of them being Ventura's *Feux de joie*, and who appeared in *Paris chante toujours*, also had Mediterranean origins, born André Deyhérassary in 1912 in Biarritz in the Basque country.
³ 'I really don't know why critics want to prevent shop girls from enjoying Tino Rossi's charm, and the escape from reality that he offers them.'
⁴ 'His warm, fluid and simple voice./His silky voice, full of warm inflections/moves women deeply.'
⁵ 'The king of the crooners. His voice has an exceptional range of two and a half octaves and is probably the most beautiful we have ever known in this genre since the beginning of the century.'
⁶ 'A new romanticism comprising songs and guitar strings.'
⁷ The biographical information on Rossi is indebted to an extensive and well-researched website by Claude Rizzo-Vignaud: http://tinorossi.monsite-orange.fr/index.html.

major Paris-based singing star. Rossi was part of the Corsican tableau, 'Corse, île de beauté' ('Corsica, Beautiful Island'), singing among other songs 'Ô Corse, île d'amour' ('Corsica, Island of Love'), affecting a pseudo-Corsican costume that became his trademark, 'ce costume qui aurait fait rire un habitant de Sartène, mais qui allait séduire les Françaises: une chemise bouffante, une veste accessoire que j'étais décidé à tenir négligemment sur une épaule, le pantalon bouffant, des bottes, et ma guitare pour faire joli et typique'[8] (Rossi 1974: 69–70). His identity as a singer was therefore a mixture of Southern French and Corsican in a generalized Mediterranean identity, an identity that resurfaces in his films, particularly those before 1945. In *Au son des guitares* he plays a naïve Corsican fisherman ensnared by a sophisticated Parisian woman. This plot is echoed in *Naples au baiser de feu* in which Rossi plays an Italian singer duped by a vamp (Viviane Romance); in *Le soleil a toujours raison* and *Le Gardian* he plays a Camarguais torn between his fiancée and a bewitching gypsy. In *Le Chant de l'exilé* (in which Luis Mariano has a small part) he is a Basque who seeks refuge in the Sahara. In *L'Île d'amour*, a remake of the silent film of the same name by Berthe Dagmar and Jean Durand starring Pierre Batcheff (1928), he plays a Corsican, as he does in *Marlène*. In *Deux amours* he plays two brothers who live in a Provençal village, in *Au pays du soleil* he is a Marseillais, and even in his last major film, *Son dernier Noël*, he plays a singer returning to where he grew up in Nice. Over his film career then he demonstrates a free-floating Mediterranean identity; in his first major film, *Marinella*, when asked to sing on stage he suggests that this might not be appropriate because 'j'ai même un peu d'accent',[9] but it is never clear in the film what his origins are. In subsequent films his accent can vary from slightly inflected to a relatively broad Midi accent; but in the films set in the Midi, his accent is never as broad as some of the other Provençal 'types' alongside whom he plays. This Mediterranean identity changed in the post-war films. The famous singers he plays in *Sérénade aux nuages*, *Le Chanteur inconnu*, *Envoi de fleurs* (a biopic of Paul Delmet) and *Tourments* are all Paris-based with no trace of Mediterranean origins.

In many of his films Rossi plays an unknown singer who rises to fame through his singing skills, echoing to some extent his real trajectory as a singer; indeed, his character in his first film as a star, *Marinella*, is called Tino, emphasizing the correlation between the real singer and his character. In this film, as in many others, characters comment on the singing voice of Rossi's characters: 'Vous avez une jolie voix'[10] the boss's secretary says to him as he leaves at the end of his working day, and an eccentric English woman says 'vous avez un diamant dans la gorge',[11] that she wants to dance with him, to which he responds self-effacingly 'je danse mal'.[12] Another frequent comment in the films is the comparison of his voice to that of the 'rossignol' or nightingale, the

---

[8] 'This costume would have made an inhabitant of Sartène laugh, but it would seduce French women: a baggy shirt, an accessorized jacket that I decided to hold casually over my shoulder, baggy trousers, boots and my guitar to give a pretty and typical look.'
[9] 'I've even got a bit of an accent.'
[10] 'You've got a nice voice.'
[11] 'You've got a diamond in your throat.'
[12] 'I dance badly.'

French term lending itself to the pun on Rossi's name: in *Fièvres* his manager says that Rossi's character Jean who is performing in Mozart's *Don Juan* sings 'comme un rossignol sur la branche'[13] (0.13) in a flashback to his career as an opera singer; and in the later *Destins*, André's mother similarly points out how he sings 'comme un rossignol' (1.07). A few years later in *Deux amours* attention is still being drawn to his character's voice as the circus director says to Sylvain, who is thinking of running away from home, 'vous avez un trésor dans la gorge'.[14] The typical mise en scène for the performance of the songs comprises Rossi's character standing relatively still, surrounded by a crowd of mainly female admirers, their adulation often emphasized by scenes in which a friend of Rossi's character or his manager is responding to letters, for example, in *Envoi de fleurs* and in *Fièvres*, or autographing photos as happens in *Marinella* where his manager complains ruefully that there are 347 of them.

The films often call on the trope of self-effacement, typical both of Rossi's films and Mariano's, but particularly apt for Rossi who was frequently described by journalists who interviewed him as 'un grand timide'[15] (Stane 1941: 6). In many of Rossi's films fame comes at the cost of privacy, and the narratives frequently dwell on his characters' attempts to protect themselves from public view. In *Marinella*, Tino refuses to be identified publicly and sings behind a screen so that we see only his shadow. He falls in love with a rival upcoming singer who herself wears a mask. The denouement depends on their revealing on stage who they are, not only to each other but to their public. In *Marinella*, his first film as a star, the self-effacement is key to the revelation of new talent, whereas in later films, once Rossi was better established as a film star, his characters try to escape. In *Lumières de Paris* and *Sérénade aux nuages*, Rossi plays a famous Italian singer who escapes to the countryside so as to avoid his fans and hangers-on. *Fièvres* recounts in flashback the life of a famous singer who was having an affair while his wife was dying, and who has retired broken-hearted to a monastery, where he plays the organ and sings classical pieces, something we shall return to. In *Mon amour est près de toi* and the later *Le Chanteur inconnu* he is a famous singer who becomes an amnesiac. In all of these films, Rossi plays both the singer and his shadow, who rejects fame or has forgotten it. The rejection of fame and the attempt to escape women admirers reflects what happened to Rossi throughout his career, where, like Mariano later, he was harassed by fans, as is well-documented in biographies, with stories of scarlet letters, attempts to tear souvenirs from his clothes, women throwing themselves under his car, and so on (see Rossi 1974: 90–95; Trimbach 1978: 34; Delange 1985: 33–5; Bonini 2003: 59–63).

Rossi explains his success as a combination of singing style and an appeal to the emotions: 'Il n'existait pas à l'époque de chanteur de charme. J'ai apporté un style qui manquait au music-hall. Mais, en toute sincérité, je crois que j'avais avant tout "senti"

---

[13] 'Like a nightingale on a branch.'
[14] 'You've got a treasure in your throat.'
[15] 'A really shy one.'

le public. Pour toutes les femmes, j'ai changé l'amour. Leur amour'¹⁶ (1974: 95). For his (generally) female admirers, Rossi could do no wrong, as the number of his films and the number of tickets sold for them suggest: twenty films as star in eighteen years, with an average of 2.8 million tickets per film. As a character says to him in one of his last films, *Son dernier Noël*, 'les hommes vous débinent mais les femmes vous écoutent'.[17] That said, his fan club, 'L'Association des amis de Tino Rossi' appears to have had a considerable number of men, according to its President, Mlle Ramel (Delpeuch 1941: 5).

Film critics may have admired his voice, but they were scathing about his acting abilities, despite the acting lessons that Rossi took with the well-known actor and theatre director Charles Dullin (Rossi 1974: 101–2). As the critic of *Opéra* commented, Rossi 'a indéniablement une jolie voix, mais il fait son petit travail avec si peu de conviction, il est tellement absent de ses chansons, que j'ai immanquablement l'impression que c'est toujours la même qu'il chante'[18] (Rougeul 1946). The sameness that Rougeul complains of is not helped by two factors. First, Rossi's songs tend to be ballads that generally climax in the high tenor register, and his voice lacks an expressive quality; a review of *Fièvres*, for example, recognizes that his voice is 'pure et séduisante' but points out that 'elle remplace l'expression par le timbre'[19] (R. de B. 1942: 48). Second, he tends not to move much when performing; as a review of *Le Chanteur inconnu* complained, Rossi's acting style demonstrated a 'jeu dépouillé à force d'être inexistant'[20] (Sauvage 1946). Spectators often felt the same way. A piece in *Mon Film*, for example, among the many letters enthusing over Rossi's voice and the pleasure it gave them, also included the following comment from 'Angèle S': 'Tino Rossi a un très joli timbre de voix, c'est doux et berceur: mais je trouve son chant monotone, et, au bout d'un moment qu'il chante, je ne l'entends plus',[21] and 'Ginette N' wrote that 'il est trop immobile ... , jamais sa figure ne bouge. Il embrasse une femme avec autant d'indifférence qu'il boirait un bock'[22] (Sylvain 1946: 9).

His lack of movement could have been compensated by the kind of dancing by other characters on screen, familiar in the operettas of the early 1930s, or the big-budget spectaculars of Luis Mariano, but when the chorus girls dance it is generally with low-key choreography. In *Destins*, for example, he is asked to rehearse his 'Schubert' (0.18); we see him dressed in period costume playing Schubert's 'Serenade',[23] the piano lid opens with a superimposed small screen in which eight ballerinas in long white dresses

---

[16] 'There weren't any crooners at the time. I brought a style that the music hall didn't have. But in all sincerity I think that above all I had a feel for the public. I changed the notion of love for all women. Their love.'
[17] 'Men run you down, women listen to you.'
[18] 'Undeniably he has a nice voice, but he delivers with so little conviction, he is so not there when he sings, that I always feel that he's singing the same thing every time.'
[19] 'Pure and seductive/replaces expressiveness with tone.'
[20] 'His acting is so stripped down that it is non-existent.'
[21] 'Tino Rossi has a really nice tone of voice, it's soft and soothing: but I feel that his singing is monotonous and after a while I stop hearing him.'
[22] 'He is too still, he never moves. He kisses a woman in the same indifferent way he might drink a beer.'
[23] It is the fourth song from the posthumous collection 'Schwanengesang' or 'Swan Song' D957, arranged by Franz Liszt, with lyrics by Henri Martinet adapted from the original poem by Ludwig Rellstab.

parade with adagio moves in a colonnaded atrium, mainly attitudes derrières, followed by sixteen dancers in black evening dress who walk elegantly lifting their arms into fifth position, while a couple in evening dress execute a pas de deux. The most interesting aspect of this sequence is not the choreography but the superimposition of the dance sequence inside the piano lid, which has the effect of containing what little movement there is as Rossi sits still at the piano. As we do not even see him sing, it is implied that the dance sequence represents what the music evokes for him as he plays it. Not only is the dancing slow but it is separate from his own limited movements at the piano, emphasizing Rossi's characteristic rigidity. Even in the finale of films with a musical number on stage there is a similarly slow procession of dancers. In *Sérénade aux nuages*, Sylvio, after his escapade to the country, returns to his normal singing activities in Paris with a medley. We see him riding a stationary bike in a film studio as he sings 'Tango d'un soir' ('One Night Tango'), followed by him doing a radio recording of 'Étrange mélodie' ('Strange Tune'), then an autographing session of the record, to finish with him performing another of the key songs of the film, 'Écoutez' ('Listen'), on a theatre stage (1.22), where he is dressed in a white suit and surrounded by women dancers in long dresses holding large ostrich feather fans. As was the case with the Schubert sequence in *Destins* the dancers move slowly around the stage in long shot, without the close-ups of faces or legs commonly used by operetta films of the 1930s.

The only dance and song sequence that demonstrates some liveliness in his films is the finale of *Marinella*, his first film, in which he and the 'unknown singer' who is his professional rival but also literally the girl next door whom he knows well, meet up on stage while he sings the title song, a 'rumba d'amour' as the lyrics have it. Rossi's character, Tino, is dressed in a white bolero-ruffled shirt, and the dancers wear rumba dresses open mid-thigh. Unusually, Rossi sways in time with the rumba rhythms when close to the other dancers, but, more typically, stands stiffly when separated from them. The dancers' choreography is subtler than in his later films: half of them wear white and are associated with Tino, the other half wear black and are associated with the 'unknown singer', Lise (Yvette Lebon), and they criss-cross as they leave the stage in Berkeley-style parades, black-and-white mixing so as to emphasize the lovers coming together. But this level of activity is not found in his later films, which led his critics to comment frequently on the woodenness of his performance.

In *Le Chanteur inconnu*, in which Rossi plays an amnesiac singer, the camera takes the place of Rossi's character, a procedure adopted the same year by Robert Montgomery's Hollywood film *The Lady in the Lake* (1947). This procedure emphasized the principle of self-effacement we have referred to, but its unconvincing artificiality encouraged some particularly vituperative reviews, which we quote to give a sense of the critical establishment's view of his films more generally:

> Tino Rossi chante, puisqu'il est là pour cela et reste fort souvent – et heureusement – 'le chanteur inconnu'.[24] (*Franc-Tireur* 1947)

---

[24] 'Tino Rossi sings, because that's what he's there for and he often stays, thank Heavens, 'the unknown singer'.

L'obstination des producteurs à vouloir faire de Tino Rossi un comédien est une chose infiniment émouvante en soi.²⁵ (*Le Canard enchaîné* 1947)

Comble de l'adresse les rares scènes où – tout de même – Tino Rossi est obligé de jouer, André Cayatte est parvenu à le rendre vivant et naturel.²⁶ (*Paris-Presse* 1947)

And finally we quote an extract from a longer review from a critic who had purportedly never seen Rossi on screen, and whose piece scorns Rossi's fan base as well as Rossi's appearance and wooden acting:

Je sais comme tout le monde que des millions d'admiratrices s'enivrent à ce ruisselet de charme, que des incurables lui écrivent: 'Vous voir et mourir…', que, à la sortie des music-halls des dames saines de corps et d'esprit se disputent l'honneur de le toucher. … J'ai vu un monsieur mûr, replet, qui chante, une main sur le cœur. Quand il a fini, il semble bien ennuyé de devoir rester là, marcher, parler. Il bouge peu, d'ailleurs, car son costume des dimanches le gêne aux entournures, et il parle le moins possible … Est-ce sa faute s'il n'a qu'une voix et si ses enthousiastes le voient, qui pourraient se contenter de l'entendre, veulent le voir et le voient svelte, expressif et beau? … Qui sait? On fera peut-être un jour avec lui ou plutôt autour de lui un bon film: *Le Chanteur invisible*. Comparé aux précédents, il paraît que celui-ci, où on l'entend plus qu'on ne le voit, marque d'étonnants progrès.²⁷ (*Spectateur* 1947)

In that film he plays Julien, a famous opera singer who is an amnesiac living a simple life in Portugal as a fisherman called Paolo. His singing skills attract the attention of an itinerant film projectionist who turns him into a famous singer. As Paolo hears a variety of songs he used to sing, he eventually recollects what happened to him as Julien: he was attacked by a jealous rival while on his honeymoon cruise and thrown overboard. The plot therefore reprises the tension between fame and obscurity on which so many of Rossi's films are based, but uses music as a stimulus for memory. In a sequence that crosses space, time and technology, his ex-fiancée, Renée (Maria Mauban), suspecting that Julien is not dead after all, listens to the 'unknown singer' on the radio at the same time as she plays a record of the same song by Julien (0.46; Figure 10.1). The otherwise

---

²⁵ 'The determination shown by producers to turn Tino Rossi into an actor is infinitely moving.'
²⁶ 'In the few scenes where Tino Rossi is nonetheless supposed to act, André Cayatte shows consummate skill in making him appear alive and natural.'
²⁷ 'I know like everyone that millions of female admirers get drunk on this trickle of charm, that addicts write to him saying' to see you and die', that ladies who are of mind and body fight to touch him at the music-hall exits. I saw an older rounder gentleman, who sings with his hand over his heart. When he stops, he seems rather bored having to stay there, having to walk and talk. He doesn't move much, actually, because his Sunday best is a bit tight, and he talks as little as possible. Is it his fault if he only has one voice and that his fans see him, when they could be content with listening to him, want to see him and see him as someone slim, expressive and handsome? Who knows? Maybe one day someone will make a good film with him, or rather around him: *The Invisible Singer*. Compared with his previous films, apparently this one, in which you hear him more than you see him, shows remarkable progress.'

Figure 10.1 Renée compares the two performances on disc and on radio in *Le Chanteur inconnu* (Courtesy René Chateau).

scathing critic of *Le Spectateur* commented favourably on the innovative nature of this 'duo avec soi-même, harmonie curieuse'[28] (1947).

The procedure is a variant on the principle of repetition that we saw previously in the big-band films, and which are a constant in Rossi's films as well. Key songs are woven through the soundtrack, and were subsequently commercialized on radio or record. In *Sérénade aux nuages*, for example, 'Tango d'un soir' ('One Night Tango') and 'Étrange mélodie' ('Strange Melody') are repeated numerous times. The film opens with Sylvio singing 'Tango d'un soir', the camera pulling back to reveal that he is singing the song on a film set, the film set changing to a recording studio, a film, a music-hall stage and a concert stage as the song carries on. Mobbed by fans, he seeks refuge in a restaurant where a violinist plays the same song; an orchestral version can be heard on the radio in the taxi he takes to go home, only to find his manager playing the tune on the piano. Later, when he escapes to the countryside, he enters an inn where the clients are listening in rapt attention to the same song (Figure 10.2). At the end of the film we see him once more making the film of the song as we had done at the start of the film, as we pointed out earlier. Such intense repetition is unusual though; generally, key songs are heard three times, as is the case with 'Bella ragazzina' and 'Sous le ciel de mon beau pays' ('Beneath My Country's Beautiful Sky') in *Au son des guitares*, or the title song in *Marinella*.

Partly, no doubt, to demonstrate that Rossi was not without acting skills, and partly to diversify the standard plot of the self-effacing singer, two of Rossi's post-war films show him going further than playing the same character in *Le Chanteur inconnu*. In *Destins* and *Deux amours*, he plays two completely different characters, one a famous singer who attracts women and the other his twin but moral and physical opposite. In *Destins* the twin is Fred, a recently released criminal, with sweaty skin and twitching eye, who extorts money from his family man singer brother André. In a desperate attempt to raise more money to cover his gambling debts, Fred abducts his nephew, but wracked with guilt, returns the boy and leaves André's life forever (see Figure 10.3).

---

[28] 'Duo with himself, curious harmony.'

Figure 10.2 'Tango d'un soir' repeated in *Sérénade aux nuages* (Courtesy René Chateau).

In *Deux amours* Rossi plays both Sylvain, the handsome assistant to the Mayor, and his ironically named brother, Désiré, a simple carpenter with a moustache, curly hair and a limp, both of them in love with the same woman (see Figure 10.4). Although our attention is constantly drawn to the technical difficulty of splicing shots of the two characters played by Rossi in scenes where they both appear, the ploy works to some extent; in both films, the non-singing brother is the more interesting character in narrative terms, precisely because of the contrast between him and the normal singer character played by Rossi. In *Deux amours*, there is a final melodramatic sequence where Désiré, learning that Sylvain is going to become a father, leaves with the circus that has come to town, and which Sylvain had been thinking of joining. We see Désiré being made up as a clown with face paint, and smacked about the face as practice for the slapstick gags that await him; the final close-up is particularly moving (Figure 10.5; 1.28). The narrative ploy of the circus is nostalgic: the heyday of circus films was the 1930s, as Colin Crisp points out (2002: 168). Indeed, *La Ronde des heures* (Alexandre Ryder, 1931) was by all accounts one of the most popular films of the 1930s, starring one of the well-known tenors of the period, André Baugé; he plays a singer who, like Désiré, runs away with the circus to become a clown after losing his voice. The film was remade by the same director and released in 1950, fourteen months after *Deux amours*, partly we can assume because of the success of Rossi's film.

The trope of the self-effacing singer is underlined by the use of classical music numbers. We saw for example how André in *Destins* sits rigidly at the piano while the activity of the sequence occurs in a small screen superimposed inside the lid of the piano he is playing. Classical music pieces are often used to indicate a painful past which the Rossi character would rather forget. In *Le Chanteur inconnu*, for example, walking onto the empty stage of the theatre where he will perform as the unknown singer, he has a flashback to his previous life as a famous opera singer: we see him sing the 'Aubade' from Lalo's opéra comique *Le Roi d'Ys* (0.39), and two of the key songs are set to classical pieces. 'Loin de ton cœur' ('Far from Your Heart') has music by Brahms, the well-known Waltz in A Flat Major opus 39 no.15, with modern lyrics by Jacques

Figure 10.3 Fred and André in *Destins* (Courtesy René Chateau).

Figure 10.4 Sylvain and Désiré in *Deux amours* (Courtesy René Chateau).

Figure 10.5 Désiré in *Deux amours* (Courtesy René Chateau).

Larue. We hear it twice at the beginning of the film, first as a record, then with 'Paolo' singing over the record, then in the sequence when Renée compares the record she has with the song on the radio, and again at the end of the film, when he has fully recovered his memory. Chopin's Étude opus 10 no.3, familiarly known as 'Tristesse', here with lyrics by Jean Loysel, triggers the defining memory of his identity, and he sings it later in the story with lyrics that only he and Renée know, in his attempt to find her; but the story ends badly, as he rejects her and his past for the woman with whom he has been living, as a result of which Renée commits suicide.

The most forceful example of this trope of classical music signalling a painful past occurs in *Fièvres*. The film opens with Rossi's character as a monk playing the organ and singing one of the songs for which Rossi was best known, Schubert's 'Ave Maria', followed by another sacred text, 'O sacrum convivium' ('mens impletur gratia et futurae gloriae nobis pignus datur')[29] set to the music of Handel's 'Largo', from the opera *Xerxes*; the Abbott comments 'il a souffert'[30] (0.10). The story of Jean the famous singer who lost his wife to illness while having an affair with another woman is told in flashback, and at the end of the film classical music returns as we hear the monk he has now become singing once more, as he had at the start, 'O sacrum convivium'.

As we have seen, Schubert figures frequently in Rossi's films, no more so than in one of Rossi's less successful films, directed by Marcel Pagnol, *La Belle Meunière*, a part rendering of Schubert's twenty lieder in the song cycle *Die schöne Müllerin*, based on Wilhelm Müller's collection of poems of the same name. In it he plays the role of Schubert who in search of inspiration follows a stream to a mill where he falls in love with the miller's daughter, Brigitte, played by Pagnol's wife, Jacqueline Pagnol; he loses her to the local lord whose wealth seduces her. Only nine of the twenty songs in Schubert's cycle are included in the film, although the composer, Tony Aubin,

---

[29] 'The soul is filled with grace and a pledge of future glory is given to us.'
[30] 'He has suffered.'

used some of the melodies from those not included in his score for the film, and the soundtrack also includes other Schubert pieces, such as 'Der Lindenbaum' ('The Linden Tree') from another song cycle, *Winterreise* (*Winter Journey*), and the same serenade as in *Destins*, with Rossi this time accompanying himself on guitar rather than piano. We also hear the Trout Quintet as Schubert spies on Brigitte swimming naked in the stream (0.34), and the Unfinished Symphony when Schubert tries to persuade her to leave with him and she refuses (1.24). The film's relative lack of success was because unlike Rossi's other films, there were no modern-sounding potential hit songs, just reworkings of some well-known and many less well-known classical pieces. But there was another major reason for the film's lack of success.

It was one of the first French films to be made in colour. Pagnol had originally made it in black and white, but attracted by the Roux brothers' research into colour film he processed the film using their methods, which involved attaching a composite lens to the camera comprising four smaller lenses filtering red, blue, green and yellow. As Dudley Andrew explains, 'each 35mm frame was actually a composite of four 16mm black-and-white images. When the same module was attached to the projector, the image would be reconstituted in color' (1979: 45; for more technical details see Martin 2013). The results were less than satisfactory, partly because film theatres were ill-equipped to deal with the process (Frouart 1987), and the majority of the reviews at the time focused on the use of colour rather than on Rossi's performance, complaining of the blurring of the image as colours leaked from their objects (Feron 1947), and of an unnatural yellow making it look like the characters had jaundice (Lauwick 1948).

When comments focused on Rossi's performance they expressed incredulity that a singer associated with the Mediterranean sun could satisfactorily convey Schubert's tormented life, and that unlike Rossi's previous films in which songs were always motivated in some way by the narrative, in *La Belle Meunière* they functioned more like musical interludes in a sentimental story: 'On imagine mal le grand compositeur susurrant des airs doucereux à longueur de journée et de nuit pour plaire à sa belle'[31] (Delville 1949). Later commentators, once the film had been restored using Eastmancolor, saw its kitsch value: 'Il n'est pas interdit … pour peu qu'on goûte assez le "kitsch", d'apprécier à leur juste valeur les roucoulades de Tino, susurrées dans le décor insensé d'une Autriche d'opérette'[32] (Le Saux 1987) – reminding us that only fifteen years before the codes of the French operetta made this kind of musical acceptable.

Rossi is remembered less for his films than for his songs, and for one song in particular, even for younger generations: 'Petit Papa Noël'. This song has the same status in France as Irving Berlin's 'White Christmas' sung by Bing Crosby in the film *Holiday Inn* (Marc Sandrich, 1942). Originally composed by lyricist Émile Audiffred and composer Henri Martinet in 1944 as a prayer by a child asking for his father's return from the war, the lyrics were rewritten by Raymond Vincy as a child's prayer to Father Christmas begging him not to forget the presents. Rossi sings the song as a lullaby in *Destins*, first during a long tracking shot from an empty dining room through doors

---

[31] 'It's difficult to imagine the great composer whispering sugary melodies day and night for his sweetheart.'
[32] 'As long as you like kitsch, you will like Tino's cooing in the absurd décor of a Viennese operetta.'

Figure 10.6 'Petit Papa Noël' in *Destins* (Courtesy René Chateau).

that open onto his son's bedroom where he sings his son to sleep (0.15), then a second time as a spectacular musical number in the theatre where he is performing. During this number the scene switches to the room where his brother Fred listens to André's performance as his nephew, whom he has abducted, lies in bed next door (1.23).

Fred, filled with remorse for the abduction, and having killed his lover who pushed him to it, returns the child; the final scene of the film repeats the first lullaby scene as the camera pulls back in a long tracking shot that reverses the first scene (1.33; see Figure 10.6). With over 5.8 million singles sold in France, it is the bestselling single of all time in France. As Rossi ruefully commented later: 'Toute ma vie, j'ai chanté l'amour et mon plus gros succès, je le dois à une chanson pour enfants! Le miracle de cette chanson, c'est sa simplicité. On parlait toujours du Père Noël mais les trois mots "Petit Papa Noël" ont vraiment touché tous les enfants!'[33] (Trimbach 1978: 62).

Of the Three Tenors, Rossi is the most important, not just because of the success of 'Petit Papa Noël', which led to a Golden Disc in 1949, or because he received the Légion d'Honneur in 1952. He normalized the romantic singer across a variety of media, and made possible the success of Guétary and Mariano, the three of them constituting the last major success of the popular singer in the first half of the century, alongside Piaf and Trenet. In the next chapter we turn to the other two tenors, Guétary and Mariano.

---

[33] 'I've sung love songs all my life and my biggest success is a children's song! The song is miraculously simple. We were still referring to Father Christmas but the three words "Petit Papa Noël" really moved children!'

11

Georges Guétary and Luis Mariano

Georges Guétary

Whereas Rossi is now best remembered for a single song, Georges Guétary is remembered by film-establishment critics for starring alongside Gene Kelly in *An American in Paris*. A reviewer for *Positif*, for example, commented briefly in his diary on Guétary's death, positioning him relative to that film, even if acknowledging his considerably more extensive European career: 'On apprend la mort de Georges Guétary. Certains n'oublient pas ses deux grands numéros dans *Un Américain à Paris*. Mais il fut aussi la vedette de quelques opérettes filmés en France, en Grèce, en Allemagne'[1] (Masson 1997: 74).[2]

Like Rossi and Mariano, Guétary took singing lessons in Paris, in his case with the well-known opera singer Ninon Vallin, as well as acting classes in René Simon's acting school. He made his debut as a singer in Jo Bouillon's jazz orchestra before joining Mistinguett's revue at the Casino de Paris in 1937. During the war he began his career in stage operetta in 1941 with the reprise of *Toi c'est moi* – the same operetta that Pills and Tabet had staged in 1934 and made into a film in 1936 – followed by his own production of *La Course à l'amour* in 1942. Reviews complimented him on his 'jolie voix'[3] (Honegger 1941; Leroi 1942). The reviewer of one of the main Paris dailies commented on his 'timbre délicatement chaleureux et un aigu de rossignol'[4] (Berlioz 1942), 'rossignol' being a term also frequently used for Tino Rossi. Another reviewer, while also complimenting Guétary's 'jolie voix', commented that he had 'un léger accent qu'il faudrait faire disparaître'[5] (Daix 1942). But like both Rossi and Mariano, Guétary chose to retain his Mediterranean accent, enhancing his exoticism; as James Kirkup wrote in his obituary, 'the public loved his "Mediterranean" voice, rolling its "r's" like the River Garonne running over its pebbles' (1997). He made his

---

[1] 'Georges Guétary has died. He was best known for his two great numbers in *An American in Paris*. But he was also the star of a few film operattas in France, Greece and Germany.'
[2] Guétary, in fact, has three musical numbers in the film, not two: the trio 'By Strauss', the duo 'S'Wonderful', and the number that he is most remembered for, 'I'll Build a Stairway to Paradise'. A number of songs that he was due to sing were eventually dropped (Padilla 2010: 74–5).
[3] 'Nice voice.'
[4] 'His warm and delicate tone and nightingale high notes.'
[5] 'A slight accent that he needs to lose.'

first recordings during the war with compositions by Francis Lopez, many of which were very successful, such as 'Robin des Bois' ('Robin Hood', 1943), 'À Honolulu' ('In Honolulu', 1945), and 'Chic à Chiquito' (1945), which was one of the signature songs in his first film, *Le Cavalier noir*.

Like Mariano, Guétary was principally a stage performer of operettas. After *Toi c'est moi*, he produced all of his subsequent sixteen operettas, whether staged in France, London or New York. Some of these were very successful, such as *Bless the Bride* in London's Adelphi Theatre (1947), which had 886 performances over two years, or *La Route fleurie* (1952), which played in Paris for four years. Other operettas were less successful, such as *Arms and the Girl* (1950) which played on Broadway for only 134 performances; but Guétary was awarded a Tony as Best Foreign Performer, and it led to him being chosen by Arthur Freed for the role of Henri Baurel in *An American in Paris*, a role that he almost turned down (Guétary 1981: 133–5). The second of Guétary's Broadway shows, *Portofino*, opened on 21 February 1958, but closed after only three performances, despite Guétary's appearance on the Ed Sullivan Show at the beginning of the month (Inman 2006: 90).[6]

Guétary and Mariano's operettas vied with each other during the early 1950s, and the press liked to pit them against each other. But they knew each other well and were friends (Guétary 1981: 158–9). *Mon film* ran many pieces on him in their regular column 'Les amours de nos vedettes';[7] the main purpose of one published in 1948 was to counter the rumour that they were bitter rivals (Corday-Marguy 1954: 14).[8] Unlike Mariano, however, who, as we shall see, regularly turned his stage operettas into films, Guétary never did so, his films disappointing him; talking about *Plume au vent*, he comments that 'comme bien d'autres auxquels j'avais participé, ce film ne répondit pas à mes espérances'[9] (1981: 159).

And unlike Rossi, whose characters in most of his films are singers, Guétary plays a singer – and so naturalizing his singing performances – in fewer of his films.[10] His early films are costume films in which he plays suave noblemen: in *Le Cavalier noir* he is a Spanish nobleman, whose heritage has been taken by the King of France, and he has turned smuggler to recoup what he has lost. In his next film, in which he teamed once more with director Gilles Grangier and composer Francis Lopez, *Trente et quarante*, he is a nineteenth-century Italian nobleman who happens to write songs and with whom

---

[6] He remained in the United States, appearing twice more on the Ed Sullivan Show, alongside the Everly Brothers on 2 March and Frankie Vaughn on 30 March (Inman 2006: 90).
[7] 'Loves of the stars.'
[8] 'Les amours de nos vedettes' were all produced by Paule Corday-Marguy: (1946: 8–9; 1949: 8–9; 1951: 8–9; 1953: 8–9; 1956: 14).
[9] 'Like many of my films, this one didn't live up to my expectations.'
[10] *Jo la romance, Une fille sur la route, Plume au vent, Le Chemin du paradis, Amour, tango, mandoline*. We are excluding the sketch films in which he plays himself, and which we have not listed in Table 10.1: *Paris chante toujours* (Pierre Montazel, 1951), *La Route du bonheur* (Maurice Labro and Giorgio Simonelli, 1953), and *C'est arrivé à 36 chandelles* (Henri Diamant-Berger, 1957). We are also excluding the Austrian film *Vergiß wenn Du Kannst* (Hans König, 1956), in which he has a cameo part as a singer; the film was shown only in Northern France in its original German-language version.

the daughter of a French aristocrat falls in love; and he is Italian again in the two-film series directed this time by Jean Boyer, *Les Aventures de Casanova*, pursuing those adventures in Paris.

In his next two films, once more directed by Grangier, he moved away from the swashbuckler persona. In *Jo la romance* he plays a singer, Georges Hyverlin, who gives up singing to work in his father's car factory, before returning to his singing career; in *Amour et compagnie* he is an accountant and amateur singer. It was only following the success of *An American in Paris* that he played, as Rossi had so often before him and Mariano was to do, a famous singer tired of being besieged by his fans; in *Une fille sur la route* he is Carlos Cortez who escapes to the south of France for some respite, and betrays himself by coaching a group of young campers putting on a show. *Plume au vent*, in which Guétary returns to the amateur singer character, was a Franco-Spanish production; he stars opposite the Spanish star Carmen Sevilla, who had previously starred alongside Luis Mariano in *Andalousie*, *Violettes impériales* and *La Belle de Cadix*. His three following films were German co-productions: *Baron Tzigane*, which many commentators consider to be his best film, is a film adaptation of the Johann Strauss operetta. In the same year, he was a restaurant owner in Greece in *Liebe ist ja nur ein Märchen*, known in France as *Amour, tango, mandoline*, and in 1956 was one of the three friends in a remake of the 1930 MLV *Le Chemin du paradis*. His final film, *Une nuit aux Baléares*, was also based on a stage operetta. Despite the fact that these last films attracted significant numbers of spectators (Table 10.1), Guétary subsequently focused entirely on stage operettas.

Whereas one of Rossi's signatures was a certain stiffness of the body, Guétary's signature is movement, both in terms of his singing which is frequently accompanied by dancing, and in terms of the plot which frequently places him in exterior locations. In the first shot of his first film, for example, *Le Cavalier noir*, we see him riding from far off across a wide plain as he sings 'Chic à Chiquito' (Chiquito is his horse), a song that returns ten minutes later as he strides past virginal blonde Solange's window for an assignation. The song is reprised again in the countryside when he calls his horse to him having had a narrow escape from the soldiers pursuing him (0.23). Four of the five songs of the film are sung in exteriors: apart from this one, there is 'Cavalier' as he arrives in the smuggler camp (0.25), and 'La plus belle' ('The Most Beautiful Woman') as he goes to meet Solange (1.00), the only song occurring in the confines of a room being his duet with Solange, 'Avec l'amour' ('With Love'), a few minutes later as they dance in her boudoir. Part of the reason for so many exteriors is most likely to have been cost-cutting. One reviewer calls the film mediocre, but praises the use of authentic exteriors, even if some of the camouflage of modern features is obvious (G. S. 1945). Similar comments were made about two of Guétary's less successful ventures, *Amour et compagnie* and *Amour, tango, mandoline*, both of which are set in the Mediterranean, the first in Cannes and the second in Greece. A reviewer of *Amour et compagnie* lambasted the film, scorning it as 'cinéma alimentaire',[11] verging

---

[11] 'Jobbing cinema.'

on the xenophobic with comments on the international cast: 'M. Guétary, qui parle français avec un accent étranger, cause avec Mme Thamar qui a un fort accent moins définissable encore et une troisième personne, Française, qui parle anglais, un anglais de chez Berlitz … Si vous ne me croyez pas, allez voir cette tour de Babel'[12] (Lauwick 1950). The only saving grace for this reviewer was Johnny Hess's music and the 'charmantes vues de la Côte d'Azur'.[13] Similarly, *Amour, tango, mandoline*'s 'insipid' storyline (Labarthe 1957) has little to praise except the frequent exteriors in some of Greece's major tourist attractions, including the Temple of Poseidon on Cape Sounion. Guétary plays an inconstant restaurant owner. His friend Fritz says 'il a toujours des femmes qui tournent autour de lui',[14] and comments at the end of the film: 'Son destin est de chanter et de parcourir le monde',[15] cementing the link between the mobility of desire, geographical mobility and the way that singing enables both.

The link between mobility and natural settings is at its most obvious in *Une fille sur la route*, also located in Cannes. The first twenty minutes of the film show his character, Carlo, besieged by fans. They are anchored in the number 'Toutes les femmes' ('All Women') which we see Carlo rehearsing, the lyrics pointing out that 'toutes les femmes rêvent toujours à moi':[16] we see twins hiding in his apartment, echoed in the misogynistic lyrics of the song ('elles sont toutes les mêmes'),[17] followed by the Countess's comment in equally poor taste when he discovers a Black woman and a Japanese woman hiding under the furniture: 'Les femmes vous en font voir de toutes les couleurs'[18] (0.11). Like Rossi in some of his films, Carlo escapes to the country, picking up the hitchhiker Annabel (Lilian Bert) who does not recognize him, and after finding that there is no room in hotels in Cannes, he returns to the campsite where he had dropped her off. Much of the film is shot in exteriors, emphasizing the mobility of the characters' performances, as well as emphasizing their bodies, whether the shorts worn by everyone at the campsite or in the grounds of the Countess's home, where her friends have suntan lotion rubbed over their bikini-clad bodies (0.41), or, indeed, Guétary himself who appears wearing only swimming trunks when Carlo and Annabel go for a swim in the sea (0.53). Carlo's cavalier attitude to women at the start of the film is resolved at the end, as he finally falls in love with the free-spirited Annabel, singing to her 'J'ai besoin de te voir pour chanter'[19] (1.25).

We find a similar mobility in *Plume au vent*, in which Guétary is Claude, the 'feather in the wind' of the title, a romantic dreamer constantly pursued by and pursuing the women of the Basque village where he lives, 'un vrai village d'opérette'[20] we are told in

---

[12] 'M. Guétary speaks French with a foreign accent, and talks with Mme Thamar who has an even more indistinguishable accent and a third person, French, who speaks Berlitz-style English. If you don't believe me, just go and see this tower of Babel.'
[13] 'Charming views of the Côte d'Azur.'
[14] 'Women are always sniffing around him.'
[15] 'His destiny is to sing and to travel the world.'
[16] 'All women dream about me.'
[17] 'They are all the same.'
[18] 'Women give you a colourful time.'
[19] 'I need to see you to sing.'
[20] 'A real operetta village.'

Figure 11.1 'On peut blaguer l'amour' in *Plume au vent* (Courtesy René Chateau).

a voice-over at the start of the film. One of his friends inherits a pharmacy in Paris, but feels incapable of running it, as a result of which the three friends go to Paris, and Claude pretends to be his friend, falling in love with Héléna (Carmen Sevilla), an old acquaintance from his childhood who works as an assistant in the shop. As was the case with *Le Cavalier noir*, song and movement work together to establish the elegant mobility that characterizes Guétary's performances. In an early scene of the film Claude is composing a song, 'Simple et douce' ('Simple and Sweet'), based on the songs of the birds he can hear as he lies in a field far from the village (0.6), and carries on singing it as he walks through the trees in a long tracking shot; later in the film he sings 'Canoë' as he floats down the river in a canoe (1.17). Even when songs are sung in interiors, Guétary's character dances, such as the trio 'Et ouf, on respire!' ('Phew, We Can Breathe!') with his two friends (0.24), or his duet 'Je n'embrasse pas les garçons' ('I Don't Kiss Boys') in the pharmacy with Héléna during which the two dance around the shop's furniture (0.40). 'On peut blaguer l'amour' ('You Can Lark Around with Love', 0.11) takes place in a cluttered work area full of his friends; Guétary's character constantly moves around, and frequently breaks into balletic dancing, at one point waltzing with an older peasant woman who enters the room, much as Gene Kelly does in the 'By Strauss' sequence in *An American in Paris* (Figure 11.1).

This is not the only echo of *An American in Paris*. In a digression from the main plot (0.47), the three friends go to Paris with Claude's girlfriend Alicia (Jacqueline Pierreux), who is rehearsing a show in a small theatre. She persuades the director to put on a more spectacular show involving the three friends, who demonstrate what they can do by singing a lively trio 'S'il n'y avait au monde' ('If in the World There Was Only'), whose chorus – 'S'il n'y avait au monde qu'une seule fille blonde, le choix pour les garçons serait simple'[21] – motivates the parade of a variety of showgirls across the small

---

[21] 'If there were only one blonde in the world, boys wouldn't have to choose.'

stage. Claude opens the backdrop curtain to reveal a map of Paris as he sings solo 'C'est tout Paris' ('This Is Paris'). As the number progresses two more backdrop curtains are raised, each time revealing an improbably deeper and more spectacular stage, much as occurred in *La crise est finie* (Chapter 3). When the second curtain is raised we see the beginnings of a staircase and the small chorus line has multiplied its numbers as the dancers swirl around Claude. He gestures off-stage, and again improbably, we see him now in black tails dancing with a range of showgirls wearing designer clothes as the song refers to Paris as a centre of fashion. A third curtain is raised to reveal a long staircase which he climbs flanked by the showgirls; it is a direct reference to 'I'll Build a Stairway to Paradise' in *An American in Paris* (1.01; Figure 11.2), in which Henri also starts the number in front of the curtain which lifts to reveal the stage and the staircase.

Figure 11.2 'C'est tout Paris' in *Plume au vent* (Courtesy René Chateau).

Figure 11.3 'I'll Build a Stairway to Paradise' in *An American in Paris* (Courtesy Warner Home Video).

When *Plume au vent*'s number finishes, there is a close-up of Claude's face suggesting that what we have seen was him imagining a spectacular musical number, which only serves to underline its function as a nostalgic recall of the number in *An American in Paris* (Figure 11.3).

The most startling sequence in *Plume au vent* is a dream sequence (Figure 11.4), which demonstrates mobility at several levels. The three friends give Héléna a sleeping draught because they want to transport her from Paris back to the village (0.58). As she drifts off to sleep, they tell her that she looks like 'une vraie princesse de légende, une Belle au Bois Dormante ... nous autour de vous comme des troubadours ... il ne manque plus qu'une chanson',[22] and Claude launches into 'Simple et douce', the song he was composing at the start of the film. Héléna floats through the clouds and lands in a fairy-tale wood with very obviously cardboard trees, where she meets Claude dressed in cod-medieval costume (tights, high collar and cape). As in fairy tales, the troubadour romance turns into a nightmare as evil creatures pursue her, and she falls through the clouds as she chases a vanishing Claude, to wake up next to the three friends in a field close to the village, where they will join a village festival with traditional Basque dancing. The sequence parallels the three friends' drive to Paris in Alicia's car earlier in the film, but in fantasy mode. Alicia has been exchanged for the harder-to-get Héléna, and the sequence confirms Héléna's love for Claude and for her village, functioning as a nostalgic return to the simplicity of rural life contrasted with Paris; however, her status as an independent shop assistant in Paris is abandoned, and the spectacular stage show exchanged for folk dancing. We might be forgiven for preferring the former.

Figure 11.4 The dream sequence in *Plume au vent* (Courtesy René Chateau).

---

[22] 'A real fairy-tale princess, a Sleeping Beauty, us around you like troubadours, all we need now is a song.'

The final film we will explore is the adaptation of the 1885 Strauss operetta *Baron Tzigane*, which had already been twice adapted for the screen in Germany, first in 1927 directed by Frederic Zelnick and starring future filmmaker William Dieterle as Sándor, and then again in 1935 directed by Karl Hartl, with Anton Walbrook as Sándor. Rabenalt's version was an MLV, with Gerhard Riedmann as Sándor in the German-language version and Guétary as the only French performer in the French version. Like *Le Cavalier noir*, it is a costume film in which Guétary once more plays a nobleman who has lost his estate after the war, and returns to claim it, and is once more caught between a blonde and a brunette, this time Anita the blonde daughter of the pig farmer who has stolen much of his estate, and Saffi (Margit Saad) the gypsy girl who resists him, but with whom he falls in love by the end of the film. Filmed in Eastmancolor, it has a freshness that the earlier film lacked. It attracted as many spectators as Guétary's late-1940s films, and more than another filmed operetta by the same director with Luis Mariano released the same year, *Der Zarewitsch*, based on Léhar's 1927 operetta of the same name. It led to a debate by well-known critics on the genre of the filmed operetta and its continued success with audiences; in itself this constituted a major shift of perception, as the critical establishment had generally been dismissive of the popular films of the Three Tenors, as we saw in particular with the reactions to Rossi's films. Jean d'Yvoire, editor of the Catholic-inspired journal *Télé-Ciné*, and one of François Truffaut's bêtes noires (Dixon 1993: 81–2), considered that the genre of the filmed operetta 'a vieilli et ne nous touche plus guère'[23] (1955). This view was shared by Jacques Doniol-Valcroze, the influential co-founder with André Bazin of *Cahiers du cinéma*, who wrote a lengthy article in *France Observateur*, the left-leaning magazine which was to become *Le Nouvel observateur*. For Doniol-Valcroze the film was typical of 'un genre particulièrement démodé, plat et cinématographiquement peu valable'[24] (1955). But he was forced to admit that the films remained popular: 'Là où les choses se compliquent c'est quand on constate le succès du Châtelet, lieu de prédilection, avec le Casino de Paris, de toute une partie de la province française.'[25]

Claude Mauriac, the influential cinema critic of *Le Figaro*, also wrote a long and more positive review, admiring the film's naiveté and 'innocence': 'Le film s'il est souvent ridicule ne cesse pas d'être plaisant. À cause d'abord de Johann Strauss, qui n'a rien perdu de sa sensuelle fraîcheur. En raison aussi d'un Eastmancolor dont les tons pastel s'accordent bien avec cette Hongrie d'opérette. ... La seule façon de n'être point désillusionné avec un film de ce genre est de n'en point trop attendre'[26] (1955). Another reviewer pointed out in similar fashion that the film's charm was that it gave ninety

---

[23] 'Has aged and we don't find it touching anymore.'
[24] 'A genre that is particularly old-fashioned, dull and cinematographically limited.'
[25] 'It's a bit more complicated when you consider the huge success of the Châtelet, the place cherished, along with the Casino, by many people from the provinces.'
[26] 'The film may be ridiculous but it doesn't prevent it from being pleasurable. First because of Johann Strauss, whose music has not lost its sensual freshness. And then because of Eastmancolor whose pastel tones work well with this Hungary from operetta. The only way not to be disappointed by this kind of film is not to expect too much from it.'

minutes of song and dance accompanied by music 'pas trop sirupeuse, charmante et sans prétention'[27] (Garson 1955).

Arguably the film's strength was its recalling of the filmed operettas of the 1930s; indeed, one of the film's songs, between the tutor Honoré and Anita, the pig farmer's daughter, begins as a *parlé-chanté* (0.32), which as we saw in Chapter 3 was one of the features of the French musical in that decade. But it was not just the appeal to the past that attracted spectators; as Mariano's films demonstrate, the appeal was also that of the exotic 'éternel séducteur'[28] (Guétary 1981: 203).

Luis Mariano

More popular than either Rossi or Guétary in the 1950s was the Spanish tenor Luis Mariano, who specialized in the film adaptations of his popular stage operettas performed on a variety of Paris stages, such as the Théâtre du Châtelet, the Palais de Chaillot and La Gaîté Lyrique. He rose as Rossi waned, with a string of very successful films in the early 1950s (Table 10.1). *Andalousie* was the bestselling French film of 1951; *Violettes impériales* the second bestselling film of 1952, with *Rendez-vous à Grenade* doing well in the same year. *La Belle de Cadix* was the fourth bestselling French film of 1953, as was *Le Chanteur de Mexico* in 1956 (for an extended analysis of the success of the latter film, see Creton and Kitsopanidou 2014).

Mariano was born in the Basque country on the Spanish side of the border. The family emigrated to Bordeaux after the Spanish Civil War, where Mariano began singing in cabarets. In 1942 he went to Paris, where he studied classical opera singing. His first small singing role in films was in a Tino Rossi film, *Le Chant de l'exilé* (André Hugon, 1943). By the end of the war he was recording songs on vinyl, and shared the bill with Montand and Piaf at the Gala des Catherinettes in the Palais de Chaillot in November 1945. He is better known for his operettas, the first of which, *La Belle de Cadix*, opened in December 1945 and was adapted for the screen eight years later. The music was by Francis Lopez, who collaborated with Mariano throughout his career. Due to run for six weeks, it remained for over five years, and was reprised in the late 1950s with a total of over 15,000 shows. One of its best-known songs, 'Maria Luisa', written for his sister of the same name, sold 1.25 million copies.

Mariano combined stage operettas and films during the 1950s, along with extensive tours nationally and internationally during this decade and into the 1960s. He toured France, Algeria and Tunis for eight months in 1946, and the United States in 1949, where he returned in 1958 to be introduced by Frank Sinatra on US TV's The Ed Sullivan Show. He regularly attracted audiences of 100,000, and like Rossi would regularly be mobbed by large crowds of admirers, as he complains in his autobiographical writing and as is frequently mentioned in reviews. This was in part because of his exposure

---

[27] 'Not too syrupy, charming and unpretentious.'
[28] 'Eternal seducer.'

beyond the stage and the big screen. He frequently appeared on the covers of the main industry magazines, such as *Mon Film* and *Cinémonde*. In 1947 the popular magazine *Cinévogue-Cinévie* started an agony column entitled 'Luis Mariano vous répond',[29] and from 1948 to 1956 he had a regular agony column, entitled 'Lettres à Luis Mariano',[30] in *Cinémonde*, whose readership was principally female (Sellier 2014). The formula was so successful that it was translated to French TV in 1950, where he was regularly invited on shows such as Nohain's *36 chandelles* (Chapter 9). Finally, Mariano's fan club, modelled on Rossi's, started in 1948 with 6,000 subscribers, and finished with over 30,000 by his death; there are still a number of active fan websites devoted to Mariano.[31]

There are a number of reasons for Mariano's success. First and foremost, there is the music. Francis Lopez's compositions are 'hispanismes sans prétention',[32] as one critic said of the stage version of *Andalousie* (Brillant 1947), and Raymond Vincy's lyrics are equally unpretentious, such as the title song of *Fandango* which was a major hit: 'Fandango du pays basque/Fandango simple et fantasque/Pour te danser dans les bras d'un garçon/Une fille ne dit jamais non.'[33] This was also the case for 'Rossignol' from *Le Chanteur de Mexico*, whose songs were played on the radio for several years: 'Rossignol de mes amours/Quant ton chant s'élèvera/Mon chagrin s'envolera/Et l'amour viendra peut-être.'[34]

But Mariano's success was mainly due to his voice, a bel canto tenor with unequalled purity in the top registers, as this account of *La Belle de Cadix* makes clear: 'Luis Mariano, ténor à la voix cuivrée, au 'si bémol' somptueux, reprend la tradition de chanteurs de grand style des opérettes à grand spectacle. Il a une voix magnifique, aussi jolie dans sa plénitude que dans ses demi-teintes. Et son phrasé est toujours nuancé avec goût'[35] (*Télé-Soir* 1946). Mainstream film critics may well have derided the films as mass cultural products aimed at women, as they had done for Rossi, but they were prepared to acknowledge his exceptional voice, as is evidenced by the critique of *La Belle de Cadix* which deplored the film version but complimented Mariano's voice: 'Dénigrer le jeu, la voix et l'aspect de M. Luis Mariano passe aux yeux de certains pour une preuve de délicatesse. Je cours bien

---

[29] 'Luis Mariano Answers You.'
[30] 'Letters to Luis Mariano.'
[31] Les Amis de Luis Mariano (http://luismariano.superforum.fr/); Association du souvenir à Luis Mariano (http://aslm.free.fr/), Luis Mariano (http://www.luismariano.com/mariano/).
[32] 'Unpretentious hispanisms.'
[33] 'Fandango from the Basque country/Fandango simple and whimsical/To take you dancing into a boy's arms/A girl never says no.'
[34] 'Nightingale of my love/When you start singing/My sorrow will take flight/And love will perhaps come.'
[35] 'Luis Mariano has a copper-bottomed voice, a sumptuous B flat major in the tradition of grand style operetta singers. He has a magnificent voice, as lovely in full flight as in quieter passages. And his phrasing is always tastefully tempered.'

volontiers le risque de leur déplaire: M. Luis Mariano me plaît beaucoup. Sa voix est un perpétuel ensoleillement'[36] (*Comœdia* 1954).

The word 'sunshine' signals an important aspect of Mariano's star persona, that of the exotic. To some extent, all three of the Three Tenors are exotic given their origins; but Mariano is more so. His exoticism is that of the Latin lover as Françoise Mallet-Joris pointed out: 'Il exerçait la fascination du séducteur latino-américain de l'entre-deux-guerres, avec son œil de velours, son sourire éclatant, sa voix chaude et ses cheveux bruns plaqués'[37] (cited in Rouhaud and Patchi 2006: 50). Reviews throughout his career stress his likeness to Ramon Novarro and even more to Rudolph Valentino: he was almost contracted in 1946 to star in a film on Valentino in Hollywood, but decided against it when it became clear that the contract required him to stay in Hollywood and make four further films. The comparison is instructive. Miriam Hansen (1986) has demonstrated the sexual ambiguity and ethnic alterity of Valentino in the post-war period of sexual liberalization and interrogations of masculinity. She shows how the spectatorial gaze is constantly drawn to Valentino through his dancing and feminine costumes. Similarly, Mariano is the focus of our gaze when he sings, and occasionally dances, more so than Rossi, who as we pointed out earlier, tends to stand stiffly when he sings. And although Mariano often wears relatively sobre costumes, he was also well known for his spectacular and extravagant costumes (Figure 11.5), often in the matador style with tight trousers, a wide belt (the *faja*), short jacket, the whole liberally scattered with lace. Indeed, Mariano made his own costumes according to his biographers:

> Il se donne un style, mi-hidalgo, mi-torero. Sa tenue de scène, romantique à souhait, choque certains conventionnels des tours de chant. ... Il arbore en effet un costume avec boléro. Ce n'est autre que le reste d'un vieux smoking trop court. Après avoir coupé le bas de la veste, lui-même, et rallongé les manches avec des rangées de dentelles, il confectionne un jabot grâce aux franges des rideaux maternels.[38] (Rouhaud and Patchi 2006: 45)

And then there are the cod-Middle Ages costumes, such as the tights and high collar of 'Rossignol' in *Le Chanteur de Mexico* (Figure 11.6), or the rather more risqué costume of 'Boumgali' in *Je n'aime que toi*, where Mariano wears nothing more than a leopard-skin loin-cloth and a crown of feathers: 'Mariano chante à demi-nu, en Tarzan, au milieu de la jungle, une samba-boléro échevelée, "Boumgali". Cela a de quoi exciter et

---

[36] 'Disparaging M. Luis Mariano's acting, voice and appearance passes for some as a mark of refinement. I'm happy to run the risk of disappointing them: I like M. Luis Mariano a lot. His voice is non-stop sunshine.'
[37] 'He had the fascination of the inter-war Latin lover, with his velvet eyes, his brilliant smile, his warm voice and his slicked back hair.'
[38] 'He created a style midway between that of a Spanish gentleman and a torero. His stage costume was incredibly romantic and shocked some who had conventional views about song recitals. He wore a costume with a bolero, which was no more than an old smoking jacket that was too short. After cutting the bottom of the jacket himself and lengthening the sleeves with lace, he made a jabot using fringes from his mother's curtains.'

Figure 11.5 Mariano's Hispanic and exotic costumes (Courtesy René Chateau and StudioCanal).

Figure 11.6 Mariano sings 'Rossignol' in *Le Chanteur de Mexico* (Courtesy StudioCanal).

désespérer tout à la fois ces jeunes femmes qui, jusque-là, n'avaient vu que ses dents'[39] (Rouhaud and Patchi 2006: 79).

Mariano's operettas and films are frequently set in exotic locations: Mexico, Jamaica and, especially, Spain. Part of the point of the stage operettas was escapism through spectacle, those performed in the Théâtre du Châtelet in particular requiring a range of tableaux set in different countries, something that Mariano's films could engage with even more forcefully. Indeed, Mariano played on his Spanishness in ways that Rossi and Guétary did not on their Mediterranean origins, for example, keeping his Spanish accent on purpose. But his exoticism was tempered by an appeal to ordinariness.

---

[39] 'Half-naked like Tarzan in the middle of the jungle, Mariano sings a wild bolero, "Boumgali". This excited young women who had never seen more than his teeth, as much as it drove them to despair.'

It is not unusual for the narrative of films about singers to be about their rise from obscurity to fame and fortune, as we have seen with the films of Rossi. While this is also the case for some of Mariano's films (*Fandango, Le Chanteur de Mexico*), in more of his films he is an already established singer (*Je n'aime que toi, Pas de week-end pour notre amour, Rendez-vous à Grenade, La Belle de Cadix*). But one of the key aspects of Mariano's star image is his ordinariness; as was frequently said of him, he was 'Monsieur Tout-le-monde', an ordinary guy. His films as a group therefore display much the same tension as Rossi's between the celebrity singer and the ordinary guy who wants to escape the pressures that celebrity brings. Either he is an ordinary guy who rises to fame and fortune, but retains his ordinariness, or, if he is already a famous singer, the narrative either has him trying to escape attention by retiring to the country (*Pas de week-end pour notre amour*), or else places him in situations that suggest a lower status (the barber Figaro in *L'Aventurier de Séville*, the hairdresser in *Quatre jours à Paris*), or an attempt to avoid high status, typically by consorting with gypsy girls in preference to women of higher status (*Violettes impériales, La Belle de Cadix, L'Aventurier de Séville*). In those films where he is not a singer, he is normally in a powerful position as a result of his high financial status or relatively tenuous connection with the upper classes; but he plays characters who are retiring, or who seem retiring largely as a result of larger-than-life comic foils, such as Jean Tissier, the egotistical film director in *La Belle de Cadix*, or Bourvil in *À la Jamaïque* where Mariano plays a rich plantation owner, or again in *Sérénade au Texas*, where, in both films, Bourvil is the buffoon.

Mariano's 'ordinariness' is also emphasized by the relationship between the films and Mariano's real-life situation. Many of the films refer to aspects of Mariano's life that would have been common knowledge, if not to the general public then to his fans. In *Rendez-vous à Grenade*, for example, the hero's house is the spitting image of Mariano's real house, the car he drives is Mariano's own distinctive Cadillac, the music of the film uses themes from previous films. The most frequent allusion to Mariano's real situation in the films is in the way that he attracts women, either intentionally or, more often than not, unintentionally, reminding the spectator of the way Mariano was constantly mobbed by crowds of admirers wherever he performed. In *Pas de week-end pour notre amour*, where he plays a famous singer who is trying to escape those very crowds, there is the following dialogue: 'Elles sont toutes folles de toi. …/Elles se consoleront, je ne suis pas Dieu le Père après tout./Pour elles tu n'en es pas loin. …/ Ta carrière passe avant ta famille. Frank, tu ne pourras jamais te marier.'[40] His films therefore function almost as pastiches of Mariano's star image off-screen, in ways that the films of Rossi and Guétary did not. The dialogue we have just quoted is doubly ironic. Given Mariano's status as a romantic singer, it was hardly surprising that there were frequent rumours concerning relationships with his co-stars, such as Martine Carol and Carmen Sevilla. But Mariano never married, and it is likely that he was gay, a

---

[40] 'They're all mad about you./They'll get over it, after all I'm not God the Father./You're pretty close as far as they're concerned./Your career comes before your family. Frank, you'll never be able to marry.'

subject of considerable speculation both during his lifetime and afterwards, and which contributed to his exotic aspect.

Mariano's star image displays a curious tension between the effeminate and the chaste. Unlike Novarro and Valentino, he does not smoulder; on the contrary, he was well known for his dazzling white smile, and impish eyes, frequently commented on by reviewers and admirers. Mariano was not at all the dangerous lover, but, rather, the carefree unthreatening youngster. Surrounded by women in his day-to-day life as well as in his films, he never married, was very publicly a family man dominated by his mother, and for the early part of his career by his female agent, Jeanne Lagiscarde, as well as being very close to his sister. He rarely commits fully to a woman in his films; when he does, the final kiss is half-hearted. He was also known to be extremely religious, travelling with a statuette of the Virgin Mary and attending Mass, and having at one time thought of becoming a priest. A survey in *Cinémonde* of the Mariano songs preferred by readers – 'Santa Maria' and 'Maria Luisa' (the latter dedicated to his sister) – suggests that his fans were attracted by a sensitive, religious and loving Mariano (Mirambeau 2004: 223–4).

Mariano's Spanishness with all its religiosity, plays into both his ordinariness and his exoticism, and is a fundamental element of his star persona. Spain opened up its doors to tourists in the 1950s. While there were 700,000 visitors, mainly British and French, to Spain in 1950, by 1959 this had risen to 4 million. Once the preserve of the nobility in the Romantic period, Spain was now the country of choice for ordinary French families; this was immortalized in Louis de Funès's successful 1958 comedy about an irascible taxi driver who goes to Spain for his holidays, *Taxi, roulotte et corrida* (2.5 million tickets). Mariano's Spanishness – he retained his Spanish accent on purpose to accentuate it – played into this thirst for an 'ordinary exoticism', while at the same time being Basque meant that he was neither Spanish nor French but somewhere in between, as reassuringly French as he was Spanish. As Mirambeau points out, 'L'Espagne, c'est "comme chez nous", mais "ailleurs", avec une autre langue et des castagnettes'[41] (2004: 220). There is a revealing comment made in *Cinémonde* at the time of Mariano's visit to the United States. He tells his admirers that he left a plush hotel for a cheaper one where he could cook his own food. But complaining that the Americans do not have any garlic, he says that he wrote to his mother so that she could send some, ending 'ça sent bon la France (et l'Espagne)'[42] (Mirambeau 2004: 221).

Mariano therefore represents a new masculine ideal specific for the 1950s: exotic, erotic and feminized, but also ordinary enough to be accessible to all. Just as in the 1920s a new generation of young and effeminate leading men appeared in the wake of WW1, such as Jaque Catelain and Pierre Batcheff, so too it can be argued that the new leading men of the 1950s such as Mariano (as well as Jean Marais and Gérard Philipe) represented a less warrior-like and more innocent masculinity appropriate for a consumer culture in which women had an increasingly important part to play

---

[41] 'Spain is like "chez nous" but also "elsewhere", with another language and castagnettes.'
[42] 'France (and Spain) smell good.'

domestically. As Mirambeau says, Mariano represented a return to normality and incarnated 'un nouvel idéal masculin. Un "Monsieur-tout-le-monde" d'extraction modeste, discret, travailleur, gentil et sensible'[43] (2004: 120). The moral values he embodied – 'la gentillesse, le dévouement, la conscience professionnelle, la dévotion à la mère et à la famille'[44] (Sellier 2014: 42) ensured the devotion of a predominantly female public during the 1950s.

This changed at the end of the 1950s and in the early 1960s. What had seemed to be a relatively stable and homogeneous genre anchored in high-profile singers began to fragment in three distinctive directions. Singers remained at the heart of the first strand, but were more international than had been the case with Rossi and Mariano. Zizi Jeanmaire, for example, had a significant American career, and exemplifies the attempt to produce American-inflected musicals in this period, recalling what had happened in the early 1930s. A second strand was the rise of the *yéyé* singers catering to new youth audiences that were less gendered than those of the Three Tenors. Finally, the New Wave demonstrated an auteurist and deconstructive approach to the genre, more realist than spectacular, with actors rather than well-known singers.

---

[43] 'An "Ordinary Guy" from a modest background, discrete, hard-working, kind and sensitive.'
[44] 'Kindness, devotion, professional integrity, devoted to his mother and his family.'

12

The transition to the modern musical

Folies-Bergère

Towards the end of the 1950s, as the films of Mariano were beginning to lose momentum, there was a sudden flourish of spectacular Hollywood-style musicals. The most successful of these with 3.5 million tickets sold was *Folies-Bergère* (1957), a reply to, and in part a replay of, *An American in Paris*. The *Cahiers du cinéma*'s review considered that the film was as good as the average Hollywood film musical, even if what was missing was 'un charme ... , le sens du rythme, la juste intuition du moment où la danse doit intervenir et pour quelle durée'[1] (E. L. 1957: 52). François Truffaut was more scathing, complaining that Decoin's camerawork resembled 'un éléphant paralytique qui ne se déplace qu'en titubant pesamment' compared with Minnelli's 'aigle qui peut virevolter gracieusement'[2] (1957). Eddie Constantine plays Bob, a US soldier in Paris trying to become a cabaret singer. He settles down with showgirl Claudie (Zizi Jeanmaire), and the film tracks the ups and downs of their careers as entertainers in music-hall revues. As we shall see the film is as French as it is American, with Jeanmaire seen as the revelation (see the title of Truffaut's review); many reviews describe her as the new Arletty: 'Même câlinerie gavroche, même tact dans la tendresse, même vif-argent dans les veines, mêmes longues, minces et troublantes jambes de soie, même éclat'[3] (Brulé 1957).

There are several spectacular stage numbers which take full advantage of Technicolor with very colourful costumes, such as the two opening numbers, 'Ça va faire du bruit' ('It Will Be Noisy') and 'Dépêchez-vous' ('Hurry') as well as the later 'Vendanges au village' ('Village, Harvest', 0.33). Jeanmaire is showcased in two numbers (Figure 12.1). The first is the ballet 'Sport d'hiver' ('Winter Sports'), choreographed by Roland Petit, which starts with her emerging from a snowman before a pas de deux (0.36). The second is a reprise of the successful number from her 1950 American tour, 'Je suis une croqueuse de diamants' ('I'm a Golddigger', 0.51). Constantine, who unlike Jeanmaire was not a dancer, sings more numbers than she does, but many of them, particularly

---

[1] 'Charm, a feel for rhythm, knowing exactly when dance is necessary and for how long.'
[2] 'A paralytic elephant that lurches heavily all over the place/an eagle that circles gracefully.'
[3] 'Same insolent flattery, same subtlety in affection, same quicksilver in the veins, same long, slim and silkily unsettling legs, same radiance.'

Figure 12.1 Jeanmaire's two showcase numbers in *Folies-Bergère* (Courtesy of LCJ Éditions).

in the first half of the film, are heard as brief snatches and neatly woven into the fast-moving narrative, such as Bob's attempts to sing in French with short bursts of songs – 'La Pipe à pépé' ('Pappy's Pipe') and 'Sous les pieds' ('Under My Feet') (0.24) – followed a few minutes later by the rapid editing of him singing in a variety of cabarets with snatches from what are supposed to be Russian and Spanish songs (0.28).

There are many self-referential nods in the film, such as the moment when Bob and Claudie are walking in the streets of Paris and she says 'toutes ces lumières, on dirait des diamants' ('These streetlights are all like diamonds', 0.15), referring to Jeanmaire's American show; a few minutes after the number itself, we see her on a TV screen advertising 'les bas Diamants' ('Diamond Stockings', 0.59). The room where Bob practises his singing has posters of Piaf, Chevalier, Jacques Pills, Trenet, and ... Eddie Constantine (0.23). The humour evidenced here underpins the transnational aspect of the film: Jeanmaire's success in France was sealed after her work in the US. There was the 1949 ballet *Carmen*, choreographed by Petit, which ran for seven months in New York, followed by the previously mentioned show, *La Croqueuse de diamants*, and a couple of films, both choreographed by Petit: *Hans Christian Andersen* with Danny Kaye (Charles Vidor, 1952) and *Anything Goes* with Bing Crosby (Robert Lewis, 1956). Constantine, on the other hand, was the exact reverse: an American who began a successful career in Parisian cabarets and achieved fame in a series of French B-films as the detective Lemmie Caution.

There are numerous echoes of American musicals in *Folies-Bergère*, such as the three soldiers on leave in Paris at the start of the film echoing the three sailors of *On the Town* (Gene Kelly and Stanley Donen, 1949). But the tension between the US and French aspects of the film is at its clearest in its final ten minutes which in backstage musical style bring several complete numbers to the music-hall's stage. The first of these is a replaying of the 'Girl Hunt' number in *The Band Wagon* (Vincente Minnelli, 1953) with Jeanmaire and Constantine as the Astaire–Charisse couple (Figure 12.2). Not only is Constantine dressed in the same white suit as Astaire, and Jeanmaire in a similar split-thigh dress as Charisse,

Figure 12.2 Echoes of 'Girl Hunt' in *Folies-Bergère* (Courtesy of Warner Home Video and LCJ Èditions).

but much of the narrative of the number, choreographed once again by Petit, is also calqued on 'Girl Hunt' (choreographed by Michael Kidd). This is particularly apt: in the American film it is a parody of Mickey Spillane pulp crime novels, and Constantine was best known in France for his Lemmy Caution roles in the B-film crime thrillers of the early 1950s. However, whereas Jeanmaire dances as sensuously as Cyd Charisse, Constantine is a clumsy echo of Astaire's sleek balletic moves, although it is possible to see these echoes as parody as much as homage or emulation. This homage-cum-parody is followed by two musical numbers that could not be more French, however, both associated with Mistinguett: 'La Java' (1.25) and 'Ça, c'est Paris' ('That's Paris', 1.26). Nostalgically French though they may be, they are presented in the same style as the Hollywood musical spectacular, the latter number in particular, with its gigantic staircase emerging from the base

Figure 12.3 'La Java' and 'Ça, c'est Paris' in *Folies-Bergère* (Courtesy of LCJ Èditions).

of the Eiffel Tower echoing the 'I'll Build a Stairway to Paradise' sung by Guétary in *An American in Paris* (Figure 12.3).[4]

The film was so successful that Zizi Jeanmaire starred in Decoin's *Charmants garçons*, choreographed once more by Petit, later the same year (December 1957, 1.9 million tickets), in which she plays a nightclub singer-dancer who works her way through a number of men. Once again Jeanmaire was applauded by reviewers; Claude-Marie Trémois, for example, commented on how a film that could have been merely saucy was considerably less shallow thanks to Jeanmaire's 'honnêteté païenne qui rend le film amoral certes, mais non sordide'[5] (1957).

The most striking aspect of *Folies-Bergère* is less its homage to the US musical than its emphasis on a very French music-hall tradition. That appeal to the past, enshrined in

---

[4] For more details on the Franco-American crossover in the film, see Pillard (2014).
[5] 'Heathen open-heartedness that certainly makes the film amoral, but not sordid.'

Jeanmaire's versions of Mistinguett's classic songs, is echoed in the remake of two Marseille operettas in the last half of the decade. *Trois de la Canebière* (1955, 2.8m tickets) and *Trois de la marine* (1957, 2.7m tickets) were both directed by Maurice de Canonge; they both starred the stage operetta singer Marcel Merkès and a familiar face from the Ventura films, Henri Génès. *Honoré de Marseille* (Maurice Regamey, 1957, 3.8m tickets) came out at the beginning of 1957 and clearly traded on the success of *Trois de la Canebière*, but was more a comedy than a film musical with only a few songs sung by Fernandel.

The end of the 1950s saw a shift away from the more dominant operetta films of the Three Tenors and the Hollywood-style musicals that frequently reprised the operetta films of the 1930s through to the 1950s. These new films had different types of singers, such as Turkish-born Dario Moreno in the mambo-inflected film *Oh! Qué mambo* (John Berry, 1959) with its four songs (see Gendrault 2014 for the mambo trend in cinema during the 1950s), and Gilbert Bécaud in *Casino de Paris* (André Hunebelle, 1957), considered by some to be the heir to Maurice Chevalier (J.-G. P. 1957), but who acted in very few films. *Casino de Paris*, an operetta-style film, also starring Vittorio de Sica at his most laconic as a famous playwright with Bécaud playing his secretary, was considered by reviewers to be much less successful than *Folies-Bergère*; Jacques de Baroncelli misogynistically dismissed Bécaud and the kind of female audience he presumed that Bécaud appealed to: 'Bécaud hurle, gesticule, grimace, se pâme, se disloque, défaille, rugit, bondit, gémit, halète. ... C'est ainsi que l'aiment les demoiselles'[6] (1957). Georges Sadoul more perceptively, but wrongly in our view, criticized the film for belonging to a different era, that of the nineteenth-century operetta (1957), although the energetic swing orchestra musical numbers are very much of their time; indeed, 'La Machine à écrire' ('The Typewriter') begins with the rhythmical sound of the typewriter used by Bécaud's character, recalling a similar procedure in *Le Chemin du paradis*, but develops as a high-energy song with Bécaud leaping around the room and on and off the furniture.

The *yéyé* and Johnny Hallyday

The most significant shift of the period, however, was to films that appealed to youth audiences. The first few years of the 1960s saw the development of the *yéyé* phenomenon, a term coined by the sociologist Edgar Morin (based on the English term 'yeah' frequently used in songs), who was the first to acknowledge the aspirations of the post-war baby boomers (Morin 1963). Like the *Zazous* during the Second World War and their attraction to swing and bebop jazz, the youth culture of the 1960s was intrinsically bound to American music, in this case rock 'n' roll. Unlike the *Zazous*, however, the youth culture of the 1960s was a considerably more extensive phenomenon, for several reasons. There was a post-war baby boom leading to many more teenagers in the 1960s

---

[6] 'Bécaud yells, throws his arms around, grins, goes into ecstasies, lurches about, faints, roars, leaps, moans, pants. ... That's how young women like it.'

than in the 1950s. The 1960s were also the height of France's post-war economic boom, the *Trente Glorieuses* as they were known, the thirty years stretching from 1945 to the oil crisis of 1974. The boom led to the widespread practice of giving teenagers pocket money, which they then spent on the new music technologies of the period, the emerging vinyl market and transistor radios. As David Looseley points out, 'by the early 1960s, a brash new culture was thrusting itself upon public attention, centred on music, with the arrival of vinyl records, English-language pop, music-oriented peripheral radio stations like Europe 1 (1955), and finally television' (2007: 265). A range of singers adapted American rock 'n' roll to the French context, often reprising the tunes, but with French lyrics. Among these were Françoise Hardy, Eddie Mitchell, Sheila, Sylvie Vartan and most importantly Johnny Hallyday. Just as the Gallicized jazz of the big bands underpinned the *Zazou* subculture during the Second World War, so too this Gallicized rock 'n' roll underpinned the new youth subculture, including the phenomenon often referred to as *Salut les copains*.

Originally a radio programme on Europe 1 that began airing in 1959, *Salut les copains* also became a magazine in 1962. The radio programme and the magazine promoted the *yéyé* singers. When circulation figures reached a million for its twelfth issue in 1963, a free concert was hurriedly organized for 22 June 1963 in the Place de la Nation. Although there had been very little advertising, between 150,000 and 200,000 young people attended to listen to a range of rock 'n' rollers, including top-billed Hallyday and his girlfriend Sylvie Vartan who had been flown up from the Camargue where they were shooting the musical *D'où viens-tu, Johnny?* (Noël Howard, 1963). Unsurprisingly, given the number of people attending, there was some damage to property around the venue; this was much exaggerated in the press, and led to a media panic. Commentators saw the phenomenon as an extension of the *blouson noir* (black leather jacket) subculture that had emerged in the late 1950s (Copfermann 1962): working-class youth who modelled themselves on the black-leather-jacket-wearing Marlon Brando of *The Wild Ones* (Laslo Benedek, 1953) or the anomic James Dean of *Rebel without a Cause* (Nicholas Ray, 1955).[7]

The *Salut les copains* phenomenon, however, was considerably less confrontational than the *blousons noirs*. Whereas these were largely a working-class phenomenon, the *copains* emerged from the white-collar class which had mushroomed during France's economic boom (Briggs 2006: 52–60). In a famous article for *Le Monde* after the concert the sociologist Edgar Morin pointed out that the hedonistic aspect of youth culture also included an attachment to consumer goods and therefore to potential conformism, the one held in tension with the other:

> L'exaltation du yé-yé peut porter en germe la fureur du blouson noir, le refus solitaire du beatnik, mais elle peut être aussi la préparation purificatrice à l'état de salarié marié, casé, intégré. ... Cette contradiction ... correspond bien à

---

[7] For some contemporary recollections of that concert with onstage photos, see Brigaudeau (undated). For an overview of the *yéyé* phenomenon, see Jouffa and Barsamian (1983). For work on *Salut les copains*, see Quillien (2009) and Tinker (2010).

l'adolescence, âge de la préparation à l'état adulte et du refus de l'état adulte, âge ambivalent par excellence qui porte toujours en lui la possibilité de la révolte de la jeunesse et son probable conformisme. ... Le sens finalement dominant de l'extase désirée, appelée par le yé-yé, est le jouir; ce jouir sous toutes formes englobe (et se déverse dans) le jouir individualiste bourgeois: jouir d'une place au soleil, jouir de biens et de propriété – le jouir consommateur, enfin.[8] (1963)

The role of *Salut les copains*, radio programme and magazine, became one of 'social ordering', which 'attempts to instil a sense of social order and good citizenship within its young readers, and is particularly critical of delinquent and anti-social behaviour' (Tinker 2007: 300); Tinker concludes that it 'expresses a solid determination to order youth and prepare readers for adulthood' (2007: 306; for a more extensive analysis see Tinker 2010). This position corresponded to socially and sexually conservative attitudes of teenagers and young women, as Jonathyne Briggs has shown in his study of the major stars of *Salut les copains*, Vartan, Sheila and Françoise Hardy, concluding that 'far from forming some kind of sexual avant-garde, French rock and roll often underscored and reinforced existing gender divisions and sexual roles through sound' (2012: 547). We will see similar tensions in the major film we will be exploring, *D'où viens-tu, Johnny?*

Just as the youth subculture during the Second World War manifested itself in both music and films, so too for the *yéyés* (Le Pajolec 2009). All the *yéyé* stars flirted with cinema, but as the titles of two articles on the subject suggest it was 'un rendez-vous manqué'[9] (Le Pajolec 2009; Faucon 2015) and did not lead to a substantial corpus of films: Eddie Mitchell et les Chaussettes noires in *Les Parisiennes* (Marc Allégret, Claude Barma, Michel Boisrond, Jacques Poitrenaud, 1962); Sylvie Vartan, Johnny Hallyday's partner, in *Un clair de lune à Maubeuge* (Jean Chérasse, 1962) and *D'où viens-tu, Johnny?*; Françoise Hardy in *Château en Suède* (Roger Vadim, 1963) and *Une balle au cœur* (Jean-Daniel Pollet, 1966); and Sheila in *Bang Bang* (Serge Piollet, 1967), also with Françoise Hardy. *Cherchez l'idole* (Michel Boisrond, 1964) was a celebration of these new pop idols in the tradition of the sketch film.

Unlike the singer-focused films we have explored in previous chapters, stretching from Piaf through to Rossi and Mariano, the majority of these films flopped. Le Pajolec suggests that this was mainly due to the mediocrity of both the narratives and the directors, with the singers playing themselves as a gambit to attract youth audiences. This does not entirely explain the films' lack of success, as similar criticisms were levelled

---

[8] 'The high spirits of *yéyé* carries the seeds of the *blouson noir*'s rage, the solitary refusal of the beatnik, but it can also be the purifying preparation for the employee who is married, settled, integrated. This contradiction corresponds with adolescence, the age when you prepare for adulthood and when you also refuse adulthood, an ambivalent age par excellence which always entails the possibility of youthful revolt and likely conformism. The dominant sense of the *yéyé*'s wish for ecstasy is pleasure; that pleasure in all its forms includes and diversifies itself in the individualist pleasure of the bourgeois: the pleasure of a place in the sun, the pleasure of material goods and property – consumer pleasure in the end.'
[9] 'A missed opportunity.'

at the films of the Three Tenors, which, as we have seen, were extremely successful. The additional factors are, first, the fact that the *yéyé* phenomenon was subcultural and located in youth culture rather than the broader culture of the Three Tenors that made them attractive to broader female audiences; and second, the mismatch between the *yéyé* subculture based firmly around music and the idolization of the singers on the one hand, and the very traditional narrative forms of cinema in which the singers and their songs played only a small part.

Johnny Hallyday was seen not only as the most important of the *yéyé* singers, but also as the one who had the most sustained engagement with cinema throughout his life, although as an actor rather than a singer. There were some high-points in that regard: he was a world-weary fight promoter in Jean-Luc Godard's *Détective* (1985), and was nominated for a Best Actor award in the European Film Awards for his role as a bank robber in Patrice Leconte's *L'Homme du train* (2002), which Hallyday considered to be his first serious role as an actor (Tesson 2002). During the *yéyé* years, he acted in four feature films, although only one of these could be defined as a film musical. *Les Parisiennes* is a sketch film with four sketches focusing on four types of Parisian women. Hallyday's sketch is 'Sophie', directed by Marc Allégret, in which he plays a singer distraught at the loss of his guitar and with whom a schoolgirl (Catherine Deneuve) falls in love. Hallyday sings two songs written by Charles Aznavour and Georges Garvarentz, 'Retiens la nuit' ('Keep the Night') and 'Sam'di soir' ('Saturday Night'), both of which were also commercialized as 45s. The walls of his bedsit in the film display American influences with posters of Las Vegas, San Francisco and a range of US singers. In *Dossier1413* (Alfred Rode, 1962), a mediocre police thriller, he is a singer in a cabaret and we see him perform two songs with his quartet: 'Une boum chez John' ('A Party at John's') on stage at L'Ange noir (1.03), and 'Laisse les filles' ('Leave the Girls') on the screen of a Scopitone in a bar (0.23). Similarly, in *Cherchez l'idole*, a chase film modelled on *Paris chante toujours* and *Boum sur Paris*, a stolen diamond is hidden in a guitar, this serving as a pretext to showcase a range of singers playing themselves, including Eddie Mitchell, Sylvie Vartan, and Hallyday who sings just one song, 'Bonne chance' ('Good Luck'), as he travels in his bus to a concert in Carcassone. The only film of this period that could be defined as a film musical is the relatively successful *D'où viens-tu, Johnny?* (Noël Howard, 1963), in which Hallyday has the starring role as a singer pursued by gangsters to his childhood home in the Camargue.

The choice of Noël Howard as director was significant, as it lent an American flavour to the film: he had been assistant director for a range of major Hollywood films, such as *Land of the Pharaohs* (Howard Hawks, 1955), *Love in the Afternoon* (Billy Wilder, 1957), *The Journey* (Anatole Litvak, 1959), *Solomon and Sheba* (King Vidor, 1959), *King of Kings* (Nicholas Ray, 1961) and the UK film *Lawrence of Arabia* (David Lean, 1962). The music was a collaboration between Eddie Vartan (Sylvie Vartan's brother, who had launched her career in 1961 and composed songs for Hallyday), Jean-Jacques Debout (who plays one of the musicians in the film) and Hallyday. The film is a curious amalgam of film noir, French Western and singer film, echoing Elvis Presley's films of the period, such as *King Creole* (Michael Curtiz, 1958) in which a young singer gets involved with gangsters, the Western *Flaming Star* (Don Siegel, 1960), in which

Presley's mixed-race character is caught between allegiances, *Wild in the Country* (Philip Dunne, 1961) in which his troubled character returns to the care of his uncle, and *Kid Galahad* (Phil Karlson, 1962) in which he plays a boxer whom gangsters try to turn.

The first quarter of an hour is a pre-credits sequence filmed in black and white, during which Johnny's group perform the first of the film's four songs, 'À plein cœur' ('From the Heart'), in a café owned by a drug-dealing boss who uses the youngsters as mules. Johnny discovers he has been duped when he opens the case he has been asked to deliver; he throws the drugs into the Seine, and escapes to his family's place in the Camargue, at which point the film changes from a gritty urban thriller to a Western in Eastmancolor as we see Johnny reintegrating himself in picture-postcard Camarguais life with extended sequences of him galloping on his horse, rounding up bulls, wrestling them, baiting them in the ring (Figure 12.4). The setting inflects the film towards an American-style Western, this being literally underscored by a sequence in which Johnny gallops with the cowboys to a score that resembles Jerome Moross's score for *The Big Country* (William Wyler, 1958) after he has sung the second song of the film, 'Pour moi la vie va commencer' ('Life Will Begin for Me', 0.29), which celebrates the return to his family home. But as director Howard pointed out in interview, in an attempt to justify the use of black and white, the Western is not a French genre, because as soon as a character has a gun in his hand it presupposes a police thriller, hence in his view the necessity of the black-and-white prologue with the gangsters in Paris (Ledieu 1963). Timothy Scheie has explored what might otherwise seem to be an oxymoron in his work on the French Western, pointing out that the genre is not only 'variable, scant and discontinuous' but also unstable 'when Western tropes and situations mix with those of other genres (comedies, gangster films, musicals, Camarguais regional dramas)' (2016: 318; see also Scheie 2019). *D'où viens-tu, Johnny?* exemplifies this generic mix with its combination of gangster film, musical and Camarguais drama. The contrast between city and country echoes the binary of urban East and Wild West in the American Western. Paradoxically, though, the Camargue setting also makes the

Figure 12.4 Johnny as 'cowboy' in *D'où viens-tu, Johnny?* (Courtesy René Chateau).

film very French, recalling Rossi's 1946 film set in the Camargue, *Le Gardian*, which also traded on local colour, whether the cowboys and bulls or the Pagnolades with 'typical' Provençal characters. In that respect, the film perpetuates the kind of tension between Hollywood and French styles that we have seen throughout the history of the French film musical.

By French standards the film did well at the box office with 2.8 million tickets sold, equalling the success of many of Mariano and Guétary's late-1950s musicals. As had been the case with the Three Tenors, part of that success would have been because fans wished to see their pop idols on screen, not least because 'Pour moi la vie va commencer' was broadcast on radio before the film was released, and a 45rpm was released alongside the film with the four songs of the film; they were also released on a 33rpm which included Eddie Vartan's score. As had frequently been the case with Rossi's films, this film's dialogues draw attention to Hallyday's voice, in this case when he sings the third song of the film, a nostalgic ballad, 'Rien n'a changé' ('Nothing Has Changed'), for his childhood girlfriend Magali, who comments admiringly 'T'as une jolie voix tu sais'[10] (1.08).

The film was roundly critiqued by establishment critics, however, although this was not because of Hallyday's performance. Vartan's screen presence was misogynistically described as no better than 'un ectoplasme' (Baroncelli 1963), her acting ability resembling that of 'une savate'[11] (M.D. 1963), and one critic remarked caustically that Hallyday 'joue aussi mal que Tino Rossi'[12] (Bory 1963); but most reviewers gave Hallyday qualified praise:

> [Il] n'est pas antipathique ni trop maladroit. On lui a donné un texte réduit à quelques phrases tirées de son vocabulaire usuel.[13] (M.D. 1963)

> Il n'est pas plus mauvais qu'un autre, même il fait des débuts prometteurs; dès qu'il chante, il passe l'écran.[14] (Sengissen 1963)

> [Il] se tire assez convenablement des embûches de son rôle d'essai[15] (Synchro 1963).

> [Il] ne s'en est pas mal tiré. Il a de l'allure, un manque d'assurance très sympathique.[16] (Chazal 1963)

The main charge against the film, unlike those of Rossi, was its juvenile flavour. As *Le Monde*'s reviewer commented, 'Johnny, c'est un peu Tintin qui aurait grandi et qui ne se couperait plus les cheveux. Chez l'un et l'autre la gentillesse, l'honnêteté morale,

---

[10] 'You've got a nice voice you know.'
[11] 'A slipper.'
[12] 'Acts as badly as Tino Rossi.'
[13] 'He's not disagreeable or too clumsy. He's been given dialogue pared down to his usual vocabulary.'
[14] 'He's no worse than anyone else would have been; he actually shows some promise; as soon as he sings, he has some presence on screen.'
[15] 'He gets through the traps of this first role reasonably well.'
[16] 'He manages quite well. He looks good and his lack of confidence is very endearing.'

l'astuce et l'esprit d'aventure sont les mêmes'[17] (Baroncelli 1963). The director, Noël Howard, made this clear in an interview (Ledieu 1963), saying that the film had been aimed at eight to eighteen-year-olds, which explains the lack of love scenes, something that the film was criticized for. The charge that the film was juvenile if not puerile underlines a key development in France's response to the development of 1960s youth culture, analysed by Morin, as we pointed out earlier: the recuperation of youth in revolt. *L'Aurore* announced that Hallyday would be playing 'un blouson noir gentil'[18] (*Aurore*, 1963); indeed, the word 'gentil' applied to Hallyday occurs frequently in press reviews. The preview of the film in L'Olympia in Paris took place on 15 October 1963 in the presence of four ministers, including Jean Sainteny, the minister for war veterans, and the proceeds from the sale of programmes were used for veterans' welfare (Le Pajolec 2009: 194). On the same day Hallyday and Vartan announced that they were almost engaged, which led one commentator to write that 'le twist se range du côté de la famille et de la patrie'[19] (Bory 1963), and another to say that the film was 'un bréviaire scout'[20] (Chapier 1963).

Part of the film's problem, as several commentators pointed out, was that it was made for a new generation by an older generation. Paule Sengissen lamented the fact that the writer of the scenario, Yvan Audouard, was 'rigoureusement incapable de comprendre le phénomène yéyé'[21] writing that Hallyday needed 'un scénariste de sa génération, un réalisateur astucieux comme Jacques Rozier'[22] (1963). The title of Jean Collet's article for the same magazine reiterates the problem: 'Les Idoles du yé-yé au cinéma de papa'[23] (1963). Jean-Louis Bory caustically remarked that the film's function was to recuperate a potentially dangerous youth culture: 'Cette peinture d'une jeunesse déplorablement conformiste, est d'une fadeur éprouvante. On eût souhaité de beaux éclats, de beaux élans, du rire, du feu. Hélas! C'est un film vieux. Un film de vieux, qui ont utilisé Johnny et Sylvie pour remettre la main sur la jeunesse'[24] (Bory 1963). It certainly seems odd to see Hallyday wrestling bulls and riding in pristine white jeans and jacket, demarcating him from those around him as the focal point of interest, but also suggesting a clean-cut image very different from the black leather jackets associated with the *blousons noirs*.

This tension is best exemplified in a sequence where the diegetic singing comments on the action. Magali's boyfriend, and Johnny's closest friend as a child, Django, in the film's subplot, is jealous of Johnny, believing that he will win Magali back, despite Magali's protestations that she and Johnny go way back and are just friends. This

---

[17] 'Johnny's a bit like a grown-up Tintin who has let his hair grow long. Both of them are friendly, morally upstanding, and the cleverness and spirit of adventure are the same.'
[18] 'A kind *blouson noir*.'
[19] 'The twist is aligning itself with the family and the nation.'
[20] 'A scout's prayer book.'
[21] 'Absolutely incapable of understanding the *yéyé* phenomenon.'
[22] 'A scriptwriter from his own generation, a clever director like Jacques Rozier.'
[23] 'The *yéyé* pop idols sell out to daddy's cinema.'
[24] 'This sketch of a deplorably conformist youth is testingly dull. You long for outbursts, effusions, laughter, fire. Alas! It's an old film. A film for old people, who have used Johnny and Sylvie to get a grip on youth.'

culminates in a stand-off between the two in a restaurant (1.15; see Figure 12.5). The guitarist Manitas de Plata is on stage with his flamenco group, and is joined by a very drunk Django. Johnny comes to take him back to Magali, but Django takes out his knife. Johnny walks slowly towards him as the flamenco singer comments on what is happening, and Django eventually drops the knife. The potentially hyper-melodramatic nature of the sequence is partially offset by a careful mix of low-angle and close-up shots in the cinematography, and the curiously stagey exoticism of the flamenco singer standing almost between them and commenting on the action. The dramatic tension is punctured when Johnny picks up a guitar and sings 'Ma guitare' ('My Guitar') in playback, the contrast between the flamenco and what sounds like a juke-box, as one reviewer wrote (Synchro 1963), demonstrating a potentially debilitating lack of talent.

But for us, this moment of the film marks a critical moment for the history of the French film musical. It demonstrates a tension between cinema and pop music: the sequence is set up to generate a highly dramatic moment of reckoning in narrative terms, and is all but ruined when Hallyday 'does' a song whose jaunty rhythm and vanilla lyrics undermine what could have been the kind of dramatic stand-off found in standard Hollywood Westerns, as can be seen from the first stanza: 'Ma guitare s'enflamme de joie/Quand tu es là/Ma guitare, fredonne en bleu/Devant tes grands yeux.'[25] The song is to all intents and purposes beside the point, functioning even more than might be normal in singer films as an unintegrated musical moment aimed at youth radio rather than cinema audiences. Indeed, Le Pajolec has suggested that *yéyé* music is more suited to emerging short forms, such as the Scopitone,[26] the forerunner of contemporary music videos (2009: 194); certainly the disjunction between dramatic flamenco and juke-box spectacle in this sequence demonstrates a critical transition.

Figure 12.5 Johnny and Django fight in *D'où viens-tu, Johnny?* (Courtesy René Chateau).

---

[25] 'My guitar burns with joy/When you are here/My guitar hums in blue/When I see your big eyes.'
[26] See Herzog (2007) for more on the Scopitone.

Isolated though this film may be as the only significant musical of the *yéyé*s, nonetheless it marks a significant shift in the development of the French film musical. It is the last of the singer-focused musicals that we have traced from the realist singers through to the jazz singers and then the Three Tenors. After this film, the film musical takes a modern turn with the films of Jacques Demy. With Jacques Demy, the musical became auteurist rather than popular, as had been the case with many of the films we have explored so far, and the musical moments more carefully integrated. In that sense, *D'où viens-tu, Johnny?* is past-facing but, paradoxically, also marks a critical historical transition, away from the film musical as it had developed since the 1930s, to the modern film musical that begins with the films of Jacques Demy. There were only four months between the release of *D'où viens-tu, Johnny?* in October 1963 and *Les Parapluies de Cherbourg* in February 1964; but in our view, everything changed in those four months.

13

Jacques Demy

Just at the time that the film musical appeared no longer to be in tune with the evolution of audience tastes, Jacques Demy renewed the genre, producing no less than six from the mid-1960s to the late 1980s; other directors connected with the New Wave and beyond flirted with the genre. Demy's best-known and by common accord most remarkable musicals are *Les Parapluies de Cherbourg*, which was considered innovative and very French, and *Les Demoiselles de Rochefort*, which is often seen as a homage to the Hollywood musical.

Selling 1.2 million tickets each, they attracted far fewer spectators than the spectacular musicals of the 1950s.[1] His later musicals, as, indeed, the other musicals by New Wave directors and beyond, were even less successful (Table 13.1). In this chapter we will focus principally on Demy's musicals, for three reasons: First, because they represent a significant moment in the evolution of the genre, as the musical focused on the singer changed to being the auteur musical; Demy wrote his own lyrics, and had what amounted to a repertory company around him, whether actors – Danielle Darrieux, Catherine Deneuve, Jean Marais, Jacques Perrin, Michel Piccoli – or other key personnel, such as Michel Legrand for the music, Bernard Évein for set design, Annie Maurel as script girl, Rosalie Varda for costumes; second, because Demy's musicals inspired many of the musicals made after 2000; and finally, because they changed from being an acquired taste where academic work is concerned, during his lifetime and in the decade after his death in 1990, to being of major interest since 2000. In this chapter, we will consider the films of Jacques Demy, and in the next chapter those of other directors connected with the New Wave, and some others (Table 13.1).

Prior to 2000, the standard works on Demy were biographical (Berthomé 1982, revised editions 1996 and 2014a; Taboulay 1996). Since then there have been a number of major studies (Bogart 2001; Boulangé 2007; Père 2010; Bouarour 2018), several of which explore Demy's work from a queer perspective (Duggan 2013; Waldron 2013; Hill 2014; Mulligan 2017), studies of specific films (Jullier 2007; Lefèvre 2013;

---

[1] By comparison, in 1964, there were 15 French films in the top-20 bestsellers, with the Louis de Funès comedy *Le Gendarme de Saint-Tropez* in first place with 7.8m tickets sold. In 1967 there were 16 French films in the top-20 best-sellers, with the Louis de Funès comedy *Les Grandes Vacances* in first place with 7m tickets sold.

Table 13.1 Film Musicals by New Wave Directors and Others

Une femme est une femme	1961	Jean-Luc Godard	0.6m
Les Parapluies de Cherbourg	1964	Jacques Demy	1.2m
Les Demoiselles de Rochefort	1967	Jacques Demy	1.2m
Les Idoles	1968	Marc d'O	Not known
Peau d'âne	1970	Jacques Demy	2.2m
Chobizenesse	1975	Jean Yanne	0.6m
L'une chante, l'autre pas	1977	Agnès Varda	0.3m
Tous vedettes!	1980	Michel Lang	Not known
Une chambre en ville	1982	Jacques Demy	0.2m
Sandy	1983	Michel Nerval	Not known
Paroles et musique	1984	Élie Chouraqui	1.7m
Parking	1985	Jacques Demy	0.1m
Golden Eighties	1986	Chantal Akerman	Not known
Trois places pour le 26	1988	Jacques Demy	0.3m
Rendez-vous au tas de sable	1990	Didier Grousset	0.09m
Haut bas fragile	1995	Jacques Rivette	0.05m

Guillamaud 2014), a journal special number and an exhibition in 2013,[2] as well as many journal articles (e.g. Lazen 2004; Becker and Williams 2008; Hill 2008a, b; Henneton 2012; Virtue 2013, 2016) and significant book chapters (Lindeperg and Marshall 2000; Stilwell 2003; Herzog 2010, Peacock 2010). This explosion of academic work is, as Nick Rees-Roberts has suggested (2008: 109), partly due to a revival of interest in Demy's work by gay directors, their work being strongly marked by Demy's signature themes, such as bisexual romance, and signature mise en scène, such as the use of intense colour schemes. It is also partly due to the promotion of his work by his wife, Agnès Varda, both in film – her *Jacquot de Nantes* (1991) is a film version of his autobiographical notebooks, her *Les Demoiselles ont eu 25 ans* (1993) is a documentary in which the original cast return to Rochefort, and *L'Univers de Jacques Demy* (1995) is a documentary about her late husband's life and cinema – and in the curation of the complete films of Demy in a DVD box set (2008), which made his films available to a wider public.[3]

In terms of their place in the history of the French film musical, Demy's musicals are a coherent and extensive body of work at a key point in the evolution of the genre towards a more atomized, but also more 'auteurized', modern form. Whereas the musicals of the pre-1960s period focused largely on the singers, especially in the case of the Three Tenors, with Demy there was a substantive and sudden transition away from the singer towards the auteur-director, consonant with the *politique des auteurs* espoused by the *Cahiers du Cinéma*. As a result, standard works on his films use wordplay to emphasize the coherence of Demy's 'world', which is a 'Demy-monde'

---

[2] 'Le monde enchanté de Jacques Demy', exhibition at Cinémathèque française-Musée du cinéma, Paris, 10 April–4 August 2013.
[3] Although this also led Jean-Pierre Berthomé to complain about the skewed 'reinvention' of Demy by Varda (Berthomé (2014b)).

'en-chanté'; appropriately given the auteurist turn, we even find the pun 'Demy-urge' (Anderson 2013: 99). The pun 'en-chanté', used by Demy himself, is a play on the idea of singing – 'chanter' – and that of fairy-tale 'enchantment'; the notion of a 'Demy-monde' plays on the term 'demi-monde', and it contrasts starkly with the idea of the fairy tale. As Robynn Stilwell explains, the term 'carries with it connotations of twilight and shade, of alluring sin, of the hard, real exchange of sex and money that still does not preclude romance and love' (2003: 123).

Most major studies of Demy's films incorporate work on his musicals as part of a broader approach focused on all of his films. A major disadvantage of this approach is that the later musicals are treated more cursorily than the early and more successful musicals. In what follows, we will show how the three later musicals reprise the narratives and themes of the first three as Demy attempted to replicate their success. While this does not change the standard view of his late musicals that they are in general considerably less successful than the early musicals, it does confirm an obsessive authorial interest in specific themes as well as an intensification of the melancholic nostalgic gesture already in evidence in the first three musicals.[4]

Les Parapluies de Cherbourg is arguably Demy's best-known film, as the number of books specifically devoted to it suggests (Berthomé 1995; Jullier 2007; Guillamaud 2014), and arguably the best-known French film musical, 'probably the only non-English-language musical that could be considered part of the generic canon' (Stilwell 2003: 129). It won both the Prix Louis Delluc in 1963 and the Palme d'Or in Cannes in 1964, as well as being nominated for five Oscars in 1966; French reviews were almost entirely positive (Mulligan 2017: 214–5). The film is unusual in that all dialogue is sung, with very few set pieces as would normally be found in standard musicals; 'J'attendrai' ('If it Takes Forever') is 'the most melodically distinctive' song (Stilwell 2003: 132). The decision to make a through-sung film was in part because Demy and composer Michel Legrand wished to make something approaching a 'popular' opera film. As Demy commented, 'je ne crois pas à l'opéra pour faire un film populaire parce qu'on ne comprend pas ce qui s'y dit. Essayons de trouver un équivalent de l'opéra au cinéma où chaque mot soit compréhensible, clair'[5] (in Berthomé 1995: 15), and Legrand emphasized that they had to avoid the 'operatic', leading to something more akin to the *parlé-chanté* that we have already seen in some of the film musicals from the 1930s. There is an ironic reference to one of the standard French operas in *Les Parapluies de Cherbourg*, when Guy tells his friends that he and Geneviève will be attending *Carmen*, to which one of his friends responds: 'J'aime pas l'opéra. Le ciné c'est mieux.'[6] The film is also unusual in that despite Demy's wish to make a 'realist' musical, there is a strong emphasis on saturated, non-realist colours that are used to code the narrative and the characters (Peacock 2010; Mulligan 2017: 220–6), and whose brooding interiors echo

---

[4] Demy's first feature *Lola* was originally intended to be a musical in colour.
[5] 'I do not believe you can use opera to make a popular film because you can't understand what is said. Let's try to find a version of opera in cinema where each word would be comprehensible, clear.'
[6] 'I don't like opera. Cinema is better.'

Vincente Minnelli's musicals (Stilwell 2003). Unlike Hollywood musicals, however, Legrand's music is eclectic, ranging across a variety of contemporary musical styles: 'Swing, big band, rythmes afro-cubains, héritage post-romantique, réminiscences baroques, chanson même'[7] (Berthomé 1995: 41).

Rather like Varda's *Cléo de 5 à 7* (1962), *Les Parapluies de Cherbourg* focuses on a young woman and her relationship with a man who either is already a soldier fighting in the Algerian War in the case of Varda's film or becomes one in Demy's case; indeed, the structure of the film depends closely on the War with its three subtitled parts ('Departure', 'Absence', 'Return'). Unlike other films that alluded to the Algerian War, however, Demy chose not to focus on a particular moment, such as the days before the departure, as Jacques Rozier did in *Adieu Philippine* (1963), or the difficulty in returning to everyday life, as was the case in Alain Resnais's *Muriel ou le temps d'un retour* (1963) or Robert Enrico's *La Belle Vie* (1964). Instead, the film charts the gradual destruction of the two lovers' idyll by war. Car mechanic Guy (Nino Castelnuovo) loves Geneviève (Catherine Deneuve), the young daughter of a single mother who owns an umbrella shop. They plan to marry, but he is drafted to Algeria; she discovers she is pregnant and eventually marries a rich older man and moves to Paris. When Guy returns, he marries Madeleine who had been secretly in love with him before. In the bittersweet ending of the film Guy and Geneviève meet again by chance, both with their young children, but go their separate ways.

The through-sung music emphasizes the melancholic aspects of the romance and the claustrophobia of the mise en scène. There are no exuberant and utopian expressions of joy as we might have expected in Hollywood musicals; there is, rather, an insidious gnawing away of happiness by the quotidian realities of life. The film's interweaving of 22 leitmotivic themes not only underscores the dystopian aspect of a lost romance and the physical cost of the Algerian War in the background (Guy returns with a limp), but also manages to 'juxtapose past and present, recall the past in the present, anticipate the future, accompany the protagonists' hopes, contrastively undermine their reality' (Lindeperg and Marshall 2000: 103). The interweaving also functions like a musical web in which the characters are caught, as much as they are by the saturated claustrophobic interiors. Melancholia, dystopia, confinement, nostalgia are the defining features of the film, as they will be in varying ways for the other musicals by Demy.

Les Demoiselles de Rochefort by contrast appears very different. It opens with a vibrant dance by the troupe of travelling players in Rochefort's town square, Place Colbert. Twin sisters Delphine (Deneuve) and Solange (Françoise Dorléac, Deneuve's sister in real life) are the 'demoiselles' of the title, both dreaming of Mr Right and a move to Paris; they perform a number at the fair (1.34) which is a direct reference to Marilyn Monroe and Jane Russell's duo 'Two Girls from Little Rock' in *Gentlemen*

---

[7] 'Swing, big band, Afro-Cuban rhythms, post-romantic, baroque inflections, French *chanson*.' Berthomé analyses the themes in considerable detail (1995: 41–52).

Prefer Blondes (Howard Hawks, 1953; Figure 13.1); at the end of the film they leave for Paris with the fair. The twins' mother, Yvonne (Danielle Darrieux), runs a café where various characters meet. She longs for Simon (Michel Piccoli) whom she left ten years before and who unbeknownst to her has just opened a music shop in Rochefort. Demobbed sailor Maxence (Jacques Perrin), who is a painter, dreams of his ideal woman who from one of his paintings we realize is Delphine. Solange meets Andy (Gene Kelly), an old friend of Simon who has travelled to Rochefort to visit him. The film interweaves the romances between these various couples (Yvonne–Simon, Solange–Andy, Delphine–Maxence).

Although both of Demy's early musicals are located in the provinces (Cherbourg and Rochefort, respectively), and both have Demy's signature use of colour, *Les Demoiselles de Rochefort* is mostly filmed in sunny exteriors as opposed to *Les Parapluies de Cherbourg*'s claustrophobic interiors, and has set-piece dance and song-and-dance sequences as opposed to the earlier film's reliance on singing only. The cameo appearances of Gene Kelly in the film, along with George Chakiris and Grover Dale from *West Side Story* as part of the dance troupe, point the film more firmly in the direction of the Hollywood musical than did *Les Parapluies de Cherbourg*, especially the Donen-Kelly musicals *On the Town* (1950) and *An American in Paris* (1951). Sailors appear in Kelly's cameo street scene, echoing *On the Town* (Becker and Williams 2008: 310) and 'the opening gestures of Andy and Solange's pas de deux in the music shop are lifted from "Our Love Is Here to Stay" on the banks of the Seine in *An American in Paris*' (Stilwell 2003: 136). In some respects, the film may appear then to be a regression to the 'mean' represented by the Hollywood musical, yet another attempt, as critics were fond of saying in the 1930s, to replicate the success of the Hollywood musical.

Figure 13.1 Echoes of *Gentlemen Prefer Blondes* in *Les Demoiselles de Rochefort* (Courtesy of 20th Century Fox and Arte Éditions).

In our view this is not the case; rather, the film is clearly a complex homage, as many critics have pointed out (see, for example, the title of Diane Henneton's 2012 article); but it is also a pastiche of the tropes of the Hollywood musical. Following Georgia Mulligan (2017) we are using the word 'pastiche' in Richard Dyer's sense of a knowing imitation that does not necessarily distance us from the work; rather, pastiche

> imitates formal means that are themselves ways of evoking, moulding, and eliciting feeling, and thus in the process is able to mobilise feelings even while signalling that it is doing so. Thereby it can, at its best, allow us to feel our connection to the affective frameworks, the structures of feeling, past and present, that we inherit and pass on. That is to say, it can enable us to know ourselves affectively as historical beings. (2007: 180)

Les Demoiselles de Rochefort quite clearly signals its relationship to the Hollywood musical while differentiating itself. It is a backstage musical without a proper stage and almost unrehearsed: we only see occasional rehearsals, and they occur in exteriors rather than in a studio. The show itself is less like a show, even from the French point of view with its history of backstage film musicals located in music halls, than it is a traditional open-air *fête foraine*, with various song-and-dance activities going on, such as a stylized basketball display, a chorus of young girls dressed in sailors' costumes backing ballet dancers, dancers representing a boat company, then a Honda stand which is used for the twins' Monroe-Russell routine 'Chanson d'un jour d'été' (Summer's Day Song'). The choice of Danielle Darrieux as the owner of the café around which much of the film revolves forcefully recalls the tradition of the 1930s French film musicals in which she starred.

Then, as Stilwell astutely points out, the multiple couple pairings mentioned earlier are an exploration and deconstruction of 'the generic traits of couple-formation' (2003: 134) familiar in Rick Altman's theorization of the Hollywood musical as a dual-focus narrative that keeps the couple apart before bringing them together in the happy-end climax. In *Les Demoiselles de Rochefort* there are three couples: the older couple formed by Yvonne and Simon's story is set in the past, and they do meet at the end of the film, as do Solange and Andy. On the other hand, the meeting between Delphine and idealistic dreamer Maxence is only hinted at as the two of them leave Rochefort. It is tempting to see these examples as deficient relative to the Hollywood musical, as does Stilwell when she comments on the music and the dancing. For her, Legrand's 'song-like' melodies diminish the 'energy that comes from extended syncopations, asymmetrical rhythms, and dissonant intervals' (Stilwell 2003: 136) that we find in Bernstein's music for *West Side Story*; Norman Maen's choreography for *Les Demoiselles de Rochefort*, while borrowing from Jerome Robbins's work for the Donen-Kelly musicals, does so 'unimaginatively' (2003: 136); and Dale and Chakiris's energetic dance style is in tension with the lacklustre choreography as it is with 'Legrand's narrow-gauge flowing music' (2003: 137). Even Berthomé expresses considerable disappointment with the choreography, saying that Maen clearly feels uncomfortable dealing with the vast space of Rochefort's square, and that the choreography in more intimate spaces lacks inspiration or originality (2014a: 199). The twins' duet after the ballet class they have given to the children in their apartment is a good example of these tensions. Presented as an energetic 'number' in Hollywood musical style as they sing directly to the camera and use musical props (piano, trumpet), Deneuve and Dorléac's 'dancing' is little more than restricted movements into model-like poses; and the song itself is somewhat jarringly interrupted by *parlé-chanté* as the twins talk about collecting Boubou from school, before a final sung stanza. In some ways it is hardly surprising that Pauline Kael considered that the film showed how 'a gifted Frenchman who adores American musicals misunderstands their conventions' (Kael 1994: 208).

The other way of looking at this supposed misunderstanding is to accept that Demy's film is certainly a homage but also a pastiche, a playful deconstruction of the Hollywood musical, similar in this respect to our comments on the relationship between *La crise est finie* and *Gold Diggers of 1933* in Chapter 3. The dialogue and song lyrics, written by Demy, are occasionally and for no obvious reason in the noble poetic form of the alexandrine with its two hemistiches of six syllables, much to Legrand's chagrin: 'Il n'y a rien de pire car l'alexandrin a une espèce de régularité rythmique qu'il faut s'ingénier à briser'[8] (in Berthomé 2014a: 196); the form is particularly out of place in a dinner party sequence (1.24). Further instances of Demy's playfulness are the puns and wordplay scattered throughout the dialogue. Frequently cited in academic work is the pun combining Demy's favourite town, Nantes, and Maxence's leave, 'je vais en perm' à Nantes', sounding like the word 'permanent', the idea of permanency being the exact opposite of his status as a sailor on leave. Demy's playfulness extends to a self-deprecating awareness of the lameness of the pun as Maxence repeats and comments on it subsequently, saying 'ça ne vous fait pas rire du tout' to Solange who responds 'c'est de l'esprit de quatre sous'.[9]

And then, finally, we could argue that Demy's film has a darker side than this playfulness might have suggested, which also deconstructs the utopian nature of the Hollywood musical: one of the minor characters in the café is a quiet retiree, Monsieur Dutrouz; he turns out to be the axe-murderer who is referred to in the newspaper and commented on by patrons of the café. As Dutrouz murdered the woman he loved when she spurned him, this makes the film veer towards the grisly horror genre of *grand guignol* as Stilwell tentatively suggests (2003: 135). He is not the only dark character of the film, however. Guillaume Lancien, the pretentious owner of an art gallery lusts after Solange. His name recalls that of the gentleman criminal Lacenaire from Marcel Carné's *Les Enfants du paradis* (1945); indeed, at one point, Lancien quotes Carné's character.

However much *Les Demoiselles de Rochefort* is indebted to the Hollywood musical, it is also a very French affair in its surreal use of language, its deliberate nods to French cinema and theatrical traditions, and the eclectically French score by Legrand. The glossy surface of the Hollywood musical is not just intertwined with 'Frenchness' and

---

[8] 'There's nothing worse because the Alexandrine has a kind of rhythmical regularity that you have to work hard to break.'
[9] 'It doesn't make you laugh at all./It's second-rate.'

apparently amateurish choreography; it is lovingly and subtly subverted as a glaze is crackled or crazed, the effect in ceramics being due to 'critical tensile stresses in the coating ... caused by a mismatch of the thermal expansion coefficient of the glaze and the body' (McColm 1984: 117). This metaphor functions well to explain the way in which *Les Demoiselles de Rochefort* is as fundamentally French as *Les Parapluies de Cherbourg*; its 'Americanness' is all surface, and that surface is 'crazed' by the French tensions introduced by Demy and Legrand. The twins' number at the *fête foraine* illustrates this point (Figure 13.1): the twins are dressed more or less to resemble Monroe and Russell, and like them they sing on a stage; but their stage allows us to see cars through the back curtain, and shots of the crowd remind us of the very European and Brueghelian trope of the community brought together in a traditional festivity. This is less the Hollywood folk musical, with its focus on community, than a pull towards realism characteristic of Demy's musicals, even when they appear at first sight to be no more than fantasy, as is the case with *Peau d'âne*.

Peau d'âne returns us to a very French context, as it is a reworking of a traditional fairy tale by Charles Perrault (1628–1703) dating from 1694. With its questionable focus on incest (a key component of the original fairy tale), it is a fairy tale as much for adults as for children. Demy follows Perrault's tale closely: after his wife's death, the King of the Blue Kingdom (Jean Marais) falls in love with his daughter, the Princess (Catherine Deneuve) and insists on marrying her. She seeks the advice of the Lilac Fairy (Delphine Seyrig) who counsels her to set as a condition the making of three wedding dresses. When the King manages to fulfil these conditions, the Princess asks him for the skin of the donkey that defecates gold; with some reluctance he does so, and the Princess escapes into the forest wearing the skin as a disguise. She is seen by the Prince of the Red Kingdom (Jacques Perrin) who falls in love with her, and she bakes a cake in which she places a ring for him. The Prince's father (Fernand Ledoux) proclaims that the Prince will marry the woman whose finger can fit the ring, leading to the wedding of the Prince and Princess.

As was the case with *Les Demoiselles de Rochefort*, *Peau d'âne* is shot through with references to Hollywood films and American culture more generally. Disney's *Snow White and the Seven Dwarfs* (1937) was the first film Demy saw as a child, and he pointed out how the cake-baking sequence (0.59) was inspired by that film (Berthomé 2014a: 245). The Fairy's dress with its high collar echoes that of Disney's Queen, the glass coffin used in *Peau d'âne* for the Princess's mother recalls that used for Snow White, and the Princess singing 'Amour amour' by a well with perching doves in the castle courtyard (0.9) is a nod to Snow White fetching water from the well with similarly perching doves, although in each case, as can be seen from Figure 13.2, Demy exaggerates the echo, either by changing the shapes (a round glass coffin, Donkey Skin's exaggeratedly 'medieval' dress, the Lilac Fairy's elongated collar) or by insisting on colour (the Lilac Fairy's very lilac collar, her anachronistic Jean Harlow hair colour and hairdo, the use of characters with blue or red skin).[10] Demy's exposure to pop

---

[10] For this and other intertextual references, see Waldron (2013: 88–90).

Figure 13.2 References to *Snow White and the Seven Dwarfs* in *Peau d'âne* (Courtesy of Walt Disney and Arte Éditions).

and psychedelic culture in his two-year stay in Los Angeles no doubt influenced the intensification of an existing sensitivity to colour coding (see Pace 2013): the Blue Kingdom's service personnel and horses are coloured blue, while the Red Kingdom's are coloured red, signifying a key binary for Demy: 'D'un côté le sang royal, le sang bleu, conservateur; et de l'autre cette espèce de prince un peu révolutionnaire et tout cet univers rouge'[11] (in Berthomé 2014a: 243).

There are also clear references to French films, principally Jean Cocteau's first two films: Jean Marais who plays the Blue King recalls the Beast of Cocteau's fairy tale *La Belle et la Bête* (1946), as do the frequent use of mirrors and slow motion

---

[11] 'On the one hand royal blood, blue blood, conservative; on the other the sort of revolutionary prince and all that red universe.'

(see Taboulay 1996: 100; Berthomé 2014a: 246), while a specific scene, that of the Prince being advised by a rose that speaks through a mouth (0.45) recalls the mouth in the palm of a hand from the surreal *Le Sang d'un poète* (1932). These major intertextual references quite clearly queer the film, pulling it towards icons of French gay culture, as several recent studies have pointed out (Duggan 2013: 46–50; Rosenthal 2013). As we shall see, Cocteau's later film based on the Orpheus myth is recalled in Demy's *Parking* in which Marais plays a similar role to that of the Blue King and the Beast.

But these echoes form part of a much more complex web of apparently incompatible and playful anachronistic contrasts. Characters mentioned in passing at the trying on of the ring (1.12) are historical and literary characters recognizable to a French audience. These historical references jostle alongside the extracts from modern poems the Blue King reads to the Princess by those he calls 'les poètes de demain':[12] Cocteau's *Ode à Picasso* (1919) that playfully evokes the Ancient Muses using modern utensils, followed by an extract from 'L'Amour' (Love) by Guillaume Apollinaire (1899). The Lilac Fairy is associated with modern technology: she has a telephone, she compares her diminishing powers to a fading light bulb, and she arrives with the Blue King at the Prince and Princess's wedding in a helicopter. Costumes and music, as Berthomé points out (2014a: 248), mix periods and styles: the Princess and the Queen wear eighteenth-century costumes while the Prince wears early-sixteenth-century costumes; the Blue King's costume with exaggeratedly large shoulders is designed to remind us of Cocteau's Beast, while the Red King's doctors and the peasants are dressed in seventeenth-century costumes. As was the case with *Les Demoiselles de Rochefort*, Legrand mixes musical styles (baroque, jazz and pop) and musical references (Disney-like glissandos on the harp for the Lilac Fairy, echoes of Georges Auric's score for Cocteau's *La Belle et la Bête* for the three dresses) to match the confusing temporalities of the costumes.

Finally, Demy's use of stars complicates the issue even more. While it was inconceivable that adult audiences would not have been aware of the queer implications of the Cocteau–Marais references, it is equally inconceivable that they would have been unaware of the implications of perversity publicly connoted by Deneuve, who had her first child with Roger Vadim at the age of nineteen in 1963, and had starred as the schizophrenic murderess in *Repulsion* (Roman Polanski, 1965) (see Downing 2007), and as the perverse high-class prostitute of *Belle de jour* (Luis Buñuel, 1967) (see Evans 2007), which won the Golden Lion in Venice. Demy turns the passive heroine into a more active potentially feminist Princess, in that she 'unlocks' the Prince's desire rather than the other way round, but also into a woman who appears to be tempted by her father's offer of marriage (Weiner 2007), giving her modern agency as well as a perverse twist. Seyrig's star persona was, like Deneuve and Marais, associated with auteurist directors; she had starred in two iconic 'art' films by Alain Resnais: *L'Année dernière à Marienbad* (1961) and *Muriel ou le temps d'un retour* (1963), as well as playing a smaller role as a prostitute in a film by Buñuel, *La Voie lactée* (1969). Her role

---

[12] 'Tomorrow's poets.'

in *L'Année dernière à Marienbad* in particular, as a mysterious woman whom the man of the narrative may or may not have slept with and may or may not have raped, inflect *Peau d'âne* towards a meditation on fantasy and its relationship with historical time. In that respect, the film is an ironic, tongue-in-cheek comment on women's roles in the kind of traditional narrative represented by the fairy tale.

Much like *Peau d'âne*, Demy's next musical was a cherished project which he started in 1955 as a novel, and resurrected twenty years later; but his preferred collaborators decided not to take part, Legrand because he did not like the story, Deneuve because she wanted to sing her role rather than be dubbed as she had been in the three previous musicals by Demy, Gérard Depardieu because Deneuve backed out (Berthomé 2014a: 294–9). They were eventually replaced by Michel Colombier, Dominique Sanda and Richard Berry. As Geoff Andrew pointed out much later, the changes in personnel, coupled with 'the background – a violent dockers' strike – to the tale of a doomed adulterous amour fou' (2011: 19) meant that the film not only did not do well in France, but remains little known outside of France. And yet, as Andrew says, 'this dark, deliriously intense liebestod' has 'truly operatic power' (2011: 19). The action is concentrated in a 48-hour period: the dockers of Nantes are on strike, one of their leaders being François Guilbaud (Berry) who has made his girlfriend Violette pregnant. She believes that he will marry her, but François meets Édith (Sanda), unhappily married to television shop owner Edmond (Michel Piccoli), and, unbeknownst to him, the daughter of his landlady, Margot Langlois (Danielle Darrieux). They enjoy a night of passion, and the next day, François breaks with Violette, as does Édith with Edmond, who slits his throat in front of her. The three women meet up in the apartment and watch as François is shot during the demonstration in the street outside; brought up to the apartment, he dies and Édith kills herself.

The film is anchored in the past. The strikes in Nantes that form the background to the story occurred in 1955, as a caption makes clear at the start of the film. The doomed hero François who dies in an apartment after being shot by the police is a clear echo of *Le jour se lève* (Marcel Carné, 1939), and the shot of the dead lovers lying side by side of the Cocteau-scripted *L'Éternel Retour* (Jean Delannoy, 1943) starring Jean Marais. The location of the film in Nantes reminds us of Demy's breakthrough film *Lola*, and several elements echo *Les Parapluies de Cherbourg*: the through-sung score, the claustrophobic interiors (designed by Bernard Évein in both films), the single mother (here there are two, Édith's mother and Violette's mother), the pregnant daughter, the dystopian trajectory. With the exception of the songs sung by the strikers at the beginning and the end of the film, the score is, in fact, even more through-sung than *Les Parapluies de Cherbourg* in a kind of permanent recitative, even though there are some twenty recognizable motifs. As Berthomé points out, these motifs circulate between characters rather than being leitmotifs (2014a: 347), so that the music hems the characters in a web. The political songs sung by the strikers at the start and at the end have the same effect: the situation naturalizes the singing – strikers often do sing songs – but the book-end nature of these songs also serves to enclose the melodramatic action so that the characters are in more ways than one boxed in.

Similarly, the mise en scène crushes the characters: Évein's design accentuates the bourgeois interior of Margot's apartment partly through the saturated colours, but also by bringing the ceiling down by a metre (Berthomé 2014a: 338). His use of colour also contributes to the oppressive feel of the film, the most striking example of this being the lurid greens of Edmond's shop and clothes (0.27), which contribute to the film's 'feeling of simmering madness and sadness' (Mulligan 2017: 250). Margot's apartment is a mausoleum, its plush carpets and heavy furniture emphasizing the tomb-like space with its tributes to a vanished way of life for the widowed Margot, abandoned by the death of her husband and the suicide of their son.

The melodramatic sense of oppression is paralleled by the background of political oppression. The serried ranks of strikers confronting similarly serried ranks of CRS recalls *Le jour se lève*, as well as the events of May 1968, making this film the most political of Demy's musicals; indeed, Danielle Darrieux's character, Margot, a penniless Baroness, living in a very bourgeois apartment, paradoxically makes clear to François what had only been implied in Demy's previous films, a loathing of bourgeois propriety and attraction to what the French call 'le peuple': 'J'emmerde les bourgeois, je ne leur appartiens pas.'[13]

Une chambre en ville and *Les Parapluies de Cherbourg* are both through-sung dystopian musicals. *Parking*, Demy's next musical, is closely related to *Peau d'âne* by its anchoring in myth and the presence of Jean Marais in an authoritarian patriarchal role, the Blue King in the earlier film and Hades in *Parking*. Like several other films by Demy, Cocteau is referred to not just in the dedication, which alludes to fairy-tale narratives – 'À Jean Cocteau qui aimait ces mots magiques: "Il était une fois ..."'[14] – but also in the very clear parallels between Demy's film and Cocteau's *Orphée* (1950). *Parking* has the characteristics of a backstage musical, as we see Orpheus (Francis Huster), who is in this version of the myth a pop star, rehearsing his songs and giving two concerts. Eurydice (Keïko Ito) is a sculptress who dies of a drug overdose rather than a serpent's bite. In the myth Orpheus is killed by the Maenads because he has switched his allegiance from Dionysus to Apollo; in the film they are coded as lesbians, laughably enraged because Orpheus has failed to give them the tickets he promised for his concert. Hell is represented by an underground parking in which there is a stereotypical office reception with computers; the colour scheme for Hell involved a laboratory process that decolourized all hues except red, with the result that red objects shine brightly almost like neon lights in an otherwise desaturated environment in which everything else is a variant of pallid green. These were not the only unfortunate choices Demy was obliged to make for reasons of cost. Francis Huster as Orpheus was allowed to sing his own songs, with disastrous results: it is difficult to believe in Orpheus's success as a pop star when he frequently sings out of tune, with little vocal projection, accompanied by peculiar facial distortions.

---

[13] 'Fuck the bourgeoisie, I don't belong with them.'
[14] 'For Jean Cocteau who liked the magic words: "Once upon a time ...".'

Figure 13.3 'Entre vous deux': the bisexual moment in *Parking*'s recording studio (Courtesy of Arte Éditions).

The major development in *Une chambre en ville* was its political overtones; *Parking* too shows a clear development in that non-heteronormative relationships previously only hinted at in the most oblique way in earlier films, for example, in the frequent references to Cocteau and Marais, are here on display: it is suggested that Orpheus is bisexual, torn between Eurydice and his sound engineer Calaïs (Laurent Malet). We see Orpheus and Calaïs sharing loving smiles as he sings 'Entre vous deux' ('Between the Two of You') in the studio (0.32; Figure 13.3), the song very clearly alluding to Orpheus being caught between Eurydice and Calaïs (see Berthomé 2014a: 379–81 for an extended analysis of the song, which he considers the best song of the film). Later Orpheus and Calaïs kiss during the party after the first concert (0.56), although this idyllic moment is melodramatically undermined: Orpheus returns home immediately after the studio session to find that Eurydice has overdosed. Mulligan points out that the film seems to be pushing us to the assumption that the kiss between the two men is 'the film's disaster, which precedes or somehow precipitates a sequence of accidents and deaths, in line with the film's subtextual engagement with AIDS' (2017: 137).

Demy's final musical, *Trois places pour le 26*, is the most Hollywoodian of the six. A backstage musical, it stars Yves Montand as himself returning to his home city Marseille to stage an autobiographical stage musical; the title refers to three tickets for the show for Marion (Mathilda May) who works in a perfume shop, and two of her friends. In keeping with one of the standard narratives of the backstage musical, Montand's stage partner falls ill, and is replaced by Marion. Unknown to either Montand or Marion, Marion is his daughter by Mylène (Françoise Fabian), his first love, who still lives in Marseille. Marion triumphs and in a reprise of the incest theme of *Peau d'âne*, father and daughter make love after the show. Their conversation in the morning reveals who they really are to each other. But there is no drama; Marion takes her mother to the train station to meet Montand and the three of them leave for Paris where the show will be staged.

Apart from the beginning and end of the film which take place in exteriors outside the train station – and which recall the opening scenes of *Les Demoiselles de Rochefort* – the film was shot in studios, recalling the great Hollywood musicals of the 1940s and 1950s. Like them, and unlike Demy's earlier musicals with *parlé-chanté*, the film has a series of song-and-dance set pieces. One of the early songs, 'Ciné qui chante' ('Cinema that Sings'; 0.22) recalls Hollywood musicals both in its mise en scène and in quotations from well-known musicals, such as when Montand, in hat and tails like Astaire, dances tap and sings 'Singin' in the Rain', then 'Heaven, I'm in heaven, and my heart beats' from 'Cheek to Cheek' in *Top Hat* (Mark Sandrich, 1935). We see him watching a blonde doing a Marilyn Monroe impersonation as she sings 'I wanna be loved by you' from *Some Like It Hot* (Billy Wilder, 1959), and then 'Je ne pourrai jamais vivre sans toi' from the title song of Demy's first musical, *Les Parapluies de Cherbourg*, with a final line 'ce que je préfère c'est le musical'[15]. Michel Legrand commented in a DVD interview that he and Demy 'wanted to make a real musical, in truly American style' (cited in Henneton 2012: 226).

However, as both Henneton and Berthomé (2014a: 397–400) point out, Demy plays with the codes of the Hollywood musical. The musical numbers are generally motivated by the action and the dancing is similarly contained within realist space, recalling Demy's attachment to quotidian reality, most in evidence in his first two musicals. There is a startling blur between reality and fantasy in the use of Montand, who plays himself in what is a faithful account of his autobiography, but this 'reality' is inserted in a fictional and stereotypical Hollywood-style musical. As Henneton points out, this is further complicated by the fact that on stage Montand plays the role of Montand, but he becomes Demy's fictional character when off-stage. The final irony is that the musical functions on the principle of uniting the heterosexual couple; but the couple constituted by the film is not the father-daughter couple which has been at the forefront of the action through the film, but the father-mother couple who are brought back together right at the end of the film, not having seen each other prior to the conclusion.

The film is Demy's most nostalgic; it is nostalgic for the Hollywood musicals it alludes to as it plays with their conventions, but it is also nostalgic for Demy's own work. The most telling, and in our view the best number of the film, is the extraordinary 'Lorsqu'on revient' ('When You Come Home'), which is as quiet and reflective as 'Ciné qui chante' is noisily exuberant. Whereas in the latter number, there are nods to Hollywood musicals, replete with sailors passing in the background, in the former song Montand, singing a cappella to start with, laments the passing of time. The two songs encapsulate the two sides of Demy, both rooted in nostalgia, but with one looking back melancholically on time past, the other exulting in the expression of present joy (Figure 13.4).

---

[15] 'I prefer the film musical.'

Figure 13.4 Versions of the past: 'Lorsqu'on revient' (left) and 'Ciné qui chante' (right) in *Trois places pour le 26* (Courtesy of Arte Éditions).

Table 13.2 The Six Musicals of Jacques Demy

Les Parapluies de Cherbourg	through-sung dystopian	*Une chambre en ville*
Les Demoiselles de Rochefort	integrated backstage utopian	*Trois places pour le 26*
Peau d'âne	fairy-tale myth & Marais	*Parking*

Demy's six musicals form a coherent body of work, suffused with the themes and tropes found in all of his films. As a group the last three mirror the first three (Table 13.2). *Les Parapluies de Cherbourg* and *Une chambre en ville* are both through-sung musicals, impregnated with a dystopian vision, whose backdrop is political unrest (the Algerian War in the first, popular strikes in the second). Both *Les Demoiselles de Rochefort* and *Trois places pour le 26* both play with the conventions of the Hollywood musical, and integrate well-known stars as part of their fabric (Kelly, in the first, Montand in the second). And then finally, the other two musicals are both based on well-known tales, and both have gay icon Jean Marais at their heart.

Other directors of the period, whether connected with the New Wave or not, flirted with the musical, as we shall see in the next chapter. But Demy's engagement with the genre– six of his thirteen feature films are musicals – is a major moment in the genre's history. Coming at a moment when the New Wave insisted on authorial status for the director, Demy's musicals not only rebooted the genre, but also reinvented it. They brought to the fore the inevitability of the genre's relationship with the Hollywood musical, prevalent in many French film musicals as we have seen, while also teasingly undermining it in a number of ways: the constant reminders of the Hollywood musical, whether, for example, through specific American personnel in *Les Demoiselles de Rochefort* or with quotations from Hollywood films in *Trois places pour le 26* never dilute the 'Frenchness' of Demy's musicals. Demy's playful lyrics, Legrand's Gallicization of American musical tropes, and provincial locations all embed the musicals in a very French context. Then, as Mulligan points out, his musicals exaggerate the campness of the Hollywood film musical, through excessive costume in *Peau d'âne* and Demy/Évein-specific décor and colours. Although the following comments by Mulligan are made in relation to *Les Demoiselles de Rochefort*, it can be argued that they apply to all of Demy's musicals, which are 'focused on performance rather than essence, surface rather than depth' and as a result make 'visible the mechanisms through which the American musical constructs heterosexuality' (Mulligan 2017: 162–3).

Unlike the films of the New Wave directors, which as Geneviève Sellier argues (2008), are masculinist in intent and execution – as can be seen from the importance of the crime genre for many of the directors – Demy's musicals are 'perverse' (a term frequently used for his films by critics). They engage with more women-oriented genres, particularly the combination of melodrama and musical in the films we have been exploring. They have therefore been seen as more marginal, both in terms of their relationship to the New Wave – Demy, along with Varda, Marker and Resnais, are usually termed 'Left Bank' New Wave to distinguish them and their preoccupations from the *Cahiers* New Wave – and in terms of French film history more generally. It is for that reason that we have resisted the temptation to bundle Demy's films and those by his New Wave contemporaries in the same chapter.

14

Around Demy

Godard and Rivette

A few years before Demy's first musical, Jean-Luc Godard also played with the genre of the film musical. The opening credits of *Une femme est une femme* show a black screen with a list of mostly single upper-case words in a variety of colours:

IL ÉTAIT
UNE FOIS
BEAUREGARD [producer]
EASTMANCOLOR
PONTI [producer]
FRAN CHEMENT SCOPE
GODARD
COMÉDIE FRANÇAISE
COUTARD [cameraman]
MUSICAL
LEGRAND [composer]
THÉÂTRAL
EVEIN [production design]
SENTIMENTAL
GUILLEMOT [editor]
OPÉRA
LUBITSCH [surname of character Émile]
14 JUILLET [title of film by René Clair]
CINÉMA

The surnames of personnel mixed with 'comédie', 'musical' and 'opéra', among others, suggest that the film we are about to see is a film musical. At one point in the film Angela (Anna Karina), after Alfred (Jean-Paul Belmondo) has asked her why she is sad, responds 'parce que je voudrais être dans une comédie musicale',[1] and we see her sketch a couple of dance moves as she adds that her dream musical would be with

---

[1] 'Because I would like to be in a film musical.'

Cyd Charisse and Gene Kelly, choreographed by Bob Fosse (0.15). But there is only one sustained musical number in the film and this deconstructs what we might expect from a musical, just as the dance sketch had done: she works as a striptease artist in a seedy café, and sings a number (0.9), the piano stopping mid-phrase, and the camera pointedly not showing her naked, her face at the end of the number in close-up lit by coloured lights (Figure 14.1).

Godard's purpose is to interrogate the very foundations of the genre, as *Prénom Carmen* (1984) was later to do with his film version of the opera *Carmen*, a film in which the music we hear is Beethoven's late quartets rather than Bizet (see Powrie 2007a). His interrogation applies partly to the sustained musical numbers normally found in the genre – here they are not sustained, only gestured at – as well as to the utopian fantasy underlying musicals. As Felicity Chaplin explains, Godard's comment in a 1962 interview that when making the film he was thinking of 'néo-réalisme musical' (Bergala 1998: 224) suggests that the film should be seen less as a radically deconstructed version of a film musical and more as a neo-realist exploration of the daily lives of three Parisians, in which the principal neo-realist element is occasionally deconstructed by film musical fragments (Chaplin 2013). Demy attended to the lives of ordinary people in *Les Parapluies de Cherbourg* by having everything sung; Godard does the opposite.

The only other New Wave filmmaker to work with the musical was Jacques Rivette, more than thirty years later, with *Haut bas fragile*. *Une femme est une femme* was about three Parisians: Angela, her boyfriend Émile (Jean-Claude Brialy) and Alfred, the man

Figure 14.1 The two 'musical' numbers in *Une femme est une femme* (Courtesy Universal Music StudioCanal).

who wants to have an affair with her. Rivette's film is also about three Parisians, but this time three women; and in another echo of Godard's film, Anna Karina appears as Sarah, the owner of a saloon, and sings a couple of songs, 'La Fille à l'envers' ('Upside Down Girl') and 'L'Amant perdu' ('Lost Lover'). The film's disjointed narrative links a series of vignettes during which Louise (Marianne Denicourt), a little rich girl just out of a coma, Ninon (Nathalie Richard), the impetuous good-time girl, and Ida (Laurence Côte), an orphan and daydreamer looking for her birth mother, end up reinventing themselves. Song-and-dance musical numbers comment on the various episodes, although the first one, teasingly, does not occur until one hour into the film, and they often appear to be wilfully rough at the edges. The *Cahiers du cinéma* reviewer commented on the way that the characters are constantly in motion, but how much of the time that motion is not motivated, and appears gratuitous (Moullet 1995: 47).

The actors circle around each other tentatively in semi-dance steps as their conversations slip hesitantly into song. Jonathan Rosenbaum terms this 'documentary roughness – a respect for real durations, for moments that are empty as well as full' (1996), and another reviewer talks of the 'gaucherie touchante' and 'grâce maladroite'[2] of the song-and-dance routines (Horguelin 1995: 22). The focus of the film is precisely the song-and-dance routines, however rough they may be:

> The occasional narrative intrigues that engage the three women become mere pretexts for musical performances in which our attention is focused on the pleasure of sensual body movements of the characters that rock rhythmically or pose gratuitously as required by the demands of the music. *Haut bas fragile* mobilizes American dance and musical styles to produce the abstract pleasure associated with a performance aesthetic. (Wiles 2001: 98)

Rivette's models for the film were MGM musicals like *Give a Girl a Break* (Stanley Donen, 1953) made on shoe-string budgets in pre-existing decors (Rivette 1995a). Most of the songs are by the singer Enzo Enzo, who had won the Best Singer of the Year award at the 1995 French equivalent of the Grammys, the Victoires de la musique, a few months before the film was released. Rivette said in an interview that he had fallen in love with one of the songs on her second album, 'Les Naufragés volontaires' (Rivette 1999), so ended up using it along with three other songs from the album; Enzo Enzo's composer, François Bruant, composed the other numbers for the film. The lyrics of 'Les Naufragés volontaires' refer to lovers shutting the world out to enjoy their own company. Rivette's film feels similarly enclosed as the three women live their day-to-day lives, their gauche song-and-dance routines emerging as if spontaneously improvised, almost, but not quite as though we might have performed them ourselves. Much like Godard's fascination in *Une femme est une femme* with Karina, Rivette's focus is less on narrative or genre, and more on the performance of particular bodies

---

[2] 'Touching clumsiness', 'awkward grace'.

in space, echoing some of his other films: 'J'ai envie de filmer les comédiens de haut en bas ... , les pieds sont aussi importants que la tête'[3] (Rivette 1995b).

Unlike Godard's film, however, which, despite its whimsy, is an austere interrogation of generic conventions, and only glancingly a musical, Rivette's film uses the film musical to explore emotion and the way that bodies articulate the tentative back-and-forth moves in relationships. In that sense it is, like Godard's, an anti-musical, not least because of its anchoring in quotidian reality, as Luc Moullet points out. The sometimes almost imperceptible shifts into song and dance are anchored in 'thèmes de peu d'envergure, une sorte de mouvement naturel fondé sur le trivial, le rien, au contraire du film musical traditionnel, où le passage au ballet est lié à la naissance du grand amour, à un état d'âme excessif ou à un événement majeur'[4] (1995: 47). What links these two musicals to each other, to Demy's early musicals, and to the two 'feminist' musicals we now turn to, is the focus on what might be conceived of as 'ordinary' people in their daily lives, helped at least in part by the fact that the actors in them were at the time of the films themselves not stars, as had been the case with Demy's early musicals.

Varda and Akerman

L'une chante, l'autre pas is one of Varda's least known films, a feminist musical as Varda herself labelled it (2014a: 77). It focuses in part on the struggle for the legalization of abortion. A feminist musical group, Orchidée, takes the struggle into towns and villages throughout France. They perform nine songs in the course of the film. In the same way that Demy wrote the lyrics for his songs, so too the words for this film were written by Varda herself, and they sound like feminist tracts with their 'paroles militantes',[5] as Varda called them (1994: 110–1). Despite that, a number of contemporary women critics took the film to task. Françoise Audé in her influential *Ciné-modèles, cinémas d'elles* called the music 'charmante plutôt que mordante', brushing the film off as 'sucré'[6] (1981: 145). The film is as much rooted in its time as Demy's *Parking*. Looking back in 1994, Varda comments that the band's tour of France seems 'datée, baba cool, militante et désuète'[7] (1994: 110). Not only is the film dated, but Varda herself has dismissed its importance within the larger body of her work, locating it within a very specific conjuncture: 'J'ai seulement fait le point ... en proposant une fiction documentée sur la lutte des femmes entre 1969 et 1976'.[8] (1994: 110).

---

[3] 'I want to film actors from top to bottom, the feet are as important as the head.'
[4] 'Small-scale themes, a sort of natural movement based on the trivial, on the nothing much, unlike the traditional film musical in which the transition to ballet is linked to the beginning of a great love, to extreme emotion or a major event.'
[5] 'Militant lyrics.'
[6] 'Charming rather than biting', 'sugary.'
[7] 'Dated, hip, militant and old-fashioned.'
[8] 'I just took stock and proposed a documentary fiction on women's struggles between 1969 and 1976.'

We are in 1962. The film articulates feminist politics of the period through the relationship of two women. Pomme, a schoolgirl, befriends Suzanne, the stay-at-home mother of two children. More resilient and resourceful than the quieter Suzanne, she pays for Suzanne's abortion by lying to her parents, and supports her morally when Suzanne's photographer-lover Jérôme commits suicide. Pomme wants to be a singer, and we see her taking part in a rock 'n' roll recording session. More than a decade later, in 1976, Pomme has become a protest singer for the all-woman band Orchidée, while Suzanne works in a family planning clinic. The two women meet again at a demonstration for the legalization of abortion associated with the Mouvement pour la Liberté de l'Avortement et de la Contraception (Movement for Free Abortion and Contraception). Pomme marries Darius, an Iranian, whom she had met on a trip to Amsterdam where she had gone for an abortion. She and Darius move to Iran briefly, but they break up, because he expects her to be a stay-at-home wife. The film is about Pomme and Suzanne's enduring friendship, despite a decade-long separation during which they communicate by postcard, and their common struggle for women's rights. That struggle is complementary, and reflects the film's title. Suzanne, the quieter of the two, is shown listening to women as they come to her for help in the family planning clinic. Pomme, on the other hand, is more outgoing; we see her expressing her views forcefully throughout the film, partly through the protest songs with their militant lyrics. Alison Smith neatly encapsulates this difference: 'What is interesting about Suzanne to the audience is what she *does* with her situation – what is important about Pomme is more often what she *is* or presents herself as being' (1998: 109; Smith's emphasis).

As DeRoo (2009) points out, the film undermines the conventions of the genre. Musicals are generally not 'political' in the militant sense. The longest song of the film is 'Amsterdam-sur-eau' ('Amsterdam on the Water'), sung by Pomme as she and the acquaintances she has made at the abortion clinic decide to take a sightseeing tour on the Amsterdam canals. Its lyrics focus on abortion and read more like a poetic political tract. DeRoo lists other familiar Brechtian strategies, such as the use of props that undermine theatrical illusion in the song 'La Femme-bulle' ('Bubble Woman') and draws out their implications: 'Varda's reluctance to provide a single resolution to feminist issues mirrors her refusal to employ a single narrative thread or to resolve the story neatly with a happy, uncomplicated ending. Varda's film reminds us of the aesthetic and political significance of speaking in the plural, confronting and continually undermining expectations in order to deny the idea of a complete resolution' (2009: 259). The film is open-ended, without any obvious resolution or closure in the manner of a standard narrative. Life goes on. Suzanne was a single mother at the beginning of the film, but she is settled with Pierre at the end. Pomme, who was married to Darius, has split up with him, and is herself now a single mother. The epilogue's voice-over, by Varda herself, explains how the children are growing up, but how the challenges of being a woman remain.

The songs as a group function to destabilize any notion of a fixed female identity. The first twenty minutes of the film dwell on Suzanne and her partner Jérôme, who is a photographer. We see row upon row of women and children in the black-and-white portraits pinned to his walls. Suzanne explains that he cannot sell enough of them to make ends meet. He comes across as a head-in-the-clouds, stereotypically tortured artist. Jérôme says in the first few minutes of the film that he is trying to capture the truth of the women he photographs. Pomme, however, comments robustly that all of the women in the photos are sad and presented as victims. Jérôme also tries to 'capture' Pomme, stripping her naked in both the literal and the figurative sense; but he is unsuccessful, complaining that he cannot get through to her 'truth'. Jérôme literally frames the women, rendering them immobile, like an entomologist might frame butterflies, their differences and individualities rendered the same through framing, the black-and-white colour, and the poses he has asked his subjects to adopt. We could almost say that he 'monotonizes' his subjects. The film's project is to construct a female-centred identity rather than one imposed by a man.

The contrast between masculine and feminine ways of representing the world is established early on in the film with music. Pomme, keen to pursue a career as a singer, is hired as part of the backing vocals for a recording session. We see the bare-chested lead singer wearing dark glasses and chewing gum, imbued with his self-image as a rock 'n' roll star. The lyrics of the song are ironic; we hear 'c'est le rock n roll, c'est une affaire d'hommes'.[9] The song goes on to describe a self-contained boys' own world where fun is, as the lyrics put it, for boys to chew gum while clapping their hands. What both Jérôme and the singer have in common is an attachment to a fixed image: that of his subjects whom Jérôme tries to fix as objects, and that of his fixed self-image for the rocker. The film will develop antitheses to these fixed objects. Jérôme's photos are echoed and counteracted in the film by the many colourful postcards that the two women exchange during their decade-long separation. This is very different from Jérôme's attempt to capture the so-called truth of his subjects, which only succeeds in turning them into objects. The function of the postcards is to locate a variety of moments in space and time, abolishing both in the act of communication, the postcards' splashes of colour contrasting vividly with Jérôme's black-and-white photos.

In the case of the music, the rock 'n' roll is superseded in the remainder of the film by a very different kind of music: first the Amsterdam song and then Orchidée's acoustic folk. This is posited as the exact opposite of the rock 'n' roll in a number of fairly obvious ways: the location of the songs constantly changes as the group tours, unlike the claustrophobic and cluttered recording studio; the group, indeed, is more often outside than inside, in farmyards and village squares, on small make-shift stages, with tiny audiences. And the focus of the songs is not the bubblegum, shades and bare-chested posturing of the rock 'n' rollers; it is the world of women and their search for identity in movement, indeed, identity in a movement (Figure 14.2).

When Varda said in an interview for the *Cahiers du cinéma* that she had 'tout fait passer dans les chansons'[10] (2014b: 84), she was referring primarily to the political message. In this film, the music 'makes everything pass', including false images and

---

[9] 'It's rock 'n' roll, it's a man's business.'
[10] 'Put everything into the songs.'

Figure 14.2 The contrast in musical styles in *L'une chante, l'autre pas* (Courtesy of Arte Éditions).

posturing self-images, to produce a sense of continually redefined and itinerant female identities.

A decade later Chantal Akerman made *Golden Eighties*. It was an unexpected film for a filmmaker better known for uncompromisingly art-house films such as *Jeanne Dielman, 23 quai du Commerce, 1080 Bruxelles* (1975), a slow-moving 201-minute-long film in which Delphine Seyrig plays a single mother who does sex work from home so as to support herself and her son. By contrast, *Golden Eighties* is in appearance a light musical, with song lyrics by Akerman herself, and music by Marc Hérouet. As Marion Schmid puts it: 'With its colourful costumes and setting, bright lighting, rapid editing and quickly alternating song-and-dance numbers, the film displays an aesthetic of excess in stark contrast to the director's minimal, sober style of the preceding decade. *Golden Eighties* is a charming exercise in viewer seduction, an unashamed spectacle of femininity and a bold pastiche of melodrama and the musical' (2010: 80). The film had

Figure 14.3 The girls' and boys' choruses in *Golden Eighties* (Courtesy of Cahiers du cinéma).

a complex gestation, with a semi-documentary mock-up, *Les Années 80* (Schmid 2010: 69–73). Seyrig is Jeanne; she and her husband Monsieur Schwartz (Charles Denner) run a clothes boutique in a shopping mall where there is also a hairdresser and a café. The former is run by Lili (Fanny Cottençon), a 'kept woman' whose shop belongs to her married lover, Jean (Jean-François Balmer), and the latter run by Sylvie (Myriam Boyer). The mall is like a goldfish bowl, at basement level with tall glass shop windows facing into the atrium, so that the characters spend their time looking at and gossiping about each other. The gossip is about relationships: sentimental Sylvie has a long-distance lover from whom she receives airmail letters; the Schwartz's son Robert (Nicolas Tronc) is passionately in love with Lili, much to his parents' exasperation; Robert is loved, in turn, by both Mado (played by Belgian pop singer Lio, who pointedly does not sing) and her friend Pascale (Pascale Salkin). The American Eli (John Berry), who had met Jeanne thirty years before, recognizes her and tries to rekindle their passion. The film is a careful choreography around these relationships: Lili plays Robert against her older lover; Robert proposes to Mado in a fit of pique; Jeanne begins to fall for Eli once more. 'Three months later' as a title tells us, Robert has become like his father, a shopkeeper dressed in a suit, and returns to Lili when about to be married with Mado; Sylvie's lover is still in Canada; and Jeanne has rejected Eli's advances, preferring the stability, but also the boredom of her life with her husband. The main characters have musical numbers as we might expect; but in addition the nine female shampoo girls and a group of four male teenagers comment on the action like Greek choruses, often bursting into song as they do so (Figure 14.3).

From the opening titles onward the film gestures to those of Demy, but to those of Truffaut as well. The titles of *Les Parapluies de Cherbourg* had umbrellas crossing the screen; Akerman's film has women's legs crossing the screen. One of the film's songs, 'Il pleut' ('It's Raining'), sung by the shampoo girls as men in raincoats come down the stairs into the mall (0.42), recalls *Les Parapluies de Cherbourg*. Sylvie's café which acts as a focal point where characters meet recalls Mme Yvonne's café in *Les Demoiselles de Rochefort*, and both Yvonne and Sylvie prefer living in their dreams (Fowler 2000: 110). Seyrig evokes the Lilac Fairy of Demy's *Peau d'Âne*, as well as Fabienne Tabard in

Truffaut's *Baisers volés*, with whom Antoine (Jean-Pierre Léaud) is madly in love, and Charles Denner reminds us of his roles in other films by Truffaut: *La Mariée était en noir* (1968) and *L'Homme qui aimait les femmes* (1977). The arrival of the American Eli recalls that of Gene Kelly's character in *Les Demoiselles de Rochefort*. Indeed, when he reminisces about the past with Jeanne he briefly sings 'It Had to Be You', a song sung by Kelly in *Living in a Big Way* (Gregory La Cava, 1947), corresponding both to the post-war period Eli evokes when he and Jeanne met and, negatively, to that film's narrative in which Kelly's character marries his girl, while Eli, as he recalls, was too shy to declare his love to Jeanne. But the fact that it is John Berry imparts a very different feel to the story: as a member of the Communist Party Berry was blacklisted by the House Un-American Activities in 1951, and spent most of the rest of his career working in France, where he directed the 'mambo' film *Oh! Qué mambo* (1959) starring Dario Moreno and *À tout casser* (1968) starring Johnny Hallyday; in the 1980s he directed the adaptation of the 1980 feminist-inspired novel by Dorothée Letessier, *Le Voyage à Paimpol* (1985), starring Myriam Boyer, who is Sylvie in *Golden Eighties*. Not only was he American and linked to musical films, but he was also, more importantly, linked to radical politics. Instead of Demy's bittersweet dreamy and utopian musicals, or Truffaut's resolutely apolitical films, the feel of Akerman's film is that of sociopolitical satire.

This begins with the title of the film: recalling *Gold Diggers of 1933* (see Chapter 3), and its focus on materialism as a means of warding off the economic crisis, Akerman's film is also a reflection on the materialist 1980s. France like other countries was going through a recession which the government attempted to solve by de-indexing wages and liberalizing financial institutions, leading to extreme poverty for some and extreme wealth for others. This is gestured at by the film's location in a shopping mall and the emphasis on material goods (the Schwartz's clothes boutique) and appearances (their boutique and Lili's hairdressing salon). But the film is not 'political'; the economic crisis is sidelined in favour of what we could call the crisis of sentiments. As the critic of *Les Inrockuptibles* pointed out, *Golden Eighties* could be seen as prophetic, given the rapid Americanization of French culture in the 1980s, but nonetheless the film 'n'est pas politique. Plus qu'une galerie marchande ... c'est une galerie d'amour que filme Chantal Akerman. C'est ce qui meut les personnages, c'est ce qui les rend vivants'[11] (Nicklaus 1986). The film revolves around 'love' and what love might mean in its three 'ages': for the youngster Robert, against his parents because they want him to 'settle down' rather than have a steamy affair with red-dressed scarlet woman Lili; for the two independent women, Sylvie who dreams of her lover in Canada, contrasted with Lili's hard-headed pragmatism as a 'kept woman'; and finally third-age love, as Jeanne rejects Eli's attempts to rekindle their passion saying that she is too old. We are made aware of the all-pervasiveness of love from the first scene of the film in which a woman

---

[11] 'Is not a political film. More than a shopping mall, Chantal Akerman has filmed a love mall. Love is what moves the characters, making them come alive.'

sits on some stairs and kisses equally passionately the men who sit on either side of her, saying 'que j't'aime, que j't'aime'.[12]

Unlike Rivette's musical, in which the characters' dance movements emerged as if spontaneously from 'natural' movement, Akerman's film is highly stylized: the characters' movements are carefully choreographed. This is very clearly the case when the film resembles a standard musical most with chorus formation dances. But the non-dance movements of the characters in the mall often appear contrived, such as when characters attempt to speak to each other but are pulled apart by the crowds in the atrium. Their dialogue also feels contrived: they speak in clichés – 'on est toujours seul dans la vie',[13] says Lili (0.24), 'grandir, s'agrandir, ou mourir',[14] says M. Schwartz (0.22) – with occasionally more pointed comments: 'Le bonheur, le bonheur, c'est quoi après tout?/Vous ne croyez pas que tout ça c'est que de la publicité?'[15] (0.11). Indeed, two reviewers astutely pointed out that the dialogue sounds like song lyrics (Ferenczi 1986; Villetard 1986: 38). The song lyrics, set to bouncy pop rhythms that feel more 1970s than 1980s, are frequently as comical as they are clichéd: for example, when Robert is laughed at by Lili, the boy's chorus chant derisively 'Robert, camembert tout vert'[16] (0.30).

Akerman, like Demy, is interested in 'ordinary' people and their lives, but her approach is distinctively ironic and derisive; the word that French reviewers frequently used was 'acidulé', meaning 'tart' or 'bitter' (e.g. Breton 1986). At one level, we are aware that everything in her film is postmodern surface: the characters' feelings have the same emotional and ethical value as material objects such as the dresses in the Schwartz's boutique; and like the dresses, those feelings are literally on show in the mall, as performed as the objects for sale. As Steven Shaviro astutely points out, 'the film's gestures are all marvellously transparent. Each of them is a perfectly realized pose, free of ambiguity or depth', and what the characters do or say 'seems framed in ironic "quotation marks"' (2007: 14). This does not mean that the film is simplistic, however. Adrian Martin emphasizes its complex mix of 'endless consumption, glitzy all-pervasive commodification of emotion, showbiz femininity, regressive longings for the perfect romance, a certain delicate kind of camp sensibility' (1989). Nor does the satire of the 'simple' passion of ordinary people exclude sincerity of emotion, as many reviewers were quick to point out; the film's sentimentalism has a 'grâce débordante'[17] (Le Morvan 1986). Despite the derision that pervades the film, Akerman manages to maintain both a critical distance and a sensitive appreciation of the 'unexamined' life of ordinary people, demonstrating empathy for the 'irreducible facticity of the empirical everyday' (Shaviro 2007: 17). Her ironic clichés are not a pastiche of feeling, but a pastiche of the language we are obliged to use to express feeling. The film paradoxically sets up a contrast between lightness of expression and heaviness of feeling, so that feeling often appears light, just another commodity that one can buy/buy into.

[12] 'I love you so much, I love you so much.'
[13] 'Everyone's alone in life.'
[14] 'Grow, expand, or die.'
[15] 'Happiness, happiness, what's that after all?/Don't you think that it's nothing but advertising?'
[16] 'Robert, green camembert.'
[17] 'Overwhelming beauty.'

Figure 14.4 Sylvie and Jeanne's emotional musical moments in *Golden Eighties* (Courtesy of Cahiers du cinéma).

There are two musical moments, however, where the film takes us from postmodern irony to deep emotion, and both are anchored in the performance of the two women concerned (Figure 14.4). An early event in the film is the arrival of a letter to Sylvie from her distant love in Canada, which is the first major song of the film, 'Plus rien ne compte' ('Nothing Matters Any More'). She begins to read the letter, which quickly turns into a rhymed poem, lifting her gaze to the camera as if she had already memorized it, and finally segueing almost imperceptibly from reading the letter to singing it, still without looking at it (0.3). The plangent melody, her soulful eyes, her little-girl voice, and even the brief shot of her friends at the bar swaying from side to side, and, finally, the letter in the form of a paper aeroplane flying in slow motion, all contribute to the intensity of this musical moment. The second musical moment is a song sung by Jeanne, 'Cette nuit' ('That Night'; 0.51). Like Sylvie's song, it is about the absence of the lover, in this case reprising her story with Eli, who left her without declaring his love. In the song Jeanne spends the night dreaming of him, but cannot keep him close once day has broken. Like Sylvie, Jeanne sings straight to the camera at the end of the song, like her she sings hesitantly, her voice breaking occasionally. Unlike Boyer, however, Seyrig's distinctively husky voice imparts a sensual resonance to the final repeated chorus: 'J'en ai le souffle court, j'ai envie de faire l'amour'.[18] One reviewer pointed out Seyrig's 'gravité à prononcer des choses simples, sa simplicité à affirmer des choses graves'[19] (Villetard 1986: 38). Jeanne's hymn to a lost love transcends irony and cliché, thanks to the extraordinary grain of Seyrig's voice.

Popular musicals

As had been the case in the 1930s and 1940s, film musicals during the Demy period also focused on singers and entertainers, although many were satires of the entertainment industry. *Les Idoles* (Marc'O, 1968), for example, was a satire of the

---

[18] 'I'm short of breath, I want to make love.'
[19] 'Gravity in saying simple things, her simplicity in saying grave things.'

yéyé singers and the industry around them, based on Marc'O's 1966 theatre show, and edited by Jean Eustache with André Téchiné as assistant director. Bulle Ogier plays Gigi la Folle (a France Gall lookalike) and Pierre Clémenti, the character Charly le Surineur (a mix of Jacques Dutronc and Johnny Hallyday), his name echoing that of Mack the Knife ('Mac le Surineur' in French) in the Brecht–Weill opera. The film focuses on a press conference during which they reveal how their careers have been artificially crafted by their managers. As Jonathan Rosenbaum commented when the film was re-released in 1973, it was not a particularly profound critique and resembled filmed theatre (1973: 2).

Chobizenesse (Jean Yanne, 1975) was a similar satire of the entertainment industry. Yanne is the director of a music hall who uses money from arms magnates to support his revue. He tries various sketches that backfire; at one point the magnates suggest that he include a sketch on bazookas, leading to one of the film's more surreal songs in which the skimpily dressed singers are dressed as soldiers and caress their bazookas erotically as they sing 'O bazooka que tu m'excites' ('O bazooka you make me horny'). He eventually decides to use the money to support 'Art' in the form of a disturbed composer, as a result of which he and the composer are shot at the end of the film by the police, egged on by the angry arms magnates. A flavour of Yanne's irreverent approach can be found in the philosopher names of the skimpily clad dancers – Célia Bergson, Gigi Nietzsche and Paulette Kant – as well as the name of the composer who produces Baroque cantatas: Jean-Sébastien Bloch with a wife whose name, like that of Johann Sebastian Bach, is Anna Magdalena.

The film managed half a million spectators, largely due to the popularity of some of Yanne's previous (non-musical) satires, *Tout le monde il est beau, tout le monde il est gentil* (1972), a satire on the mass media with four million tickets sold, and *Les Chinois à Paris* (1974, 1.7 million), a satire on the French Resistance. Yanne's anarchic humour may have worked with the previous topics, but misfired with *Chobizenesse* which was seen by reviewers as little more than a series of sketches without a clear guiding thread, and a lacklustre performance by Yanne himself: 'C'est un film terne, ennuyeux, monotone … . Jean Yanne lui-même traverse son film comme un fantôme: visiblement, il n'est pas à l'aise. Son personnage est dénué de toute crédibilité, tant il met peu de conviction à le jouer'[20] (Rémond 1975: 71). *Le Monde*'s critic was even less kind: 'Les acteurs jouent mal (exprès?), les numéros de music-hall sont d'une laideur pseudo-féllinienne, la musique est quelconque'[21] (Siclier 1975). Some reviewers cast him as a kind of populist auteur, one going so far as to call him a modern-day Molière with his derisive (and often self-derisive) humour (Monange 1975). Although clearly not an auteur in the *Cahiers du cinéma* sense, the film was nonetheless seen as an auteurist production, because Yanne not only directed and acted in the film, but also composed all the lyrics and music, including the opening song with its punningly

---

[20] 'The film is dull, boring, monotonous. Jean Yanne himself is like a ghost in his film, visibly ill at ease. He acts with such a lack of conviction that his character lacks all credibility.'

[21] 'The actors can't act (maybe on purpose?), the music-hall numbers are as ugly as something out of Fellini, the music is mediocre.'

salacious lyrics that became something of a hit: 'Il a chobibi, chobibi /Il a chaud partout bibi, chaud bibi, chobibi /Chaud du zizi jusqu'aux fesses, chobibi, chobibi /Car il est dans le show bibi, chobibi, chobibi.'[22]

Later in the period, in the comedy *Rendez-vous au tas de sable* (Didier Grousset, 1990) removal man Nickel (Richard Gotainer, who wrote the script and the song lyrics) dreams of being a rock star and enters a rock music competition with his friends as the group The Electric Pass-Moutains, the best sequence being the competition itself, with its parody of Marylin Manson in the number 'Marylin ou Marylou' (Figure 14.5).

There were also film musicals that were neither comedies nor satires. Michel Lang was a popular filmmaker whose first feature *À nous les petites Anglaises* (1976), a non-musical about two teen schoolboys who spend their summer in the UK supposedly to learn English but seducing girls as the title suggests, sold 5.7 million tickets. *Tous vedettes!* (1980), a musical with seven musical numbers, was his fourth feature. Three friends decide to produce a musical for Broadway, one of them falling for his wife's mother, Lucille, a former Hollywood star, played by Leslie Caron, echoing Caron's Hollywood career. After the first failure, Lucille helps the trio to achieve success.

In *Paroles et musique* (Élie Chouraqui, 1984), which with its 1.7 million tickets sold can be considered a reasonable success for a film musical in this period, struggling pop music duo Jérémy (Christophe Lambert) and Michel (Richard Anconina) each meet the woman of their dreams, Margot (Catherine Deneuve) and Corinne (Dayle Haddon). Margot is a workaholic mother of two. Margot works in an entertainment

Figure 14.5 Parody of Marylin Manson in *Rendez-vous au tas de sable* (Courtesy Richard Gotainer).

[22] 'He's hot everywhere, hot from his willy to his bum, because he's in showbusiness.'

agency, run by Yves (Jacques Perrin); her American writer–husband has left her temporarily. Corinne is the daughter of the head of a recording company. Margot hires the duo, and much of the film is devoted to the duo's attempts to achieve success, so that we see a range of auditions as the role of the women in the duo's lives becomes less of a focus. Deneuve's hard-working career woman was originally intended to be a major focus of the film; however, much to her dismay she was sidelined by the duo in the finished film as Chouraqui changed the script in the light of the charisma generated by Lambert and Anconina (Deneuve 1986), no doubt also because of the public profile of the two actors: Lambert was an international star after *Greystoke: The Legend of Tarzan, Lord of the Apes* (Hugh Hudson, 1984), which had garnered 3.5m spectators in France, and Anconina had won a Best Actor César for his role in *Tchao Pantin* (Claude Berri, 1983, 3.8m tickets sold).

The focus on the singer duo resulted in a film that is more of a musical than it might otherwise have been. The seven musical numbers sung by the duo all have English lyrics and are by Michel Legrand, who together with Perrin and Deneuve evokes the early Demy musicals. We see the duo's success as they perform at one of Margot's shows, with brief cutaways to her nodding in approval as they sing one of the more lively songs of the film, 'Leave it to Me' (0.17); or their recording of 'We Can Dance' during which we see Deneuve reflected in the recording booth window (Figure 14.6).

Figure 14.6 Margot and Corinne sidelined in *Paroles et musique* (Courtesy UFG).

Most of the songs are standard pop numbers, whether they are upbeat like 'Psychic Flash' (0.37) or ballads like 'I'm With You Now' (0.51). One of the more complex combinations of music and editing occurs at the end of the film in a 7-minute long telephone conversation. Margot and her children have gone to New York to be with her husband; Jérémy, unable to forget her and, urged by Michel, flies to New York. Jérémy rings Michel and we hear his voice-over as we see images of what happened in flashback, intercut with images of Michel listening (1.33). Jérémy rings Margot from the street outside her apartment, and she tells him not to come up but to meet her in the restaurant opposite, where he has lunch with the whole family. A solo electric piano plays a minor tune, stopping and starting, and we realize that it is diegetic because it is Michel who has been tapping it out on a keyboard. He asks Jérémy to listen to the full song of which the tune forms a part, the ballad 'One More Moment', and the song shifts from being diegetic to non-diegetic as we see grainy images of the duo's future success.

Chouraqui was associate director and actor in a number of Claude Lelouch's films in the 1970s, and like similar songs in Lelouch's films, 'One More Moment' comments sentimentally on the action, in this case the final breakdown of Margot and Jérémy's relationship retold in the shaggy-dog style telephone conversation. But it also binds the fragments of the conversation together: Michel listening to Jérémy's voice, the images of what happened, with Jérémy's voice-over, the occasional replaying of the conversations Jérémy had had with Margot, the interruption of the song, before the sequence segues into composition mode as Michel tries it out on Jérémy, and finally the foregrounding of the song as it shifts into a full musical number that manages to bring a broken past and a successful future together.

Not all popular musicals of this period were as focused on male friendship and posturing, with women relegated to the role of muses and onlookers while the men failed, doubted themselves, blamed the women and ended up being successful as long as the women did not ask too much of them. *Sandy* (Michel Nerval, 1983) was a refreshing contrast. Like *Paroles et musique* and *Rendez-vous au tas de sable*, it is about young singers trying to succeed, this time as Rolling Stone-type rockers, who recruit their lodger Zoe, played by British singer Sandy Stevenson, as lead singer when they realize that she has a good voice. We see her early in the film playing soulful ballads at the piano, while the band play thumping rock but without songs. By the end of the film she joins them and they end up by giving a concert in the Olympia in Paris. Perhaps unsurprisingly, this female success story was a flop.

In this chapter we have tried to correct the commonly held view that the film musical of the 1960s and beyond is best represented by those of Jacques Demy. While his early 1960s musicals are undoubtedly among the most innovative in the history of the genre, we need to remember that they emerged from a clear tradition, even if they worked against that tradition; and that his later musicals – particularly his most 'unsuccessful' musical, *Parking* – should be placed in the context of the many film musicals focused on the music industry of the late 1970s and 1980s. When set against *Paroles et musique*, for example, the most successful of the films in this chapter, *Parking* appears as a remarkably original contribution to the genre.

15

The opera film and the modern classical music film

Although opera films were a staple of Italian cinema, during the 1950s, there were no significant opera films produced in France after Gance's *Louise* until the 1980s, many of them produced by Daniel Toscan du Plantier, the director general of Gaumont from 1975 to 1984 (see Table 15.1). As we saw with Gance's two musicals, in both opera and biopics, the major issue is the integration of the music into the narrative, given that it is, in theory, the attraction for the spectator; the debate around opera films was particularly intense in the 1980s as they suddenly proliferated, a standard view being that they were too different from stage operas, democratization being trumped by vulgarization (Brèque 1987: 27), as expressed in the following caustic metaphors by Pierre Cadars: 'Le tourisme en bus climatisé, le banquet dans un fast-food, l'amour contre la montre'[1] (1987: 41).

The opera film

Among the reasons for the development of the opera film, there is 'the growth of higher education worldwide, increased prosperity and demographic factors' (Wood 2005: 190), as well as industry-specific factors, such as the requirement to develop new markets, in this case an international market, foreign languages with or without subtitles being less of an issue for Anglophone audiences in particular (Duault 1987: 3). Television also played an important role in the dissemination of opera on screen (Citron 2000: 40–2, 50–2); there are directors who specialize in TV opera films, for example, Jean-Pierre Ponnelle or Petr Weigl. The list in Table 15.1 is not definitive, but a representative list of opera films with theatrical distribution by well-known directors. In what follows, we will consider the films by Rosi, Mitterrand, d'Anna, Żuławski and Jacquot.

By far the most successful of the opera films was *Carmen*. The year 1983–4 was that of Carmen films: Carlos Saura's flamenco version (May 1983) won the Palme d'Or in Cannes; Peter Brook's pared-down triptych (November 1983) *La Tragédie de*

---

[1] 'Tourism in a climate-controlled coach, a banquet in a fast-food outlet, love against the clock.'

Table 15.1 Opera Films, 1975–2001

Year	Title	Composer	Director	Country	Spectators
1975	Moses und Aaron	Schönberg	Jean-Marie Straub, Danièle Huillet	W Germany/ Austria/ France/ Italy	Not known
1975	Trollflöjten	Mozart	Ingmar Bergman	Sweden	864,328
1980	*Don Giovanni	Mozart	Joseph Losey	France/Italy/ W Germany	1,055,012
1982	Parsifal	Wagner	Hans-Jürgen Syberberg	W Germany/ France	Not known
1982	La Traviata	Verdi	Franco Zeffirelli	Italy	973,555
1984	*Carmen	Bizet	Francesco Rosi	France/ Italy	2,200,601
1985	*Orfeo	Monteverdi	Claude Goretta	France/ Italy/ Canada/ Switzerland	Not known
1986	Otello	Verdi	Franco Zeffirelli	Netherlands/ Italy/ the United States	Not known
1987	Macbeth	Verdi	Claude d'Anna	France/ W Germany	Not known
1987	Aria	Lully	Jean-Luc Godard et al	UK	13,287
1988	*La Bohème	Puccini	Luigi Comencini	France/ UK/ Italy	102,095
1989	*Boris Godounov	Mussorgsky	Andrzej Żuławski	France/ Spain/ Yugoslavia	Not known
1995	*Madame Butterfly	Puccini	Frédéric Mitterrand	France/ UK/ Germany	291,590
1997	Von heute auf morgen	Schönberg	Jean-Marie Straub, Danièle Huillet	France/ Germany	Not known
2001	*Tosca	Puccini	Benoît Jacquot	Italy/ France/ UK/ Germany	261,540

(*=produced by Daniel Toscan du Plantier)

Carmen used a small chamber orchestra; Jean-Luc Godard's *Prénom Carmen* (January 1984) used Beethoven string quartets as diegetic music and won Venice's Golden Lion; Rosi's film (March 1984) won a number of Césars awards including Best Film and Best Sound. Albert López directed a soft-porn version, *Carmen nue* (August 1984). Rosi's film was different from the other Carmens of the 1980s. Whereas the others all in one way or another questioned the myth which Carmen had become, principally by backgrounding Bizet's music, almost to the point of non-existence in Godard's case, or by paring the opera down until it resembled something else, as was the case with Brook, Rosi's film presented itself as a realist illustration of the opera, with location shooting in the Spanish towns of Seville, Ronda and Carmona, typically Spanish scenes illustrating the entr'acte, and frequently obtrusive natural sounds.

While many reviewers found the film refreshing, the film's constant appeal to realism irked others: 'To sit before a live performance of *Carmen* in the opera house is one thing, but to sit before this exactingly slow imitation suggests listening to a concert of phonograph records while looking through a book of colored photographs of Spain' (Curtiss 1984). If some commentators felt that the shuffling of feet, the clip-clop of horse's hooves, the chattering of crickets, and the burbling of birds anchored the music in the 'real', most, even those who admired Rosi's realism, found such features distracting. This reaction underlines the difficulty of the opera film which naturalizes the body of the singer, leading to a disjunction between the melodramatic intensity of performance, and the claims of the everyday with its mundane attachment to ordinariness. For Marshall Leicester, however, there is a productive interplay between *Carmen*'s noise track, which approximates the characters' awareness of being-in-the-world, and the music, which moves towards an 'unselfconscious ecstasy' where the world is, as it were, drowned out in a moment of epiphany (1994: 269), recalling Georges Thill's view of the musical numbers in *Louise* (Chapter 7).

The film's image track uses – as had both Prosper Mérimée, the author of the novella, and Bizet, who adapted Mérimée's novella – a nineteenth-century travelogue by the Baron Charles Davillier (1874), illustrated by Gustave Doré (Powrie 2007b). Many shots, and particularly those of the entr'actes, are patterned on Doré's drawings of Spanish scenes. The historical 'real' is therefore filtered through Doré's particularly emphatic and Romantic sensitivity and aligns the film with 1980s heritage films, as is the case with *Madame Butterfly*.

Madame Butterfly adopts the same attitude to location and sound as *Carmen* (we hear crickets when the music fades), but the camerawork is very different. The camera is rarely still, with constant crane and tracking shots, the latter winding through the Japanese house giving the impression of a labyrinth of interlocking boxes. Mitterrand's justification for this was to maintain a link between interior and exterior so that the film was 'ouvert comme une maison japonaise, regarde toujours au-dehors, tel Cio-Cio San durant son attente'[2] (1995: 16). His attempt to adopt one of Gance's solutions, the roving camera, is neutralized by the insistence on showing off the lovingly recreated

---

[2] 'Open like a Japanese dwelling, always looking out, like Cio-Cio San as she waits.'

Japan. The detailed and obsessive recreation of the past is all the more curious given the theatrical and performative aspects of opera. This is less the case with the following films, each of which rejects the artificial realism of *Carmen* and *Madame Butterfly*.

Macbeth is a through-composed version of Verdi's opera whose originality lies in its nightmarish mise en scène. Most of the action takes place in a cavernous castle that looks more like an underground prison, with torches and fires piercing the gloom, the characters caught in a labyrinth of stone stairs and low-arched tunnels. Some of the most striking sequences are those with the witches. In the opening sequence on the heath, for example, we see the mud-spattered witches in loincloths emerging from holes in the battlefield on all fours like feral beasts; in their cave, later in the film (1.19), they scramble up the tall iron bars that imprison them like monkeys. The contrast between the richness of Verdi's score and a nightmarish mise en scène avoids the heritage-film 'realism' of *Carmen* and *Madame Butterfly*, although not as remarkably as the last two films we will analyse.

Boris Godounov is an opera about guilt and the madness it engenders, in some respects being very similar to the Macbeth narrative. And as in d'Anna's film, Żuławski uses labyrinthine castle spaces with dark tunnels and torchlights to similar effect, as, for example, during the chorus 'Slava! Slava! Slava!' (0.17). But the most important feature of the film is its rejection of the kind of realism found in *Carmen* (Figure 15.1). The opening sequence begins with the premiere of the opera in 1874, the audience being in period dress, among them an anxious Mussorgsky. The curtain rises and we see a modern film camera on a dolly tracking across the stage, followed by the ripping of a canvas curtain that reveals realist exteriors with horses galloping across the screen. At different points of the film, we see period decor with modern light projectors and camera teams, whether in the forest (0.26), or in the transition to Act 2, where Boris steps from surreal period decor onto the theatre stage, walking through technicians as he does so (0.38), or in the shadows during the duet between Marina and the Pretender ('O Tsarevich, I implore you'), who are naked and cavorting on the bed (1.07). We also occasionally see Soviet-looking soldiers in modern dress patrolling with their guns; there is a particularly harrowing sequence with bedraggled serfs behind modern concrete posts and barbed wire (0.11); but we also see Marina playing in her transparent bath with a blue plastic duck (1.02). The film ends, predictably one might argue, with a return to the theatre where the opera is being shown, but the audience are now in modern dress, although Mussorgsky is still among them (1.48).

It is not just the decor that undermines any sense of realism; as with *Madam Butterfly*, the camera hardly ever stops moving, giving a sense of 'manic recklessness', as one reviewer puts it, pointing out that 'characters sing while rutting vigorously [1.07], and one character completes an aria while plummeting from a minaret' [0.20] (Cairns 2016); when the camera does stop, it is generally to focus briefly on the singer in an extreme and harrowing close-up.

The camera movement is part of a rigorous aesthetic choice, however; Żuławski complains in the DVD documentary that the visual track and the music in opera films often appear to run in parallel, rather than synergistically. He therefore decided to match musical phrases with single shots, leading to highly complex pans and tracks.

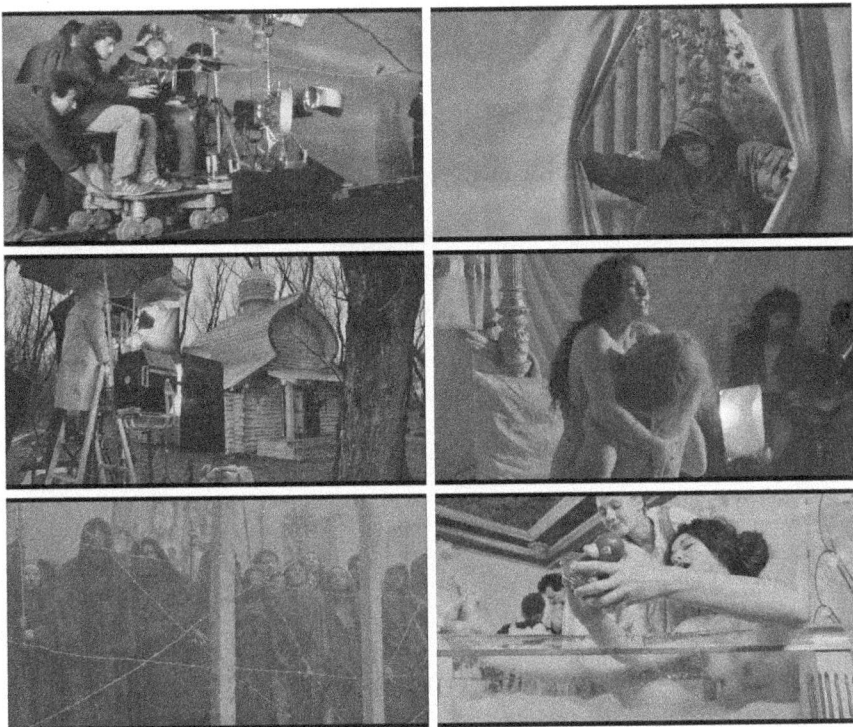

Figure 15.1 Anti-realism in *Boris Godounov* (Courtesy Gaumont).

This makes *Boris Godounov* a remarkable achievement, matched only, in our view, by the last opera film we will analyse, Jacquot's *Tosca*.

Like *Boris Godounov*, *Tosca* focuses on the performative and constructed nature of opera. The real locations of the three acts of the opera (the Basilica of Sant'Andrea della Valle, the Palazzo Farnese and the Castel Sant'Angelo) were reconstructed in a Cologne studio – a similar procedure to Gance's studio set for *Louise* – but with vast uncluttered spaces surrounded by darkness, so that the characters emerge as if from the backstage of a theatre.[3] In these vast spaces, the focus is also on costume and on isolated items of decor, such as Tosca's long-trained red dress, contrasted starkly with Scarpia's black costume, or the sequence when Scarpia looks at a distorted image of himself in the knife he has been using for his supper (0.49). The film makes no attempt to hide the playback: we frequently see mismatches between what we hear and what the singers' lips are doing; moreover, on several occasions the characters sing but we hear them repeating the words as ordinary dialogue over the singing (0.20, 0.26), or in a variant

---

[3] A similar studio set was adopted by Goretta for *Orfeo*, although much less successfully (see Friche (1987: 85–6).

effect, we hear them singing but do not see them doing so, as if their song is a kind of inner monologue (0.35).

Most startling of all is the three-stranded approach to what we see: the full colour studio sequences are punctuated by brief, stuttering and grainy colour sequences of the locations of the film, and by overexposed black-and-white sequences of the orchestra rehearsing in the recording studio. The orchestra sequences, in particular, insist on the constructed nature of what we see, as if the opera can only exist in our imagination: at the climax of the film, for example, as Tosca leaps to her death over the parapet into the darkness, her red train following her in a cloud of dust, we cut to the singer, Angela Gheorghiu, in the recording studio, sighing now that all is done, and chatting with her fellow singers.

One sequence in particular stands out as a remarkable moment of pure cinema in which theatre, music, camerawork and editing combine in ways that no other opera film has ever done. At the close of Act 1, Scarpia, the evil police chief, gloats as he imagines conquering Tosca and getting rid of her lover Cavaradossi (Figure 15.2). The camera circles around Scarpia in the main film strand, circles under the cupola of the Basilica in the grainy strand, and holds the rehearsing orchestra in the black-and-white strand. The circling camera could be taken to signify Scarpia's lust for Tosca, enfolding him to the point where he 'takes off' on wings of lust; but it could equally well signify the ascendency of the sacred in the battle with the profane, representing Tosca battling with Scarpia. The film creates a moment of perfect ambiguity in a whirligig of heightened emotion. It achieves what Gance set out to do with Charpentier's *Louise*, an opera like *Tosca* dating from 1900. Both rejected the realism that dogs so many opera films; but where Gance's *Louise* strains to allow heroic melodrama its full rein, and in the end feels more like a chocolate box, Jacquot's *Tosca* not only celebrates melodrama, but also interrogates it in postmodern mode as emotional fantasy.

Looking back at the development of the French opera film, it is very tempting to see *Louise* and *Tosca* as the beginning and the end of what was possible for the opera film, with the various films in between as interesting but failed experiments. Both *Louise* and *Tosca* mimic the melodrama and theatricality of opera by rejecting exteriors and focusing, instead, on studio sets that push what we see towards melodramatic fantasy anchored in artistically reimagined sets. But then we could ask what makes a staged opera with its sets different from a filmed opera with its sets. Apart from the temptation of realism – which means the use of exteriors and natural diegetic sounds – that most opera films display, and which Rosi's *Carmen* managed so well, the attraction of the more successful opera films lies in their fractured reality, whether the mise en abyme of *Boris Godounov* with its references to the twentieth century, or the flagrant use of the studio in *Louise*, *Boris Godounov* and *Tosca*.

Siegfried Kracauer considered the opera film to be 'a collision of two worlds detrimental to both' and that at best it could only be 'an eclectic compromise between irreconcilable entities – a sham whole distorting either the opera or the film or both' (1960: 154). He follows these comments with his view of what works and what does not work in *Louise*, the main element being, as in the view of Gance's contemporaries, the 'significant camera work'. He singles out one and only one

Figure 15.2 The three strands in the close of Act 1 in *Tosca* (Courtesy BBC).

sequence that in his view manages to achieve 'a precarious equilibrium between music and imagery', the father's aria towards the end of the film, a kind of lullaby in which he laments Louise's passage from childhood into a wilful independence and during which she sits on his knees as he rocks her (1.11): 'The camera approaches the two closely, isolates their faces, and ... draws us into the very vortex of inarticulate childhood, whose memory the song itself evokes' (154; Figure 15.3).

Figure 15.3 The close-up of father and daughter in *Louise* (Courtesy René Chateau).

The most successful opera films combine several elements: the interrogation of realism through elaborate and obvious studio sets and/or mise en abyme; the use of mobile camerawork; and, most importantly, in conjunction with these, as Kracauer points out earlier, the use of close-up which draws us into the emotion vehicled by the song and its percolation through the body of the singer. Ultimately, the difference between a staged opera and an opera film lies in the difference between distance and closeness. The proscenium arch coupled with the ritualistic elements of 'going to the opera' produces the distance of a performed rite, while the closeness afforded by the close-up in most opera films breaks that distance down leading to the opposite of ritual distance: the intimacy of human emotion felt through the combination of song and facial expressions.

The modern classical music film

Of the films dealing directly with classical music in the 1980s, four are particularly interesting as their focus is on musical performance. Three of these are biopics, a genre we will return to in our conclusion. *Tous les matins du monde* (Alain Corneau, 1991) tells the story of the composer Marin Marais as the pupil of Monsieur de Sainte-Colombe during the reign of Louis XIV. There are three films by Gérard Corbiau: *Le Maître de musique* (1988), set at the beginning of the twentieth century, and as the title suggests, telling the story of a (fictional) music teacher; *Farinelli* (1994), on the famous eighteenth-century castrato; and *Le Roi danse* (2000), on the relationship between Louis XIV and his master of music.

Corbiau began his career as a music specialist making TV films in Belgium, a fact that allowed at least one French critic to be dismissive about his second feature film, *Le Maître de musique*, commenting that the film's telefilm-type close-ups, the fact all the actors with the exception of José van Dam were dubbed, and that the stuffy style made its success with almost half a million spectators all the more surprising (Thirard 1989: 69). Another complained about the clichés in both the plot and the dialogue (Chevassu 1988: 28): in the 1900s an ageing singer retires and takes only two pupils on, but is dismayed when they enter into a competition organized by his arch-rival who wants revenge for the musical duel that ruined his career. With its French-language dialogue and focus on music clearly aiming at an international rather than Belgian audience (see Mosley 2001: 182), and its high-status locations (the châteaux of Chimay and La Hulpe in Belgium), the film played into the emerging heritage genre of the 1980s.

At the same time, it looked nostalgically backwards to Luchino Visconti's *Morte a Venezia* (1971) with its frequent use of Gustav Mahler's music, recalling the parallel between Visconti's dying composer Gustav von Aschenbach and Corbiau's Joachim Dalleyrac, the singer at the end of his career and soon to die. At the end of Visconti's film, we hear Mahler's *Adagietto* from the Fifth Symphony; in Corbiau's film, we hear Dalleyrac singing 'Ich bin der Welt abhanden gekommen' ('I am lost to the world') from Mahler's Rückertlieder as his body is taken down a river for burial, immediately followed, during the end credits, by the *Adagio* from Mahler's Fourth Symphony (1.29). Both of these pieces occur earlier in the film, the *Adagio* when Dalleyrac's young pupil, Sophie, declares her love for him, and they end up kissing (0.37), and later when Sophie is alone in her hotel room waiting for the competition and she and Dalleyrac's other pupil, Jean, end up kissing (0.57).

However, it is 'Ich bin' that dominates, its stanzas stretched across the film. We hear the first stanza during the pre-credits sequence; the second stanza when Dalleyrac has a turn during a lesson with Sophie (0.13) – on which occasion we hear only the orchestra without the lyrics that would normally have been there – the first stanza again when all three drive to the competition and Dalleyrac refuses to stay, realizing that his career, his love, and his life are at an end (0.54); and then the final stanza during the funeral boat scene as mentioned earlier. The lied therefore bookends the film, almost as if it were the determining narrative underpinning, with musical closure achieved only with Dalleyrac's death. The final words of the song push us to see the film as an illustration of the song: 'Ich leb' allein in meinem Himmel/In meinem Lieben, in meinem Lied!'.[4] Not only is Dalleyrac well and truly dead to the world, but as these final words emphasize, the film has been about his journey from the social world, to one last love (Sophie), and, finally, to the only thing that remains, the song that we have heard throughout the film.

The music does not illustrate the maudlin narrative so much as direct what we see and create the emotion we are supposed to feel: 'The film is not decorated with music, but structured through it. Music becomes the dynamic propeller of the plot' (Lawaetz 1989: 150). Indeed, when Dalleyrac is teaching Sophie, he tells her that she should be so engrossed in the music that she should not be aware of him walking past her, saying 'rien n'existe plus que votre voix et le chant'[5] (0.27). The instruction not to see what is in

---

[4] 'I live alone in my heaven/In my love, in my song!'
[5] 'Nothing exists any more except your voice and the song.'

front of us but to focus on the music is exactly what the film is asking us to do, with its pedestrian dialogue and predictable heritage-film decor overshadowed by the beauty of the music.

A few years later, in the wake of the adaptation of Peter Shaffer's *Amadeus* (Milos Forman, 1984), recounting the struggle between Salieri and Mozart, Corneau's *Tous les matins du monde* reprised the master–pupil narrative, setting it in seventeenth-century France. The film was a surprise for a number of reasons: it was directed by a man better known for making police thrillers; it dealt with unfashionable baroque music; and it attracted over two million spectators, this being an unusually high number for a film focusing on music. Two of the leads, Gérard Depardieu and Anne Brochet, had recently starred in a very successful heritage film, *Cyrano de Bergerac* (Jean-Paul Rappeneau, 1990), and in appearance *Tous les matins du monde* forms part of the heritage-film genre that had emerged during the mid-1980s. But the film is more like an art-house film – which makes its success all the more unusual – in that the style is austere, with nearly all shots using a fixed camera, and a highly literary voice-over narration by Marais/Depardieu. Many shots are unambiguously painterly, using lighting familiar in the work of Georges de la Tour or Philippe de Champaigne, as well as ostentatiously incorporating a still life painting by Lubin Baugin (1612–63), *Nature morte aux gaufrettes* (c. 1630), which plays an important role in the narrative, as it represents Sainte-Colombe's dead wife, and its recreation with real objects summons her ghost while he plays.

The tension between heritage spectacle and art-house echoes the main tension in the film between social ambition (Marais) and reclusive spirituality (Sainte-Colombe). The former is represented by ornate court costumes and a brief snatch of Lully's well-known *Marche pour la cérémonie des Turcs* ('March for the Turkish Ceremony', 1670). This was originally incorporated in the incidental music for Molière's *Le Bourgeois Gentilhomme* (1670), a play that satirizes a social climber, and by association critiques Marais's desire to be a successful royal musician. This is contrasted with a dozen viol pieces by Marais and Sainte-Colombe, played by Jordi Savall, unknown to most of the cinema audience, although that rapidly changed after the film's success.[6] Arguably, the narrative matters less than the moments when the two men play viol pieces, as we understand that Sainte-Colombe is trying to find a musical language that transcends the vanity of the world, and that Marais has to move beyond brilliant technique that the Court will admire to the expression of loss through his playing. He realizes this in the moving penultimate sequence when he visits his teacher, who tells him that 'la musique est simplement là pour parler de ce dont la parole ne peut parler; en ce sens elle n'est pas tout à fait humaine'[7] (1.35). Their two previously opposing world views coincide in the celebration and exorcism of loss as they play Sainte-Colombe's 'Le Tombeau des regrets' together.[8]

---

[6] Savall's records of viol music by Marais and Sainte-Colombe sold 5000 copies prior to the film, and 25000 after it, the soundtrack of the film also selling 100,000 copies (Denis 2010: 34).
[7] 'Music is simply here to speak what words cannot; in that sense music is not entirely human.'
[8] See Denis (2010) for a thorough exploration of the various contexts for the film.

Farinelli repeats the seventeenth-century music and the biopic genre of *Tous les matins du monde*. It is a measure of how popular the baroque had become following Corneau's film that 20,000 copies of *Farinelli*'s soundtrack were sold in two weeks (Guénée 1995: 10), and the film itself had 1.3 million spectators. The film is once more about the relationship between two musicians, the castrato Carlo Broschi (1705–82) and his composer brother Riccardo. Although there are some historically verifiable points of contact, the film is largely fictional, focusing on the brothers' relationship. Farinelli attracts women sexually because his singing is orgasmic for them: during the first major aria we hear in the film, his brother's 'Ombre fidele anch'io' ('As a Faithful Shadow I'll Be') from *Idaspe*, Farinelli holds a high note (A5) on the 'a' of 'addoro' for 25 seconds, as a result of which two women in the audience swoon from pleasure (0.20), and the Countess tells him afterwards that he is responsible for her first 'orgasme musical' (0.27). But as a castrato Farinelli cannot achieve orgasm; he gives women musical pleasure while his brother completes the sex act. With its baroque music and its various subtitled languages (Italian, French, German and English), the film is identifiably art-house, and there is the kind of spectacle that is associated with heritage cinema; Farinelli's public appearances with exotic headdresses in the first half of the film (0.17, 0.35, 0.44; Figure 15.4) cause the diegetic audience to murmur in appreciation, cueing our own admiration. But the focus on sex and the complex relationship Farinelli has with his brother (who had him unknowingly castrated to preserve the voice that would bring fame to his mediocre compositions) turn it into eroticized melodrama.

An example of the film's heady melodrama occurs towards the end of the film. Handel, who is at the opera waiting to hear Farinelli perform, has just revealed to Farinelli that Riccardo had had him castrated. Farinelli almost has a breakdown before

Figure 15.4 Farinelli sings 'Ombra fedele anch'io' (Courtesy TF1 Studio).

going on stage, where he performs 'Lascia ch'io pianga' ('Let Me Weep') from Handel's *Rinaldo*. As he sings we see flashbacks to his childhood, including the castration, with the young Farinelli lying drugged in a bath of milk. When he comes to the phrase 'e che sospiri la libertà'[9] he holds a high note (C6) on the first syllable of 'libertà', Handel swoons as the women had done earlier in the film, and we see blood rising to the surface of the bath in which the young Farinelli lies (1.31). The scene is echoed a few minutes later in the film by the slow-motion escape of a herd of white horses when Riccardo, having met with his brother after three years' absence, realizes that he has lost the score which he had been composing all of his life in atonement for the castration of his brother (1.35). Given that Farinelli's castration has historically been linked with a riding accident, and that he apparently had a stud farm with Hungarian stallions later in life, there is some factual motivation for the image of the bolting stallions. But we also frequently see horses in Farinelli's nightmares, and Handel sports a cane with a horse's head to which the camera constantly draws attention (Bergeron 1996: 168–9), so that the equine theme swamps what we see (and, indeed, what we hear). A similar type of image-laden saturation can be seen in the addition of an unhistorically verified character, the young boy Bénédicte, whose stunted body moves Farinelli. We see him being laced up in a corset to hold his body up, and he describes himself as 'un escargot privé de sa coquille'[10] (1.10), a metaphor that is immediately taken up 'to grotesque effect' (Bergeron 1996: 174):

> At a banquet, servants are shucking oysters as fast as they can be consumed. A long, almost pornographic, close-up offers one of the still-living creatures for our scrutiny – *sans coquille*. Quivering from a perfect silver fork, the shelled mollusc is either a fragile vocal chord or a horrible, missing genital. The sick-making spectacle of oyster and knife hardly puts too fine a point on the mystery of the 'missing thing' this film seeks to resolve. The director, like an overzealous social worker, forces the spectator to confront, once and for all, the very thing that the castrati apparently never let their audiences forget. (174)

These two episodes are good examples of what Martha Feldman might have had in mind when she described the film as 'at once majestic and inane' (2014: 410), the music being majestic, and the hyper-saturated costumes and exaggeratedly excessive psychology being inane. The music is majestic mainly because of the recreation of a castrato voice; this was done digitally by morphing two voices, the Polish soprano Ewa Mallas-Godlewska and the American countertenor Derek Lee Ragin. Part of the fascination of the film is the splicing together of two separate voices to create a voice that is no longer possible, echoing the cutting off of the castrato's testicles to create what Riccardo calls the voice of an angel (1.18). As Naomi André points out, the recreated voice 'was familiar enough to modern ears to sound believable, and yet

---

[9] 'And sigh for my lost freedom.'
[10] 'A snail deprived of its shell.'

it evoked a sound and technical capability that was almost unbelievable and virtually impossible' (2006: 18).

And yet, rather like the film's manipulation of historical fact to create a biography that is in many respects false, the voice we hear is artificial. Recalling the opposition between ambition and technique on the one hand and spirituality on the other in *Tous les matins du monde*, it is the reason for Handel's antipathy towards Farinelli. He comments: 'La voix d'un castrat est la manifestation de nature bafouée, détournée de son but pour tromper. Vous avez mis votre voix au service d'une virtuosité sans âme, à la seule dévotion de l'artifice'[11] (1.08). Similarly, the voice we hear in the film is not anyone's voice; it is the voice of a digital process, and feels emotionless and machine-like. Bergeron points out that the high C we hear and which makes Handel swoon (or have a stroke; it is not clear), 'penetrates – cuts like a knife' (1996: 181). Just as a knife cut Farinelli so that no one could hear his adult singing voice, so too the audience of the film do not hear a human voice, but only a reconstituted absence, which marks the film as mere spectacle, without the very human 'grain' of the voice that Barthes identified as what touches us when we hear someone sing (1982), compounding the absence we experience of a singer's body in a film as opposed to the theatre.

Corbiau followed *Farinelli* with *Le Roi danse*, which focuses on the relationship between Louis XIV and his court composer Lully. The King uses Lully's music to dance to, so as to ensure that he is literally centre stage at court. In a concerted effort to support the King's politics of spectacle and the move to undermine religious bigotry, Lully and Molière collaborate briefly on a new theatrical genre for the court, the comedy ballet. All three men suffer loss: the King stumbles during a dance, and stops dancing; Lully outsmarts Molière for the King's favours; Molière dies on stage. Unlike Corbiau's two previous films, the first of which was fictional and the second of which fictionalized much of Farinelli's life, *Le Roi danse* is broadly factual (Alion 2000: 124). Although it deals with much the same period as *Tous les matins du monde*, it feels much more like a standard heritage film targeting an international audience.

The musical pieces, rather like Gance's *Louise*, are spectacular moments subservient to a narrative focusing on the power of words to craft a melodramatic intrigue in which Lully's presumed homosexual leanings are what tie him to the King. The fact that the King and Lully are 'au bord d'une crise de nerfs permanente'[12] (Loiseau 2008) pulls the focus away from music towards the relationship between Lully and the King, and Lully and his friend, but also his rival, Molière. Indeed, we could argue that the relationship between the composer and the playwright is a metaphor for the problem of pre-eminence of dialogue and narrative over sound and music. Although the two of them collaborate to produce comedy ballets that meld words (Molière) and music (Lully), there is eventually a struggle between words and music, in which music appears to win. Lully, tired of playing second fiddle to Molière, persuades the King to grant him authority over the playwright. A boastful Lully tells Molière: 'Toute parole

---

[11] 'The voice of a castrato is the manifestation of Nature flouted, its goal diverted so as to deceive. You have put your voice in the service of a soulless virtuosity, devoted only to artifice.'
[12] 'Permanently on the edge of a nervous breakdown.'

sur laquelle j'ai composé de la musique est maintenant ma propriété. ... Ma musique ne passera plus après tes mots'[13] (1.29). The victory is Pyrrhic, however: Molière dies, but Lully is gradually abandoned by the King, and dies after puncturing his foot with his conducting staff and contracting gangrene.

Music, and particularly song, has been associated with nostalgia and loss. It is therefore unsurprising that all of the films discussed in this chapter focus on loss. Loss at another level also occurs, and is frequently commented on: the fragmentation of the music, and the loss of an immersive musical experience. Even when the film is the rendering of a whole work, as is the case with the opera films, it is clear that something is lost: the opera is cut down in length and it is impossible to recreate the 'liveness' associated with theatrical performance. The opera film will always be a palimpsest and a masquerade gesturing to something other than what it is.

---

[13] 'All words that I have set to music are now my property. My music will not play second fiddle to your words.'

16

The modern auteur musical

Demy marks a turn towards the modern musical; Resnais's *On connaît la chanson* marks the beginning of the nostalgic turn that many modern auteur musicals demonstrate. With Resnais it is the use, first, of well-known song snippets and then, in a subsequent film, the recycling of a 1920s operetta; with Ozon, similarly, it is the recycling and reworking of a 1960s boulevard play focused on musical performances by his eight female actresses. Maïwenn by contrast works against the nostalgic strain by taking Ozon's idea of a focus on women to produce a documentary-style musical focused on well-known contemporary women actresses. Finally, we focus on three queer film musicals, two of which deal with AIDS, and/or which are in part nostalgic homages to the films of Demy made some thirty-five years before. Two of these films did very well at the box office, as can be seen in Table 16.1, and as we shall see, several of them garnered substantial awards, suggesting both the importance of auteur films for the French industry, and the renewal of film musicals as a genre since the mid-1990s.

Resnais

Resnais had flirted with the musical form in *La vie est un roman* (1983) in which characters briefly burst into song and which has occasional musical numbers, such as a song by the avant-garde singer-composer Cathy Berberian, 'Air de la nourrice' ('The Nurse's Song'). The film did not do well at the hands of the critics; exactly the opposite occurred for *On connaît la chanson*, however, as it attracted considerable interest from critics and audiences alike, partly because of its innovative use of songs. It won a number of Césars including Best Film as well as awards for the actors (André Dussollier, Agnès Jaoui, Jean-Pierre Bacri), also winning the Louis Delluc Prize. It heralds the modern musical, despite the fact that Resnais, like Akerman before him, was considered by many to be an austere 1960s art-house filmmaker, better known for *Hiroshima mon amour* (1959) and *L'Année dernière à Marienbad* (1961).

Like Akerman's film, the plot of *On connaît la chanson* focuses on a group of characters involved romantically, although in Resnais's film the characters are from the Parisian bourgeoisie: Simon (André Dussollier) loves Camille (Agnès Jaoui), who loves Simon's boss, estate agent Marc (Lambert Wilson), who tries to sell an apartment to Camille's sister, Odile (Sabine Azéma). Odile's husband Claude is

Table 16.1 The Nostalgic Modern Auteur Musical

On connaît la chanson	1997	Resnais	2.7m
Jeanne et le garçon formidable	1998	Ducastel/Martineau	0.2m
8 femmes	2002	Ozon	3.7m
Pas sur la bouche	2003	Resnais	0.6m
Crustacés et coquillages	2005	Ducastel/Martineau	0.2m
Le Bal des actrices	2009	Maïwenn	0.3m
Les Chansons d'amour	2007	Honoré	0.3m
Les Bien-Aimés	2011	Honoré	0.3m

jealous of Nicolas (Jean-Pierre Bacri), who at some time in the past had courted Odile, and who now has become Simon's confidant. Taking his cue from Dennis Potter's 1978 TV series, Resnais asked the actors to lip-synch thirty-six snippets of pre-recorded French songs of which about a third are pre-1940, sung by Arletty, Josephine Baker, Dranem, Henri Garat, Gaston Ouvrard and Édith Piaf. Most of the songs, however, are from the mid-1960s to the early 1980s, sung by Charles Aznavour, Alain Bashung, Gilbert Bécaud, Jane Birkin, Julien Clerc, Dalida, Jacques Dutronc, Léo Ferré, France Gall, Johnny Hallyday, Serge Lama, Michel Sardou, Alain Souchon and Sylvie Vartan. The songs may have covered a broad set of styles, ranging from music hall (Ouvrard) and pop (Gall, Souchon, Vartan), to the more arty end represented by Ferré, but as a reviewer pointed out, the absence of contemporary French singers makes this film 'un grand film de vieux', 'un film qui a une certaine mémoire des choses et du monde et qui n'est pas prêt à la sacrifier au profit du culte du contemporain'[1] (Bouquet 1997: 48).

This comedy of manners sits oddly between vaudeville and the verbose and affected theatrical style the French call marivaudage. It is disrupted by snatches of songs whose lyrics comment on both the action and emotions of the characters while at the same time distancing us and them from themselves and others; the songs 'expriment et enferment à la fois le plus intime de ce que chacun ressent'[2] (Frodon 1997). The disruptive effect is clear in that the singing voices we hear are obviously not those of the actors themselves, especially when a male character lip-synchs to a female singer or the reverse. And the film is all the more odd for being a musical but not quite, as the actors lip-synch without any of the more expressive gestures or choreography we might associate with the musical. Resnais said that he loved the American film musical so much that he did not want to try and emulate it, and that in any case he wanted to avoid the excess of the musical and focus on the everyday. This, counter-intuitively, naturalized the use of song-bursts, as Resnais commented: 'On a en permanence une chanson au bord des lèvres, mais on n'est pas tout le temps prêt à danser'[3] (Gorin 1997),

---

[1] 'A film for older people'; 'a great film that refuses to sacrifice a certain memory of things and of the world to the cult of the contemporary.'
[2] 'Express and enclose the most intimate feelings.'
[3] 'We have a song on the tip of our tongues all of the time, but we're not always ready to dance.'

Figure 16.1 Simon sings 'Vertiges de l'amour' in *On connaît la chanson* (Courtesy Pathé).

and he also commented that the songs should be seen as the kind of thing we all do in the mirror (Resnais 1997b: 4).

Importantly, Resnais chose not to use song extracts that might have been deemed too deep or affecting and that might have pulled the character 'au fond du désespoir'[4] (Resnais 1997a). As a result, the film appears deceptively light, and surreally comical at times, especially when the voice of the singer is at odds with the voice of the actor: hypochondriac Nicolas visits the doctor (0.14) and sings a 1932 music-hall number, 'Je ne suis pas bien portant' ('I'm Not Well') with its rapidly articulated and heavily assonated lyrics ('J'ai la rate qui s'dilate/J'ai le foie qu'est pas droit');[5] soft-spoken Simon watches a parade of the Republican Guard and imagines himself riding with them (0.50), singing Alain Bashung's brash 1981 'Vertiges de l'amour' ('Giddy Love') (Figure 16.1). The lyrics of the songs used in the film rely on clichés; much like Akerman's musical, the film emphasizes 'appearances', the way that the characters hide their emotions in plain sight by using psychologically reductive phrases, or as one reviewer put it, the songs are 'rideaux de fumée masquant la complexité des personnages ballottés au gré du hasard, des malentendus, des délires de leur imaginaire et du regard forcément réducteur des autres'[6] (Tinazzi 1997). But for all the jollity of the song-bursts, the effect also leads to a feeling of being distanced, cut off from the characters and their concerns, who, in the end, are mostly depressive, leading to 'a shimmering set of scenes

[4] 'The depths of despair.'
[5] 'My spleen's dilating, my liver's not straight.'
[6] 'Smoke screens that hide the complexity of the characters blown hither and thither by events, misunderstandings, their wild imagination and the reductive gaze of other people.'

which induce the vertigo and malaise from which the characters themselves suffer' (Wilson 2006: 182).

Resnais's next film, *Pas sur la bouche*, is also a musical, although this time the actors do not lip-synch snippets of songs but sing the film's twenty musical numbers. Like *On connaît la chanson*, it won a number of prestigious prizes, including three Césars, and two Best Film awards (Lumière and Étoile d'Or). The film is a straight remake of a popular 1925 operetta by André Barde and Maurice Yvain, which ran for over a year in Paris (Gana 2000), and was subsequently adapted for the screen with the same title in 1931 by Nicolas Evreinoff and Nicolas Rimsky (Chapter 3). The story is a typical vaudeville farce in three acts: Gilberte (Sabine Azéma), previously married to the American Eric (Lambert Wilson) – who dislikes being kissed on the lips, hence the title of the film – is now married to Georges (Pierre Arditi), who bizarrely believes that once a woman has had sex with a man the couple will be happy forever and that she 'belongs' to him. Gilberte's spinster sister Arlette (Isabelle Nanty) is the only one who knows that Gilberte was previously married. Gilberte flirts with various suitors – middle-aged Faradel (Daniel Prévost) and young artist Charley (Jalil Lespert) – confident that this will not affect her marriage. Charley is in turn pursued by Gilberte's friend Huguette (Audrey Tautou). The precarious balance between the characters is disturbed by the arrival of Eric, who has come from the United States to do business with Georges. Act 2 is devoted to Charley's staging of a play based in Mexico, during which Gilberte tries to deter Eric's claims on her by pretending to be in love with Charley. In Act 3 the characters play out the imbroglio in Faradel's opulent bachelor flat, with the kind of comings and goings and misunderstandings typical of farce.

In an interview Resnais talked of his childhood love of operetta as one of the motivations for choosing an obscure 1925 stage operetta, specifically mentioning *Le congrès s'amuse*, *Le Chemin du paradis* (Chapter 2) and *Toi, c'est moi* (Chapter 3) (Resnais 2003a). He also paradoxically pointed out how foreign the concerns of the characters in *Pas sur la bouche* and the saucy songs might well seem to modern audiences; an example of sauciness is the concierge's song when the characters frolic in Faradel's apartment: 'En regardant par le trou/On voit des choses raides comme tout.'[7] The 'foreignness' was exacerbated by the fact that as well as keeping most of the songs, he kept the original dialogues with their references to contemporary events and places, and their very 'written' style, as one of the few sustained analyses of the film points out (Gral Dalby 2011: 94). Resnais himself consistently used the word 'frivolous' to describe the film (Attali 2003; Resnais 2003b), stressing how the film's mismatch with the 2000s was part of its surreal charm. Pressed on the sociopolitical relevance of the film, he repeatedly explained that the film suggested the bourgeoisie of the 1920s dancing on a volcano, impervious to world events (Liblot 2003; Resnais 2003b and 2003c). But the feel of the film is one of affectionate homage to the operetta in the past and to his familiar troupe of actors in the present.

---

[7] 'When you look through the keyhole/You see some really stiff things.'

Figure 16.2 Theatrical staginess in *Pas sur la bouche* (Courtesy Pathé).

In common with many of Resnais's films, there is a sense of theatrical staginess to the film (Figure 16.2); the characters are shot from above at the start of the film, as if they were entomological specimens. They move like puppets in the surreal décor with its strong emphasis on mirrors and paintings; they occasionally fade out, like ghosts. They frequently address very theatrical apartés to the audience, as well as singing directly to the audience in the closing sequence when they pop out from behind the stage curtain, echoing the finale of *Le Chemin du paradis* (Chapter 2) (Figure 16.3).

The film is a perfect example of a 1920s stage operetta with many of the tricks used by film operettas; that, coupled with its 'frivolity', is its strength, but also its weakness. As one reviewer put it, it is all great fun, but is just as likely to lead to 'bâillements polis'[8] (Gomez 2003), and is somewhat disappointing after the innovative turn to the past of *On connaît la chanson*.

---

[8] 'Polite yawns.'

Figure 16.3 Direct address to the audience in *Pas sur la bouche* (Courtesy Pathé).

Ozon and Maïwenn

8 femmes also faces towards the past. The story, from a *boulevard* play by Robert Thomas first produced in Paris in 1961, is an Agatha Christie-style whodunnit that showcases the film's eight high-profile actresses. It is set in a snowbound house at Christmas; the man of the house, Marcel, is discovered with a knife in his back, and the plot revolves around who among the eight women might have committed the crime. They start the film as theatrical types, as is emphasized by close-ups on flowers associated with each of them during the opening credit sequence, suggesting that they can be reduced to a single characteristic. There is Marcel's wife, wealthy Grande dame Gaby (Catherine Deneuve/variegated orchid), her dutiful daughter Suzon (Virginie Ledoyen/pink rose) and younger daughter Catherine (Ludivine Sagnier/daisy), their sour maiden aunt Augustine (Isabelle Huppert/thistle), their alcoholic grandmother Mamy (Danielle Darrieux/pansy), the cook Madame Chanel who is a person of colour (Firmine Richard/sunflower), the scheming chambermaid Louise (Emmanuelle Béart/white orchid), and Marcel's femme fatale sister Pierrette (Fanny Ardant/red rose). But quite apart from reducing its original two-and-a-half-hour length by dropping, as he put it, what he did not like and keeping everything that made him laugh (Mellini 2002: 51), Ozon complexifies Thomas's play significantly.

He does this first with the intertextual layers created by the postmodern generic mix, second by his choice of actresses, and third by the apparently disruptive use of a signature song performance for each of them. In generic terms, this last element shifts the mix of vaudeville farce and whodunnit towards the musical. But more obvious than this is the choice of actresses that gestures nostalgically towards the history of French cinema, producing a complex and disruptive archaeological layering. To see Deneuve singing once again would immediately have reminded audiences of her three films with Demy (Chapter 13); moreover, Ozon's film replicates the difficult mother-daughter relationship she had with Darrieux's character in Demy's *Les Demoiselles de Rochefort*. In addition, Deneuve twice says the same thing to Ledoyen – 'te voir, c'est à la fois une joie, et une souffrance'[9] – that a man had said to her in two of Truffaut's films, *La Sirène du Mississippi* (1969) and *Le Dernier Métro* (1980). Thibault Schilt points out the paradox that ensues:

> As soon as she utters those words, Deneuve seems more affected by the memory of Truffaut and the films she made with him than her diegetic conversation with her daughter. Similarly, the abnormally long (twenty-two-second) close-up shot of Ardant (who overhears the line) that concludes the scene suggests it is the memory of her late companion that brings her to tears rather than the fictional context of the film. (2011: 72)

Moreover, when she and Ardant roll on the floor as they catfight (1.31), they are replaying the end-of-film fight scene between Bernard (Gérard Depardieu) and Mathilde (Ardant) in Truffaut's *La Femme d'à côté* (1981). Finally, we see the maid Louise holding a photo of Romy Schneider, who starred in a number of Claude Sautet's films in the 1970s,[10] and whom Béart replaced as Sautet's favoured star for his last two films[11] after Schneider's death in 1982. Ozon explained in an interview that the reference was motivated by his childhood love of Schneider's *Sissi* films and by the fact that Schneider and Deneuve were often contrasted in the 1970s (Ozon 2002a: 21).

These intertextual historical layers give the characters depth, although that depth is of a centrifugal nature, frequently taking us out and away from the film and its hackneyed storyline, engaging our interest in the actresses as actresses rather than as characters. Indeed, Ozon, referencing France's version of the reality TV show *Big Brother*, suggested that the interest of the film was at least partly the dynamic between the actresses as actresses rather than the characters they play:

> L'idée c'était aussi de faire un documentaire sur des actrices ensemble. Que ce soit presque une expérience comme *Loft Story* où on enferme huit actrices ensemble

---

[9] 'Seeing you brings me joy, but also makes me suffer.'
[10] *Les Choses de la vie* (1970), *Max et les ferrailleurs* (1971), *César and Rosalie* (1972), *Une histoire simple* (1978).
[11] *Un cœur en hiver* (1992), *Nelly et Monsieur Arnaud* (1995).

et on regarde ce qu'il se passe. ... Il y avait l'idée, notamment à travers la danse et la chanson, que les actrices s'abandonnent, et qu'il y ait quelque chose qui leur échappe et que je réussisse à capter ça sur chacune.[12] (Ozon 2002b)

This approach clearly worked. The film had twelve César nominations; it did not win in any of the César categories, but Ozon won the Best Director Lumière award. Unusually, however, the eight actresses won the Berlin Silver Bear award and the European Film award as a group.

Each of the eight actresses has her song (Figure 16.4), and as was the case for Resnais, the songs were originally by performers popular in the 1960s and 1970s.[13] The songs function in the same way as in the traditional Hollywood musical, as pauses in the narrative. Because the film was not initially marketed as a musical, the songs come as a surprise and more as a disruption than in the traditional musical. That disruption is complex, however, as the songs also function cohesively in a number of ways. The overly performed nature of the musical moments may well distance the audience from the actresses; but paradoxically, because each actress sings the song herself, spectators, according to Ozon, are likely to feel closer to her, as well as experiencing an increase of the emotion the spectator may feel for the character embodied by the actress, because of what Roland Barthes calls the 'grain' of her voice, that grain giving us access to the actress's body (Ozon 2002b). The impact of the songs on audiences can be judged by the fact that they turned the film into what Darren Waldron calls a 'karaoké musical' (2010: 71). The website and the DVD had karaoke versions of the songs, which then elicited YouTube films of fans miming the songs, arguably further disrupting the film as a coherent whole by dissociating the songs from the narrative.

Disruptive though they may be, the songs nonetheless have a clear narrative function, as Ozon pointed out: 'Une scène chantée accélère la narration et révèle le personnage'[14] (Mellini 2002: 52). This is particularly the case of Huppert's rendering of Françoise Hardy's intensely confessional 'Message personnel', which Augustine sings to Mamy, Suzon, Mme Chanel and Catherine as they sway in time to the music (0.25). Filmed partly in close-up so that we see tears rolling down her cheeks, the camera pulls back so that we see Augustine incorporated in the group of women, partly because the song has allowed the group to understand this bitter spinster character, as Augustine

---

[12] 'The idea was to make a documentary on actresses working together, something like *Loft Story* in which you lock up eight actresses and watch what happens. The idea was that the actresses should let go through song and dance so that I could record what they no longer controlled.'

[13] Sagnier: Sheila's 'Papa t'es plus dans le coup' ('Dad, You Don't Know What's Going On', Sheila, 1963) (0.7).
Huppert: 'Message personnel' ('Personal Message', Françoise Hardy, 1973) (0.25).
Ardant: 'À quoi sert de vivre libre' ('What's the Use of Living Free', Nicoletta, 1975) (0.32).
Ledoyen: 'Toi mon amour, mon ami' ('You, My Love, My Friend', Marie Laforêt, 1967) (0.47).
Richard: 'Pour ne pas vivre seul' ('Not to Be Alone', Dalida, 1972) (1.00).
Béart: 'Pile ou face' ('Heads or Tails', Coryne Charby, 1987) (1.08).
Deneuve: 'Toi jamais' ('You Never', Michael Mallory, Sylvie Vartan, 1976) (1.25).
Darrieux: 'Il n'y a pas d'amour heureux' ('There Is No Happy Love', Georges Brassens, 1946) (1.39).

[14] 'A song moves the story along and reveals the character.'

Figure 16.4 The eight songs of *8 femmes* (Courtesy StudioCanal).

emphasizes in the ensuing dialogue: 'Vous pensez toutes que je vous déteste. C'est pas vrai, j'aime tout le monde. Mais personne ne comprend ma façon d'aimer, on croit que c'est de la haine.'[15]

A final and key issue is the film's queer contexts. Ozon's handling of the female characters has led to considerable debate and charges of misogyny in his use of patriarchal stereotypes (Waldron 2010: 73). But arguably the very excess of their performances, at their most obvious in the performance of the songs, tips those performances into camp subversion; the choice of certain songs also queers the film, as several of the original singers – Dalida, Hardy, Laforêt and Vartan – are cult figures for the LGBT community (see Guilbert 2018: 52–4 for Dalida and 85–6 for Hardy). Lesbianism is not part of Thomas's play, but features prominently in Ozon's film. Pierrette and Madame Chanel

---

[15] 'You all think I hate you. It's not true, I love everyone. But no one understands my way of loving, so you think it's hate.'

Figure 16.5 Pierrette and Gaby kiss after their catfight in *8 femmes* (Courtesy StudioCanal).

are lovers, and the latter's song refers specifically to gay relationships: 'Pour ne pas vivre seul/Des filles aiment des filles/Et l'on voit des garçons/Épouser des garçons';[16] and Pierrette and Gaby kiss passionately and lengthily after their catfight (Figure 16.5). Moreover, as Schilt points out, the lack of male characters in the film means that there is a constant female-on-female gaze that 'intensifies the film's queer tension, sometimes forecasting lesbian romances that the text will later divulge (Chanel/Pierrette; Gaby/Pierrette), other times advancing possibilities that remain unfulfilled (Augustine/Louise; Gaby/Louise)' (2011: 75). As we shall see with the films of Ducastel and Martineau and those of Honoré, the liminal queerness in Demy's musicals becomes much more evident in these later auteur musicals.

Like *Pas sur la bouche* and *Le Chemin du paradis*, *8 femmes* ends with a very theatrical gesture, as the eight women line up holding hands as if at the end of a play, reminding us of the origins of the film in a stage show (Schilt 2011: 77; see Figure 16.6), but also emphasizing female solidarity. That solidarity is a key component of the next film we wish to consider.

Like *8 femmes*, *Le Bal des actrices* has song-and-dance performances by the actresses, which is why we are considering it in this section. It is an auteur film in the genre of auto-fiction. Maïwenn is both the director of the film as well as playing a director of the film we are watching, but she is also one of the twelve actresses whose life as actress and as woman is explored by the film. In the poster of the film we see naked actresses

---

[16] 'So as not to live alone, girls love girls, and sometimes we see boys marry boys.'

Figure 16.6 The eight women line up holding hands in the last shot of *8 femmes* (Courtesy StudioCanal).

posing artfully, literally laid bare; one reviewer aptly called the film 'un *8 femmes* à vif'[17] (Bauche 2009: 53). Ozon's film had documentary embedded in its conception, as we saw; Maïwenn's film presents as a pseudo-documentary, blurring reality and fiction, as Isabelle Vanderschelden explains:

> Her camera films 'real' actresses at work and in private contexts, going behind the scenes, probing at sensitive aspects of their real/imagined star images. What she unearths varies from one actress to the next: sometimes hilarious, as when Karin Viard wants to have a career in Hollywood but cannot speak English; sometimes more emotional, as when Romane Bohringer is shown struggling to make a living from acting after being very successful, or Muriel Robin is unable to accept being typecast as a comic actress; sometimes surprising, as when Marina Foïs bluntly discusses her physical image and (fictional?) use of botox, or Charlotte Rampling unexpectedly sings JoeyStarr's rap song. Julie Depardieu and Mélanie Doutey add a further gendered dimension to the array of roles by bringing the motif of the desire for motherhood into the narrative. (2012: 251–2)

Each actress plays herself, but the role is modified by fictional aspects. We recognize some of this as what we might know of the actress's real life, such as the sequences with Robin or Lin-Dan Pham, or what we might have surmised, such as Rampling's difficulties in finding roles as an older woman; but other sequences are pure fantasy, such as Doutey's depression and interest in Hindu spirituality, or Julie Depardieu's sterility and fantasied pregnancy.

[17] '*8 Women* in the raw.'

Moreover, the boundaries between fiction and reality are confused even more by mise en abyme as we see a film within the film: Maïwenn is making a film about actresses which is the very film we are watching; unsurprisingly, then, we see cameras in nearly every sequence (with the exception of the family scenes involving Maïwenn and her real-life partner JoeyStarr at the time of making the film). Maïwenn takes this trope one step further: sometimes what we see is what we assume to be what Maïwenn-as-character has filmed, this occasionally leading to considerable epistemological confusion, as, for example, in the sequence filming Viard acting in a film by Bertrand Blier during which we become aware that there are three levels of filming: Maïwenn as director of the film, Maïwenn as character making the same film in which she is filming Blier making his film. The confusion climaxes at the end of the film when the actresses turn on Maïwenn furiously, accusing her of having made the film about herself rather than about them (1.33).

Unlike *8 femmes*, the songs are all from the 2000s, some composed for the film; but as was the case with Ozon's film, they function as pauses.[18] The documentary sequences follow the traditional tropes of the genre, with interviews of subjects, hand-held cameras and generally neutral colours. The musical numbers could not be more different from the documentary aesthetic of the rest of the film. They are colourful fantasies in the style typical of Hollywood Technicolor musicals of the 1940s and the 1950s (Figure 16.7); indeed, *Singin' in the Rain* is frequently alluded to in the film, not least in a sequence involving a vocal coach (0.15). Like Ozon's musical numbers, they jar with the rest of the film, but like Ozon's film they work with the characters, for example, Depardieu's number in which her desire for a child translates into her wallowing in a sea of baby dolls (0.47). Like Ozon's film, then, the musical numbers create an unresolved tension at several levels, not least that of genre. This is teasingly made clear in the film's dialogue when Maïwenn-as-character tries to raise money for the film with a sceptical producer who asks her why she wants to call the film *Le Bal des actrices*:

— Parce que je vais mettre des séquences où elles vont parler de leurs rêves mais en chansons, et en dansant. Tu vois, un peu comme une comédie musicale.
— Tu fais quoi, un documentaire ou une comédie musicale?
— Un documentaire.
— Un documentaire sous forme de comédie musicale?
— Voilà![19]

---

[18] Maïwenn, 'Le Bal des actrices' ('The Actress's Ball') (0.1); Muriel Robin, 'Le Rêve' ('Dream') (0.21); Karin Viard, 'I Can't Speak English' (0.24); Lin-Dan Pham, 'Les parents ne nous comprennent pas' ('Parents Don't Understand Us') (0.41); Julie Depardieu, 'Dans les films' ('In Films') (0.47); Mélanie Doutey, 'La Pin-Up du mois' ('This Month's Pin-Up') (0.53); Jeanne Balibar, 'Changer d'air' ('Change of Scene') (1.03); Charlotte Rampling, 'Revivre' ('To Live Again') (1.14) ; Romane Bohringer, 'Mille et une femmes' ('One Thousand and One Women') (1.19).

[19] 'Because in some of the sequences they will talk about their dreams but in song and dance./So what are you making, a documentary or a musical?/A documentary./A documentary in the form of a musical?/That's it!'

Figure 16.7 The musical numbers in *Le Bal des actrices* (Courtesy M6 Vidéo).

The queer musical

8 femmes has queer themes running through it, whereas the films we wish to consider in this section are more obviously queer, dealing much more directly with queer relationships and with AIDS, either directly or indirectly. Indeed, *Jeanne et le garçon formidable* refers specifically to the AIDS direct-action advocacy group Act Up, showing demonstrations in Paris (0.29). These musicals are part of the emergence of queer French cinema in the 1990s, signalled early in the decade by the AIDS-themed *Les Nuits fauves* (Cyril Collard, 1992, 2.8m tickets) and well enough established by the middle of the decade by some successful queer-themed comedies such as *Gazon maudit* (Josiane Balasko, 1995; 4m tickets) and *Pédale douce* (Gabriel Aghion, 1996, 4.2m tickets). Ducastel and Martineau's second feature, the gay AIDS-focused road movie *Drôle de Félix* (2000), although not popular with audiences (it had only 85,000 spectators) became academics' totemic queer film,[20] and to a large extent cemented the visibility of queer cinema since the millennium, thanks also to some mainstream comedies such as *Le Placard* (Francis Veber, 2001, 5.3m tickets) and *Chouchou* (Merzak Allouache, 2003; 3.9m tickets).[21]

Jeanne et le garçon formidable was Ducastel and Martineau's first feature, and *Crustacés et coquillages* their third. The latter does not deal with AIDS. The title of the film and the songs that all revolve around the title are a direct reference to Brigitte Bardot's 1962 song, 'La Madrague'. The film's songs gently parody Bardot's in much the same way that the narrative parodies vaudeville farces with its focus entirely and relentlessly on sex: the father of the family rediscovers the male lover of his youth, the son wrestles with his possible homosexuality, the mother's lover keeps popping up unexpectedly, and everyone is outed in the utopian finale with its Demy-like costumes and singing actors. The other films we will consider do have AIDS as a component, although not always foregrounded. *Jeanne et le garçon formidable* revolves around free spirit Jeanne (Virginie Ledoyen) who flits from relationship to relationship until she meets Olivier (Mathieu Demy). Their passion is cut short when he declares that he is HIV-positive and later dies. In *Les Chansons d'amour*, Julie (Ludivine Sagnier) and Ismaël (Louis Garrel) are in a relationship that is collapsing. They engage in a threesome with Alice (Clotilde Hesme), but shortly afterwards Julie dies unexpectedly of a heart attack. Ismaël meets Erwann (Grégoire Leprince-Ringuet) and after a protracted romance they end up making love. Honoré's next musical, *Les Bien-Aimés*, covers a long time span, from the 1960s through to the 2000s. Madeleine (Ludivine Sagnier) has a daughter, Véra, with Jaromil, but in 1968 she discovers that he is unfaithful and leaves him and Prague where they live to return to Paris, where Véra marries

---

[20] Ince (2002), Pratt (2004), Grandena (2006), Swamy (2006), McGonagle (2007), Provencher (2008), Archer (2013), Grandena (2013).
[21] It is of course debatable to what extent some of these films are 'queer'. We are adopting the broadest possible definition so as to place the musicals that interest us in their context of popular film production. For the debates around the definition of queer film, see Rees-Roberts (2008).

François ten years later, but maintains an occasional relationship with Jaromil (the older Madeleine is played by Catherine Deneuve, the older Jaromil by the filmmaker Miloš Forman, and the older François by the singer Michel Delpech) (who like Lio in *Golden Eighties* is the only one not to sing). Jaromil dies after being hit by a car during one of his Paris trips to see Madeleine. Véra's life also contains tragedy. Played by Chiara Mastroianni in the 1990s, she is in a relationship with Clément (Louis Garrel), but starts a relationship with the American Henderson (Paul Schneider) who tells her that he thinks he may be HIV-positive. The two of them and Henderson's lover engage in a threesome in a Montreal hotel, after which Véra commits suicide.

Many commentators thought it paradoxical to combine the pressing issue of AIDS with the musical. However, the filmmakers defended their choice, stressing the musical's lyrical life-affirming capacity. As Martineau said of *Jeanne et le garçon formidable*, 'le recours à la comédie musicale était une façon de nous délivrer de la mythologie du sida'[22] (Pliskin 1998), and as Honoré said of the use of songs in *Les Chansons d'amour*, 'passer par des chansons me permettait d'atteindre un certain lyrisme sans pour autant verser dans la mièvrerie'[23] (Frois 2007). We will consider the role of the dystopian everyday and its mediation through song later. But first we will consider the way in which the queer musicals very clearly display their relationship to those of Demy; indeed, Nick Rees-Roberts considers them to be a 'Demy revival' (2008: 109; see also Cadalanu 2018), and reviewers emphasized this aspect above all others, either to commend it – '*Jeanne et le garçon formidable* est le film que Jacques Demy aurait tourné s'il avait eu 20 ans aujourd'hui'[24] (Lefort 1998) – or occasionally to complain about it, claiming that the insistent references distance the spectator from the film (Morain 1998).

In *Jeanne et le garçon formidable* Olivier's hospital room is specifically painted a Demy-like blue; similarly, the décor of the repainted villa at the end of *Crustacés et coquillages* and the colours of the costumes in the finale also echo Demy. In *Jeanne et le garçon formidable* Olivier is played by Mathieu Demy, Jacques Demy's son. The political references that involve Act Up demonstrations, as well as the death of Olivier, echo the striking workers of Demy's *Une chambre en ville*, as does Jeanne's voice-over for a tango when she realizes that she is out of place in an up-market nightclub, her 'J'me sens pas bien dans cet endroit./Peut-être c'est pas ma place de danser avec des bourgeois'[25] (0.20) echoing Margot's diatribe against the bourgeoisie. When Jeanne walks through the streets of Paris she is accosted by a man who tells her she is beautiful, and dances in an extended tracking shot with him (1.18), just as Delphine does with the men in *Les Demoiselles de Rochefort*.[26] But the main parallels are, first, the anchoring in the banal gestures and events of the everyday, encapsulated by a transparent Demy

---

[22] 'Using a film musical was a means of freeing ourselves from the AIDS mythology.'
[23] 'Songs allowed me to achieve a certain lyricism without lapsing into sentimentalism.'
[24] '*Jeanne et le garçon formidable* is the film that Jacques Demy would have made if he were twenty years old today.'
[25] 'I don't feel good in this place, maybe it's not my thing to dance with bourgeois.'
[26] See Oyallon-Koloski (2014: 96–7) for a more extended analysis of the parallel, as well as an in-depth study of dance forms in the film.

reference when Jeanne drinks a cup of tea and sings 'passe-moi le sucre, c'est trop amer',[27] echoing the 'passe-moi le sel'[28] of *Les Parapluies de Cherbourg*; second, the parallels between Jeanne and the twin sisters of *Les Demoiselles de Rochefort* with their carefree attitude to life; third, the backdrop of major events that significantly affect the characters, such as the Algerian War in *Les Parapluies de Cherbourg* and the AIDS epidemic in *Jeanne et le garçon formidable*; and then, finally, the overall feel of the two films where 'the chance meetings and missed opportunities that are also an integral part of Demy's world point to sexual cruising as a key part of both Jeanne's lifestyle and its narrative representation' (Rees-Roberts 2008: 109).

Honoré also very visibly references Demy's films. He himself drew attention to the way in which *Les Chansons d'amour*'s tripartite structure is modelled on that of *Les Parapluies de Cherbourg* (Honoré 2007a). Julie's surname, Pommeraye, references the Passage Pommeraye in Nantes which Demy filmed in *Lola* and *Une chambre en ville*. The choice of Catherine Deneuve's real-life daughter, Chiara Mastroianni, for roles in both *Les Chansons d'amour* and *Les Bien-Aimés* is a clear reference to Deneuve's roles in Demy's first three films, something that Honoré emphasizes when he uses the same paper crown worn by Deneuve in *Les Parapluies de Cherbourg* (0.46) in a scene with Mastroianni in *Les Chansons d'amour* (0.19; Figure 16.8). *Les Bien-Aimés* reprises the Demy references with the opening credits of criss-crossing feet in the shoe shop that echo the criss-crossing umbrellas in the opening credits of *Les Parapluies de Cherbourg*, and the shop closely resembles the umbrella shop of *Les Parapluies de Cherbourg*, just as Julie's costume and very 1960s makeup with heavy mascara and eye-liner in *Les Chansons d'amour* are patterned on Deneuve's Geneviève. Sailors appear in the street in *Les Chansons d'amour* as they do in *Les Demoiselles de Rochefort*.

Demy is not the only intertextual reference, however. Honoré said in an interview that he felt close to the New Wave aesthetic (2007b) and there are many obvious references to New Wave films in *Les Chansons d'amour*: the opening credits show only surnames in heavy white block type, a clear reference to Godard's films of the 1960s; three characters sharing a bed is an allusion to *La Maman et la putain* (Jean Eustache, 1973)

Figure 16.8 The paper crown worn by Deneuve in *Les Parapluies de Cherbourg* and Mastroianni in *Les Chansons d'amour* (Courtesy Arte Éditions and BAC Films).

[27] 'Pass me the sugar, it's too bitter.'
[28] 'Pass me the salt.'

both in *Les Chansons d'amour* and in *Les Bien-Aimés*, Julie's white coat to Anna Karina's in *Une femme est une femme*, and three characters reading under the bedcovers to a bedroom scene between Antoine (Jean-Pierre Léaud) and Christine (Claude Jade) in *Baisers volés* (François Truffaut, 1968). As one critic said, the plethora of intertextual references, while charming, can become boring (Lefort 2007), and threatens to overwhelm the narrative; they are arguably unnecessary to signal the anchoring of the characters in their time, which is one of the characteristics of the New Wave so admired by Honoré. Like those New Wave films, there are conspicuous references to social and political realities. This is particularly the case for AIDS, although *Jeanne et le garçon formidable* also gestures to immigration issues with the office cleaners' song (0.4), and *Les Chansons d'amour* to major political upheavals such as the Prague Spring of 1968 and 9/11. These impart a sense of actuality, but the intertextual references keep pulling us back to a nostalgic cinematic past.

The songs, however, mediate the tension between nostalgic past and generally dystopic present by creating a generic tension, already evident in Demy's bittersweet films, between 'la comédie grave et la tragédie optimiste' (Murat 1998: 22), a paradoxically serious lightness or gracefulness; as Demy said of his films: 'Je voudrais qu'on accepte cette légèreté mais qu'on ne la prenne pas à la légère'[29] (cited in Taboulay 1996: 93). As we shall see later, this key notion of 'lightness' is also part of Honoré's vocabulary. In true Demy fashion, Martineau composed the lyrics for the 16 songs of *Jeanne et le garcon formidable*, whose musical styles range widely from North African raï to tango and java. Moreover, some songs echo those of Demy: 'L'Homme de mes rêves' (0.6) in which Jeanne explains that she is waiting for her dream man echoes 'La Chanson de Delphine' in *Les Demoiselles de Rochefort*, and 'Le Garçon formidable' (0.26) in which she recounts meeting Olivier echoes 'La Chanson de Solange' in the same film (Lagabrielle 2016: §8). The romantic 'lightness' of these songs, which is inherited from the lightness of *Les Demoiselles de Rochefort*, is offset by songs about AIDS, more appropriate to the darker atmosphere of *Les Parapluies de Cherbourg*, such as 'La vie réserve des surprises' ('Life Can Surprise Us'), sung early in the film (0.10) by Act Up activist François who has lost a lover to AIDS, and the paradoxically jaunty 'La java du séropo' ('The Java of the HIV-Positive Man') (0.32) in which Olivier reveals to Jeanne that he is HIV-positive, using terminology lifted from Act Up leaflets, such as Olivier lambasting the powers that be for their failures: 'Si y a un coupable/C'est pas le pauvre diable/qui un jour m'a donné/Sa s'ringue contaminée. ... C'est la faute à Pasqua/C'est la faute à Cresson/C'est la faute à l'État/C'est la faute aux prisons.'[30] A similar development from utopian lightness to its combination with dystopian darkness occurs in *Les Bien-Aimés*, whose song 'Une fille légère' (1.05), sung by Madeleine and Véra, also speaks of 'lightness', playing on the double meaning of a loose woman (Madeleine in 1964

---

[29] 'I would like this lightness to be accepted but I don't want it to be treated lightly.'
[30] 'The person to blame isn't the poor blighter who gave me a contaminated needle one day, it's Pasqua's fault, Cresson's fault, the State's fault, the prisons' fault.' Charles Pasqua was minister of the interior from 1986 to1988 and introduced anti-immigration laws. Édith Cresson was briefly prime minister between 1991 and1992 and supported anti-immigration measures.

occasionally turns tricks) and a graceful woman: 'Telle fille, telle mère/Je suis restée/ Une femme légère/Pour m'éviter/Le poids du cœur et ses mystères/Les amours comme des sacs de pierre/Tout ce qui pèse tout ce qui nuit/Jamais faire pitié juste envie.'[31]

All of these auteur musicals rework their source material and update it, by their AIDS narratives in the case of *Jeanne et le garçon formidable* and *Les Bien-Aimés*, and by the feminist frames of reference in the case of Ozon and Resnais; indeed, Resnais described *Pas sur la bouche* as a feminist operetta (Lorrain 2003). But however much they reject 'l'effet bulle des comédies musicales'[32] (Honoré 2007a), the sense of utopian possibilities that reject the dystopia of quotidian reality, ultimately they present themselves as doubly nostalgic gestures: first, to the operetta genre that was dominant in the 1935–55 period on both stage and screen; and second, in the case of Resnais and Ozon, to popular songs of the 1960s in particular, and in the case of Honoré and Ducastel/Martineau, to a filmmaker, Demy, whose major successes were all in the 1960s. In the next chapter we consider musicals that demonstrate a less nostalgic turn, by filmmakers not so obviously considered auteurs.

---

[31] 'Like daughter, like mother, I am still a loose/graceful woman, so as to avoid the weight of the heart and its mysteries, loves like bags of stones, everything that lies heavy and harms you. Never inspire pity only envy.'

[32] 'The bubble effect of film musicals.'

17

The fairy-tale musical and the documentary musical

The musical has always overlapped with other genres, and this is even more true of the self-conscious contemporary 'postmodern' musical. In this chapter we will contrast two very different types of the modern musical and their interactions with other genres, notably the rom-com, the teen movie and the documentary. The first genre is the popular fairy-tale musical. This category is one of Altman's three categories of Hollywood musical and is sufficiently broad so that it serves to identify a strand of the French film musical, particularly since the musicals of Jacques Demy. Many contemporary musicals present as fairy tales, interrogating the contemporary through different types of sublimation. This generally leads to a tension between the requirement of an atemporal and idealized context, on the one hand, and the exigencies of the real world, on the other. The second type of musical we will consider could not be more different as it is fully engaged in aspects of the real: these are the series of semi-documentary musicals by Tony Gatlif, anchored in the world of the Romani people; and finally the unusual sub-genre of the documentary musical, *Chante ton bac d'abord*.

The popular fairy-tale musical

We will consider four mainstream films: *Filles perdues, cheveux gras* (Claude Duty, 2002), *On va s'aimer* (Yvan Calbérac, 2006), *Toi, moi, les autres* (Audrey Estrougo, 2011) and *Laurent et Safi* (Anton Vassil, 2017); and an auteur film, *Sur quel pied danser* (Paul Calori et Kostia Testud, 2016). They have in common often explicit references to the fairy tale in their dialogue as well as a similar narrative arc: the real world is presented as dystopian and the film works to affirm a utopian happy end characterized by both professional and personal success, in the latter case by the constitution of the couple, hybridizing the musical with the *rom-com*.

Filles perdues, cheveux gras focuses on the love lives and professional lives of three women, Marianne (Amira Casar), Natacha (Marina Foïs) et Élodie (Olivia Bonamy), who are, as the title suggests, 'lost', and who find themselves not through the usual heteronormative relationship but, more unusually for this type of narrative, through their friendship. Élodie is out of work, Natacha is an alcoholic, and Marianne is in love with a troublemaker. The three actresses sing the six songs composed for the film.

Marianne's first song (0.17) refers to her life as the exact opposite of the fairy tale she longs for: 'Une histoire de corps, c'est tout ce que l'on vivait. Un conte de fées *hard core*. L'héroïne est fatiguée.'[1] The film is built on a series of comedy sketches, no doubt partly due to Duty's previous experience as a short-film maker and then director of short-film production for Canal+ from 1996 to 2001. It includes a Disney-fairy-tale animated sequence (0.32) about Princess Pocaya who falls in love with the sun, as a result of which she shuns all men and eventually becomes blind, the moral of the sequence being that too much idealistic escapism is not good for you.

The tone of the film is an odd mixture of parody and self-derision. The final sequence caricatures the tropes of the fairy tale with star dust and a song that might or might not be ironic: 'Qu'une force céleste nous transcende.'[2] The critic of *Les Inrockuptibles*, comparing the film to the musicals of Ozon (as several critics unsurprisingly did, given that Ozon's film was released in the same year) and Akerman, emphasized its ambivalent tone; the film 'a des airs de version prolo-Ikea du film d'Ozon … , le toc des décors comme des chansons très variétoche chantées (volontairement?) faux cachant un réel soin de construction au service d'un *nonsense* plus ou moins digeste. … Un rejeton inédit né du *Golden Eighties*'[3] (Masson 2002). Others were less kind, seeing the film as an incoherent mix of insipid caricatures (Chou 2002), although many admired Marina Foïs's performance; her buffoonish rendering of drunkenness in 'L'Alcool' (1.06) is one of the film's better moments.

On va s'aimer focuses on two couples: Laurent (Julien Boisselier) and Camille (Mélanie Doutey), and his friend François (Gilles Lellouche) and new girlfriend Élodie (Alexandra Lamy) with whom Laurent falls in love when he meets her for the first time. The film's narrative is built around the heteronormative permutations made possible by the two couples, with a sexual frankness unusual for a fairy-tale narrative; homosexuality, however, is restricted to secondary characters: Christophe, Élodie's ex, now gay, and Frédérique, Camille's lesbian art teacher. Homosexual relationships are used as Aunt Sallies: François, who has just slept with Camille, suggests to Laurent that she might have been unfaithful to him with her lesbian art teacher, and sees Camille in his mind's eye as a butch lesbian with face piercings and shaved head (0.59). What might therefore appear as a relatively contemporary presentation of the couple is deep down very traditionally heteronormative, the various ups and downs being resolved by marriage.

Towards the end of the film we see François, who is a primary school teacher, giving a lesson whose title on the blackboard is 'Princes and Princesses'. One of the children asks him whether they married, had children and lived happily ever after, to which François replies:

Ça c'est les fins de contes de fées. Dans la vie les fins de contes de fées, tu vois, ça n'existe pas. C'est des mensonges qu'on vous met dans la tête. Et si vous commencez

---

[1] 'We were in it for the sex, that's all. A hard-core fairy-tale in which the heroine is exhausted.'
[2] 'May a heavenly force exalt us.'
[3] 'Looks like a working-class-Ikea version of Ozon's. The fake-artificial nature of the décor and of the middle-of-the-road pop songs sung out of tune (on purpose?) hiding carefully constructed nonsense that just about passes. The odd offspring of *Golden Eighties*.'

à y croire, vous allez au-devant de grandes désillusions, c'est moi qui vous le dis. Parce que l'amour, c'est triste à dire, mais ça n'a rien d'éternel.[4] (01.21)

But this is immediately contradicted as François goes to meet Élodie outside where they make up, this being followed by the final wedding sequence, during which Laurent and Camille also make up as they dance.

The songs, sung by the actors themselves, are all well-known pop hits,[5] which emphasizes the mismatch between the song-and-dance sequences and the rest of the film. The choreography makes the mismatch all the more obvious; with two exceptions, dance is performed by figures dressed in black who come from nowhere and whose purpose appears to be the externalization of the main characters' emotions, as can be seen in the sequence 'Je te le dis quand même' among others (Figure 17.1).[6]

Like *Filles perdues, cheveux gras*, there were mixed reactions. If one critic thought that the musical sequences 'pèsent des tonnes, et ces histoires de cœur et de cul, très magazine féminin chic, paraissent à la fois banales et artificielles'[7] (A.F. 2006), others were more impressed, comparing the film to musicals by Demy and Resnais: 'Une comédie fraîche et pimpante, ponctuée çà et là d'intermèdes musicaux savoureux au cours desquels les personnages expriment leurs sentiments en entonnant des tubes, à mi-chemin entre les comédies enchantées de Jacques Demy et *On connaît la chanson* d'Alain Resnais'[8] (J.-P. G. 2006).

Toi, moi, les autres reworks the familiar story of the Prince and the Shepherdess, as well as hybridizing the musical with the Hollywood-influenced teen movie. Rich kid Gabriel (Benjamin Siksou), son of the police chief, lives a life of idleness, and is

Figure 17.1 Choreography by figures dressed in black in *On va s'aimer* (Courtesy TF1 Studio).

---

[4] 'That's what happens in fairy tales. In real life there are no fairy-tale endings. They're lies, and if you start to believe them you'll be disappointed, I can tell you. Because love, sad to say, is not eternal.'
[5] 'Le Coup de soleil' ('Sunstroke', Richard Cocciante, 1989), 'Je te le dis quand même' ('I'll Tell You Anyway', Patrick Bruel, 1990), 'Femme que j'aime' ('Woman That I Love', Jean-Luc Lahaye, 1982), 'Ça valait la peine' ('It Was Worth It', Coralie Clément, 2001), 'Pour le plaisir' ('For Pleasure', Herbert Léonard, 1981), 'Sensualité' ('Sensuality', Axelle Red, 1993), 'Tout doucement' ('Slowly', Bibie, 1985) et 'On va s'aimer' (We Will Love Each Other', Gilbert Montagné, 1984).
[6] For more on this film, see Lagabrielle (2018: 116–8).
[7] 'Are really heavy, and these glossy women's magazine-style stories about love and sex seem both banal and artificial.'
[8] 'A fresh and smart comedy punctuated here and there with charming musical interludes during which the characters express their feelings while singing pop songs, half-way between Demy's enchanted musicals and Alain Resnais's *On connaît la chanson*.'

due to marry his childhood girlfriend Alexandra (Cécile Cassel), until he meets Leïla (Leïla Bekhti), daughter of Maghrebi immigrants. Leïla is a law student whose mother has died and whose father struggles to make a living for her, her brother and the grandmother in their small flat. There is a political subplot involving Leïla's hairdresser friend Tina (Marie-Sohna Condé), who is under threat of deportation back to Senegal, the decision depending on Gabriel's police chief father. As was the case with the two previous films, the narrative moves from the difficulties of real life to a utopian fairy-tale resolution, with copious references to fairy-tale tropes in the dialogue; for example, a hairdresser complains that she has been waiting forever for her 'prince charmant' (0.9), Leïla's kid brother asks whether she has been to Gabriel's castle (0.38). In the end, all conflicts are resolved, however: Leïla and Gabriel overcome the class gap, she benefits from his wealth and he benefits from her ambition, leaving his life of idleness behind to take up law studies; and the family under threat of deportation earn a reprieve at the last possible moment when they are on the plane ready to take off back to Senegal. The film was scripted and directed by women – Audrey Estrougo directed, and co-wrote the script with Juliette Sales and Aline Mehouel – exemplifying the importance of women in contemporary French rom-com and their influence on the genre (see Harrod 2012), although the film reinforces standard male/female roles.

As was the case with *On va s'aimer*, the songs are mostly well-known pop songs, clearly intended to please middle-of-the-road audiences,[9] although unusually for a French musical they are also dance sequences, more reminiscent of Hollywood musicals. However, the dance sequences are filmed in the style of music videos, intended to please younger audiences, as can be seen in the first song-and-dance sequence to Delpech's 'Pour un flirt', the meet cute when Leïla takes her brother to hospital after he has been hit by Gabriel's car. There are abrupt shifts from earthy to neon colour schemes, pink-dressed nurses in formation dancing surrounding Gabriel (Figure 17.2). As *Le Monde*'s critic observed, the film suggests 'une vision publicitaire du monde, trop toc et pressée pour émouvoir, trop saturée de clichés pour se prétendre authentique, trop pétrie de bons sentiments pour prendre la mesure de la complexité des choses'[10] (Mandelbaum 2011). The politically correct narrative strand on illegal immigrants, recalled at the end of the film by documentary footage, is equally disruptive, and equally stereotypical:

> The heroine, even though she is presented as a 'strong woman', fails in her attempt to support the regularization of the illegal migrants' papers, despite her putting all her heart and energy into the task. It is the young man who comes up with the plan by which the deportations are prevented in the same way that it was he who

---

[9] 'Pour un flirt' ('For a Flirt', Michel Delpech, 1993), 'Le Temps de l'amour' ('Time for Love', Jacques Dutronc, 1980), 'Tout le monde' ('Everyone', Zazie, 1998), 'La Bonne Étoile' ('Lucky Star', Matthieu Chedid, 2003), 'Si tu n'existais pas' ('If You Didn't Exist', Joe Dassin, 1975), 'Un autre monde' ('Another World', Jean-Louis Aubert, 1984), 'J'attendrai' ('I Will Wait', Claude François, 1966), 'Sauver l'amour' ('Save Love', Daniel Balavoine, 1985), 'Quand on n'a que l'amour' ('When All You Have is Love', Jacques Brel, 1957).

[10] 'An advertising view of the world, too fake and rushed to be moving, too clogged with clichés to be authentic, too steeped in good intentions to address complex realities.'

re-enrolled Leïla in the competitive law examination when she had decided to give up. The same can be said of his role in the saving of the illegal immigrants: it seems that in this too the myth of the prince, who has the gift of magic powers, has lost none of its force. (Lagabrielle 2018: 123)

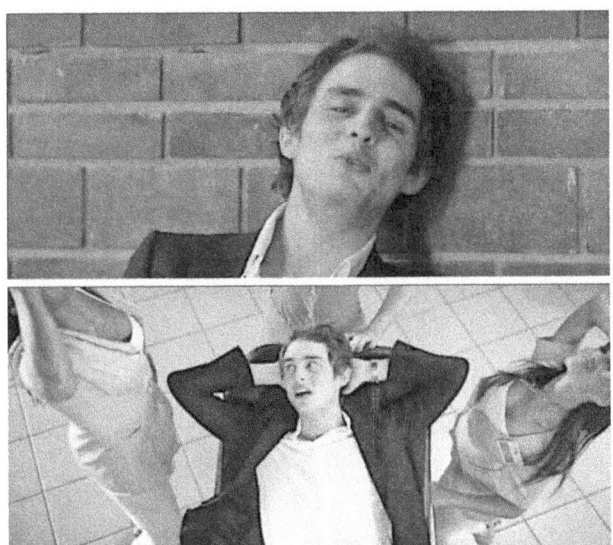

Figure 17.2 The first song-and-dance sequence in *Toi, moi, les autres* (Courtesy Universal StudioCanal Video).

Laurent et Safi is a French–Malian co-production, released in the Ivory Coast in 2015 and in France two years later. Like Estrougo's film, it is a Prince and Shepherdess romance, but with a much stronger emphasis on immigration and integration. Safi (Tatiana Rojo) is looking for Mr Right in Paris's African quarter, Château Rouge, without much success. She meets ambitious Laurent (Xavier Jozelon), due to marry his boss's daughter, through a dating website. Reprising some of the themes that made *Qu'est-ce qu'on a fait au Bon Dieu?* (Philippe de Chauveron, 2014) successful, the film dwells on the cultural differences between the two families, as the couple has to overcome prejudices held by the parents on both sides of the cultural, social and racial divide: Laurent's White bourgeois parents and Safi's Black Malian parents. The music mixes traditional French, zouk and rap, the songs' languages covering both the French and Bambara languages. The film won a number of prizes, including the first prize at the Cannes International Pan African Film Festival, but was heavily criticized in France for what some saw as its sitcom clichés (Narbonne 2017). The film was more successful in the Ivory Coast because it foregrounded well-known Ivorian pop songs and major stars, detailed in the press kit, such as the singer Teeyah, film star Michel Gohou and celebrity Habib Dembélé (B-Mol Productions 2017).

Considerably more interesting is *Sur quel pied danser*, whose directors graduated from the Fémis film school, and whose film has an auteurist signature. Julie (Pauline Étienne) is taken on as a warehouse clerk in a luxury shoe factory where she meets truck driver Samy with whom she falls in love. There are rumours that the factory will be closing, and Julie decides to fight alongside her co-workers. Unlike the French-produced films we have considered in this chapter, the songs, sung by the actors, are not well-known pop songs, but songs written specifically for the film by contemporary composers and lyricists (Agnès Bihl, Jeanne Cherhal, Clarika, Olivier Daviaud, Albin de la Simone, Jean-Jacques Nyssen, Polo, Olivia Ruiz). The film was shown at a range of festivals in France and internationally (Cabourg, Palm Springs, Minneapolis-Saint Paul, Sonoma, Hawaii, Filmfest DC). Critics, while pointing out the influence of Demy's *Une chambre en ville*, appreciated the way that the film was in many respects more realist than Demy's (Allard 2016; Douhaire 2016). Like the other fairy-tale musicals we have considered, however, the film did not manage to combine the lightness of song-and-dance convincingly with the social and political drama, as the withering *Cahiers du cinéma* review makes clear:

> Le film ressemble trop souvent à une publicité joyeuse et vintage pour les souliers d'antan et manque complètement le coche de son inscription politique contemporaine. … L'enjeu collectif est rapidement rebattu sur celui d'une amourette gnangnan. Et du côté de la comédie musicale, la poignée d'ouvrière qui dansent et chantent ne sont pas assez puissantes, nombreuses ou emportées par la mise en scène pour que l'ensemble ne prenne pas rapidement la forme d'un hommage inoffensif et fourre-tout aux canons du genre.[11] (Tuillier 2016)

The films of Tony Gatlif

In the second part of this chapter we discuss an outlier director whose films are neither musical films nor film musicals while adopting the tropes of both. They focus on the Romani people and music plays a significant ethnographic role, as it is an important component of Romani identity. As a result, Gatlif's work has attracted considerable academic attention, particularly in relation to issues of exile and transnational mobility.[12] His fiction films are unusual in that they are almost documentary in style, and whereas in many of the film musicals we have discussed, a major issue is the disconnect between musical numbers and narrative, in Gatlif's films the Romani

---

[11] 'The film is too often like a happy vintage ad for the shoes of yore and completely misses the boat where the political aspect is concerned; the collective action is quickly subsumed in a mushy love affair. And where the film musical side is concerned, the handful of dancing and singing women workers are just not strong enough, numerous enough or carried by the mise en scene for the whole thing not to be fairly quickly a harmless hotch-potch of what you might expect from the genre.'

[12] See Dobreva (2007), Blum-Reid (2008), Holohan (2011), Rosello (2012), Andreescu and Quinn (2014), Mielusel (2015), Berger (2016) and Davies Hayon (2017).

community is a musical community; music is the anchoring context for the narrative, creating and supporting the community within which the fiction evolves. In what follows, we focus on three of his films: *Latcho Drom* (1993), *Gadjo Dilo* (1998) and *Swing* (2002).

Latcho Drom was selected for the *Un certain regard* section of the 1993 Cannes festival. It is an ambitious overview of the Romani people as a whole, both a history and a journey across Romani communities in eight countries, with a range of musical traditions: the Kalbelia of India with a range of traditional instruments: the dholak, ghatam, tamboura and sarangi; the Ghawazi of Egypt with string and percussion instruments and a belly dance; the Roma of Istanbul with the Turkish clarinette; the Romanian group Taraf de Haïdouks with their political songs against Ceausescu; the Hungarian Roma and their tense interactions with non-Roma; the Slovakian Roma and the Porajmos or Nazi genocide of the Romani people; the annual pilgrimage of the Romani to Saintes-Maries-de-la-mer in France; and finally flamenco dancers in Spain (Figure 17.3). Midway between fiction and documentary, Gatlif uses non-professionals to act out self-contained symbolically important aspects of Romani culture in each of which there is a scripted micro-narrative. In the Hungarian chapter, for example, which illustrates the tensions between the Romani and others, a mother is crying and her son crosses the road to ask the Roma to play some music to cheer her up. The clumsiness of a fiction/documentary mix was superseded in the eyes of critics by the film's authenticity, as the following flattering review by the *Cahiers du cinéma* makes clear:

> *Latcho Drom* est le film le plus vrai de l'année. ... je trouve un tel film irréfutable. Bien qu'artistiquement, *Latcho Drom* soit impur, voire maladroit, son sujet même rend toute falsification impossible. La ferveur mystique avec laquelle ces manouches de plusieurs coins du monde, chantent, dansent, *sont* leur musique, dépasse tous les distinguos entre réel et fiction. C'est peut-être même l'un des rares cas où un documentaire ne peut être suspecté de fausseté ou de manipulation. Peu importe la manière dont Tony Gatlif élabore des mises en scène (légères) autour des Gitans, peu importe les saynètes qui illustrent didactiquement. ... Ce qui compte, c'est que dès l'instant où les Gitans ... *entrent* dans leur musique, tous les simulacres possibles et imaginables du cinéma disparaissent.[13] (Ostria 1993, 70; his emphasis)

Gadjo Dilo explores the encounter between France and the Roma. Stéphane (Romain Duris) travels across Romania looking for a singer he once heard on one of his father's records. He meets an old musician, Izidor, who introduces him to Romani culture. As with *Latcho Drom*, music accompanies major events, whether

---

[13] '*Latcho Drom* is the most truthful film of the year. It is irrefutable. Even if artistically it is impure, even clumsy, its very subject makes falsification impossible. The mystical enthusiasm with which these gypsies from all corners of the world sing, dance, are their music, surpasses any distinction between reality and fiction. It's perhaps even one of the rare cases where a documentary cannot be suspected of falsehood or manipulation. It doesn't matter that Tony Gatlif stages (slight) didactic sketches for the gypsies. What matters is that as soon as the gypsies enter into their music, all imaginable cinematic pretences disappear.'

Figure 17.3 The Romani people in *Latcho Drom* (Courtesy ContactFilm). Left to right: India, Egypt, Turkey, Romania, Hungary, Slovakia, France, Spain.

public – a wedding (0.40), a funeral (0.48) – or private, such as when Stéphane builds a phonograph to play music by Izidor's father (0.53). The whole film is constructed as an initiatory musical quest; Stéphane collects recordings of Romani music on his travels, repeating what he tells us his father did many years before. Moreover, the narrative functions as a mise en abyme of what Gatlif is doing in his film. The ethnographic impulse is as pronounced as it was in *Latcho Drom*, not least because of the use of non-professional actors complemented by Duris's apparently improvised performance.

In *Swing*, Max (Oscar Copp) wants to buy a guitar. He meets Swing (Lou Rech) who tries to persuade Max that the guitar he has for sale belonged to Django Reinhardt. Subsequently, Max is taught how to play the guitar by Miraldo (Tchavolo Schmitt) in exchange for Max's services in writing his letters. Swing and Miraldo initiate Max into Romani culture, especially the music, and its importance for the culture. In his journal Max notes that he has learnt a new chord with Miraldo, who told him 'qu'avant, tout le monde savait jouer de la musique, même les enfants'¹⁴ (0.34), naturalizing music as a community activity for the Romani. Music also signifies freedom and communion with nature, and Gatlif shows himself to be 'un remarquable paysagiste d'inspiration panthéiste, capable de délivrer des plans qu'aurait pu signer Terrence Malick'¹⁵ (Loutte 2002). In front of a kennel, Dr Liberman (Ben Zimet), sings, using the wire fences as strings, then stops and remarks that 'chaque fois que je vois du barbelé ou du grillage, ça me fait mal au ventre'¹⁶ (0.31). Later, Max and Swing take a rowboat to trespass on land belonging to Électricité de France and play music on the gramophone they have brought with them (0.58). The film is even more documentary-like than *Latcho Drom*, not least because its location in Neuhof, a shanty town near Strasbourg, brings to the fore the issue of the integration of the Romani in French society. The film also naturalizes ethnographic documentation through the device of Max's journal, which he gives to Swing at the end of the film, the journal, like the quest in *Gadjo Dilo*, functioning as a mise en abyme of the film itself.

The documentary musical

The films of Gatlif are semi-documentary; David André pushes the tension between the realism we might associate with the documentary and the artificial utopia of the musical even further. His *Chante ton bac d'abord* (2014) focuses on a group of five teenagers in the run-up to their final exams at the Lycée Mariette in Boulogne-sur-Mer. Adolescent angst is set against the context of economic decline in France's industrial North. The film's title is a transparent reference to the non-musical fiction *Passe ton bac d'abord* (Maurice Pialat, 1978), which also focused on a group of teenagers and the economic decline of the late 1970s in the northern town of Lens. The film is a good example of contemporary documentary (see Bruzzi 2000), and illustrates what Nichols identifies as the 'performative mode' (2001). The direct opposite of the 'observational mode', the performative mode depends on the involvement of the filmmaker and a subjective point of view. The events we see in *Chante ton bac d'abord* are all re-enacted, everything being carefully scripted and staged on the basis of the teenagers' lives and feelings, notably in the song sequences. The combination of musical and documentary is due to André's twin interests as both journalist and documentary filmmaker, and song composer (e.g. for Dani and Marianne James). The film is as a result so unusual that reviewers described it as a UFO (Durand 2014), or questioned its generic category (Ekchajzer 2014; Mal 2014).

André is the composer of the eleven songs sung by the teenagers, recorded live on mobile phones with a piano and guitar, before being orchestrated and mixed in a

---

[14] 'Before, everyone knew how to play music, even the children.'
[15] 'A remarkable landscape artist with pantheist inspiration, capable of producing Terrenc Malick-type shots.'
[16] 'Every time I see barbed wire or wire fences, I feel sick in my stomach.'

studio. Rather like the songs in Honoré's films, André's songs are used to express what the dialogue cannot; they are not so much an escape from quotidian reality as a step back from, and reflection on, it. The songs speak of the following:

1. The teenagers' worries about the impending exams, and about the future in more general terms: 'Partir d'ici' ('Leaving Here'), sung by Caroline (0.34) and the chorus 'C'est quand le présent' ('When Is the Present?'; 0.39).
2. Life's troubles, as when Alex sings about the cancer he contracted as a child (0.29), or Nico and teenage angst in songs inspired by Rimbaud and Gainsbourg (0.19 and 0.52).
3. Relationships with parents, as with Gaëlle who tries to reassure her father that her studies are going well in 'Ne t'en fais pas' ('Don't Worry'; 0.46).
4. Nostalgia about a fast-vanishing childhood, as in the chorus song towards the end of the film: 'De nous à vous/On aurait voulu/Que ça dure encore un peu/Juste encore un peu'[17] (1.18).

Whereas with so many other musicals, the issue for reviewers and audiences was the tension and lack of integration of the musical numbers, oddly perhaps for this film the reverse appears to have been the case. Dystopian disenchantment and utopian re-enchantment, as one reviewer put it, are dissolved in the term key to Demy's films – enchantment:

> Plutôt que de déchanter et s'abandonner à la mélancolie, ils ont décidé de la mettre en chansons. ... Comme si l'envol d'une voix triste ... portait la promesse, illusoire mais intense, d'un réenchantement. Le film induit d'ailleurs en creux ce sentiment que le désenchantement et le réenchantement sont au fond un peu la même chose: ce que les deux mots partagent – l'enchantement – est plus fort que ce qui les sépare – un préfixe un peu flou.[18] (Durand 2014)

The integration of the everyday in a genre normally characterized by the spectacular and the artificial is very much the hallmark of the films of Jacques Demy and of Christophe Honoré. In that respect *Chante ton bac d'abord*, even though it is a documentary, could be considered the culmination of the New Wave's auteurist attempt to naturalize the film musical. As we shall see in our conclusion, however, the popular film musical of the 1930–60 period has returned, although in a different guise.

---

[17] 'From us to you/We would have wanted/It to last a little longer/Just a little longer.'
[18] 'Rather than giving way to disenchantment and melancholy, they have decided to put melancholy to music. As if the soaring of a sad voice carried the illusory but intense promise of a re-enchantment. The film leads you to feel that disenchantment and re-enchantment are in the end much the same thing and that what separates them – a prefix – is less important than what they share: enchantment.'

18

Conclusion

The musical and nostalgia

In this conclusion we focus on biopics to demonstrate the hybridization of genres in the contemporary period, although it is worth pointing out that in addition to the kind of hybridization with documentary discussed in Chapter 17, there has been a significant crossover with rom-coms as well as comedies. In the case of rom-coms, films such as *Modern Love* (Stéphane Kazandjian, 2008) or the AIDS-related *Clara et moi* (Arnaud Viard, 2004) have occasional Demy-like musical numbers (see Harrod 2015). We will focus briefly on *La Famille Bélier* (Éric Lartigau, 2014) as one of French cinema's most popular films in recent times (7.5 million tickets sold) to illustrate hybridization in contemporary film musicals before discussing the prevalence of the contemporary musical biopic.

La Famille Bélier

Paula (Louane Emera) and her family – her father (François Damiens), mother (Karin Viard) and younger brother – are farmers near Lassay-les-Châteaux, in the Mayenne region. All are deaf with the exception of Paula, who plays an indispensable role as interpreter for the family, for example, when they need to phone the insurance company. She is a member of the school choir directed by an embittered teacher (Éric Elmosnino); he is a fan of Michel Sardou, whose heyday was in the 1970s and 1980s, saying at one point that 'Michel Sardou est à la variété française ce que Mozart est à la musique classique: intemporel'[1] (0.20). As Ginette Vincendeau points out, Sardou is still popular 'with an older, conservative audience' (2015: 80). When her teacher pushes her to take part in a radio competition, Paula is torn between her vocation as a singer and her duty to her family who cannot understand her love of music. Additional plot strands include Paula's emerging love for Gabriel, a fellow student in the choir, as well as her father's bid to be elected to the town council so as to protect his farming community against big business. Not only did the film garner well over the million spectators that are the threshold for success in the industry, but Louane Emera also won the César for most promising female newcomer.

---

[1] 'Michel Sardou is to French variety what Mozart is to classical music: timeless.'

The film meshes the rom-com and the teen movie with the film musical, as had *Toi, moi, les autres*. It is also part of the emerging trend of films based in rural communities, such as *Saint Amour* (Benoît Delépine and Gustave Kerven, 2016) and *Les Vétos* (Julie Manoukian, 2020), making it very different from the tendency of contemporary comedies to focus on ethnic issues – for example, *Intouchables* (Olivier Nakache and Éric Toledano, 2011) and *Chocolat* (Roschdy Zem, 2016), and in the film musical genre, *Laurent et Safi* (Anton Vassil, 2015) – or on queer issues, such as *Les Garçons et Guillaume, à table* (Guillaume Gallienne, 2013) (see Harrod and Powrie 2018: 7).

Song is a major focus of the film, as might be expected, and is both absent and present at the same time. Paula's parents do not have access to her singing voice, as is reflected in several sequences. For example, at the choir's concert the finale consists of Paula and Gabriel singing 'Je vais t'aimer' ('I Will Love You'); we hear the beginning of the song (1.17) but it gradually fades away to silence, suggesting her parents' experience of it, and bringing home their exclusion from their daughter's musical world. In the following sequence the family return home and Paula sings the song again; her father places his hand on her throat to feel the song, innovatively making it as much a tactile experience as an auditory one. And then in the audition for Radio France when she sings 'Je vole' ('I Am Flying'), a song about a child leaving home, Paula signs the lyrics for her parents who are in the 'audience'. We see tears falling from her parents' eyes; as Vincendeau comments, 'not subtle – but pleasurable and moving' (2015: 81), and this partly because of the nostalgia attached to Sardou's song.

The almost exclusive choice of songs by Sardou makes the film nostalgic, in the same vein as *Les Choristes* (Christophe Barratier, 2004), which we will consider later. But unlike *Les Choristes*, whose songs are nearly all contemporary compositions by Bruno Coulais, *La Famille Bélier* recycles the songs of Sardou while adapting them to a more contemporary context, using two procedures theorized by Catherine Rudent (2019). The first of these is what she calls 'abrasion', by which she means the careful selection of songs that excludes what made Sardou a controversial right-wing figure in his time,[2] the relatively restrained singing and accompaniment to the songs, and especially the reworking of stylistic elements to make the songs seem less outdated. For example, in 'Je vole', 1970s features such as spoken lyrics and a rock instrumental bridge are dropped for the film. The second procedure discussed by Rudent is what she calls 'transigeance musicale, c'est-à-dire [la] soumission à des influences musicales extérieures non choisies'[3] (2019: 305), by which she means stylistic features corresponding to global pop music of the 2010s, such as the use of high notes or musical ornamentation (316). Moreover, the film subordinates Sardou's music to Emera's star persona, developed through her television performances in *L'École des Stars* (2009) and *The Voice* (2013), which drew her to Lartigau's attention (308). Rudent's hypothesis is that these procedures update Sardou for contemporary youth audiences (306). The

---

[2] He was accused of racism for his song 'Le Temps des colonies' ('The Time of the Colonies'), of being in favour of the death penalty for 'Je suis pour' ('I'm for It'), a song about a murdered child; feminists outraged by his misogynist views frequently demonstrated at his concerts.
[3] 'Musical transigeance, i.e. submission to unchosen external musical influences.'

hypothesis is more broadly valid for a number of films that recycle well-known songs from the French variety repertoire, such as *On va s'aimer, Toi, moi, les autres*, and in a different register, *On connaît la chanson*. Nostalgia thus becomes a complex affair whereby music of the past is filtered through a contemporary lens, altering its pastness and potentially renegotiating it musically and ideologically within a ludic postmodern framework. This also applies to the biopic.

Biopics

The post-2000 period witnessed an explosion of biopics, including musical biopics, as well as sustained interest in the genre across a range of national cinemas.[4] We have already come across musical biopics in this book, although they have all been in the classical music area – *Un grand amour de Beethoven, La Symphonie fantastique, La Valse de Paris* – and then much later the classical music films of the 1980s: *Farinelli, Tous les matins du monde, Le Roi danse*. The post-2000 musical biopics, however, are nearly all of popular performers rather than classical music composers. We shall consider them briefly, because they arguably belong more to the genre of the biopic and its crossover into heritage cinema rather than to a separate film musical genre. We will then consider the musicals of Christophe Barratier before concluding. Like many of the musical biopics, Barratier's films are nostalgic and backward-looking, which raises the question as to whether the film musical has become exhausted as a genre, mutating with the biopic, as with other genres, into a range of hybrid genres.

Starting in the mid-1990s, when the modern auteur musical appeared, there have been in our estimation around ninety biopics of which only eleven are musical biopics or related genres (Table 18.1),[5] mostly but not exclusively dealing with singers (*Opium* is about Jean Cocteau's relationship with Raymond Radiguet, while Dumont's 2017 film is about Joan of Arc),[6] in which we include what we are calling the pseudo-biopic.

Raphaëlle Moine considers that *La Môme* in 2007 signals the beginning of the surge in biopics (2017: 17). Starting with what we could consider the beginning of the modern film musical in 1997 with *On connaît la chanson*, there were about twenty in the period between 1997 and 2007, while between 2007 and 2017 there were sixty (an average of six per annum instead of two); it is in this second period that most of

---

[4] See Bingham (2010), Polaschek (2013), Brown and Vidal (2014), Minier and Pennacchia (2014), Epstein and Palmer (2016), Moine (2017), Pettey and Palmer (2018).
[5] There were fourteen biopics in 2016 alone. The majority of the ninety or so biopics are focused on artistic figures including painters, sculptors and designers (12: Paul Cézanne, Coco Chanel, Camille Claudel, Facteur Cheval, Paul Gaugin, Artemisia Gentileschi, Toulouse Lautrec, Rembrandt, Auguste Renoir, Séraphine Louis, with two on Yves Saint Laurent), writers (13: Anton Chekhov, Denis Diderot, Alexandre Dumas, Marguerite Duras, Jean de la Fontaine, Romain Gary, Violette Leduc, Molière, Alfred de Musset, the Marquis de Sade, Françoise Sagan, Georges Sand, Albertine Sarrazin), and broadly 'political' figures (11: Carlos the Jackal, Mademoiselle de la Charce, Joan of Arc, Louis XIV, Patrice Lumbaba, Madame de Maintenon, Marie-Antoinette, François Mitterrand, Napoleon, Nicolas Sarkozy, Vercingetorix).
[6] The 2019 Dumont film is part 2 of Joan of Arc's story, released as a TV film with only one week's theatrical release

Table 18.1 Biopics and Pseudo-biopics (asterisked)

*Podium	Yann Moix	2003	3.6m
*Jean-Philippe	Laurent Tuel	2006	1.3m
*Quand j'étais chanteur	Xavier Giannoli	2006	0.9m
La Môme	Olivier Dahan	2007	5.2m
Gainsbourg (vie héroïque)	Joann Sfar	2010	1.2m
CloClo	Florent-Emilio Siri	2012	1.8m
Opium	Arielle Dombasle	2013	0.02m
Dalida	Lisa Azuelos	2016	0.8m
Django	Étienne Comar	2017	0.5m
Jeannette, l'enfance de Jeanne d'Arc	Bruno Dumont	2017	Not known
Barbara	Mathieu Amalric	2017	0.4m
Jeanne	Bruno Dumont	2019	Not known

the musical biopics were released, as can be seen in Table 18.1. These consecrated well-known popular singers (Figure 18.1), made obvious by the fact that the titles of the films are their stage-names (Gainsbourg, Dalida, Django, Barbara) or the nicknames by which they were known in the media ('La môme' for Piaf, Cloclo for Claude François). As might be expected, the biopics of well-known singers weave songs and biography together, the one motivating the other, and like the fictional musicals starring well-known singers from Trenet through to Mariano, these films chart the singers' rise to fame, with the difference that they are what Bingham calls warts-and-all biopics (Bingham 2011) that generally highlight well-known personal tragedy: the murder of Piaf's impresario Louis Leplée, the death in an accident of her lover Marcel Cerdan, her descent into drug-fuelled depression; Dalida's abortion and the impossibility of subsequently becoming pregnant, the suicide of her lovers and her own suicide; Claude François's irascible megalomania, narcissism, autocratic behaviour, tantrums, his indictment for tax evasion; Gainsbourg's alcoholism and so forth. Their prevalence suggests a different way of dealing with recent history, compared with other types of history films, such as the heritage film, which we will consider later. They 'suggest a shift in emphasis from the meta-historical to an emphasis on biography as the most appropriate vehicle for stories that can offer points of identification to the viewer, thus making him or her susceptible to a renegotiation of collective memory' (Radner 2014: 308).

As Moine points out, there is frequently a difference between biopics of male subjects and those of female subjects (2017: 100–06). Women singers are portrayed as victims, while men singers are portrayed as heroic geniuses. Often this is accompanied by differences in narrative structure: La Môme and Dalida rely on flashbacks, fragmenting the women's stories and making them seem tossed around by 'destiny', deprived of agency, while the Gainsbourg and François biopics are broadly linear, their narratives focused on the construction of genius, as well as, in both cases, the tiresome trope of the star's serial seduction of women.

Linearity could easily lead to a loss of cinematographic quality, a descent into the televisual docu-drama, as we work our way through a range of celebrities with the

Figure 18.1 Biopics of popular performers (Courtesy TF1 Studio, Universal StudioCanal Video, Pathé, Gaumont). From left to right: *La Môme, Gainsbourg (vie héroïque), Cloclo, Dalida, Django, Barbara.*

songs that in some cases Gainsbourg wrote for them in the biopic devoted to him (Fréhel, the Frères Jacques, Juliette Gréco, France Gall, Brigitte Bardot, Jane Birkin, Georges Brassens), or the singers that we see in *Cloclo* (Johnny Hallyday, Gilbert Bécaud, France Gall, Frank Sinatra, who reworked one of François's songs into 'My Way'). *Gainsbourg* avoids this partly by the introduction of an alter-ego cartoon character drawn by the young Gainsbourg and with whom Gainsbourg debates throughout the film (Burgoyne 2014). *Cloclo* avoids the televisual with inventive long takes, such as a four-and-a-half-minute-long single take as he leaves home, is assailed by fans, drives to his office, where he is assailed by more fans (1.27); this is followed a little later by an almost three-minute-long single take as the camera follows his wife Isabelle offering guests macaroons in his converted windmill home in Dannemois, the camera briefly following a waiter, then another guest as we change floors before returning to Isabelle and then to François, who leaves the party to find his son hiding in an upstairs bedroom (1.38). Both of these shots emphasize the ever-present coterie of fans or followers that invade François's private spaces, to some extent mitigating his furious outbursts as the life he tries so hard to dominate spirals out of his control.

The biopics we have so far mentioned are variants of heritage cinema (see Moine 2017: 117–26), something that takes them even further away from previous film musicals, especially those focused on popular performers of the 1940s and 1950s like Rossi or Mariano. *Django*, with its attention to period detail and slightly sepia colour palette, is almost indistinguishable from mainstream heritage cinema; disappointingly, it focuses on a single episode of Reinhardt's career in 1943, when the Germans forced him to perform for them and he decided to escape to Switzerland. The main point of the film is less Reinhardt's biography than the critique of Nazi repression of the Roma. Correlatively the musical interest of the film is less the occasional and nicely done performances of Reinhardt's Quintet than his composition of a funeral mass for organ memorializing the persecution of the Romani people. Thought lost, it was reconstituted from a brief outline by Australian composer Warren Ellis (a member of the group Nick Cave and the Bad Seeds) with Reinhardt's grandson David Reinhardt; we see Reinhardt composing it on a church organ (1.15), and then conducting an orchestra and choir when it is performed in the last sequence of the film and over the end credits (1.47).

The only biopic mentioned so far that strays from realist biographical presentation is *Gainsbourg (vie héroïque)*. As the reviewer of *L'Express* commented, in contrast with *Cloclo*'s standard treatment, its approach was refreshing, and he suggested that this might be a productive route for future biopics, wishing that 'un biopic ne se limite pas à un savoir-faire technique, mais soit également doté de partis pris artistiques, tant visuels que narratifs'[7] (Carrière 2012). Some do precisely this, although they tend to be more obviously art-house or avant-garde. *Barbara*, for example, was dismissed as a 'sorte d'anti-biopic intello pour happy few'[8] (Comte 2017; Morice 2017). Its director, Mathieu Amalric, playfully labelled it a 'bio-utopic' (Guichard 2017). Amalric also plays a director within the film who is making a film on Barbara, whose role in the film-within-the-film is taken by Brigitte (Jeanne Balibar). The film we are watching, unlike the other biopics mentioned earlier, is non-linear; we hear songs by Barbara, sung by her but also by Balibar, and the film weaves footage of the real Barbara, for example, a clip of the feature film she made with Jacques Brel, *Franz* (Jacques Brel, 1971), and extracts from a documentary by Gérard Vergez, *Barbara ou ma plus belle histoire d'amour* (1973).[9] As is the case with the biopics we have already considered, the actors playing the singers closely resemble them, and Balibar is no exception. In contrast with the other biopics we have commented on, however, *Barbara* constantly mixes levels of reality so that we are not always certain whether what we are seeing is Amalric's film or the film-within-the-film or extracts from footage of Barbara herself. This uncertainty is emphasized not just by Balibar's resemblance to the singer, but by Brigitte's constant attempts to emulate the singer's gestures and voice, as well as by the use of documentary-style filming (both hand-held camera and grainy 1970s-style film stock).

Musical biopics are not confined to singers. *Jeannette, l'enfance de Jeanne d'Arc* is a biopic about Joan of Arc, clearly indicated in the opening credits as a 'film musical' (in French, meaning a 'musical film'), although it was generally called 'une comédie musicale' by reviewers (meaning a 'film musical'), renewing with the instability of generic terminology that we saw at the beginning of the sound era. Like *Barbara*, it is uncompromising art-house cinema that rejects mainstream and popular aesthetics.

---

[7] 'A biopic should not just be technically good, but should also be artistic both visually and narratively.'
[8] 'A sort of intellectual anti-biopic for the happy few.'
[9] See https://www.ina.fr/video/CPF09007876.

The film is set in the dunes of the Pas-de Calais under a luminously blue sky, its dialogue and songs based on two texts by the Catholic poet and playwright Charles Péguy, his play *Jeanne d'Arc* (1897), and its reworking into something that resembles a poem in 1904. The actors are all non-professionals, in terms of both acting and singing. Their performance alternates between deadpan dialogue, off-key and frequently off-rhythm live singing or *parlé-chanté*, and dervish-like dance-steps with much lifting of arms and lowered swinging heads – 'headbanging straight from Hellfest' as one French reviewer, using English terminology, and referring to the annual French heavy-rock festival, put it (Kaganski 2017). It was choreographed by Philippe Decouflé, best known for the opening and closing ceremonies of the Albertville Winter Olympics in 1992. Much of the music is by the composer Igorrr (Gautier Serre), known for his mix of musical genres, particularly death metal and heavy metal, whose growling guitars accompany many of the 'songs' in what *Variety*'s reviewer called 'retro noise pollution' (Debruge 2017). The film was received with a mixture of respect for what Dumont appeared to be trying to do, some reviewers seeing it as a boldly minimalist recuperation of a Joan of Arc figure adopted by the Front National, and a return to early cinema through its echoes of a passion-play aesthetic. Dumont released the second and less musical part in May 2019. This time the musical accompaniment included some songs by progressive-pop singer Augustin Charnet, and a cameo from pop singer Christophe.

An equally off-beat musical, *Opium*, focuses on the relationship between Jean Cocteau and the writer Raymond Radiguet in the early 1920s; it is loosely based on Cocteau's journal about his treatment for opium addiction (1930), which Cocteau (Grégoire Colin) reads in voice-over. The film's narrative is non-linear, constructed like an opium-induced dream, with half a dozen musical interludes in black and white sung by Cocteau's mythological characters; the film's director, Arielle Dombasle, plays Mnemosyne. The songs are extracts from Cocteau's plays and poems set to music; indeed, two of them, 'Les Voleurs d'enfants' ('Kidnappers') and 'La Toison d'or' ('The Golden Fleece') were recorded by Cocteau himself to a jazz accompaniment, and presented by him on those recordings as 'poèmes d'opéra'.[10] Reviewers were divided, some calling the film pretentious and amateurish (Mintzer 2013), others admiring the film's inventiveness (Rouchy 2013).

The final type of musical biopic we will consider is the pseudo-biopic. Two of these focus on well-known singers, Claude François in *Podium* and Johnny Hallyday in *Jean-Philippe*, but through the bias of fictional characters who have a fixation on the singers. In *Podium*, based on the director's novel of the same name (2002), Bernard Frédéric (Benoît Poelvoorde) plays a Cloclo lookalike. We hear and see performed a range of songs from the 1970s and 1980s, mainly by Claude François, but also by Michel Polnareff, Julien Clerc and Sheila. *Jean-Philippe*'s plot is more complex: Fabrice Luchini plays Fabrice, an office-worker who is a fan of Johnny Hallyday, but who has an accident and wakes up in an alternate reality in which Hallyday never became a star, but remained Jean-Philippe Smet.

---

[10] 'Opera poems.'

Fabrice decides to find Hallyday and turn him into the star he is familiar with. At the end of the film, he has another accident and on his return to work realizes not only that Hallyday exists as a star, but that he himself is a famous actor called Fabrice Luchini, further confusing the levels of reality. Hallyday plays himself, and we hear and see performed many of Hallyday's songs; and we also briefly see Bernard Frédéric from *Podium* (again played by Poelvoorde) performing as Claude François in a talent show (both films were produced by the same company, Fidélité Films).

A third pseudo-biopic is *Quand j'étais chanteur* in which Gérard Depardieu plays an ageing singer popular with older audiences who spends his time touring the Auvergne; although his character is fictional, it was based on a real singer, Alain Chanone (Lainé 2015). His late career break comes when he is invited to be the warm-up act for the real singer Christophe (playing himself), but backs out at the last minute. Depardieu sings seventeen songs himself, and as one critic pointed out, acquits himself rather well, suggesting that part of the pleasure of the film was seeing a majestic performance from Depardieu, compensating for a number of previous poor films of the star. The same critic also admired the way that Christophe's presence in the film (he advises Depardieu's character, as well as singing his 'Les Paradis perdus' ['Lost Paradises']), apart from demonstrating the director's admiration for the singer, also managed to create 'ce qui devient trop rare dans le cinéma français: un bon film à fort potentiel populaire'[11] (Badache 2006). The film is suffused with nostalgia for well-known songs from the 1960s and 1970s, among them 'Comme un garçon' ('Just Like a Boy', Sylvie Vartan, 1967), 'L'Anamour' (Serge Gainsbourg, 1969), 'Salma Ya Salama' (Dalida, 1977), and 'Vous les femmes' ('You Women', Julio Iglesias, 1979). The title of the film, however, comes from pop singer Michel Delpech's 1975 album of the same name in which the singer, then aged 30, imagines himself aged 73 in 2019, and looks back nostalgically on his past glories.

There are a few films that are not straightforward biopics but fictional films that celebrate and star the real singers in more substantive ways than *Jean-Philippe*. Michel Delpech plays himself in *L'Air de rien* (Grégory Magne and Stéphane Viard, 2012). One of his fans, Grégory (Grégory Magne), moves heaven and earth to bring about a comeback, and arranges concert performances in very provincial locations in the Auvergne. We hear Delpech sing a number of his hit songs from the 1970s, including 'Quand j'étais chanteur', as well as 'Que Marianne était jolie' ('Marianne Was So Pretty', 1973), 'Le Chasseur' ('The Hunter', 1975) and his last major success 'Le Loir-et-Cher' (1977). Released several weeks before *L'Air de rien*, and renewing with the tradition of revue films of the 1950s, there was *Stars 80* (Frédéric Forestier, Thomas Langmann, 2012) in which fans Vincent (Richard Anconina) and Antoine (Patrick Timsit) direct a company that puts on shows of singer lookalikes, rather like *Podium*. Based on the real story of two music producers, Hugues Gentelet and Olivier Kaefer, they discover some old 45s of real pop singers from the 1980s,[12] and like the plot of *L'Air de rien*, decide to

---

[11] 'What has been all too rare in French cinema: a good film that is truly popular.'
[12] Among some of the better-known hits we hear are the group Cookie Dingler, 'Femme libérée' ('Liberated Woman', 1984); the duo Début de soirée, 'Nuit de folie' ('Crazy Night', 1988); the

put on shows using the singers. They tour the provinces and end up, unlike Depardieu's character in *Quand j'étais chanteur*, with a triumphal concert in the Stade de France. The film sold 1.9m tickets, leading to a sequel with many of the same stars, *Stars 80, la suite* (Thomas Langmann, 2017). This did less well (0.3m tickets), but still proved the enduring attraction of recycling successful musical commodities from the relatively recent past, namely the 1970s and 1980s.

The films of Christophe Barratier

We will complete this brief review of contemporary nostalgic film musicals with two films by Christophe Barratier, which encapsulate the fascination with and recycling of past film musicals, but from earlier periods, the 1930s and 1940s. *Les Choristes* (2004), set in 1949, is the remake of the successful but forgotten *La Cage aux rossignols* (Jean Dréville, 1945) (see Vincendeau 2007 for a comparison of the two films). With its 5m tickets this film beat, in the same year, *Les Enfants du paradis* (Marcel Carné, 1945, 4.8m), as well as several film musicals by Rossi (*Sérénade aux nuages*, 3.5m; *L'Île d'amour*, 3.1m) and Guétary (*Le Cavalier noir*, 3.7m; *Trente et quarante*, 2.2m). It is the story of young delinquents in a strict special school who are coached by their teacher to become a successful choral ensemble. It is part of a small number of French films historically focusing on children, either threatened by authoritarian figures or supported by sympathetic teachers, starting with *Zéro de conduite* (Jean Vigo, 1930), *Les Disparus de Saint-Agil* (Christian-Jaque, 1938), *Scout toujours* (Gérard Jugnot, 1985), *Au revoir les enfants* (Louis Malle, 1987), the documentary *Être et avoir* (Nicolas Philibert, 2002) and *Monsieur Batignole* (Gérard Jugnot, 2002). The star of Barratier's film in the role of Clément Mathieu, the sympathetic teacher, was Jugnot, who had directed and starred in two of the previously listed films, none of which, however, was a film musical. Mathieu in Dréville's film is an aspiring writer; Barratier's remake focuses much more tightly on music as a redemptive force, not least because the film is framed by a nostalgic discussion between two of the boys, now in late middle age, one of whom, Morhange, is a successful conductor living in New York. The chorale used in Dréville's film was Les Petits Chanteurs de la Croix de Bois, established in 1903 and still active today. As the name implies – The Little Singers of the Wooden Cross – the

---

androgynous Desireless with his Europe-wide hit 'Voyage, voyage' (1986); François Feldman, 'Les Valses de Vienne' ('Viennese Waltzes', 1987); the group Gold, 'Plus près des étoiles' ('Nearer to the Stars', 1985); the group Images, 'Le Démon de minuit' ('Midnight Demon', 1986); Jean-Luc Lahaye with 'Débarquez-moi' ('Leave Me', 1987); Marc Lavoine, 'Elle a les yeux révolver' ('She Has Pistol Eyes', 1985); the Belgian group Léopold Nord et Vous, 'C'est l'amour' ('It's Love', 1987); Lio (who starred in the film musical *Golden eighties*, and whose major Europe-wide hit a few years earlier in 1980 was 'Amoureux solitaires' ['Solitary lovers']); Jeanne Mas, 'En rouge et noir' ('In Red and Black', 1987 [1985]); Gilbert Montagné with 'On va s'aimer' ('We Will Love Each Other', 1983); Peter et Sloane 'Besoin de rien, envie de toi' ('Need Nothing, Need You', 1984); Julie Pietri, 'Ève, lève-toi' ('Eve, Stand Up', 1986); and Sabrina with 'Boys (Summertime Love)' in 1987, whose accompanying video was banned in the UK for excessive nudity.

organization has piously Catholic connotations, adding to the sense of nostalgia for a France long left behind by post-war industrialization.

The two films share only one song, Jean-Philippe Rameau's 'La Nuit' ('Night'). Bruno Coulais earned a César award for the many songs he composed for the film; one of the songs, 'Vois sur ton chemin' ('Look on Your Path') was nominated for an Oscar, and sung by Beyoncé at the Academy Awards, much to Barratier's surprise (Barratier 2017). The songs were pre-recorded by another boys' chorale, Les Petits Chanteurs de Saint-Marc, which has links with Les Petits Chanteurs de la Croix de Bois, one of whose members, Jean-Baptiste Maunier, was chosen as the main soloist, Morhange, for the film. With 8.7 million tickets sold in France, and 20 million worldwide, the film was extraordinarily successful, standing out among the more successful comedies that tend to attract large audiences; indeed, Barratier adapted the story as a stage musical which toured France in 2017 with considerable success. The CD of the songs was also immensely popular, staying in first place for album sales in France for eleven weeks in 2004 (lescharts.com) and selling over four million copies worldwide (Ruelle 2017).

The film's success is due to a complex mix of music and individualism. While arguably both films celebrate the power of the underdog, Barratier's focuses on a more contemporary sense of the solitariness of the individual, dissociated and even alienated from society. Dréville's film is framed by crowds, with Mathieu trying to sell cardboard aeroplanes to passers-by at the start and married to his sweetheart at the end accompanied by the chorale. Barratier's Mathieu arrives alone at the school surrounded by Gothic mists at the start, and leaves accompanied by only one boy, Pépinot, the film ending with Pépinot and Morhange talking about their teacher in New York, a long way from Paris and even further from the location of the film in the Auvergne. But that said, the songs the chorale sings are composed by Mathieu, whose character thus manages to be both centre stage through his music and self-effacing by virtue of Jugnot's understated performance; similarly, his character frames the film, but that framing is at the end made of self-effacement as his two pupils review the man's journal.

Some reactions to the film were hostile, one reviewer saying it was just as 'cuculla-praline, gorgé de musique niaiseuse et de chœurs d'angelots'[13] (Douhaire 2005) as Dréville's film. Others, anxious to account for the film's success, pointed out how the film's narrative carefully constructs a middlebrow cultural space strategically located between the total absence of 'culture' at the start of the film and the high culture gestured at by Morhange's status as a successful conductor (Darrigrand 2004). The cocooned middlebrow space created by the film is reinforced by the effect of placing the film in 1949, as it legitimizes the absence of black faces that would otherwise have spoken to issues of racism in contemporary French society. Barratier was quick to legitimize this absence by the period of the film (Dumais 2004), although this is somewhat paradoxical given that the children in his film at times lapse into contemporary *banlieue* language. That middlebrow space is also enabled and shaped by relatively middlebrow music,

---

[13] 'Cheesy, full of silly music and singing cherubs.'

whose ordinariness – Coulais said that the music was not difficult to write and that he was 'moyennement satisfait'[14] with it (Dicale 2004) – functions as the ground for Maunier's 'voix surnaturelle' that 'envoûta la France entière et une bonne partie de la planète'[15] (Anon. 2013).

The film therefore gestures to a golden age, both that of childhood and that of a traditional France as yet unsullied by industrialization and consumerism, where Third Republic values of education are reinforced by the socializing and redemptive power of music. At the same time the film gestures to contemporary values: the self-effacing 'new man' and the importance of the individual. The film therefore, as one reviewer pointed out, creates a 'modest utopia' (Darrigrand 2004). That utopia – 'middle-class, middlebrow and middle-aged' (Vincendeau 2007: 74) – is conjured in Maunier's top notes, an abstract voice of innocence floating free of the encumbrance of a past golden age past and a safely bracketed present into an angelic but clichéd future.

Barratier followed up *Les Choristes* with *Faubourg 36* (2008) about a music hall at the crucial juncture of the Popular Front in 1936. In this backstage musical, a group of friends take over a closed-down music hall in which they used to work, with a view to putting on a musical whose proceeds will allow them to buy it back. Riding on the back of his previous film's success, *Faubourg 36* managed 1.3 million tickets, which is a little better than the average for film musicals in the contemporary period. Although its fourteen songs were all composed specifically for the film by Frank Thomas (lyrics) and Reinhardt Wagner (music), they are in the idiom of popular songs of the 1930s. More than this, the film constantly and very obviously refers to well-known films of the 1930s, as Barratier himself listed in interview (2008; see also Ousselin 2014). The setting in a Paris *faubourg* focused on entertainment recalls *Les Enfants du paradis* (Marcel Carné, 1945), the music-hall location *Quai des Orfèvres* (Henri-Georges Clouzot, 1947), the band of friends setting up a business *Le Crime de Monsieur Lange* (Jean Renoir, 1936) and *La Belle Équipe* (Julien Duvivier, 1937).

Barratier's characters are echoes of those we find in the films just mentioned and other films: Nora Arnezeder's singer Douce is a composite of Michèle Morgan's Nelly in *Quai des brumes* (Marcel Carné, 1938), Jacqueline Laurent's Françoise in *Le jour se lève* (Marcel Carné, 1939) and Florelle's Valentine in *Le Crime de Monsieur Lange*; Clovis Cornillac's proletarian hero Milou reprises Gabin's roles in the same films, Gérard Jugnot's Pigoil those of Bernard Blier, and Bernard-Pierre Donnadieu as the baddie Galapiat recalls Jules Berry's Batala in *Le jour se lève*. None of these intertextual references are musicals. But the final song-and-dance number, patterned on Busby Berkeley's films of the 1930s according to Barratier, also echoes the Hollywood-inspired *La crise est finie* (see Chapter 3).

Critical responses depended on what was thought of the nostalgic replaying of France's cinematographic past. It was seen as escapism, particularly because of the very sketchy sense of the historical period and its political problems with the rise of

---

[14] 'Not particularly happy.'
[15] 'Supernatural voice', 'captivated the whole of France and much of the planet.'

fascism – 'son cinéma, fondé sur la reconnaissance et le retour du même, est bébête'[16] (Morain 2008) – and it was also seen as a utopian aspiration for collective action in the face of the adversities visited by capitalism – 'chanter de vieilles rengaines pour retrouver l'élan d'un renouveau social, mieux vivre ensemble, croire en l'avenir'[17] (Douin 2008). Or as Roger Ebert pithily put it, 'if I had seen it before I was born, I would have loved it' (2009).

Barratier's films are interesting precisely because they raise questions about the intersection between the musical genre and utopia, and about the evolution of genres. Does the constant appeal to the past, evidenced in musical biopics and in Barratier's films, point to renewal, a generic shift in tune with the times? Or does it point to the genre running on empty, capable only of replaying well-worn tropes? We would argue that when the more experimental musicals are taken into account – whether the self-derisive pseudo-biopics or the art-house complexities of Amalric and Dumont – the musical genre is still evolving from its origins in operetta and the great singer films of the 1940s and 1950s. But the films of Barratier also show that the genre has come full circle, replaying, particularly in the case of *Faubourg 36*, the musicals of the 1930s, and amalgamating their tropes with the tropes of the Poetic Realist films of the 1930s.

Coda

The history of the film musical that we have elaborated in this book demonstrates five key points.

First, there have always been film musicals since the beginning of sound film. It is a well-established genre of French cinema, particularly in the period between 1930 and 1960, and if it has not loomed large in academic thinking (there is not a single academic piece on Tino Rossi or Georges Guétary, for example), it is partly because, as the editors of *The International Film Musical* point out, 'conventional national cinema histories ... have often concentrated on the achievements of art or auteur-driven cinemas rather than mainstream, commercial entertainment' (Creekmur and Mokdad 2013: 1). But there is a second reason for the critical neglect: contempt for overtly popular cinema is combined with contempt for genres that are deemed to be 'feminine', as we have seen, in particular, in the reactions to the work of the Three Tenors.

Second, all French film musicals are nostalgic, albeit to different degrees, in that they re-present past songs, often as proxy for a lost golden age, or they re-present the absent body of the singer as a proxy for the live performance. In both cases, they are a celebration of and longing for what has already been heard, whether it is the song heard on stage, in the street, on the radio, on record, or in previous films in the case of remakes. This is the case even for film musicals with songs composed specifically for

---

[16] 'His cinema, based on recognition and the return of the same, is corny.'
[17] 'Singing well-known tunes to rediscover social renewal, to make living together easier, to believe in the future.'

the film, which almost always hark back to specific styles or tonalities, such as the films of Honoré that evoke those of Demy. Even Demy's radically innovative films often display nostalgia for the same kind of community already celebrated by the films of René Clair.

Third, Demy marks a shift from the popular utopian musical where the focus is on the singer and the song, to the dystopian auteur musical where the focus is on the director's vision, and on an engagement with the everyday. That engagement with the everyday is both a celebration and an interrogation, whether it is Godard's emptying of the musical genre while retaining the whimsy of a contemporary everydayness, to the submerging of the operatic in everyday sounds in *Carmen*, to the incorporation of contemporary realities such as AIDS in the films of Ducastel and Martineau or Honoré, and even to a different type of everydayness in the return to Poetic Realism and the preoccupations of *le peuple* in *Faubourg 36*. The transition of 1964 then is the attempted abandonment of the utopian spectacular which helped audiences forget their troubles to a wilful commitment to what lies beneath the surface.

Fourth, the 1963–4 transition is a major social and cultural pivot point, a moment even more critical than was the end of the Second World War in 1945. Not only does 1963 signal, as we pointed out earlier in this book, the end of a particular era with the deaths of Piaf and Cocteau in October 1963, it was also the year that the first hypermarket opened in France, a Carrefour in Sainte-Geneviève-des Bois (June 1963). Carrefour, ironically given its name, meaning a crossroads, forcefully marked a different type of community, detached from the close-local – the kind of community celebrated by Clair, but which even in his time had already to some extent disappeared – to the dispersed out-of-town, the fragmentation of local community under pressure from American-style consumerist materialism. While this may make post-1964 musicals seem in this context like the American folk musical, they are embedded in a completely different social, cultural and political context.

Fifth, and as a corollary, the contemporary French film musical maintains both the utopian and the dystopian, often in the same film: the celebration of small and close communities and the attempt to prevent them from exploding and dissipating. To reprise the terms so frequently used of Demy's films, enchantment rubs shoulders with disenchantment; we could argue that the distinctive characteristic of the contemporary French film musical is the bittersweet pleasure taken in the present's erosion of the certainties of the past.

Filmography

The English title is sourced from the IMDB. Where this is not available, it is our translation. No translation means that the original title in French was used for international release. The date given is that of the first performance.

42nd Street (1933). Lloyd Bacon, USA: Warner.
8 femmes [*8 Women*] (2002). François Ozon, France: Fidélité Productions, Mars Films/France 2 Cinéma, Canal Plus, CNC, Gimages 5.
À la Jamaïque [*To Jamaica*] (1957). André Berthomieu, France: Lyrica, Films Mars, Filmel.
À moi le jour, à toi la nuit [*To Me the Day, To You the Night*] (1932). Ludwig Berger and Claude Heymann, Germany/France: UFA.
À nous deux, Madame la vie [*To Us, Madame Life*] (1937). René Guissart and Yves Mirande, France: Eden Productions.
À nous la liberté (1931). René Clair, France: Films Sonores Tobis.
À nous les petites Anglaises [*Let's Get Those English Girls*] (1976). Michel Lang, France: Films Galaxie.
Adieu Léonard (1943). Pierre Prévert, France: Essor Cinématographique Français.
Abschiedswalzer [*Farewell Waltz*] (1934). Géza von Bolváry, Germany: Boston Films.
Adieu Philippine (1963). Jacques Rozier, France/Italy: Rome-Paris Films, Unitec France, Alpha Productions, Euro International Films.
Ah! Les belles bacchantes [*Peek-a-Boo*] (1954). Jean Loubignac, France/Italy: Optimax Films, Lux Films.
L'Air de rien [*Sounds Like Nothing*] (2012). Grégory Magne and Stéphane Viard, France: les Films Velvet, Garance Capital.
Algiers (1938). John Cromwell, USA: United Artists.
Amadeus (1984). Milos Forman, USA/France/Czechoslovakia: AMLF, The Saul Zaentz Co.
Les Amants de demain [*Tomorrow's Lovers*] (1959). Marcel Blistène, France: Cinextension, Société Nouvelle Océans Films.
America di Notte [*America by Night*] (1961). Carlos Alberto de Souza Barros and Giuseppe Maria Scotese, Italy/France/Brazil/Argentina: D'An-Fran, Geralartes, Les Productions René Thévenet.
Amok (1934). Fedor Ozep, France: Pathé-Natan.
Amour et Compagnie [*Love and Co.*] (1950). Gilles Grangier, France: La Société des Films Sirius.
An American in Paris (1951). Vincente Minnelli, USA: MGM.
Andalousie [*Andalousia*] (1951). Robert Vernay, France/Spain: CCFC, UDIF, Columbia Films, CEA.
Andrei Rublev (1969). Andrei Tarkovsky, Soviet Union: Mosfilm.
L'Année dernière à Marienbad [*Last Year in Marienbad*] (1961). Alain Resnais, France/Italy/West Germany/Austria: Cocinor, Terra Films, Como Films, Cormoran Films, Argos Films, Cinétel, Silver Films, Précitel, Tamara, Cineriz.
Anything Goes (1956). Robert Lewis, USA: Paramount.

Arènes joyeuses [*Happy Arenas*] (1935). Karl Anton, France: Metropa Films.
Arènes joyeuses [*Happy Arenas*] (1958). Maurice de Canonge, France: Athos Films, Compagnie Méditerranéenne de Films, Eminente Films.
Aria (1987). Robert Altman, Bruce Beresford, Bill Bryden, Jean-Luc Godard, Derek Jarman, Franc Roddam, Nicolas Roeg, Ken Russell, Charles Sturridge, Julien Temple, UK: Lightyear Entertainment.
Arthur (1931). Léonce Perret, France: Les Films Osso.
Au fil des ondes [*Over the Radio Waves*] (1951). Pierre Gautherin, France: Cité Films.
Au pays du soleil [*In the Land of the Sun*] (1934). Robert Péguy, France: Les Films Tellus.
Au pays du soleil [*In the Land of the Sun*] (1951). Maurice de Canonge, France: Les Films Tellus.
Au revoir les enfants (1987). Louis Malle, France/West Germany/Italy: Nouvelles Éditions de Films, MK2 Productions, Stella Films, N.E.F Filmproduktion und Vertriebs.
Au soleil de Marseille [*Sun of Marseille*] (1938). Pierre-Jean Ducis, France: Productions Henri Ullmann.
Au son des guitares [*To the Sound of Guitars*] (1936). Pierre-Jean Ducis, France: Les Films Henri Ullmann.
L'Auberge du Petit Dragon (1934). Jean de Limur, France: Flora-Films.
Aventure à Paris [*Adventure in Paris*] (1936). Marc Allégret, France: Prod. André Daven, Films Osso.
Les Aventures de Casanova [*The Adventures of Casanova*] (1947). Jean Boyer, France: La Société des Films Sirius.
L'Aventurier de Séville [*The Adventurer of Seville*] (1954). Ladislas Vajda, France/Spain: Les Productions Cinématographiques/Producciones Benito Perojo.
Baisers volés [*Stolen Kisses*] (1968). François Truffaut, France: Les Films du Carrosse, Les Productions Artistes Associés.
Le Bal des actrices [*All About Actresses*] (2009). Maïwenn Le Bescot, France: Les Films du Kiosque, Canal Plus, CNC/SND Groupe M6, France 2 Cinéma, Cinécinéma, Uni Etoile 5, Banque populaire Images 8, Procirep, Angoa.
The Band Wagon (1953). Vincente Minnelli, USA: MGM.
Bang Bang (1967). Serge Piollet, France: Cité Films, Films Cinematografica.
Barbara (2017). Mathieu Amalric, France: Waiting For Cinema, Gaumont, France 2 Cinéma, Alicéléo.
Barbara ou ma plus belle histoire d'amour [*Barbara, or My Greatest Love Story*] (1973). Gérard Vergez, France: France 5.
Le Barbier de Séville [*The Barber of Seville*] (1904). George Méliès, France: Star Films.
Le Barbier de Séville [*The Barber of Seville*] (1948). Jean Loubignac, France: Codo Cinéma.
Bariole (1934). Benno Vigny, France: Henri Ullmann.
Baron Tzigane [*Gypsy Baron*] (1927). Frederic Zelnick, Germany: Zelink Films.
Baron Tzigane [*Gypsy Baron*] (1935). Karl Hartl, France/Germany: UFA, ACE.
Baron Tzigane [*Gypsy Baron*] (1954). Arthur Maria Rabenalt, West Germany: Berolina.
La Belle de Cadix [*The Belle of Cadiz*] (1953). Raymond Bernard, France/Spain: Compagnie Commerciale Française Cinématographique, CEA.
Belle de jour (1967). Luis Buñuel, France/Italy: Robert et Raymond Hakim, Paris Film Productions, Five Films.
La Belle Équipe [*They Were Five*] (1936). Julien Duvivier, France: Ciné-Arys Productions.
La Belle et la Bête [*Beauty and the Beast*] (1946). Jean Cocteau, France: Les Films André Paulvé, Discina.

La Belle Meunière [*The Pretty Miller Girl*] (1948). Marcel Pagnol, France: Société du Film La Belle Meunière.
La Belle Noiseuse [*The Beautiful Troublemaker*] (1991). Jacques Rivette, France/Switzerland: Pierre Grise Productions, George Reinhart Productions, FR3 Productions.
La Belle Vie [*The Good Life*] (1964). Robert Enrico, France: Les Films du Centaure.
Berlingot et Compagnie (1939). Fernand Rivers, France: Les Films Fernand Rivers.
Les Bien-aimés [*Beloved*] (2011). Christophe Honoré, France/UK/Czechoslovakia: Why Not Productions/France 2 Cinéma, France Télévisions, Orange Cinéma Séries, Région Ile-de-France, Sacem, Soficinéma 7, Canal Plus, Negativ, Sixteen Films.
The Big Country (1958). William Wyler, USA: Anthony Productions et Worldwide Productions.
La Bohème (1988). Luigi Comencini, France/UK/Italy: Gaumont, Rai Due.
Boîte de nuit [*Hotbed of Sin*] (1951). Alfred Rode, France: S.F.F.A.R.
Bonjour sourire! [*Hello Smile!*] (1956). Claude Sautet, France: Vox Films.
Boris Godounov (1989). Andrzej Żuławski, France/Spain/Yugoslavia: Gaumont, Erato Films, La Sept.
Boum sur Paris [*Rendezvous in Paris*] (1953). Maurice de Canonge, France: Les Films Marceau.
Bouquet de joie [*Bunch of Joy*] (1951). Maurice Cam, France: Sonofilm.
Branquignol (1949). Robert Dhéry, France: Cité-Films, Fidès, Stella Films.
The Broadway Melody (1929). Harry Beaumont, USA: MGM.
C'est arrivé à 36 chandelles [*It Happened on the 36 Candles*] (1957). Henri Diamant-Berger, France: Eden, Les Films d'Art, Les Films Fernand Rivers, Panorama Films.
La Cage aux rossignols [*A Cage of Nightingales*] (1945). Jean Dréville, France: Société Nouvelles des Établissements Gaumont.
Carmen (1910). André Calmettes, Paris: Films d'Art Pathé.
Carmen (1984). Francesco Rosi, France/Italy: Gaumont.
Carmen nue [*Carmen Baby*] (1984). Albert López, France: African Queen Productions, Vidéo Cinéma-Télévision International.
Casino de Paris (1957). André Hunnebelle, France/Italy/Germany: Criterion Films, Pathé Consortium Cinéma, Bavaria Films, Bavaria-Filmkunst, Eichberg Films, Rizzoli Films.
La Cavalcade des heures [*Love Around the Clock*] (1943). Yvan Noé, France: France Productions.
Le Cavalier noir (1945). Gilles Grangier, France: Gaumont/Société des Films Sirius.
Cavalleria rusticana (1909). Émile Chautard, France: Éclair.
Ce soir les souris dansent [*The Mysterious Melody*] (1956). Jean Fortuny, France/Spain: Eurociné, Producciones Miguel Mezquíriz.
César et Rosalie (1972). Claude Sautet, France/Italy/West Germany: Fildebroc/Mega Film/Orion Filmproduktion/Paramount Pictures.
Chacun sa chance [*Everybody Wins*] (1930). Hans Steinhoff, France/Germany: Marce Hellman Films, Pathé-Natan.
La Chanson de l'adieu [*Farewell*] (1934). Géza von Bolváry and Albert Valentin, France/Germany: Films Sonores Tobis, Boston-Films.
Les Chansons d'amour [*Love Songs*] (2007). Christophe Honoré, France: Alma Productions, Canal Plus, CNC, Cinécinéma, Cofinova 3, Cofinova 4, Coficup, Backup Films, Flach Films.
Le Chant de l'exilé [*The Exile's Song*] (1943). André Hugon, France: Les Films Collard, Les Productions André Hugon.

Chante ton bac d'abord [*We Did It on a Song*] (2014). David André, France: Brotherfilms.
Le Chanteur de Mexico [*The Mexican Singer*] (1956). Richard Pottier, France/Spain: Vauban Productions, Jason Productions, CEF, Producciones Benito Perojo.
Le Chanteur inconnu [*The Unkown Singer*] (1947). André Cayatte, France: Gray-Films.
Charmants garçons [*Charming Boys*] (1957). Henri Decoin, France: Société des Films Sirius.
Château en Suède [*Nuttey, Naughty Chateau*] (1963). Roger Vadim, France: Euro International Films (EIA)/Les Films Corona/Spectacles Lumbroso.
Le Chemin du paradis [*The Road to Paradise*] (1930). Wilhelm Thiele and Max de Vaucorbeil, Germany/France: UFA, ACE.
Le Chemin du paradis [*The Road to Paradise*] (1956). Willi Forst and Hans Wolff, France/West Germany: Berolina, CEC.
Cherchez l'idole [*The Chase*] (1964). Michel Boisrond, France/Italy: France Cinéma Productions, Mannic Films, Société des Films Sirius, UGC, Adelphia Compagnia Cinematographica.
Les Chinois à Paris [*Chinese in Paris*] (1974). Jean Yanne, France/Italy: Cine Qua Non, Productions 2000, Produzioni Europee Associate.
Chobizenesse (1975). Jean Yanne, France: Productions Yanne.
Chocolat [*Monsieur Chocolat*] (2016). Roschdy Zem, France: Mandarin Cinéma.
Les Choristes [*The Chorus*] (2004). Christophe Barratier, France/Switzerland/Germany: Vega Films, Banque Populaire Images 4, CP Medien AG, Canal+, Centre National de la Cinématographie, Dan Valley Film AG, France 2 Cinéma, Galatée Films, Novo Arturo Films, Pathé Renn Productions, Procirep.
Les Choses de la vie [*The Things of Life*] (1970). Claude Sautet, France/Italy: Lira Films, Sonocam, Fida Cinematografica.
Chouchou (2003). Merzak Allouache, France: Les Films Christian Fechner, Fechner Audiovisuel, Canal+, France 2 Cinéma, KS2 Productions.
Ciboulette (1933). Claude Autant-Lara, France: Pathé Consortium Cinéma, Cipar Films.
La Cinquième Empreinte [*The Fifth Fingerprint*] (1934). Karl Anton, France: Films Fred Bacos, Fox Film.
Clara et moi [*Clara and Me*] (2004). Arnaud Viard, France: Gloria Films, Les 1001 Marches, France 2 Cinéma.
Cléo de 5 à 7 [*Cleo from 5 to 7*] (1962). Agnès Varda, France/Italy: Ciné Tamaris, Rome-Paris Films.
CloClo [*My Way*] (2012). Florent-Emilio Siri, France/Belgium: LGM Productions, Flèche Productions, 24C Productions, StudioCanal, TF1 Films Production, Rockworld, JRW Entertainment, Emilio Films, UFilm, Belgacom.
Cœur de Lilas [*Lilac*] (1932). Anatole Litvak, France: Fifra.
Le Comte Obligado (1935). Léon Mathot, France: Eurêka Films.
Le congrès s'amuse [*Congress Dances*] (1931). Erik Charell and Jean Boyer, France/Germany: UFA.
Construire un feu [*To Build a Fire*] (1930). Claude Autant-Lara, France: Renée Meyer-See.
Crime au concert Mayol [*Palace of Shame*] (1954). Pierre Méré, France: Lutetia Films, U.E.C.
Le Crime de Monsieur Lange [*The Crime of Monsieur Lange*] (1936). Jean Renoir, France: Films Obéron.
La crise est finie [*The Crisis Is Over*] (1934). Robert Siodmak, France: Nero Films.
Cyrano de Bergerac (1990). Jean-Paul Rappeneau, France: Hachette Première, Caméra One, DD Productions, Films A2, U.G.C.

D'où viens-tu, Johnny? [*Where Are You from, Johnny?*] (1963). Noël Howard, France: Hoche Productions, Société Nouvelle de Cinématographie.
Dactylo [*The Typist*] (1931). Wilhelm Thiele, France: Pathé-Natan, Greenbaum Films.
Dalida (2016). Lisa Azuelos, France: Bethsabée Mucho, Pathé, TF1 Films Production, UMedia, Universal Music Publishing.
Dames (1934). Busby Berkeley and Ray Enright, USA: Warner Bros.
La Damnation de Faust (1904). Georges Méliès, France: Star Films.
Dédé (1934). René Guissart, France: France Univers-Films.
Les Demoiselles de Rochefort [*The Young Ladies of Rochefort*] (1967). Jacques Demy, France/USA: Parc Films, Madeleine Films.
Les Demoiselles ont eu 25 ans [*The Young Girls Turn 25*] (1993). Agnès Varda, France: Ciné Tamaris.
Le Dernier Métro [*The Last Metro*] (1980). François Truffaut, France: Les Films du Carrosse, Sédif, TF1 Films Production, Société Française de Production, Maran Films.
Destins [*Destinies*] (1946). Richard Pottier, France: Compagnie Commerciale Française Cinématographique.
Détective [*Detective*] (1985). Jean-Luc Godard, France: JLG Films, Sara Films.
Deux amours [*Two Loves*] (1949). Richard Pottier, France: Union des Distributeurs Indépendants.
Les Disparus de Saint-Agil [*Boys' School*] (1938). Christian-Jaque, France: Dimeco Productions.
Django (2017). Étienne Comar, France: Fidélité Films, Arches Films, Moana Films, Curiosa Films, Pathé, France 2 Cinéma, Rhône-Alpes Cinéma.
Don César de Bazan (1909). Victorin Jasset, France: Éclair.
Don Giovanni (1980). Joseph Losey, France/Italy/West Germany: Gaumont, Antenne 2, Opera Films, Janus Filmproduktion.
Dossier 1413 (1962). Alfred Rode, France: S.F.F.A.R.
Die Drei von der Tankstelle [*The Three from the Filling Station*] (1930). Wilhelm Thiele, Germany: UFA.
Die Dreigroschenoper [*The Threepenny Opera*] (1931). Georg Wilhelm Pabst, Germany/USA: Tobis filmkunst, Nero Films AG, Warner Bros.
Drôle de Félix [*The Adventures of Felix*] (2000). Olivier Ducastel et Jacques Martineau, France: Les Films Pelléas, Arte France Cinéma, Pyramide Productions, Canal+, CNC, Gimages 2.
Les Duraton (1955). André Berthomieu, France: Simoja, Films Metzger et Woog.
Les Enfants du paradis [*Children of Paradise*] (1945). Marcel Carné, France: Société Nouvelle Pathé Cinéma.
L'Enfer des anges [*Angels' Hell*] (1941). Christian-Jaque, France: Ciné-Alliance, Société Anonyme de Réalisation Œuvres Cinématographiques.
Énigme aux Folies-Bergère [*The Enigma of the Folies-Bergere*] (1959). Jean Mitry, France: Gimeno Phillips Films.
L'Entraîneuse [*Nightclub Hostess*] (1939). Albert Valentin, France/Germany: Les Films Raoul Ploquin, UFA.
Envoi de fleurs [*Sending of Flowers*] (1950). Jean Stelli, France: Coco Cinéma.
L'Éternel Retour [*Love Eternal*] (1943). Jean Delannoy, France: Les Films André Paulvé, Discina.
Étoile sans lumière [*Star Without Light*] (1946). Marcel Blistène, France: Société Universelle de Films, Une Production d'Eugène Tuscherer, B.U.P. Française.
L'Étrange Madame X [*The Strange Madame X*] (1951). Jean Grémillon, France: Codo Cinéma, S. G. G. C.

Être et avoir [*To Be and to Have*] (2002). Nicolas Philibert, France: Maïa Films, Arte France Cinéma, Les Films d'Ici, Centre National de Documentation Pédagogique.
Europa di notte [*European Nights*] (1959). Alessandro Blasetti, Italy: Avers Films.
La Famille Duraton (1939). Christian Stengel, France: Société de Production du Film Famille Duraton.
La Famille Bélier (2014). Éric Lartigau. France/Belgium: Jerico, Mars Films, France 2 Cinéma, Quarante 12 Films, Vendôme Productions, Nexus Factory, Umedia.
Fandango (1949). Emil-Edwin Reinert, France: Les Films Gloria/Olympia Films.
Fantasia (1940). Various, USA: Walt Disney Studios.
Farinelli (1994). Gérard Corbiau, France/Italy/Belgium/UK: Stéphan Films, MG, Italian International Films K2 SA.
Fashions of 1934 (1934). William Dieterle, USA: First National Pictures.
Faubourg 36 [*Paris 36*] (2008). Christophe Barratier, France/Germany/Czech Republic: Galatée Films, Pathé, Constantin Films, France 2 Cinéma, France 3 Cinéma, Logline Studios, Novo Arturo Films, Blue Screen Productions.
Faust (1910). Henri Andréani and Georges Fagot, France: Pathé.
Faust (1922). Gérard Bourgeois, France: Azur.
La Femme d'à côté [*The Woman Next Door*] (1981). François Truffaut, France: Les Films du Carrosse, TF1 Films Production.
Femmes de Paris [*Women of Paris*] (1953). Jean Boyer, France: Prod. Ray Ventura.
Feux de joie [*Bonfires*] (1939). Jacques Houssin, France: Florida Films, Films Derby.
Fièvres [*Fevers*] (1942). Jean Delannoy, France: Les Films Minerva.
Filles perdues, cheveux gras [*Hypnotized and Hysterical (Hairstylist Wanted)*] (2002). Claude Duty, France: Ce Qui Me Meut Motion Pictures, France 2 Cinéma, Gimages 5, Mars Distribution, More Movies.
La Fin de Don Juan [*The End of Don Juan*] (1911). Victorin Jasset, France: Éclair.
Flaming Star (1960). Don Siegel, USA: 20th Century Fox.
Folies-Bergère (1957). Henri Decoin, France: La Société des Films Sirius, Les Productions Jacques Roitfeld.
Folies-Bergère (aka *L'Homme des Folies-Bergère*) (1935). Roy Del Ruth and Marcel Achard, USA: 20th Century Fox.
Folies-Bergère de Paris (1935). Roy Del Ruth, USA: 20th Century Pictures.
Footlight Parade (1933). Lloyd Bacon, USA: Warner Bros.
Fra Diavolo (1912). Alice Guy-Blaché, France: Solax.
Franz (1971). Jacques Brel, France/Belgium: Productions Belles Rives, Ciné Vog, Elan Films.
Die Frauen von Folies Bergères [*The Women of the Folies-Bergère*] (1927). Joe Francis and Max Obal, France/Germany: Cando Films.
Frédérica (1942). Jean Boyer, France: Jason Films.
French Cancan (1954). Jean Renoir, France/Italy: Franco London Films, Jolly Films.
Gadjo Dilo [*The Crazy Stranger*] (1998). Tony Gatlif, Romania/France: Princes Films.
Gainsbourg (vie héroïque) [*Gainsbourg: A Heroic Life*] (2010). Joann Sfar, France: One World Films, Studio 37, Universal Pictures International, France 2 Cinéma, Liloi Films, Xilam Films.
Les Gangsters du château d'If [*The Gangsters of the Château d'If*] (1939). René Pujol, France: Vandas Productions.
La Garçonne [*The Tomboy*] (1936). Jean de Limur, France: Franco London Films.
Les Garçons et Guillaume, à table [*Me, Myself, and Mum*] (2013). Guillaume Gallienne, France/Belgium: LGM Productions, Rectangle Productions, Don't Be Shy Productions, Gaumont, France 3 Cinéma, Nexus Factory, uFilm.

Le Gardian [*The Herdsman*] (1946). Jean de Marguenat, France: Les Films Lutétia.
Gazon maudit [*French Twist*] (1995). Josiane Balasko, France: Renn Productions, Les Films Flam, TF1 Films Production, Canal+.
Gentlemen Prefer Blondes (1953). Howard Hawks, USA: 20th Century Fox.
Gigolette (1937). Yvan Noé, France: Les Productions Pellegrin.
Giovinezza (1952). Giorgio Pastina, Italy: Zeus Films, Bomba e cio.
Give a Girl a Break (1953). Stanley Donen, USA: MGM.
Gold Diggers of 1933 (1933). Mervyn LeRoy, USA: Warner Bros.
Gold Diggers of 1935 (1935). Busby Berkeley, USA: First National Pictures.
Gold Diggers of 1937 (1936). Lloyd Bacon, USA: Warner Bros.
Golden Eighties (1986). Chantal Akerman, France/Belgium/Switzerland: La Cecilia/Ministère Français de la Culture, Paradise Films, Centre du Cinéma et de l'Audiovisuel de la Communauté française de Belgique, Limbo Films AG.
Le Grand Refrain [*Symphonie d'Amour*] (1936). Yves Mirande, France: Metropa Films.
Greystoke: The Legend of Tarzan, Lord of the Apes (1984). Dir. Hugh Hudson, UK/USA: Warner Bros, Edgar Rice Burroughs Inc., WEA Records.
La Guerre des valses [*Vienna Waltzes*] (1933). Ludwig Berger and Raoul Ploquin, Germany/France: UFA, A.C.E.
Hans Christian Andersen (1952). Charles Vidor, USA: The Samuel Goldwyn Company.
Haut bas fragile [*Up, Down, Fragile*] (1995). Jacques Rivette, France/Switzerland/Italy: Pierre Grise Productions, Carac Films, George Reinhart Productions, Canal+/Centre National de la Cinématographie, Ministère français de la Culture et de la Francophonie, Sacem, Televisione Svizzera Italiana, Mikado Films.
Les héros sont fatigués [*Heroes and Sinners*] (1955). Yves Ciampi, France: Central Cinema Company Film, Cila Films, Terra Films.
Hiroshima mon amour (1959). Alain Resnais, France/Japan: Argos/Pathé/Como Films/Daiei Studios Motion Picture Company.
Holiday Inn (1942). Marc Sandrich, USA: Paramount.
L'Homme du train [*Man on the Train*] (2002). Patrice Leconte, France/Germany/UK/Japan: Ciné B, Zoulou Films, Rhône-Alpes Cinéma, FCC, Tubedale Films, Pandora Filmproduktion, Cinéma Parisien, Media Suits.
Ich bei Tag und du bei Nacht [*I by Day, You by Night*] (1932). Ludwig Berger, Germany: UFA.
Les Idoles [*The Idols*] (1968). Marc'O, France: International Thanos Films.
Il est charmant [*He Is Charming*] (1932). Louis Mercanton, France: Paramount.
L'Île d'amour [*Love Island*] (1928). Berthe Dagmar and Jean Durand, France: Gaumont.
L'Île d'amour [*Love Island*] (1944). Maurice Cam, France: Cyrnos Films, Productions Sigma.
L'Innocent [*The Innocent*] (1938). Maurice Cammage, France: Films Chantecler.
Intouchables [*The Intouchables*] (2011). Olivier Nakache and Éric Toledano, France: Gaumont, TF1 Films Production, Quad Productions, Chaocorp, Ten Films.
J'accuse! (1919). Abel Gance, France: Pathé.
Jacquot de Nantes (1991). Agnès Varda, France: Ciné-Tamaris, Canal Plus, Centre National de la Cinématographie, La Sept Cinéma, Sofiarp, Ministère français de la Culture et de la Communication, Conseil municipal de la Ville de Nantes, Conseil général de Loire – Atlantique, Région Pays de la Loire, ARPCA.
Je chante [*I'm Singing*] (1938). Christian Stengel, France: René Wheeler.
Je n'aime que toi [*My One Only Love*] (1949). Pierre Montazel, France: Les Films Gloria.
Jean-Philippe (2006). Laurent Tuel, France: Fidélité Productions, Bankable.

Jeanne Dielman, 23 quai du Commerce, 1080 Bruxelles (1975). Chantal Akerman, France/Belgique: Paradise Films, Unité Trois, Ministère de la Culture Française de Belgique, Centre du Cinéma et de l'Audiovisuel de la Fédération Wallonie-Bruxelles.
Jeanne et le garçon formidable [*Jeanne and the Perfect Guy*] (1998). Olivier Ducastel et Jacques Martineau, France: Les Films du Requin, Orsan Productions, M6 Films, Canal+, CNC, France 2 Cinéma, Fondation Gan pour le Cinéma, Procirep, Pyramide Productions.
Jeanne [*Joan of Arc*] (2019). Bruno Dumont, France: 3P Productions.
Jeannette, l'enfance de Jeanne d'Arc [*Jeannette: The Childhood of Joan of Arc*] (2017). Bruno Dumont, France: Taos Films, Arte Films.
Jo la romance (1949). Gilles Grangier, France: La Société des Films Sirius.
Le jour se lève [*Daybreak*] (1939). Marcel Carné, France: Productions Sigma.
The Journey (1959). Anatole Litvak, USA: Alby Pictures.
Kid Galahad (1962). Phil Karson, USA: The Mirisch Corporation.
King Creole (1958). Michael Curtis, USA: Paramount, Wallis-Hazen.
King of Jazz (1930). John Murray Anderson, USA: Universal Pictures.
King of Kings (1961). Nicholas Ray, USA: Samuel Bronston Productions.
Der Kongreß tanzt [*Congress Dances*] (1931). Dir Erik Charell, Germany: UFA.
Königswalzer (1936). Herbert Maisch, Germany: UFA.
The Lady in the Lake (1947). Robert Montgomery, USA: MGM.
Lady Paname (1950). Henri Jeanson, France: Spéva Films.
Land of the Pharaohs (1955). Howard Hawks, USA: Continental Company.
Latcho Drom (1993). Tony Gatlif, France: KG Productions.
Laurent et Safi (2017). Anton Vassil, France: B-Mol Productions.
Lawrence of Arabia (1962). David Lean, UK: Horizon Pictures.
Liebe ist ja nur ein Märchen [*Amour, tango, mandoline*] (1955). Arthur Maria Rabenalt, West Germany: Berolina.
Living in a Big Way (1947). Gregory La Cava. USA: MGM.
Louise (1939). Abel Gance, France: Société Parisienne de Production de Films.
Love in the Afternoon (1957). Billy Wilder, USA: Billy Wilder Productions.
Love Me Tonight (1932). Rouben Mamoulian, USA: Paramount.
The Love Parade (1929). Ernst Lubitsch, USA: Paramount.
Lumières de Paris [*Lights of Paris*] (1938). Richard Pottier, France: Paris Film Productions.
Macbeth (1987). Claude d'Anna, France/West Germany: Henry Lange, UNITEL, Delalus, S.F.P.C., TF1 Films Production.
Madame Butterfly (1995). Frédéric Mitterrand, France/UK/Germany: Erato Films, Idéale Audience, Imalyre, VTCOM France Telecom, France 3 Cinéma, Sony Classical.
Mademoiselle s'amuse [*Mademoiselle Has Fun*] (1948). Jean Boyer, France: Hoche Productions.
Mademoiselle Swing (1942). Richard Pottier, France: SUF.
La Maison du Maltais, [*Sirocco*] (1938). Pierre Chenal, France: Compagnie Cinématographique de France, Gladiator Films.
Le Maître de musique [*The Music Teacher*] (1988). Gérard Corbiau, Belgium: Radio Télévision Belge Francophone, K2 SA.
La Maman et la putain [*The Mother and the Whore*] (1973). Jean Eustache, France: Elite Films, Ciné Qua Non, Les Films du Losange, Simar Films, V.M. Productions.
Manon Lescaut (1912). Unknown, France: Pathé.
Le Mariage de Figaro [*The Marriage of Figaro*] (1959). Jean Meyer, France: LPC, Pathé, Comédie Française.

Marinella (1936). Pierre Caron, France: Forrester-Parant.
Marlène (1949). Pierre de Hérain, France: Union des Distributeurs Indépendants.
Marseille mes amours [*Marseille My Love*] (1940). Jacques Daniel-Norman, France: GARB Productions.
Le Masque d'Hollywood [*Woman Hunter*] (1931). Clarence Badger and Jean Daumery, USA: First National Pictures.
Max et les ferrailleurs [*Max and the Junkmen*] (1971). Claude Sautet, France/Italy: Lira Films Sonocam, Fida Cinematografica.
The Merry Widow (1934). Ernst Lubitsch, USA: MGM.
Mignon (1906). Unknown, France: Gaumont.
Mignon (1912). Alice Guy-Blaché, France: Solax.
Le Million [*The Million*] (1931). René Clair, France: Films Sonores Tobis.
Mireille (1953). René Gavault and Ernest Servaës, France: Société Chantereine d'Études Cinématographiques.
Les Misérables (1934). Raymond Bernard, France: Pathé-Natan.
Miss Helyett (1928). Maurice Keroul and Georges Monca, France: Phocea Films, Grandes Productions Cinématographiques.
Modern Love (2008). Stéphane Kazandjian, France: Galatée Films, Delante Films, Cirrus Communications.
La Môme [*La Vie en rose*] (2007). Olivier Dahan, France/UK/Czech Republic: Légende Films, TF1 International, TF1 Films Production, Okko Productions, Songbird Pictures.
Mon amour est près de toi [*My Love Is Near You*] (1943). Richard Pottier, France: Continental Films.
Il Mondo di notte [*World by Night*] (1960). Luigi Vanzi, Italy: Julia Films.
Monsieur Batignole (2002). Gérard Jugnot, France: RF2K Productions, Novo Arturo Films, TF1 Films Production.
Monte Carlo (1930). Ernst Lubitsch, USA: Paramount.
Monte Carlo Baby (1953). Jean Boyer and Lester Fuller, France/UK: Hoche Productions.
Montmartre-sur-Seine (1941). Georges Lacombe, France: Société Universelle de Films.
Morte a Venezia [*Death in Venice*] (1971). Luchino Visconti, Italy/France/USA: Warner Bros, Alfa Cinematografica, PECF.
Moses und Aaron [*Moses and Aaron*] (1975). Danièle Huillet and Jean-Marie Straub, West Germany/Austria/France/Italy: Österreichischer Rundfunk, Straub-Huillet Films, NEF, Taurus Films, Rai, ORTF, Janus Films.
Muriel ou le temps d'un retour [*Muriel, or the Time of Return*] (1963). Dir. Alain Resnais, France/Italy: Argos Films, Films de la Pléiade, Alpha Productions, Éclair, Dear Film Produzione.
Musica de siempre [*Music Forever*] (1958). Tito Davison, Mexico: ANDA, Aliancia Cinematografica Mexicana.
Musique en tête [*Music on Your Mind*] (1951). Georges Combret and Claude Orval, France: Radius Productions.
Naples au baiser de feu [*The Kiss of Fire*] (1937). Augusto Genina, France: Paris Film Productions.
Napoléon vu par Abel Gance [*Napoleon*] (1927). Abel Gance, France: Société Générale de Films.
Nelly et Monsieur Arnaud (1995). Claude Sautet, France/Italy/Germany: Les Films Alain Sarde (FAS) /TF1 Films Production/Canal Plus/Procirep/Cecchi-Gori Group Tiger Cinematografica/Prokino Filmproduktion.

Neuf garçons, un cœur [*Nine Boys, One Heart*] (1948). Georges Friedland, France: Vox Films.

Nous irons à Deauville [*We Will Go to Deauville*] (1962). Francis Rigaud, France/West Germany: Hoche Productions, Films Odéon, UFA, Comacico.

Nous irons à Monte-Carlo [*We Will Go to Monte-Carlo*] (1951). Jean Boyer, France: Hoche Productions.

Nous irons à Paris [*We Will Go to Paris*] (1950). Jean Boyer, France: Hoche Productions.

Nu comme un ver [*Naked as a Worm*] (1933). Léon Mathot, France: Gaumont-Franco Film-Aubert.

Les Nuits de Paris [*Paris Nights*] (1951). Ralph Baum, France: Spéva Films.

Les Nuits fauves [*Savage Nights*] (1992). Cyril Collard, France/Italy: Banfilm Ter, La Sept Cinéma, Société Nouvelle de Cinématographie, Sofinergie 2, Canal+, CNC, Procirep, Erre Produzioni, Orango Films, Fondation Gan pour le Cinéma.

Oh! Qué mambo (1959). John Berry, France/Italy: Boréal Films, D.M. Films, PEG Produzione.

On connaît la chanson [*Same Old Song*] (1997). Alain Resnais, France/Switzerland, UK: Arena Films, Camera One, France 2 Cinéma, Canal+ Cinéma, CNC, Cofimage 9, Sofineurope, Eurimages, Procirep, Vega Films, Alia Films, Télévision Suisse-Romande, Office fédéral de la Culture Suisse, Greenpoint, European Coproduction Fund.

On the Town (1949). Gene Kelly and Stanley Donen, USA: MGM.

On va s'aimer [*Cheating Love*] (2006). Yvan Calbérac, France: Mandarin Films, M6 Films, TF1 International.

L'Opéra de quat'sous [*The Threepenny Opera*] (1931). Georg Wilhelm Pabst and Solange Bussi, Germany/USA: Tobis filmkunst, Nero Films AG, Warner Bros.

Opium (2013). Arielle Dombasle, France: Margo Films.

Orfeo (1985). Claude Goretta, France/Italy/Canada/Switzerland: Gaumont, Erato Films, FR2, Fondation totale pour la musique, Istituto Luce-Italnoleggio Cinematografico, Société Suisse de Radiodiffusion et Télévision, Radio Canada.

Otello (1986). Franco Zeffirelli, Netherlands/Italy/USA: Cannon City Produktie Maatschappij B.V., Cannon Productions, RAI, Italian International Films.

Panique au music-hall [*Panic in the Music Hall*] (1958). Antonio Santillan, France/Spain: Vértice P.C.

Parade d'amour [*Love Parade*] (1930). Ernst Lubitsch, USA: Paramount.

Les Parapluies de Cherbourg [*The Umbrellas of Cherbourg*] (1964). Jacques Demy, France/West Germany: Parc Films/Madeleine Films/Beta Films.

Paris chante toujours [*Paris Still Sings*] (1951). Pierre Montazel, France: Société de Production de Long et Court Métrage.

Parisian Life (1936). Robert Siodmak, France: Nero Films.

Les Parisiennes [*Tales of Paris*] (1962). Marc Allégret, Claude Barma, Michel Boisrond, Jacques Poitrenaud, France/Italy: Francos Films, Incei Films.

Parking (1985). Jacques Demy, France: Garance Productions, FR3 Cinéma.

Paroles et musique [*Love Songs*] (1984). Élie Chouraqui, France/Canada: 7 Films Cinéma, FR3 Cinéma, Ministère français de la Culture français, Canadian International Studios, Téléfilm Canada, Radio Canada.

Parsifal (1982). Hans-Jürgen Syberberg, West Germany/France: TMS Films, Bayerischer Rundfunk, Gaumont.

Pas de week-end pour notre amour [*Not Any Weekend for Our Love*] (1950). Pierre Montazel, France: Les Films Gloria.

Pas sur la bouche [*Not on the Lips*] (1931). Nicolas Rimsky et Nicolas Evreïnoff, France: Comédies Filmées.
Pas sur la bouche [*Not on the Lips*] (2003). Alain Resnais, France/Switzerland: Arena Films, France 2 Cinéma, France 3 Cinéma, Arcade, Canal+, Cinécinéma, Région Île-de-France, Vega Films, TSR, Office Fédéral de la Culture, Sacem.
Passe ton bac d'abord [*Graduate First*] (1978). Maurice Pialat, France/Canada: FR3, INA, Les Films du Livradois.
Pattes blanches [*White Paws*] (1949). Jean Grémillon, France: Majestic Films.
Peau d'âne [*Donkey Skin*] (1970). Jacques Demy, France: Parc Films, Marianne Productions.
Pédale douce [*Soft Pedal*] (1996). Gabriel Aghion, France: MDG Productions, TF1 Films Production, Tentative d'évasion, Sofinergie 3, Sofinergie 4, Canal+.
Pépé le Moko (1937). Julien Duvivier, France: Paris Films, Robert et Raymond Hakim.
Les Perles de la couronne [*The Pearls of the Crown*] (1937). Sacha Guitry, France: Cinéas, Imperial Films Production.
Le Petit Café [*The Little Café*] (1931). Ludwig Berger, USA/France: Paramount.
Phi-Phi (1927). Georges Pallu, France: Natan.
Pigalle-Saint-Germain-des-Prés (1950). André Berthomieu, France: Hoche Productions.
Le Placard [*The Closet*] (2001). Francis Veber, France: Gaumont, EFVE Films, Canal+, TF1 Films Production.
Playboy of Paris (1930). Ludwig Berger, USA: Paramount.
Plume au vent [*Feather in the Wind*] (1953). Louis Cuny, France/Spain: Célia Films, Cocinor, Suevia Films-Cesáreo González.
Podium (2003). Yann Moix, Belgium/France: Fidélité Productions, K2 SA, TF1 Films Production, M6 Films.
Pouic-Pouic [*Squeak-Squeak*] (1963). Jean Girault, France/West Germany: Hoche Productions, Comacico, Films Odéon, UFA.
La Pouponnière [*The Nursery*] (1932). Jean Boyer, France: Les Studios Paramount.
Prends la route [*Take to the Road*] (1937). Jean Boyer and Louis Chavance, France: ACE.
Prénom Carmen [*First Name Carmen*] (1984). Jean-Luc Godard, France: Sara Films, JLG Films, Films A2.
Prince de Minuit [*Midnight Prince*] (1934). René Guissart, France: Lemania Films, Vedettes Françaises Associées.
Princesse Tam-Tam (1935). Edmond T. Gréville, France: Productions Arys.
Printemps à Paris [*Springtime in Paris*] (1956). Jean-Claude Roy, France: Giméno-Philips-Films.
Le Puritain [*The Puritan*] (1938). Jeff Musso, France: Derby Films.
Quai des orfèvres (1947). Henri-Georges Clouzot, France: Majestic Films.
Quand j'étais chanteur [*The Singer*] (2006). Xavier Giannoli, France: Europacorp, Rectangle Productions, France 3 Cinéma.
Quatorze juillet [*The Fourteenth of July*] (1933). René Clair, France: Films Sonores Tobis.
Quatre jours à Paris (1955). André Berthomieu, France: Filmel, Films Mars, Lyrica.
Quitte ou double [*Double or Quits*] (1952). Robert Vernay, France: Olympic Films.
Rebel Without a Cause (1955). Nicholas Ray, USA: Warner Bros.
Rendez-vous à Grenade (1951). Richard Pottier, France: Société Française de Cinématographie, La Société des Films Sirius.
Rendez-vous au tas de sable [*Rendezvous in the Sandpit*] (1990). Didier Grousset, France: Gérard Mital Productions, Films A2.

Repulsion (1965). Roman Polanski, UK: Compton Films, Tekli British Productions.
Rêves d'amour [*Dreams of Love*] (1947). Christian Stengel, France: Pathé.
Rigoletto (1909). André Calmettes, France: Pathé.
Le Roi danse [*The King Is Dancing*] (2000). Gérard Corbiau, France/Germany/Belgium: K-Star, France 2 Cinéma, MMC Independent, K-Dance, K2 SA, RTL-TVi.
Le Roi des galéjeurs [*The King of Tall Stories*] (1940). Fernand Rivers, France: Films Fernand Rivers.
Le Roman d'un tricheur [*The Story of a Cheat*] (1936). Sacha Guitry, France: Cinéas.
Roman Holiday (1953). William Wyler, USA: Paramount.
Romance de Paris [*Paris Romance*] (1941). Jean Boyer, France: Pathé.
La Ronde des heures [*Round of Hours*] (1931). Alexandre Ryder, France: Les Établissements Jacques Haïk.
La Ronde des heures [*Round of Hours*] (1950). Alexandre Ryder, France: Radius Productions.
La Rose Rouge [*The Red Rose*] (1951). Marcello Pagliero, France: Les Films Marceau.
La Roue [*The Wheel*] (1923). Abel Gance, France: Films Abel Gance.
La Route du Bonheur (1953). Maurice Labro and Giorgio Simonelli, France/Italy: Courts et Longs Métrages, Athena Cinematografica.
La Route enchantée [*The Enchanted Road*] (1938). Pierre Caron, France: Films SACA.
La route est belle [*The Road Is Fine*] (1930). Robert Florey, France: Les Établissements Braunberger-Richebé.
La Rue sans joie [*Street Without Joy*] (1938). André Hugon, France: Productions André Hugon.
La Rue sans nom [*Street Without a Name*] (1934). Pierre Chenal, France: Les Productions Pellegrin.
Saint Amour (2016). Benoît Delépine and Gustave Kerven, France: No Money Productions, JPG Films, Nexus Factory.
Sandy (1983). Michel Nerval, France: African Queen Productions, Paris Prociné.
Le Sang d'un poète [*Blood of a Poet*] (1932). Jean Cocteau, France: Vicomte de Noailles.
Scout toujours [*Still a Scout*] (1985). Gérard Jugnot, France: Arturo Productions, Films A7, Films A2.
Sérénade (1940). Jean Boyer, France: Tarcali-Films.
Sérénade au Texas [*Serenade of Texas*] (1958). Richard Pottier, France: Jason Films.
Sérénade aux nuages [*Song of the Clouds*] (1946). André Cayatte, France: Union des Distributeurs indépendants.
Le Sexe faible [*Weaker Sex*] (1933). Robert Siodmak, France: André Haguet, Nero Films.
Show Girl in Hollywood (1930). Mervyn LeRoy, USA: First National Pictures.
Si tu veux [*If You Wish It*] (1932). André Hugon, France: Films André Hugon.
Si Versailles m'était conté [*Royal Affairs in Versailles*] (1954). Sacha Guitry, France: Cocinex.
Die Sinfonie der Grosstadt [*Berlin: Symphony of a Great City*] (1927). Walter Ruttman, Germany: Deutsche Vereins-Film, Les Productions Fox Europa.
Singin' in the Rain (1952). Stanley Donen and Gene Kelly, USA: MGM.
Sins of the Fathers (1928). Ludwig Berger, USA: Paramount.
La Sirène des tropiques [*The Siren of the Tropics*] (1927). Mario Nalpas and Henri Étiévant, France: La Centrale Cinématographique.
La Sirène du Mississippi [*Mississippi Mermaid*] (1969). François Truffaut, France/Italy: Les Films du Carrosse, Productions Artistes Associés, Produzioni Associate Delphos.

The Smiling Lieutenant (1931). Ernst Lubitsch, USA: Paramount.
Snow White and the Seven Dwarfs (1937). David Hand, USA: Walt Disney Productions.
Soirs de Paris [*Paris Nights*] (1954). Jean Laviron, France: Arca Films.
Le soleil a toujours raison [*The Sun Is Always Right*] (1943). Pierre Billon, France: Miramar.
Solomon and Sheba (1959). King Vidor, USA: Edward Small Productions.
Some Like It Hot (1959). Billy Wilder, USA: Ashton Productions, The Mirisch Corporation.
Son dernier Noël [*His Last Christmas*] (1952). Jacques Daniel-Norman, France: Paris-Monde-Productions.
Sous les toits de Paris [*Under the Roofs of Paris*] (1930). René Clair, France: Films Sonores Tobis.
Stars 80 (2012). Frédéric Forestier and Thomas Langmann, France/Belgium: La Petite Reine, TF1 Films Production, Studio 37, Entre Chien et Loup.
Stars 80, la suite (2017). Thomas Langmann, France: Barnstormer Productions, La Petite Reine, Umedia.
Street of Sin (1928). Mauritz Stiller and Ludwig Berger, USA: Paramount.
Sur quel pied danser [*Footnotes*] (2016). Paul Calori and Kostia Testud, France: Loin Derrière L'Oural, France 3 Cinéma, Région Rhône-Alpes.
Swing (2002). Tony Gatlif, France/Japan: Princes Films.
La Symphonie fantastique [*The Fantastic Symphony*] (1942). Christian-Jaque, France: Continental Films.
Tchao Pantin (1983). Claude Berri, France: Renn Productions.
Titin des Martigues (1938). René Pujol, France: Productions Malesherbes/Vondas Films.
Toi, c'est moi [*You Are Me*] (1936). René Guissart, France: Pathé.
Toi, moi, les autres [*Leila*] (2011). Audrey Estrougo, France: Fidélité Films, Wild Bunch, Mars Films, France 2 Cinéma.
Top Hat (1935). Mark Sandrich, USA: RKO.
Tosca (2001). Benoît Jacquot, Italy/France/UK/Germany: Euripide Productions, Integral Films, Veradia Films, France 3 Cinéma, Axiom Films, Seven Stars System, Westdeutscher Rundfunk, Arte France.
Tourbillon de Paris [*Whirlwind of Paris*] (1939). Henri Diamant-Berger, France: Films Albert Lauzin.
Tourments [*Torment*] (1954). Jacques Daniel-Norman, France: Vascos Films.
La Tournée des grands-ducs [*The Tour of the Grand Dukes*] (1953). Norbert Carbonnaux, France: Pécéfilms.
Tous les matins du monde [*All the Mornings of the World*] (1991). Alain Corneau, France: Film Par Film, DD Productions, Divali Films, Société d'Exploitation et de Distribution de Films, FR3 Films Production.
Tous vedettes! [*All Stars*] (1980). Michel Lang, France: Gaumont, Société de Production des Films Marcel Dassault.
Tout le monde il est beau, tout le monde il est gentil [*Everybody He Is Nice, Everybody He Is Beautiful*] (1972). Jean Yanne, France/Italy: Cine Qua Non, Belstar Productions, Idi Cinematografica.
Tout va très bien Madame la Marquise [*Everything Is Fine, Madame la Marquise*] (1936). Henry Wulschleger, France: France Productions.
La Tragédie de Carmen [*The Tragedy of Carmen*] (1983). Peter Brook, France/West Germany/UK/USA: Bentwood Television Productions, Channel Four Television, Bavaria Atelier, France 2, Alby Films.

La Traviata (1982). Franco Zeffirelli, Italy: RAI, Accent Films B.V.
Trente et quarante [*Thirty and Forty*] (1945). Gilles Grangier, France: Gaumont-Alcina, Société Nouvelle des Établissements Gaumont.
Trois de la Canebière [*Three from the Canebière*] (1955). Maurice de Canonge, France: Tellus-Films, Cocinex, Noël Films.
Trois de la marine [*Three from the Navy*] (1934). Charles Barrois, France: Métropa Films.
Trois de la marine [*Three from the Navy*] (1957). Maurice de Canonge, France: Les Productions Cinématographiques, Cocinex, Noël Films.
Les Trois Masques [*The Three Masks*] (1929). André Hugon, France: Pathé-Natan.
Trois places pour le 26 [*Three Seats for the 26th*] (1988). Jacques Demy, France: Renn Productions.
Les Trois Valses [*Three Waltzes*] (1938). Ludwig Berger, France: S.O.F.R.O.R.
Trollflöjten [*The Magic Flute*] (1975). Ingmar Bergman, Sweden: Sveriges Radio.
Le Tzarévitch [*The Little Czar*] (1954). Arthur Maria Rabenalt, West Germany/France: Central Cinema Company Film, Films Roger Richebé.
Un clair de lune à Maubeuge [*Moonlight in Maubeuge*] (1962). Jean Chérasse, France: Edic, Ardennes Films, C.F.C.
Un cœur en hiver (1992). Claude Sautet, France: Film Par Film, Cinéa, Orly Films, Sedif, Paravision, DA Films, FR3 Film Productions, Investimage 3, Sofica Créations, Canal+, CNC, Sofinergie.
Un de la Canebière [*One from the Canebière*] (1938). René Pujol, France: Vondas Films.
Un grand amour de Beethoven [*The Life and Loves of Beethoven*] (1937). Abel Gance, France: Général Productions.
Une balle au cœur [*Devil at My Heels*] (1966). Jean-Daniel Pollet, France/Greece: CMC, Lambessis Films.
Une chambre en ville [*A Room in Town*] (1982). Jacques Demy, France: Progéfi, TF1 Films Production, UGC, Top n°1.
L'une chante, l'autre pas [*One Sings, the Other Doesn't*] (1977). Agnès Varda, France/Belgium/Netherlands: Ciné-Tamaris, Contrechamp, INA, INLC, Société Française de production, Stephan Films, Paradise Films, Population Films.
Une femme est une femme [*A Woman Is a Woman*] (1961). Jean-Luc Godard, France/Italy: Rome-Paris Films, Euro International Films.
Une fille sur la route [*A Girl on the Road*] (1952). Jean Stelli, France : Société Française de Cinématographie, La Société des Films Sirius.
Une histoire simple [*A Simple Story*] (1978). Claude Sautet, France/West Germany: Renn Productions, Sara Films, Société Française de Production et de Création Audiovisuelles, FR3, Rialto Films, Zweites Deutsches Fernsehen.
Une java (1939). Claude Orval, France: Société de Production du Film Une java.
Une nuit aux Baléares [*A Night in the Balearic Islands*] (1957). Paul Mesnier, France: Taurus Films.
L'Univers de Jacques Demy [*The World of Jacques Demy*] (1995). Agnès Varda, France: Ciné-Tamaris, Canal+, Centre National de la Cinématographie, Docstar, Valor 2, INA, Ministère français des Affaires étrangères.
The Vagabond King (1930). Ludwig Berger and Ernst Lubitsch, USA: Paramount.
La Valse de Paris [*Paris Waltz*] (1950). Marcel Achard, France/Italy: Lux Films France, Lux Films Rome.
Valse royale [*Royal Waltz*] (1936). Jean Grémillon, France/Germany: UFA/ACE.

Van Gogh (1991). Maurice Pialat, France : Erato Films, StudioCanal, Films A2, Les Films du Livradois.
Les Vétos (2020). Julie Manoukian, France: Les Films du 24, France 3 Cinéma.
La Veuve joyeuse [*The Merry Widow*] (1935). Ernst Lubitsch, USA: MGM.
La Vie de bohème [*Bohemian Life*] (1945). Marcel L'Herbier, France/Italy: Invicta, Scalera.
La Vie en rose (1954). Billy Wilder, USA: Paramount.
La vie est un roman [*Life Is a Bed of Roses*] (1983). Alain Resnais, France: Soprofilms, Films Ariane, Films A2, Fideline Films, Filmédis.
La Vie parisienne [*Parisian Life*] (1936). Robert Siodmak, France: Nero Films.
Violettes impériales [*Imperial Violets*] (1952). Richard Pottier, France/Spain: Les Films Modernes, Producciones Benito Perojo, Productions Émile Natan, Suevia Films-Cesáreo González.
La Voie lactée [*The Milky Way*] (1969). Luis Buñuel, France/Italy: Greenwich Film Productions, Fraia Films.
Volpone (1941). Maurice Tourneur, France: Île-de-France Films.
Von heute auf morgen [*From Today Until Tomorrow*] (1997). Jean-Marie Straub, Danièle Huillet, France/Germany: Produktion Straub-Huillet, Pierre Grise Productions, Hessischer Rundfunk.
Waltzerkrieg [*Waltz War*] (1933). Ludwig Berger, Germany: UFA.
Ein Walzertraum [*The Waltzdream*] (1925). Ludwig Berger, Germany: UFA.
West Side Story (1961). Jerome Robbins and Robert Wise, USA: The Mirisch Corporation, Seven Arts Productions.
White Christmas (1954). Michael Curtiz, USA: Paramount.
Wild in the Country (1961). Philip Dunne, USA: Jerry Wald Productions.
The Wild Ones (1953). Laslo Benedek, USA: Stanley Kramer Productions.
The Woman from Moscow (1928). Ludwig Berger, USA: Paramount.
Wonder Bar (1934). Lloyd Bacon, USA: First National Pictures.
Zéro de conduite [*Zero for Conduct*] (1930). Jean Vigo, France: Franfilmdis, Argui-Film.
Zouzou (1934). Marc Allégret, France: Les Films H. Roussillon, Productions Arys.

References

Where pagination is missing from printed texts this is because the material has been sourced from the newspaper clipping archive of the Cinémathèque.

A.B.C.D. (1937), 'La Parole est aux spectateurs', *Pour Vous*, 434: 10–11.
A.F. (2006), 'On va s'aimer', *Télérama*, 14 June.
Agel, H. (1984), *Jean Grémillon*, Paris: Lherminier.
Alion, Y. (1978), 'De la réalité à la fiction: deux Juliette en une', *L'Avant-Scène Cinéma*, 213: 6.1943
Alion, Y. (2000), '*Le Roi danse*: entretien avec Gérard Corbiau', *Avant-Scène Cinéma*, 497: 121–5.
Allard, A. (2016), 'Sur quel pied danser', *Positif*, 667: 51–2.
Altman, R. (1984), 'A Semantic/Syntactic Approach to Film Genre', *Cinema Journal*, 23 (3): 6–18.
Altman, R. (1987), *The American Film Musical*, Bloomington: Indiana University Press.
Altman, R. (1999), *Film/Genre*, London: British Film Institute/Bloomsbury.
Altman, R. (2013), 'Coda: The Musical as International Genre: Reading Notes', in C. K Creekmur and L. Y. Mokdad (eds), *The International Film Musical*, 257–4, Edinburgh: Edinburgh University Press.
Amengual, B. (1951), *L'Homme, le sentiment et les choses dans le monde de René Clair*, Alger: Travail et Culture.
Amengual, B. (1963), *René Clair*, Paris: Seghers.
Anderson, B. (1991), *Imagined Communities: Reflections on the Origin and Spread of Nationalism*, London: Verso.
Anderson, M. (2013), 'Divine Comedies', *Artforum International*, 51 (8): 99–100.
André, N. (2006), *Voicing Gender: Castrati, Travesti, and the Second Woman in Early-Nineteenth-Century Italian Opera*, Bloomington: Indiana University Press.
Andreescu, F. C. and S. P. Quinn (2014), 'Gypsy Fetish: Music, Dirt, Magic, and Freedom', *Journal for Cultural Research*, 18 (4): 1–16.
Andrew, D. (1979), 'The Postwar Struggle for Color', *Cinema Journal*, 18 (2): 41–52.
Andrew, D. (1995), *Mists of Regret: Culture and Sensibility in Classic French Film*, Princeton: Princeton University Press.
Andrew, G. (2011), 'Une chambre en ville', *Sight and Sound*, 21 (6): 19.
Anon. (2013), 'Sans fausse note', *Le Parisien*, 1 September. http://www.leparisien.fr/espace-premium/culture-loisirs/sans-fausse-note-01-09-2013-3097039.php. Accessed 5 June 2019.
Archer-Straw, P. (2000), *Negrophilia: Avant-Garde Paris and Black Culture in the 1920s*, London: Thames & Hudson.
Archer, N. (2013), 'No Place Like Home: Camping It Up in *Drôle de Félix*', in N. Archer (ed.), *The French Road Movie: Space, Mobility, Identity*, 75–88. Oxford: Berghahn.
Arnoux (1931), 'L'Opéra de quat'sous de G.W. Pabst', *Pour Vous*, 156: 9.
Aschied, A. (2012), 'Germany', in C. K. Creekmur and L. Y. Mokdad (eds), *The International Film Musical*, 45–58, Edinburgh: Edinburgh University Press.

Attali, D. (2003), 'Alain Resnais: "je revendique la frivolité"', *Le Journal du Dimanche*, 30 November.
Audé, F. (1981), *Ciné-modèles, cinémas d'elles*, Lausanne: L'Âge d'Homme.
Auriol, J.-G. (1931), 'Revue des programmes', *Revue du cinéma*, 29: 50.
Aurore (1963), 'Premier film de Sylvie Vartan: *D'où viens-tu, Johnny?*', *L'Aurore*, 20 April.
B-Mol Productions (2017), *Laurent et Safi*, press kit. http://www.hevadis.com/assets/dp-la urent-et-safi.pdf. Accessed 27 June 2019.
Badache, R. (2006), '*Quand j'étais chanteur*', *Les Inrockuptibles*, 1 January.
Balcerzak, S. (2006), 'Nationalizing and Segregating Performance: Josephine Baker and Stardom in *Zouzou* (1934)', *Post Script*, 26 (1): 13–31.
Barnier, M. (2002), *En route vers le parlant: histoire d'une évolution technologique, économique et esthétique du cinéma, 1926–1934*, Liège: Éditions du Céfal.
Barnier, M. (2004), *Des films français made in Hollywood: les versions multiples 1929–1935*, Paris: L'Harmattan.
Barnier, M. (2007), 'Versions Multiples franco-américaines à Hollywood et à Joinville', in C. Viviani (ed.), *Hollywood: les connexions françaises*, 35–51, Paris: Nouveau Monde.
Baroncelli, J. de (1957), '*Casino de Paris*', *Le Monde*, 7 November.
Baroncelli, J. de (1963), '*D'où viens-tu, Johnny?*', *Le Monde*, 4 November.
Barratier, C. (2008), 'Le Faubourg 36 de Christophe Barratier', *L'Express*, 18 September. https://www.lexpress.fr/culture/cinema/le-faubourg-36-de-christophe-barratier_83 2659.html. Accessed 5 June 2019.
Barratier, C. (2017), '*Les Choristes, le spectacle musical*: "L'histoire reste d'actualité treize ans après le film", estime Christophe Barratier' (interview with F. Randanne), *20 minutes*, 3 March. https://www.20minutes.fr/culture/musique/2024463-20170303-ch oristes-spectacle-musical-histoire-reste-actualite-treize-ans-apres-film-estime-chris tophe-barratier. Accessed 4 June 2019.
Barreyre, J. (1933), 'La Pouponnière', *Pour Vous*, 221: 4.
Barrios, R. (1995), *A Song in the Dark: The Birth of the Musical Film*, Oxford: Oxford University Press.
Barrot, O. (1985), *René Clair ou le temps mesuré*, Renens: Foma.
Barsamian, J. and F. Jouffa (1983), *L'Âge d'or du yéyé: le rock, le twist et la variété française des années 60*, Paris: Ramsay.
Barthes, R. (1982), 'Le Grain de la voix', in *L'Obvie et l'obtus*, 236–45, Paris: Seuil.
Basile, G. (2000), 'Une esthétique neuve de la chanson à l'écran', in Noël Herpe and Emmanuelle Toulet (eds), *René Clair ou le cinéma avant la lettre*, 139–52, Paris: Association Française de Recherche sur l'Histoire du Cinéma.
Bauche, N. (2009), 'Note sur les films de A à Z', *Positif*, 576: 52–3.
Becker, S. and B. Williams (2008), 'What Ever Happened to *West Side Story*? Gene Kelly, Jazz Dance, and Not So Real Men in Jacques Demy's *The Young Girls of Rochefort*', *New Review of Film and Television Studies*, 6 (3): 303–21.
Bellemare, P. (2018), 'La Symphonie fantastique', in P. Fryer (ed.), *The Composer on Screen: Essays on Classical Music Biopics*, 140–50, Jefferson: McFarland.
Belleret, R. (2013), *Piaf: un mythe français*, Paris: Fayard.
Bergala, A. ed. (1998), *Jean-Luc Godard par Jean-Luc Godard: tome 1 1950–1984*, Paris: Cahiers du cinéma.
Berger, V. (2016), '"Going Home": Mobility and Return Journeys in French and Spanish Road Movies', *Transnational Cinemas*, 7 (2): 168–82.
Bergeron, K. (1996), 'The Castrato as History', *Cambridge Opera Journal*, 8 (2): 167–84.

Berliner, Brett A. (2002), *Ambivalent Desire: The Exotic Black Other in Jazz-Age*, France, Amherst, MA: University of Massachusetts Press.
Berlioz, P. (1942), 'Toi c'est moi', *Paris Soir*, 2 January.
Berner, R. (1934), 'Chansons de films', *Cinémonde*, 314: 868.
Berner, R. (1936), 'Pills et Tabet: l'accord parfait', *Cinématographe*, 424: 904–5.
Bernier, C. (1939), 'Films musicaux', *Ciné-Miroir*, 759: 675.
Berthomé, J.-P. (1995), *Les Parapluies de Cherbourg: Jacques Demy, étude critique*, Paris: Nathan.
Berthomé, J.-P. (2014a), *Jacques Demy et les racines du rêve*, 3rd edn, Nantes: L'Atalante.
Berthomé, J.-P. (2014b), 'Un héritage confisqué? Jacques Demy et Ciné-Tamaris', *1895*, 72: 147–57.
Beylie, C. (1976), 'La Fête noire', *L'Avant-scène cinéma*, 177: 5–6.
Beylie, C. (1987), 'Louise', *Avant-Scène Cinéma*, 360: 64–5.
Billard, P. (1998), *Le Mystère René Clair*, Paris: Plon.
Bingham, D. (2010), *Whose Lives Are They Anyway?: The Biopic as Contemporary Film Genre*, New Brunswick: Rutgers University Press.
Bingham, D. (2011), 'Woody Guthrie, Warts-and-All: The Biopic in the New American Cinema of the 1970s', *Auto/Biography Studies*, 26 (1): 68–90.
Blum-Reid, S. (2008), 'Away from Home? Two French Directors in Search of Their Identity', *Quarterly Review of Film and Video*, 26 (1): 1–9.
Bock, H.-M. and M. Töteberg (2002), 'A History of Ufa', in T. Bergfelder, E. Carter and D. Göktürk (eds), *The German Cinema Book*, 129–38, London: BFI.
Bogart, B. A. (2001), 'Music and Narrative in the French New Wave: The Films of Agnès Varda and Jacques Demy', PhD diss., University of California, Los Angeles.
Boillat, A. (2014), 'René Clair et la résistance à la voix synchrone parlée: ce que nous disent les "machines parlantes" d'*À nous la liberté*!, *1895*, 72: 85–107.
Bonini, E. (2003), *Tino Rossi*, Monaco: Éditions du Rocher.
Bordat, F. (2010), 'Lubitsch et le Code', *Positif*, 595: 98–102.
Boris, G. (1937), 'La parole est aux spectateurs', *Pour Vous*, 429: 12.
Bory, J.-L. (1963), 'D'où viens-tu, Johnny?', *Arts*, 8 November.
Bouarour, S. (2018), 'Les Masculinités dans les films musicaux et les mélodrames de Jacques Demy et Vincente Minnelli', PhD diss., University of Sorbonne Paris Cité, Paris.
Boulangé, G. (2007), 'Jacques Demy dispersé: Essai de généalogie artistique raisonnée', PhD diss., University of Montpellier 3, France.
Bouquet, S. (1997), 'La vie n'est pas un roman: *On connaît la chanson* d'Alain Resnais', *Cahiers du cinema*, 518: 47–49.
Bourgeois, J. (1949), *René Clair*, Genève: Roulet.
Boym, S. (2001), *The Future of Nostalgia*, New York: Basic Books.
Brèque, J.-M. (1987), 'Le Film-opéra: vers une forme cinématographique autonome', *L'Avant-scène opéra/cinéma*, 98/360: 27–34.
Breton, E. (1986), 'Un film acidulé', *Révolution*, 331 (4 July).
Brigaudeau, A. (undated), '22 juin 1963: reconnaissance de la nation', *Franceinfo*. https://www.francetvinfo.fr/culture/johnny-hallyday/recit-22-juin-1963-johnny-enflamme-la-place-de-la-nation-c-a-ete-notre-woodstock-a-nous_2501721.html. Accessed 5 January 2019.
Briggs, J. (2006), 'Anarchie en France: Hypermodemity and French Popular Music, 1958–1981', PhD diss., Emory University, Atlanta.
Briggs, J. (2012), 'Sex and the Girl's Single: French Popular Music and the Long Sexual Revolution of the 1960s', *Journal of the History of Sexuality*, 21 (3): 523–47.

Brillant, M. (1947), '*Andalousie*', *L'Aube*, 13 November.
Brown, T. (2015), *Spectacle in Classical Cinemas: Musicality and Historicity in the 1930s*, London: Routledge.
Brown, T. and B. Vidal (eds) (2014), *The Biopic in Contemporary Film Culture*, London: Routledge.
Brulé, C. (1957), '*Folies-Bergère*', *Paris-Presse*, 16 January.
Bruzzi, S. (2000), *New Documentary: A Critical Introduction*, London: Routledge.
Buache, F. (1982), *Claude Autant-Lara*, Lausanne: L'Âge d'Homme.
Burch, N. and G. Sellier (1996), *La Drôle de guerre des sexes du cinéma français: 1930–1956*, Paris: Nathan.
Burgoyne, R. (2014), 'Gainsbourg: Puppetry in the Musical Biopic', in T. Brown and B. Vidal (eds), *The Biopic in Contemporary Film Culture*, 259–73, London: Routledge.
Cadalanu, M. (2016), 'Le Film musical français dans les années trente: constitution d'un genre?', PhD diss., Université de Caen-Normandie.
Cadalanu, M. (2018), 'Que reste-t-il de Jacques Demy?', *Positif*, 692: 142–4.
Cadalanu, M. (2019), 'Jean Grémillon à l'épreuve de l'opérette: *Valse royale*', in Y. Calvet and P. Roger (eds), *Jean Grémillon et les quatre éléments*, 133–46, Villeneuve d'Ascq: Presses universitaires du Septentrion.
Cadars, P. (1987), 'Confession partielle d'un amoureux ambivalent', *L'Avant-scène opéra/cinéma*, 98/360: 36–41.
Cairns, D. (2016), 'The Forgotten: Andrzej Żuławski's *Boris Godunov* (1989)', mubi.com. https://mubi.com/notebook/posts/the-forgotten-andrzej-zulawski-s-boris-godunov-1989. Accessed 4 September 2017.
Calvet, L. J. (1981), *Chanson et société*, Paris: Payot.
Calvet, L. J. (2013), *La Bande-son de notre histoire*, Paris: L'Archipel.
Cambier, O. (1936), 'Tino Rossi', *Cinémonde*, 390: 248.
Cambier, O. (1937), '*Prends la route*', *Cinématographe*, 434: 119.
Canard enchaîné (1947), '*Le Chanteur inconnu*', *Le Canard enchaîné*, 21 July.
Carrière, C. (2012), 'La Vie, l'œuvre et la face cachée de Claude François', *L'Express*, 13 March. https://www.lexpress.fr/culture/cinema/cloclo_1092929.html. Accessed 27 May 2019.
Caumartin, J. (1938), 'Configuration bénéfique dans la constellations de la lyre: Grace Moore, Georges Thill, André Pernet dans *Louise*', *Cinémonde*, 529: 1068–9.
Chapier, H. (1963), '*D'où viens-tu, Johnny?*', *Combat*, 31 October.
Chaplin, F. (2013), 'A Musical Neorealism: Jean-Luc Godard's *Une femme est une femme*', *Screening the Past*, 36. http://www.screeningthepast.com/2013/06/a-musical-neorealism-jean-luc-godard%E2%80%99s-une-femme-est-une-femme/. Accessed 10 April 2019.
Charensol, G. and R. Régent (1952), *René Clair, un maître du cinéma*, Paris: La Table ronde.
Chazal, R. (1963), '*D'où viens-tu, Johnny?*', *France-Soir*, 31 October.
Chevassu, F. (1988), '*Le Maître de musique*', *La Revue du cinéma*, 446: 28.
Chion, M. (2002), *La Comédie musicale*, Paris: Cahiers du cinéma.
Chou, D. (2002), '*Filles perdues, cheveux gras*', *Film de culte* [no date]. http://www.filmdeculte.com/cinema/film/Filles-perdues-cheveux-gras-324.html. Accessed 24 June 2019.
Cinémagazine (1931), '*Le congrès s'amuse*', *Cinémagazine*, 12: 78.
Cinémagazine (1932), '*Il est charmant*', *Cinémagazine*, 3: 73.
Cinémonde (1932), '*Il est charmant*', *Cinémonde*, 176: 146.

Cinémonde (1934a), 'Le congrès s'amuse (reprise)', Cinémonde, 300: 589.
Cinémonde (1934b), 'Dédé', Cinémonde, 323: 1067.
Citron, M. J. (2000), *Opera on Screen*, New Haven: Yale University Press.
Clair, R. (1928), 'Ne dites plus "metteur en scène", dites "auteur"', *Pour Vous*, 3: 3.
Claus, H. and A. Jäckel (2000), '*Der Kongress tanzt*: Ufa's Blockbuster *Filmoperette* for the World Market', in B. Marshall and R. Stilwell (eds), *Musicals: Hollywood and Beyond*, 80–97, Exeter: Intellect.
Cocteau, J. (1930), *Opium, journal d'une désintoxication*, Paris: Stock, Delamain et Boutelleau.
Coffman, E. (1995), 'Women in Motion: Dance, Gesture, and Spectacle in Film, 1900–1935', PhD diss., University of Florida.
Cohen, A.-Ch. (1986), *Martine chérie*, Paris: Ramsay.
Collet, J. (1963), 'Les Idoles du yé-yé au cinéma de papa', *Télérama*, 725, 8 December.
Combat (1947), 'Le Chanteur inconnu', *Combat*, 10 May.
Comœdia (1954), 'La Belle de Cadix', *Comœdia*, 6 January.
Comte, J.-M. (2017), '*Barbara* de Mathieu Amalric: faux biopic, vraie déception', *France-Soir*, 28 August. http://www.francesoir.fr/culture-cinema/le-barbara-de-mathieu-ama lric-faux-biopic-vraie-deception-video-critique-bande-annonce-jeanne-balibar-fil m-casting-realisateur. Accessed 27 May 2019.
Conway, K. (2004), *Chanteuse in the City: The Realist Singer in French Film*, Berkeley, Los Angeles, London: University of California Press.
Conway, K. (2013), 'France', in C. K Creekmur and L. Y. Mokdad (eds), *The International Film Musical*, 29–44, Edinburgh: Edinburgh University Press.
Copfermann, É. (1962), *La Génération des blousons noirs: problèmes de la jeunesse française*, Paris: Maspero.
Corday-Marguy, P. (1946), 'Georges Guétary rayonne: …Casanova est de retour', *Mon Film*, 107: 8–9.
Corday-Marguy, P. (1949), 'Georges Guétary veut être aimé incognito', *Mon Film*, 168: 8–9.
Corday-Marguy, P. (1951), 'Georges Guétary a immolé son bonheur à sa carrière', *Mon Film*, 248: 8–9.
Corday-Marguy, P. (1953), 'Georges Guétary oublie les femmes pour Carlos', *Mon Film*, 339: 8–9.
Corday-Marguy, P. (1954), 'Georges Guétary dissipe un malentendu', *Mon Film*, 407: 14.
Corday-Marguy, P. (1956), 'Georges Guétary, de l'opérette au tour de chant', *Mon Film*, 500: 14.
Cornu, J.-F. (2014), *Le Doublage et le sous-titrage: histoire et esthétique*, Rennes: Presses Universitaires de Rennes.
Creed, B. (2009), *Darwin's Screens: Evolutionary Aesthetics, Time and Sexual Display in the Cinema*, Melbourne: Melbourne University Press.
Creekmur, C. K. and L. Y. Mokdad (eds) (2013), *The International Film Musical*, Edinburgh: Edinburgh University Press.
Creton, L. and K. Kitsopanidou (2014), 'Le Genre "opérette" et la production française en Cinémascope des années 1950: le cas du film *Le Chanteur de Mexico* (Richard Pottier, 1956)', in S. Layerle and R. Moine (eds), *Voyez comment on chante!: films musicaux et cinéphilies populaires en France (1945–1958)*, 43–56, Paris: Presses Sorbonne Nouvelle.
Crisp, C. (2002), *Genre, Myth, and Convention in the French Cinema, 1929–1939*, Bloomington: Indiana University Press.

Curtiss, T. Q. (1984), 'Francesco Rosi's Film of *Carmen* Is Far More Colorful Than Dramatic', *International Herald Tribune*, 31 March.
D'Yvoire, J. (1955), '*Le Baron Tzigane*', *Radio Cinéma Télévision*, 3 June.
Daix, D. (1942), '*Toi c'est moi*', *Paris-Midi*, 9 January.
Dale, R. C. (1986), *The Films of René Clair*, Metuchen: Scarecrow Press.
Darrigrand, M. (2004), '*Les Choristes*, film d'avenir', *Libération*, 25 November. https://www.liberation.fr/tribune/2004/11/25/les-choristes-film-d-avenir_500654. Accessed 4 June 2019.
Davies Hayon, K. (2017), '"Je suis une étrangère de partout": The Material Realities of Exile in Tony Gatlif's *Exils* (2004)', *Studies in French Cinema*, 17 (1): 75–90.
Davillier, C. (1874), *L'Espagne*, Paris: Hachette.
De Bello Gallico, C. (1936), 'La parole est aux spectateurs', *Pour Vous*, 376: 10.
Debruge, P. (2017), 'Film Review: *Jeannette, the Childhood of Joan of Arc*', *Variety*, 21 May. https://variety.com/2017/film/reviews/jeannette-the-childhood-of-joan-of-arc-review-1202438764/. Accessed 27 May 2019.
Delange, C. (1985), *Tino Rossi*, Paris: PAC.
Delaprée, L. (1930), 'Deux films musicaux: *Le Chemin du Paradis* et *La Féerie du Jazz*', *Pour Vous*, 99: 8–9.
Delpeuch, C. (1941), 'Un mâle qui répand la terreur: le tinorossisme', *Ciné-Mondial*, 11: 5.
De La Roche, C. (1958), *René Clair: An Index*. London: British Film Institute.
Delville, O. (1949), '*La Belle Meunière*', *Le Soir*, 17 September.
Denain, O. (1937), 'Avis aux spectateurs', *Pour Vous*, 444: 10.
Deneuve, C. (1986), 'Deneuve sur Deneuve: la star intégrale', *Première*. http://toutsurdeneuve.free.fr/Francais/Pages/Interviews_Presse8089/Premiere86.htm. Accessed 15 April 2019.
Denis, S. (2010), *Analyse d'une œuvre*: Tous le matins du monde, *Alain Corneau 1991*, Paris: Vrin.
Derain, L. (1934a), '*Prince de Minuit*', *Cinémonde*, 316: 915.
Derain, L. (1934b), 'La Capricante Zouzou Josephine Baker bondit à l'horizon', *Cinémonde*, 322: 1038.
Derain, L. (1935), 'L'Âge des dentelles ou les deux *Veuve joyeuse*', *Cinémonde*, 329: 105.
DeRoo, R. (2009), 'Confronting Contradictions: Genre, Subversion and Feminist Politics in Agnès Varda's *L'une chantre, l'autre pas*', *Modern & Contemporary France*, 17 (3): 249–65.
Dicale, B. (2004), 'Bruno Coulais, no. 1 avec *Les Choristes*', *Radio France Internationale*, 14 May. https://musique.rfi.fr/musique-film/20040514-bruno-coulais-ndeg1-choristes. Accessed 5 June 2019.
Dixon, W. W. (1993), *The Early Film Criticism of François Truffaut*, Bloomington: Indiana University Press.
Dobreva, N. (2007), 'Constructing the "Celluloid Gypsy": Tony Gatlif and Emir Kusturica's "Gypsy Films" in the Context of New Europe', *Romani Studies*, 17 (2): 141–53.
Doniol-Valcroze, J. (1955), 'Le Baron Tzigane était-il bourguignon?', *France Observateur*, 4 March.
Doringe (1939), 'Grace Moore chantera dans *Louise*', *Pour Vous*, 531: 8–9.
Douhaire, S. (2005), '*La Cage aux rossignols*', *Libération*, 14 January. https://next.liberation.fr/culture/2005/01/14/la-cage-aux-rossignols_506165. Accessed 4 June 2019.

Douhaire, S. (2016), 'Sur quel pied danser', *Télérama*, 9 July. https://www.telerama.fr/cinema/films/sur-quel-pied-danser,510598.php?ccr=oui. Accessed 27 June 2019.

Douin, J.-L. (2008), '*Faubourg 36*: un éloge de la solidarité en chantant et en dansant', Le Monde, 23 September. https://www.lemonde.fr/cinema/article/2008/09/23/faubourg-36-un-eloge-de-la-solidarite-en-chantant-et-en-dansant_1098576_3476.html. Accessed 5 June 2019.

Downing, L. (2007), 'Polanski's Deneuve: "Frigidity" and Feminism', in L. Downing and S. Harris (eds), *From Perversion to Purity: The Stardom of Catherine Deneuve*, 14–28. Manchester: Manchester University Press.

Duault, A. (1987), 'Le Film d'opéra: une histoire, des questions', *L'Avant-scène opéra/cinéma*, 98/360: 3–5.

Duggan, A. E. (2013), *Queer Enchantments: Gender, Sexuality, and Class in the Fairy-Tale Cinema of Jacques Demy*, Detroit: Wayne State University Press.

Dumais, M. (2004), '*Les Choristes*: un air d'autrefois', *Voir*, 13 October. https://voir.ca/cinema/2004/10/13/les-choristes-un-air-dautrefois/. Accessed 4 June 2019.

Dumas, J. (1930), 'Le Chemin du paradis', *Cinémonde*, 109: 748.

Durand, J.-M. (2014), '*Chante ton bac d'abord*, un ovni télévisé poétique et étonnant', *Les Inrockuptibles*, 19 October. https://www.lesinrocks.com/2014/10/19/medias/medias/releve-notes/. Accessed 28 June 2019.

Dyer, R. (1977), 'Entertainment and Utopia', *Movie*, 24: 2–13.

Dyer, R. (2007), *Pastiche*, New York: Routledge.

E. L. (1957), 'Folies-Bergère', *Cahiers du cinéma*, 68: 52.

Ebert, R. (2009), '*Paris 36*', *Rogerebert.com*, 9 April. https://www.rogerebert.com/reviews/paris-36-2009. Accessed 5 June 2019.

Eisner, L. (1973), *The Haunted Screen: Expressionism in the German Cinema and the Influence of Max Reinhardt*, London: Secker & Warburg. Originally published in French in 1952.

Ekchajzer, F. (2014), '*Chante ton bac d'abord*', *Télérama*, 15 October. https://www.telerama.fr/cinema/films/chante-ton-bac-d-abord493320.php. Accessed 27 June 2019.

Elsaesser, T. (2000), 'Transparent Duplicities: Pabst's *The Threepenny Opera*', in T. Elsaesser (ed.), *Weimar Cinema and After: Germany's Historical Imaginary*, 311–29. London: Routledge.

Epstein, W. E. and R. B. Palmer (eds) (2016), *Invented Lives, Imagined Communities: The Biopic and American National Identity*, Albany: State University of New York Press.

Escoube, L. (1934), 'Zouzou', *Pour Vous*, 319: 7.

Evans, P. W. (2007), 'Buñuel Blonde', in L. Downing and S. Harris (eds), *From Perversion to Purity: The Stardom of Catherine Deneuve*, 29–44. Manchester: Manchester University Press.

Ezra, E. (2000), *The Colonial Unconscious: Race and Culture in Interwar France*, Ithaca: Cornell University Press.

Farnèse, M. (1934), 'La crise est finie, un *42nd Street* français?' *Cinémonde*, 309: 766.

Faucon, F. (2015), 'Le Cinéma et la musique yéyé, un rendez-vous manqué?', *Cinézik*, 13 July. https://www.cinezik.org/infos/affinfo.php?titre0=20150713015958. Accessed 30 March 2019.

Feldman, M. (2014), 'Castrato Acts', in H. Greenwald (ed.), *The Oxford Handbook of Opera*, 395–418, Oxford: Oxford University Press.

Ferenczi, A. (1986), '*Golden eighties*: indéfrisable sur fond de soap-opéra', *Le Quotidien de Paris*, 3 July.
Feron, B. (1947), 'Le Meunier, sa fille et l'âne', *Témoignage chrétien*, 15 October.
Feuer, J. (1982), *The Hollywood Musical*, Bloomington: Indiana University Press.
Feuer, J. (1995), 'The Self-Reflexive Musical and the Myth of Entertainment', in B. K. Grant (ed.), *Film Genre Reader II*, 441–55, Austin: University of Texas Press.
Feuer, J. (2010), 'The International Art Musical: Defining and Periodising Post-1980s Musicals', in S. Cohan (ed.), *The Sound of Musicals*, 54–63, London: British Film Institute/Palgrave Macmillan.
Fischer, L. (1977), 'René Clair, *Le Million*, and the Coming of Sound', *Cinema Journal*, 16 (2): 34–50.
Flinn, M. C. (2017), 'René Clair's City Views: Realism and Studio Paris', in *The Social Architecture of French Cinema 1929–1939*, 39–57, Liverpool: Liverpool University Press.
Fowler, C. (2000), 'Harnessing Visibility: The Attractions of Chantal Akerman's *Golden Eighties*', in B. Marshall and R. J. Stilwell (eds), *Musicals: Hollywood & Beyond*, 107–16, Exeter: Intellect.
Franc-Tireur (1947), 'Le Chanteur inconnu', *Le Franc-Tireur*, 6 May.
Francis, T. (2005), 'Embodied Fictions, Melancholy Migrations: Josephine Baker's Cinematic Celebrity', *Modern Fiction Studies*, 51 (4): 824–47.
Frank, N. (1935), '*Princesse Tam-Tam*', *Pour Vous*, 362: 10.
Frank, N. (1936), '*Le Grand Refrain*', *Pour Vous*, 410: 6.
Frémeaux, P. (1996), 'Le Front Populaire: Paris 1934–1939'. http://www.fremeaux.com/index.php?option=com_virtuemart&page=shop.livrets&content_id=6264&product_id=120&category_id=74. Accessed 15 October 2014.
Friche, M. (1987), '*Orfeo*', *L'Avant-scène opéra/cinéma*, 98/360: 85–86.
Frodon, J.-M. (1997), 'La Question de vérité, en chantant de bon cœur', *Le Monde*, 13 November.
Frois, E. (2007), 'Christophe Honoré dans le tourbillon de la vie', *Le Figaro*, 18 May.
Frouart, J.-P. (1987), '*La Belle Meunière* reprend des couleurs', *Libération*, 3 January.
G. S. (1945), '*Le Cavalier noir*', *Lettres françaises*, 14 April.
Gana, J. (2000), '*Pas sur la bouche*', *Encyclopédie multimedia de la comédie musicale théâtrale en France*. http://194.254.96.55/cm/?for=fic&cleoeuvre=237. Accessed 2 May 2019.
Garrigues, R. (1939), 'Charles Trenet, chanteur, acteur, compositeur', *Ciné-Miroir*, 719: 19.
Garson, C. (1955), '*Baron Tzigane*', *L'Aurore*, 21 February.
Gendrault, C. (2014), 'Un vent de mambo sur les écrans français: usages et reception d'un rythme venu d'ailleurs', in S. Layerle and R. Moine (eds), *Voyez comment on chante!: films musicaux et cinéphilies populaires en France (1945–1958)*, 105–12, Paris: Presses Sorbonne Nouvelle.
Godefroy, J. (1935), 'La parole est aux spectateurs', *Pour Vous*, 328: 12.
Gomez, C. (2003), '*Pas sur la bouche*', *Le Journal du Dimanche*, 7 December.
Gorbman, C. (1987), 'Music and Sound Space in *Sous les toits de Paris*', in *Unheard Melodies: Narrative Film Music*, 140–50, Bloomington: Indiana University Press.
Gorin, F. (1997), 'Le Cinglé du "musical"', *Télérama*, 12 November.
Gral Dalby, M. (2011), 'Les Mutations de la comédie musicale: à la croisée des genres', Master's thesis, Université Stendhal Grenoble 3. https://dumas.ccsd.cnrs.fr/dumas-00608043/document. Accessed 2 May 2019.

Grandena, F. (2006), 'L'Homosexuel en dehors de l'homosexualité: expressions de l'identité gay dans les films d'Olivier Ducastel et Jacques Martineau', *Contemporary French Civilization*, 30 (2): 63–86.

Grandena, F. (2013), 'The Constant Tourist: Passing Intimacy and Touristic Nomadism in *Drôle de Félix*', in M. Gott and T. Schilt (eds), *Open Roads, Closed Borders: The Contemporary French-Language Road Movie*, 39–54, Bristol: Intellect.

Green, N. (1985), *René Clair: A Guide to References and Resources*, Boston: G.K.Hall.

Groo, K. (2013), 'Shadow Lives: Josephine Baker and the Body of Cinema', *Framework: The Journal of Cinema and Media*, 54 (1): 7–39.

Guénée, P. (1995), 'Notre sélection de la quinzaine', *Cinéma* 545: 10.

Guétary, G. (1981), *Les Hasards du fabuleux*, Paris: La Table ronde.

Guichard, L. (2017), 'Mathieu Amalric parle de *Barbara*: "Ce n'est pas un anti-biopic mais un 'bio-utopique'"', *Télérama*, 5 September. https://www.telerama.fr/cinema/mathieu-amalric-parle-de-barbara-ce-nest-pas-un-anti-biopic-mais-un-bio-cutopique,n5185966.php. Accessed 27 May 2019.

Guido, L. (2015), '*Femmes de Paris* (1953): les scènes grotesques du "film de music-hall" français', in G. Le Gras and G. Sellier (eds), *Cinémas et cinéphilies populaires dans la France d'après-guerre 1945–1958*, 217–31, Paris: Nouveau Monde.

Guilbert, G.-C. (2018), *Gay Icons: The (Mostly) Female Entertainers Gay Men Love*, Jefferson: McFarland.

Guillamaud, P. (2014), *Les Parapluies de Cherbourg: Jacques Demy*, Liège: Céfal.

Hansen, M. (1986), 'Pleasure, Ambivalence, Identification: Valentino and Female Spectatorship', *Cinema Journal*, 25 (4): 6–32.

Harrod, M. (2012), 'The *Réalisatrice* and the Rom-Com in the 2000s', *Studies in French Cinema*, special issue on 'Women's Filmmaking in the 2000s', 12 (3): 227–40.

Harrod, M. (2015), *From France with Love: Gender and Identity in French Romantic Comedy*, London: I.B.Tauris.

Harrod, M. and P. Powrie (2018), 'New Directions in Contemporary French Comedies: From Nation, Sex and Class to Ethnicity, Community and the Vagaries of the Postmodern', *Studies in French Cinema*, 18 (1): 1–17.

Henneton, D. (2012), 'Jacques Demy's Musical Comedies: An Homage to the American Show Musical', *French Forum*, 37 (3): 221–39.

Herpe, N. (ed.) (1998), *René Clair*, sp. no. *1895*, 25, Paris: Association Française de Recherche sur l'Histoire du Cinéma.

Herpe, N. (2001), *Le Film dans le texte: l'œuvre écrite de René Clair*, Paris: J.-M. Place.

Herpe, N. and E. Toulet (eds) (2000), *René Clair ou le cinema avant la lettre*, Paris: Association Française de Recherche sur l'Histoire du Cinéma.

Herzog, A. (2007), 'Illustrating Music: The Impossible Embodiments of the Jukebox Film', in R. Beebe and J. Middleton (eds), *Medium Cool: Music Videos from Soundies to Cellphones*, 30–58, Durham: Duke University Press.

Herzog, A. (2010), 'En Chanté: Music, Memory, and Perversity in the Films of Jacques Demy', in *Dreams of Difference, Songs of the Same: The Musical Moment in Film*, 115–53, Minneapolis: University of Minnesota Press.

Hill, R. F. (2008a), 'The New Wave Meets the Tradition of Quality: Jacques Demy's *The Umbrellas of Cherbourg*', *Cinema Journal*, 48 (1): 27–50.

Hill, R. F. (2008b), 'Demy Monde: The New-Wave Films of Jacques Demy', *Quarterly Review of Film and Video*, 25 (5): 382–94.

Hill, R. (2014), 'Queering the New-Wave Deal: Gender and Sexuality in Jacques Demy's *A Slightly Pregnant Man*', *Post Script* 34 (1): 50–60.
Hirschi, S. (2008), *Chanson: l'art de fixer l'air du temps – de Béranger à Mano Solo*, Paris: Les Belles Lettres/Valenciennes: Presses Universitaires de Valenciennes.
Holohan, C. (2011), 'Wrong Turns: Radical Spaces in the Road Movies of Tony Gatlif', *Transnational Cinemas*, 2 (1): 21–35.
Honegger, A. (1941), '*Toi c'est moi*', *Comœdia*, 10 January.
Honoré, C. (2007a), '*Les Chansons d'amour*' [interview with J.-M. Lalanne and J.-B. Morain], *Les Inrockuptibles*, 22 May.
Honoré, C. (2007b), 'Christophe Honoré: "je n'accorde aucune importance au scénario"' [interview with I. Régnier], *Le Monde*, 23 May.
Horguelin, T. (1995), 'Les Nouveaux Mystères de Paris', *24 images*, 80: 22–3.
Icart, R. (1983), *Abel Gance ou le Prométhée foudroyé*, Lausanne: L'Âge d'homme.
Icart, R. (1988), *La Révolution du parlant vue par la presse française*, Perpignan: Institut Jean Vigo.
Ince, K. (2002), 'Queering the Family?: Fantasy and the Performance of Sexuality and Gay Relations in French Cinema 1995–2000', *Studies in French Cinema*, 2 (2): 90–7.
Inman, D. M. (2006), *Television Variety Shows: Histories and Episode Guides to 57 Programs*, Jefferson: McFarland.
J.-P. G. (2006), '*On va s'aimer*', *Téléobs*, 15 June.
J.-G. P. (1957), '*Casino de Paris*', *Radio Cinéma Télévision*, 17 November.
J.L. (1937), '*Un grand amour de Beethoven*', *Cinémonde*, 430: 27.
Jackson, J. H. (2002), 'Making Jazz French: The Reception of Jazz Music in Paris, 1927–1934', *French Historical Studies*, 25 (1): 149–70.
Jean de L'écran. (1941), 'Quand Tino Rossi chante, il ne pense pas aux femmes', *Ciné-mondial*, 11: 5.
Jeancolas, J.-P. (1982), 'Abel Gance entre Napoléon et Pétain', *Positif*, 256: 17–21.
Jeancolas, J.-P. (1983), *15 ans d'années trente: le cinéma des Français, 1929–1944*, Paris: Stock.
Jeancolas, J.-P. (2005), *Le Cinéma français*, Paris: Nouveau monde.
Jolivet, R. (1931), '*Pas sur la bouche*', *Cinémonde*, 139: 390.
Julien, E. (2009), 'Now You See It, Now You Don't: Josephine Baker's Films of the 1930s and the Problem of Color', in D. C. Hine, T. D. Keaton and S. Small (eds), *Black Europe and the African Diaspora*, 48–61, Chicago, University of Illinois Press.
Jullier, L. (2007), *Abécédaire des Parapluies de Cherbourg*, Paris: Éditions de l'Amandier.
Kael, P. (1994), 'Trash, Art, and the Movies', in *For Keeps*, 206–27. New York: Dutton.
Kaganski, S. (2017), '*Jeannette, l'enfance de Jeanne d'Arc*: le geste le plus fou de ce festival', *Les Inrockuptibles*, 21 May. https://www.lesinrocks.com/2017/05/21/cinema/actua lite-cinema/jeannette-lenfance-de-jeanne-darc-le-geste-le-plus-fou-de-ce-festival/. Accessed 27 May 2019.
Kermabon, J. (2000), '*Le Million*: une comédie musicale?', in N. Herpe and É. Toulet (eds), *René Clair ou le cinéma avant la lettre*, 167–78, Paris: Association Française de Recherche sur l'Histoire du Cinéma.
Kirkup, J. (1997), 'Obituary: Georges Guetary' [sic], *The Independent*, 20 September. https://www.independent.co.uk/news/obituaries/obituary-georges-guetary-1240 193.html

Kobal, J. (1971), *Gotta Sing, Gotta Dance: A Pictorial History of Film Musicals*, London: Hamlyn.

Kracauer, S. (1960), *Theory of Film: The Redemption of Physical Reality*, Princeton: Princeton University Press.

Kreimeier, K. (1999), *The Ufa Story: A History of Germany's Greatest Film Company, 1918–1945*, trans. R. and R. Kimber, Berkeley: University of California Press.

Labarthe, A. (1957), 'Amour, tango et mandoline', *Radio Cinéma Télévision*, 397, 25 August.

Labiche, M. (1930), 'Vive le jazz', *Cinémonde*, 82: 319.

Lagabrielle, R. (2016), 'Représentations (dés-)enchantées du sida: *Jeanne et le garçon formidable*', *Revue critique de fixxion française contemporaine*, 12. http://www.revue-critique-de-fixxion-francaise-contemporaine.org/rcffc/article/view/fx12.15/1028. Accessed 17 May 2019.

Lagabrielle, R. (2018), 'Boys Meet Girls, Paris Meets Hollywood: Opportunities Missed in French Films *En Chanté*', *Diogenes*, 62 (1): 115–27.

Lainé, A. (2015), 'Quand j'étais chanteur: découvrez celui qui a inspiré le héros du film, joué par Depardieu', *TéléStar*, 3 June. https://www.telestar.fr/culture/quand-j-etais-chanteur-decouvrez-celui-qui-a-inspire-le-heros-du-film-joue-par-depardieu-photos-124060. Accessed 5 June 2019.

Langlois, H. (2014), *Écrits de cinéma (1931–1977)*, eds B. Benoliel and B. Eisenschitz, Paris: Flammarion.

Lauwick, H. (1948), '*La Belle Meunière*', *Noir et blanc*, 11 February.

Lauwick, H. (1950), 'Amour et compagnie', *Noir et blanc*, 15 February.

Lawaetz, G. (1989), '*Le Maître de musique*: The Sounds of Music', *Sight & Sound*, 58 (3): 149–50.

Lawrence, J. (1930), '*Le Chemin du paradis*', *Pour Vous*, 114: 12.

Layerle, S. and R. Moine (2014), 'Les "Comédies-poursuites", un cycle de films musicaux entre scènes de cabaret et télédiffusion naissante', in S. Layerle and R. Moine (eds), *Voyez comment on chante!: films musicaux et cinéphilies populaires en France (1945–1958)*, 75–87, Paris: Presses Sorbonne Nouvelle.

Lazen, M. (2004), '"En perme à Nantes": Jacques Demy and New Wave Place', *Studies in French Cinema*, 4 (3): 187–96.

Ledieu, C. (1963), 'Interview with Noël Howard', *Arts*, 24 October.

Lefèvre, R. (2013), *Une chambre en ville de Jacques Demy: accords et accrocs*, Crisnée: Yellow Now.

Lefort, G. (1998), '*Jeanne et le garçon* c'est formidable', *Libération*, 22 April.

Lefort, G. (2007), 'Honoré enchantant', *Libération*, 19 May.

Lehmann, R. (1931a), 'Les Desseins de la censure: le satirique *Opéra de quat'sous*', *Pour Vous*, 139: 9.

Lehmann, R. (1931b), 'Lilian Harvey et Henri Garat dans *Le congrès s'amuse*', *Pour Vous*, 154: 8–9.

Leicester, H. M., Jr. (1994), 'Discourse and the Film Text: Four Readings of *Carmen*', *Cambridge Opera Journal*, 6 (3): 245–82.

Le Junkee (1937), 'La parole est aux spectateurs', *Pour Vous*, 432: 12.

Le Morvan, G. (1986), *L'Humanité*, 25 June.

Lenauer, Jean H. (1933), 'Le Film américain subit-il une influence européenne?', *Cinémonde*, 250: 641.

Le Pajolec, S. (2009), 'Le Cinéma et les yéyés : un rendez-vous manqué ?', in L. Bantigny (ed.), *Jeunesse oblige: histoire des jeunes en France XIXe–XXIe siècle*, 183–98, Paris: Presses Universitaires de France.
Leroi, P. (1942), '*La Course à l'amour*', *Comœdia*, 26 September.
Le Saux, B. (1987), 'La Fille du meunier, son film et l'art', *Le Matin*, 2 January.
Les Yeux bleus (1935), 'La parole est aux spectateurs', *Pour Vous*, 371: 10.
Lévi Alvares, A. (1931), 'Courrier de Berlin', *La Revue du cinéma*, 16: 59–60.
Liblot, É. (2003), 'Conversation avec Resnais' [interview], *L'Express*, 4 December.
Liehm, M. (1984), *Passion and Defiance: Italian Film from 1942 to the Present: Film in Italy from 1942 to the Present*, Berkeley: University of California Press.
Lindeperg, S. and B. Marshall (2000), 'Time, History and Memory and *Les Parapluies de Cherbourg*', in B. Marshall and R. Stilwell (eds), *Musicals: Hollywood and Beyond*, 98–106. Exeter: Intellect.
Loiseau, J.-C. (2008), '*Le Roi danse*', *Télérama*, 27 December. http://www.telerama.fr/cinema/films/le-roi-danse,52033,critique.php. Accessed 19 September 2017.
Looseley, D. (2003), *Popular Music in Contemporary France: Authenticity, Politics, Debate*, London: Bloomsbury.
Looseley, D. (2007), 'Conceptualising Youth Culture in Postwar France', *Modern and Contemporary France*, 15 (3): 261–75.
Lorrain, F.-G. (2003), 'Resnais connaît l'opérette', *Le Point*, 28 November.
Loutte, B. (2002), 'Le Tempo des gitans: *Swing* de Tony Gatlif', *Les Inrockuptibles*, 19 March.
M.D. (1963), '*D'où viens-tu, Johnny?*', *Le Canard enchaîné*, 16 November.
Magnan, H. (1959), 'Parlons Clair', *Le Canard enchaîné*, 22 July.
Mal, C. (2014), '*Chante ton bac d'abord*: entretien avec David André', *Le Blog documentaire*. http://leblogdocumentaire.fr/2014/10/17/chante-ton-bac-dabord-un-documentaire-social-en-chante-signe-david-andre-entretien. Accessed 28 June 2019.
Malherbe, H. (1937), '*Un grand amour de Beethoven*', *Pour Vous*, 426: 5.
Malherbe, H. (1939), '*Louise* à l'écran', *Pour Vous*, 563: 8–9.
Mandelbaum, J. (2011), '*Toi, moi, les autres*: une comédie sociale et musicale', *Le Monde*, 22 February. https://www.lemonde.fr/cinema/article/2011/02/22/toi-moi-les-autres-une-comedie-sociale-et-musicale_1483373_3476.html. Accessed 27 June 2019.
Manvell, R. (1973), *Masterworks of the German Cinema*, London: Lorrimer.
Marcel-Henry (1935), '*La Veuve joyeuse*: film américain, parlant français', *Cinémonde*, 328: 95.
Marguet, J. (1930), '*Le Chemin du paradis*', *Cinémonde*, 103: 650.
Marie, M. (2000), '"On va chanter encore une petite fois": *Sous les toits de Paris* comme "film manifeste" du cinéma musical et sonore en 1930', in N. Herpe and É. Toulet (eds), *René Clair ou le cinéma avant la lettre*, 153–66, Paris: Association Française de Recherche sur l'Histoire du Cinéma.
Martin, A. (1989), '*Golden Eighties*', *Film Critic: Adrian Martin*. http://www.filmcritic.com.au/reviews/g/golden_eighties.html. Accessed 22 April 2019.
Martin, P. (2013), 'Le Rouxcolor: un procédé additif de reproduction des couleurs', *1895. Mille huit cent quatre-vingt-quinze*, 71: 205–10.
Masson, A. (1997), '*Quelques jours de septembre*', *Positif*, 441: 73–4.
Masson, A. (2002), '*Filles perdues, cheveux gras*', *Les Inrockuptibles*, 1 January. https://www.lesinrocks.com/cinema/films-a-l-affiche/filles-perdues-cheveux-gras/. Accessed 24 June 2019.

Mauriac, C. (1955), 'Le Baron Tzigane', Le Figaro, 26 February.
Mawer, D. (2008), '"Parisomania"? Jack Hylton and the French Connection', Journal of the Royal Musical Association, 133 (2): 270–317.
McColm, I. J. (1984), Dictionary of Ceramic Science and Engineering, New York: Springer.
McGerr, C. (1980), René Clair, Boston: Twayne.
McGonagle, J. (2007), 'Gently Does It: Ethnicity and Cultural Identity in Olivier Ducastel and Jacques Martineau's Drôle de Félix (2000)', Studies in European Cinema, 4 (1): 21–33.
Mellini, C. (2002), 'Osons le boulevard au cinéma', Synopsis, 18: 50–53.
Méry, J. (1932), 'Il est charmant', Cinémonde, 174: 100–01.
Meyer-Plantureux, Ch. (2014), 'Le Burlesque musical "à la française": Gérard Calvi, Robert Dhéry et les Branquignols', in S. Layerle and R. Moine (eds), Voyez comment on chante!: films musicaux et cinéphilies populaires en France (1945–1958), 89–94, Paris: Presses de la Sorbonne Nouvelle.
Mielusel, R. (2015), Langue, espace et (re)composition identitaire dans les œuvres de Medhi Charef, Tony Gatlif et Farid Boudjellal, Paris: L'Harmattan.
Minier, M. and M. Pennacchia (eds) (2014), Adaptation, Intermediality and the British Celebrity Biopic, Farnham: Ashgate.
Minotaure (1946), 'Croquis à l'emporte-tête: Georges Guétary', L'Écran français, 57: 3.
Mintzer, J. (2013), 'Opium: Film Review', Hollywood Reporter, 10 March. https://www.hollywoodreporter.com/review/opium-film-review-642446. Accessed 27 May 2019.
Mirambeau, C. (2004), Saint-Luis, Paris: Flammarion.
Mitry, J. (1960), René Clair, Paris: Éditions universitaires.
Mitterrand, F. (1995), Madame Butterfly, Paris: Éditions Plume.
Moine, R. (2002), Les Genres du cinéma, Paris: Nathan.
Moine, R. (2015), 'Édith Piaf, une "Étoile sans lumière" dans le cinéma français populaire des années 1950', Contemporary French and Francophone Studies, 19 (1): 38–53.
Moine, R. (2017), Vies héroïques: biopics masculins, biopics féminins, Paris: Vrin.
Moix, Y. (2002), Podium, Paris: Grasset.
Mon Film (1960), 'Portraits de vedettes', Mon Film, 677: 53.
Monange, R. (1975), 'Chobizenesse: Molièresquement vôtre', Aurore, 29 October.
Monette (1935), 'La parole est aux spectateurs', Pour Vous, 328: 12.
Montagne, A. (2007), Histoire juridique des interdits cinématographiques en France, 1909–2001, Paris: L'Harmattan.
Morain, J.-B. (1998), 'Un Demy sous pression', Les Inrockuptibles, 22 April.
Morain, J.-B. (2008), 'Faubourg 36', Les Inrockuptibles, 24 September. https://www.lesinrocks.com/cinema/films-a-l-affiche/faubourg-36/. Accessed 5 June 2019.
Morice, J. (2017), 'Barbara de Mathieu Amalric: un poème kaléidoscopique', Télérama, 6 September. https://www.telerama.fr/cinema/barbara-de-mathieu-amalric-un-poeme-kaleidoscopique,n5190691.php. Accessed 27 May 2019.
Morin, E. (1963), 'Salut les copains', Le Monde, 6 July: 1, 11 and 7–8 July: 12.
Mosley, P. (2001), Split Screen: Belgian Cinema and Cultural Identity, Albany: SUNY Press.
Moullet, L. (1995), 'La Métamorphose', Cahiers du cinéma, 495: 46–7.
Moustier, J. (1931), 'Comment on réalise Pas sur la bouche', Cinémonde, 153: 616–7.
Mulligan, G. (2017), 'The Queer Cinema of Jacques Demy', PhD diss., University of Warwick.
Murat, P. (1998), 'Jeanne et le garçon formidable', Télérama, 22 April, 21–2.

Murger, H. (1851), *Scènes de la vie de bohème*, Paris: Librairie du Panthéon.
Narbonne, C. (2017), 'Laurent et Safi', *Première.fr*, September. http://www.premiere.fr/film/Laurent-et-Safi. Accessed 27 June 2019.
Niccolai, M. (2016), 'De l'opéra au grand écran: *Louise* de Gustave Charpentier dans la réalisation d'Abel Gance', in J. Rossi (ed.), *La Musique de film en France: courants, spécificités, évolutions*, 75–95, Lyon: Symétrie.
Nichols, B. (2001), *Introduction to Documentary*, Bloomington: Indiana University Press.
Nicklaus, O. (1986), 'Golden eighties', *Les Inrockuptibles*, 1 January. https://www.lesinrocks.com/cinema/films-a-l-affiche/golden-eighties/. Accessed 21 April 2019.
O'Brien, C. (2005), *Cinema's Conversion to Sound: Technology and Film Style in France and the U.S.*, Bloomington: Indiana University Press.
O'Brien, C. (2009), '*Sous les toits de Paris* and Transnational Film Style: An Analysis of Film Editing Statistics', *Studies in French Cinema*, 9 (2): 111–25.
Ostria, V. (1993), 'Le Blues des Gitans', *Cahiers du cinéma*, 473: 70–1.
Ousselin, E. (2014), 'Le Front populaire en mémoire: *Faubourg 36* (2008) de Christophe Barratier', *Cincinnati Romance Review*, 38: 34–47.
Oyallon-Koloski, J. (2014), 'Genre Experimentation and Contemporary Dance in *Jeanne et le garçon formidable*', *Studies in French Cinema*, 14 (2): 91–107.
Ozon, F. (2002a), 'François Ozon: se mettre en danger' [interview with Ph. Rouyer and C. Vassé], *Positif*, 492: 19–24.
Ozon, F. (2002b), 'Projection privée' [radio interview], *France Culture*, 3 February. INA catalogue no. 180502.
Pace, A. (2013), '*Peau d'Âne*: une extraordinaire exception' [interview by Matthieu Orléan] in M. Orléan (ed.), *Le Monde enchanté de Jacques Demy*, 151, Paris: Skira Flammarion.
Padilla, R. (2010), 'From Concert to Film: The Transformations of George Gershwin's Music in the Film *An American in Paris*', PhD thesis, University of Arizona.
Paris-Presse (1947), 'Le Chanteur inconnu', *Paris-Presse*, 8 May.
Peacock, S. (2010), 'The Umbrellas of Cherbourg', in *Colour*, 97–107, Manchester: Manchester University Press.
Péguy, C. (1897), *Jeanne d'Arc*, Paris: Librairie de la Revue socialiste.
Péguy, C. (1904), *Le Mystère de la charité de Jeanne d'Arc*, Paris: Gallimard.
Père, O. (2010), *Jacques Demy*, Paris: Martinière.
Pessis, J. (2014), *Josephine Baker*, Paris: Gallimard.
Pettey, H. B. and R. B. Palmer (eds) (2018), *Rule, Britannia!: The Biopic and British National Identity*, Albany: SUNY Press.
Peyrusse, C. (1986), *Le Cinéma méridional: le Midi dans le cinéma français (1929–1944)*, Toulouse: Eché.
Phillips, A. (2004), *City of Darkness, City of Light: Émigré Filmmakers in Paris, 1929–1939*, Amsterdam: Amsterdam University Press.
Pillard, T. (2014), '"Une curieuse rencontre": la "francisation" du *musical* hollywoodien dans *Folies-Bergère* (Henri Decoin, 1956)', in S. Layerle and R. Moine (eds), *Voyez comment on chante!: films musicaux et cinéphilies populaires en France (1945–1958)*, 97–104, Paris: Presses Sorbonne Nouvelle.
Pliskin, F. (1998), 'La Jeune Fille et la vie', *Le Nouvel Observateur*, 16 April.
Polaschek, B. (2013), *Postfeminist Biopic: Narrating the Lives of Plath, Kahlo, Woolf and Austen*, Basingstoke: Palgrave Macmillan.

Por, K. (2014), 'Usages de l'opérette aux débuts du parlant à Hollywood: innovations techniques et stratégies spectaculaires', *1895*, 72: 65–83.
Portis, L. (2004), *La Canaille ! Histoire sociale de la chanson française*, Paris: CNT.
Powrie, P. (2007a), 'Jean-Luc's Women (Godard, 1984)', in P. Powrie, B. Babington, A. Davies and C. Perriam (eds), *Carmen on Film: A Cultural History*, 122–31, Bloomington: Indiana University Press.
Powrie, P. (2007b), 'Social-Realist Fantasies (Rosi, 1984)', in P. Powrie, B. Babington, A. Davies and C. Perriam (eds), *Carmen on Film: A Cultural History*, 132–42, Bloomington: Indiana University Press.
Powrie, Ph. and Rebillard, E. (2008), 'Josephine Baker and Pierre Batcheff in *La Sirène des tropiques* (1927)', *Studies in French Cinema*, 8 (3): 245–64.
Pratt, M. (2004), 'Félix and the Light-Hearted Gay Road Movie: Genre, Families, Fathers and Decolonization of the Homosexual Self', *Australian Journal of French Studies*, 41 (3): 88–101.
Provencher, D. (2008), 'Tracing Sexual Citizenship and Queerness in *Drôle de Félix* (2000) and *Tarik el hob* (2001)', *Contemporary French and Francophone Studies*, 12 (1): 51–61.
Quillien, C. (2009), *Nos années 'Salut les copains': 1959–1976*, Paris: Flammarion.
R. de B. (1942), 'Fièvres', *L'Illustration*, 21 February. Reproduced in *Cahiers de la cinémathèque*, 8 (1972): 48.
Radner, H. (2014), 'The Historical Film and Contemporary French Cinema: Representing the Past in the Present', in A. Fox, M. Marie, R. Moine, and H. Radner (eds), *A Companion to Contemporary French Cinema*, 289–313, Chichester: Wiley-Blackwell.
Raynaud, C. (2007–2008), 'Foil, Fiction and Phantasm: "Josephine Baker," in *Princess Tam Tam*', *The Scholar and Feminist Online*, 6 (1–2). http://sfonline.barnard.edu/baker/raynaud_01.htm. Accessed 2 July 2019.
Rees-Roberts, N. (2008), *French Queer Cinema*, Edinburgh: Edinburgh University Press.
Régent, R. (1930), 'Le Chemin du paradis', *Pour Vous*, 105: 5.
Régent, R. (1931), 'E. Charrell, réalisateur du *Congrès s'amuse*', *Pour Vous*, 155: 7.
Régnier, G. (2009), *Jazz et société sous l'Occupation*, Paris: L'Harmattan.
Rémond, A. (1975), 'Il l'aime trop pour vouloir le trahir', *Télérama*, 1346: 71.
Resnais, A. (1997a), '*On connaît la chanson*' [interview with S. Grassin and G. Médioni], *L'Express*, 6 November.
Resnais, A. (1997b), 'Paroles et musique' [interview with D. Péron and O. Séguret], *Libération*, 12 November, 4.
Resnais, A. (2003a), '*Pas sur la bouche*' [interview with P. Mérigeau], *Le Nouvel Observateur*, 27 November.
Resnais, A. (2003b), '"Qu'on me jette dans l'enfer des frivoles"' [interview with A. Ferenczi], *Télérama*, 3 December.
Resnais, A. (2003c), '"Il y avait une folie à la Raymond Queneau dans ce livret"' [interview with T. Sotinel], *Le Monde*, 3 December.
Rivette, J. (1995a), 'Complot de famille: Jacques Rivette', *Les Inrockuptibles*, 12 April. https://www.lesinrocks.com/1995/04/12/cinema/actualite-cinema/complot-de-famille-jacques-rivette/. Accessed 10 April 2019.
Rivette, J. (1995b), 'Jacques Rivette: j'aime les films inégaux' [interview with G. Lefort and M. Rothe], *Libération*, 12 April. https://next.liberation.fr/cinema/1995/04/12/jacques-rivette-j-aime-les-films-inegaux_130500. Accessed 10 April 2019.

Rivette, J. (1999), '*Le Secret et la loi*' [interview with Hélène Frappat], *La Lettre du cinéma*, 11. Reprinted in J. Rivette, *Textes Critiques,* eds M. Armas and L. Chessel, 381–421, Paris: Post-Éditions.
Rodrigue, S. (1949), 'Attendez-vous à voir sous la perruque de Fresnay un Offenbach rigoureusement faux', *L'Écran français*, 217: 4.
Roger, P. (2000), 'Transcrire pour composer: le Beethoven d'Abel Gance', *1895*, 31 (1): 251–66.
Rolland, R. (1903), *Vie de Beethoven*, Paris: Hachette.
Rosello, M. (2012), 'French-Romani Dialogues in *Gadjo dilo*: Who Teaches European Languages and Minority Cultures?', *European Studies*, 29: 30723.
Rosenbaum, J. (1973), '*Les Idoles*', *Film Comment*, 9 (3): 2.
Rosenbaum, J. (1996), 'Ragged but Right', *Chicago Reader*, 26 July. https://www.jonathanrosenbaum.net/2017/11/up-down-fragile-directed-by-jacques-rivette/. Accessed 10 April 2019.
Rosenthal, O. (2013). 'La situation mérite attention', in M. Orléan (ed.), *Le Monde enchanté de Jacques Demy*, 161–67. Paris: Skira Flammarion.
Rossi, C. (1974), *Tino*, Paris: Stock.
Rouchouse, J. (1999), *L'Opérette*, Paris: Presses universitaires de France.
Rouchy, M.-É. (2013), '*Opium*: Arielle Dombasle rend un hommage fantaisiste et audacieux à Cocteau', *Le Nouvel Observateur*, 2 October. https://www.nouvelobs.com/cinema/20131002.CIN2121/opium-arielle-dombasle-rend-un-hommage-fantaisiste-et-audacieux-a-cocteau.html. Accessed 27 May 2019.
Rougeul, J. (1946), '*Le Gardian* au Royal-Haussmann', *Opéra*, 22 May.
Rouhaud, J. and Patchi (2006), *Luis Mariano: une vie*, Bordeaux: Éditions Sud-Ouest.
Rozat, P. (2010), 'Histoire de la télévision: une exception française?', *INA Global*, 9 December. https://www.inaglobal.fr/television/article/histoire-de-la-television-une-exception-francaise. Accessed 24 September 2018.
Rudent, C. (2019), 'Abrasion stylistique et transigeance musicale des chansons de "variété": Le cas exemplaire de *La Famille Bélier*', in S. Dufays, D. Nasta, and M. Cadalanu (eds), *Connaît-on la chanson? Usages de la chanson dans les cinémas d'Europe et d'Amérique latine depuis 1960*, 305–20, Bruxelles: Peter Lang.
Ruelle, J. (2017), '"Vois sur ton chemin": *Les Choristes* poussent la chansonnette pour la comédie musicale', *Charts in France*. http://www.chartsinfrance.net/actualite/news-103302.html. Accessed 4 June 2019.
Sadoul, G. (1957), '*Casino de Paris*, film franco-italo-hispanique, etc... de André Hunebelle; *Liane la sauvageonne*, film allemand, de Edouard Van Borsody', *Les Lettres françaises*, 695, 7 November.
Sannier, M. (1930), '*L'Amour chante*', *Cinémonde*, 107: 713.
Sauvage, L. (1946), '*Le Gardian*', *Franc-Tireur*, 3 June.
Scheie, T. (2016), 'Chez nous on the Range: Language, Genre and the Vernacular French Western (1956–61)', *Screen*, 57 (3): 316–35.
Scheie, T. (2019), 'Cowboy and Alien: The Bardot Westerns', *Studies in French Cinema*, 19 (2): 103–21.
Schilt, T. (2011), *François Ozon*, Champaign: University of Illinois Press.
Schlesser, G. (2006), *Le Cabaret 'rive gauche': de la* Rose rouge *au* Bateau ivre *(1946–1974)*, Paris: L'Archipel.
Schmid, M. (2010), *Chantal Akerman*, Manchester: Manchester University Press.

Sellier, G. (2008), *Masculine Singular: French New Wave Cinema*, trans. K. Ross, Durham: Duke University Press. Originally published in French in 2005.
Sellier, G. (2012), *Jean Grémillon: le cinéma est à vous*, Paris: Klincksieck.
Sellier, G. (2014), '"Le chéri des midinettes" : Luis Mariano dans le courrier des lecteurs de *Cinémonde* (1949–1956)', in S. Layerle and R. Moine (eds), *Voyez comment on chante!: films musicaux et cinéphilies populaires en France (1945–1958)*, 31–42, Paris: Presses Sorbonne Nouvelle.
Senelick, L. (2018), 'Orpheus in the Movie World: Offenbach on Film', in P. Fryer (ed.), *The Composer on Screen: Essays on Classical Music Biopics*, 18–34, Jefferson: McFarland.
Sengissen, P. (1963), '*D'où viens-tu, Johnny?*', *Télérama*, 722, 17 November.
Shaviro, S. (2007), 'Clichés of Identity: Chantal Akerman's Musicals', *Quarterly Review of Film and Video*, 24 (1): 11–17.
Siclier, J. (1975), '*Chobizenesse* de Jean Yanne', *Le Monde*, 27 October.
Smith, A. (1998), *Agnès Varda*, Manchester: Manchester University Press.
Sorel, J. (1932), '*Si tu veux*', *Cinémonde*, 204: 758.
Spectateur (1947), '*Le Chanteur inconnu*', *Le Spectateur*, 6 May.
Stane, F. (1941), 'Dans le sillage de Tino Rossi qui a le respect des sentiments vrais', *Ciné-Mondial*, 7: 6.
Staszak, J.-F. (2014), 'L'Écran de l'exotisme: la place de Joséphine Baker dans le cinéma français', *Annales de géographie*, 695–696: 646–70.
Stilwell, R. (2003), 'Le Demy-monde: The Bewitched, Betwixt and Between', in H. Dauncey and S. Cannon (eds), *Popular Music in France from Chanson to Techno: Culture, Identity and Society*, 123–38, Aldershot: Ashgate.
Swamy, V. (2006), 'Gallic Dreams? The Family, PaCS and Kinship Relations in Millennial France', *Studies in French Cinema*, 6 (1): 53–64.
Sylvain, M. (1946), 'Pour et contre les chanteurs de charme', *Mon Film*, 17: 9.
Synchro (1963), '*D'où viens-tu, Johnny?*', *Soir de Bruxelles*, 18 October.
Taboulay, C. (1996), *Le Cinéma enchanté de Jacques Demy*, Paris: Cahiers du cinéma.
Tachella, J.-C. (1947), 'Tino sans rosserie', *L'Écran français*, 120: 4.
Télé-Soir (1946), '*La Belle de Cadix*', *Télé-Soir*, 15 January.
Tesson, C. (2002), 'Mon premier vrai rôle', *Cahiers du cinéma*, 572: 48–51.
Thirard, P.-L. (1989), '*Le Maître de musique*', *Positif*, 338: 69.
Tinazzi, N. (1997), 'Le Tourbillon de la vie en chansons', *La Tribune*, 12 November.
Tinker, C. (2007), 'Shaping Youth in *Salut les copains*', *Modern & Contemporary France*, 15 (3): 293–308.
Tinker, C. (2010), *Mixed Messages: Youth Magazine Discourse and Sociocultural Shifts in Salut les copains (1962–1976)*, Oxford: Peter Lang.
Tournès, A. (2016), 'Visions – Révisions: Eric Pommer et le cinéma de Weimar', *Positif*, 665–666: 15–21.
Traubner, R. (2013), *Operetta: A Theatrical History*, London: Routledge.
Trémois, C.-M. (1957), '*Charmants garçons*', *Radio Cinéma Télévision*, 22 December.
Trimbach, G. (1978), *Tino Rossi*, Paris: Delville.
Truffaut, F. (1957), '*Folies-Bergère*: révélation de Zizi Jeanmaire', *Arts*, 16 January.
Tuiller, L. (2016), 'Sur quel pied danser', *Cahiers du cinéma*, 724: 62.
Vanderschelden, I. (2012), '*Réalisa(c)trices* Screening the Self: Valeria Bruni Tedeschi and Maïwenn', *Studies in French Cinema*, 12 (3): 241–55.
Varda, A. (1994), *Varda par Agnès*, Paris: Cahiers du cinéma.

Varda, A. (2014a), 'Agnès Varda Talks About the Cinema', in T. Jefferson Kline (ed. and trans.), *Agnès Varda: Interviews*, 64–77, Jackson: University of Mississippi Press.

Varda, A. (2014b), '*L'une chante, l'autre pas*: Inteview [sic] with *Agnès Varda*', in T. Jefferson Kline (ed. and trans.), *Agnès Varda: Interviews*, 78–88, Jackson: University of Mississippi Press.

Vecchiali, P. (2010), *L'Encinéclopédie: cinéastes 'français' des années 1930 et leur œuvre*, 2 vols, Paris: Éditions de l'Œil.

Vermorel, C. (1934), '*La crise est finie*', *Pour Vous*, 308: 7.

Vian, B. (1974), *Manuel de Saint-Germain-des-Prés*, Paris: Le Chêne.

Villetard, X. (1986), 'Galerie enchantée', *Libération*, 26 June, 38.

Vincendeau, G. (1987), 'The Mise-en-Scene of Suffering: French *Chanteuses Réalistes*', *New Formations*, 3: 107–28.

Vincendeau, G. (1988), 'Hollywood Babel: The Coming of Sound and the Multiple-Language Version', *Screen*, 29 (2): 24–39.

Vincendeau, G. (1998), *Pépé le Moko*, London: BFI.

Vincendeau, G. (2007), 'From *La Cage aux rossignols* (1945) to *Les Choristes* (2004): Change and Continuities in French Popular Cinema', in D. Waldron and I. Vanderschelden (eds), *France at the Flicks: Trends in Contemporary French Popular Cinema*, 63–74. Newcastle upon Tyne: Cambridge Scholars.

Vincendeau, G. (2015), '*La Famille Bélier*', *Sight and Sound*, 25 (10): 80–1.

Vincent-Bréchignac, J. (1931), '*Die 3 von der Tankstelle*', *Pour Vous*, 142: 6.

Virtue, N. (2013), 'Jacques Demy's *Les Parapluies de Cherbourg*: A National Allegory of the French-Algerian War', *Studies in French Cinema*, 13 (2): 127–40.

Virtue, N. (2016), 'Cubism and the Carnivalesque in Jacques Demy's *Demoiselles de Rochefort*', *Post Script*, 35 (2): 22–41.

Wahl, L. (1931a), '*L'Opéra de quat'sous*', *Pour Vous*, 123: 14.

Wahl, L. (1931b), '*Pas sur la bouche*', *Pour Vous*, 135: 5.

Wahl, L. (1935), '*Valse royale*', *Pour Vous*, 361: 10.

Wakeman, R. (2009), *The Heroic City: Paris, 1945–1958*, Chicago: University of Chicago Press.

Waldron, D. (2010), '"Une mine d'or inépuisable": The Queer Pleasures of François Ozon's *8 femmes/8 Women* (2002)', *Studies in French Cinema*, 10 (1): 69–87.

Waldron, D. (2013), *Jacques Demy*, Manchester: Manchester University Press.

Weiner, S. (2007), 'Demy and Deneuve: The Princess and the Post-68 Fairytale', in L. Downing and S. Harris (eds), *From Perversion to Purity: The Stardom of Catherine Deneuve*, 45–56, Manchester: Manchester University Press.

Wiles, M. (2001), 'Re-Staging the Feminine in Jacques Rivette's *Haut bas fragile* (1995)', *Studies in French Cinema*, 1 (2): 98–107.

Will, R. (2013), 'Rossini and Beethoven in Early Biopics', in N. Mathew and B. Walton (eds), *The Invention of Beethoven and Rossini: Historiography, Analysis, Criticism*, 333–54, Cambridge: Cambridge University Press.

Wilson, E. (2006), *Alain Resnais*, Manchester: Manchester University Press.

Wood, M. P. (2005), 'The Turbulent Movement of Forms: Rosi's Postmodern *Carmen*', in C. Perriam and A. Davies (eds), *Carmen: From Silent Film to MTV*, 189–204, Amsterdam: Rodopi.

Index

8 femmes   x, 206, *210–14*, 215, 216, 218, 247
42nd Street   13, 247

Abschiedswalzer [Farewell Waltz]   247
Achard, Marcel   25, 26, 79, 252, 261
Adieu Léonard   viii, 75, 76, 247
Adieu Philippine   162, 247
Adison, Fred   89
Aghion, Gabriel   218, 257
Ah! Les belles bacchantes   104, 247
Air de rien, L'   240, 247
Akerman, Chantal   9, 11, 160, 178, 181, 182, 183, 184, 205, 207, 224, 253, 254
À la Jamaïque   115, 141, 247
Algiers   58, 59, 247
Alibert, Henri   8, 10, 52, 53, 55, 56
Allégret, Marc   68, 151, 152, 248, 256, 261
Allouache, Merzak   218, 250
Altman, Robert   248
Amadeus   200, 247
Amalric, Mathieu   236, 238, 244, 248
Amants de demain, Les   66, 247
America di Notte   103, 247
À moi le jour, à toi la nuit   15, 247
Amok   58, 247
Amour, tango, mandoline   *131–2*
Amour et Compagnie   *131–2*, 247
An American in Paris   ix, 129, 130, 131, 133, 134, 135, 145, 148, 163, 247
Anconina, Richard   187, 240
Andalousie   115, 131, 137, 138, 247
Anderson, John Murray   67, 98, 161, 254
André, David   231, 250
Andréani, André   79, 252
Andrei Rublev   247
Anna (d'), Claude   254
Année dernière à Marienbad, L'   169, 205, 247

À nous deux, Madame la vie   89, 247
À nous la liberté   2, 247
À nous les petites Anglaises   *187*, 247
Anton, Karl   53, 66, 136, 223, 234, 235, 248, 250, 254
Anything Goes   146, 247
Apollinaire, Guillaume   168
Aragon, Louis   110
Ardant, Fanny   210, 211, 212
Arditi, Pierre   208
Arènes joyeuses (1935)   51, 53, 248
Arènes joyeuses (1958)   56, 248
Aria   248
Arletty   90, 145, 206
Armont, Paul   13
Arnezeder, Nora   243
Arnoul, Françoise   99
Arthur   29, 248
Aslan, Coco   91
Astaire, Fred   146, 147, 172
Auberge du Petit Dragon, L'   42, 248
Aubert, Jean-Louis   226
Audiffred, Émile   53, 126
Audran, Edmond   29
Au fil des ondes   248
Au pays du soleil (1934)   53, 248
Au pays du soleil (1951)   56, 115, 117, 248
Au revoir les enfants   241, 248
Auric, Georges   168
Au soleil de Marseille   52, 55, 56, 248
Au son des guitares   117, 122, 248
Autant-Lara, Claude   29, 30, 250
Aventure à Paris   90, 248
Aventures de Casanova, Les   131, 248
Aventurier de Séville, L'   115, 141, 248
Azéma, Sabine   205, 208
Aznavour, Charles   ix, 107, 108, 152, 206
Azuelos, Lisa   236, 251

Bacon, Lloyd   13, 36, 247, 252, 253, 261
Bacri, Jean-Pierre   205, 206
Badger, Clarence   13, 255
Baisers volés   183, 221, 248
Baker, Josephine   7, 9, 10, 67, *68–74*, 75, 77, 113, 206
Balasko, Josiane   218, 253
Balavoine, Daniel   226
Bal des actrices, Le   x, 206, *214–17*, 248
Balibar, Jeanne   216, 238
Balmer, Jean-François   182
Band Wagon, The   146, 248
Bang Bang   151, 248
Barbara   236, 237, *238*, 248
Barbara ou ma plus belle histoire d'amour   238, 248
Barbier de Séville, Le (1904)   79, 248
Barbier de Séville, Le (1948)   80, 248
Barde, André   29, 208
Bardot, Brigitte   218, 237
Barelli, Aimé   89
Bariole   74, 248
Barma, Claude   151, 256
Baron Tzigane (1927)   136, 248
Baron Tzigane (1935)   136, 248
Baron Tzigane (1954)   115, 131, *136–7*, 248
Barratier, Christophe   234, 235, 241, 242, 243, 244, 250, 252
Barrault, Jean-Louis   87
Barrois, Charles   53, 260
Bashung, Alain   206, 207
Batcheff, Pierre   117, 142
Baugé, André   2, 75, 123
Baugin, Lubin   200
Baum, Ralph   104, 256
Baur, Harry   80
Béart, Emmanuelle   210
Beaumont, Harry   13, 249
Beauvoir (de), Simone   109
Bécaud, Gilbert   149, 206, 237
Beethoven, Ludwig van   8, 9, 12, 79, 80, 81, 82, 83, 84, 85, 87, 176, 193, 235, 260
Bekhti, Leïla   226
Bell, Marie   60
Belle de Cadix, La   9, 115, 131, 137, 138, 141, 248

Belle de jour   168, 248
Belle Équipe, La   8, 101, 243, 248
Belle et la Bête, La   167, 248
Belle Meunière, La   *125–6*, 249
Belle Noiseuse, La   249
Belle Vie, La   162, 249
Belmondo, Jean-Paul   175
Benedek, Laslo   150, 261
Benedix, Julius Roderich   10
Berberian, Cathy   205
Beresford, Bruce   248
Berger, Ludwig   15, 29, 247, 253, 257, 258, 259, 260, 261
Bergman, Ingmar   260
Berkeley, Busby   13, 37, 39, 72, 73, 94, 243, 251, 253
Berlin, Irving   126
Berlingot et Compagnie   58, 249
Berlioz, Hector   79, 87, 129
Bernard, Raymond   248, 255
Bernstein, Leonard   164
Berri, Claude   188, 259
Berry, John   149, 182, 183, 256
Berry, Jules   62, 90, 243
Berry, Richard   169
Bert, Lilian   132
Berthomieu, André   89, 103, 104, 108, 115, 247, 251, 257
Beyoncé   242
Bibie   225
Bien-aimés, Les   249
Big Country, The   153, 249
Bihl, Agnès   228
Billon, Pierre   114, 259
Birkin, Jane   206, 237
Bizet, Georges   176, 193
Blasetti, Alessandro   103, 252
Blier, Bernard   243
Blier, Bertrand   216
Blistène, Marcel   60, 62, 66, 247, 252
Bluebell Girls, Les   107, 109
Bohème, La   249
Bohringer, Romane   215, 216
Boisrond, Michel   151, 250, 256
Boisselier, Julien   224
Boîte de nuit   104, 249
Bolváry (von), Géza   79, 247, 249
Bonamy, Olivia   223

Bonjour sourire!, 104, 249
Boris Godounov   ix, 85, *194–5*, 196, 249
Boucheron, Maxime   29
Bouillon, Jo   129
Boum sur Paris   64–5, 75, 103, 104, 106, 152, 249
Bouquet de joie   75, 103, 104, 249
Bourdet, Édouard   36
Bourgeois, Gérard   79, 252
Bourtayre, Henri   114
Boyer, Jean   7, 9, 36, 44, 74, 79, 90, 104, 131, 185, 248, 250, 252, 254, 255, 256, 257, 258
Boyer, Myriam   182, 183
Brahms, Johannes   123
Brando, Marlon   150
Branquignol   104, 249
Brassens, Georges   212, 237
Brecht, Bertolt   21, 22, 23
Brel, Jacques   226, 238, 252
Bretagne (de), Joseph   15
Brialy, Jean-Claude   176
Broadway Melody, The   13, 249
Brochet, Anne   200
Brook, Peter   191, 193, 260
Broschi, Carlo (aka *Farinelli*)   9, 198, 201, 202, 203, 235, 252
Broschi, Riccardo   201, 202
Brownlow, Kevin   80
Bruant, François   177
Bruel, Patrick   225
Bryden, Bill   248
Buffet, Eugénie   8, 65, 66
Buñuel, Luis   168, 248, 261

Cage aux rossignols, La   241, 249
Calbérac, Yvan   223, 256
Calmettes, André   79, 249, 258
Calori, Paul   223, 259
Calvi, Gérard   104
Cam, Maurice   58, 75, 103, 104, 249, 253
Cammage, Maurice   58, 253
Canonge (de), Maurice   56, 64, 75, 104, 115, 149, 248, 249, 260
Carbonnaux, Norbert   104, 259
Carmen (1910)   79, 249
Carmen (1984)   9, 176, *191–2*, 193, 194, 196, 245, 249

Carmen nue   193, 249
Carné, Marcel   165, 169, 241, 243, 251, 254
Carol, Martine   102, 141
Caron, Leslie   187
Caron, Pierre   9, 74, 187, 255, 258
Carton, Pauline   43
Casar, Amira   223
Casino de Paris   68, 129, 136, *149*, 249
Cassel, Cécile   226
Castelnuovo, Nino   162
Catelain, Jaque   142
Cavalcade des heures, La   75, 249
Cavalier noir, Le   9, 130, *131*, 133, 136, 241, 249
Cavalleria rusticana   79, 249
Cayatte, André   121, 250, 258
César et Rosalie   249
Ce soir les souris dansent   104, *111–12*, 249
C'est arrivé à 36 chandelles   ix, 75, 104, *106–7*, 108, 130, 249
Chacun sa chance   29, 31, 249
Chakiris, George   163
Champaigne (de), Philippe   200
Chancel, Jules   25
Chanone, Alain   240
Chanson de l'adieu, La   79, 249
Chansons d'amour, Les   x, 8, 9, 206, 219, *220–2*, 249
Chant de l'exilé, Le   114, 117, 137, 249
Chante ton bac d'abord   223, *231–2*, 250
Chanteur de Mexico, Le   ix, 115, 137, 138, 139, 140, 141, 250
Chanteur inconnu, Le   ix, 113, 117, 118, 119, *120–2*, 123, 250
Charby, Corinne   212
Charell, Erik   19, 250, 254
Charisse, Cyd   146, 147, 176
Charmants garçons   148, 250
Charnet, Augustin   239
Charpentier, Gustave   79, 84, 87, 196
Château en Suède   151, 250
Chautard, Émile   79, 249
Chavance, Louis   36, 257
Chedid, Matthieu   226
Cheirel, Micheline   91

Chemin du paradis, Le viii, 9, *15–19*, 21, 35, 115, 130, 131, 149, 208, 209, 214, 250
Chenal, Pierre 58, 254, 258
Chérasse, Jean 151, 260
Cherchez l'idole 151, 152, 250
Cherhal, Jeanne 228
Chevalier, Maurice 14, 15, 25, 58, 94, 149
Chinois à Paris, Les 186, 250
Chobizenesse 160, *186–7*, 250
Chopin, Frédéric 79, 125
Choristes, Les 234, *241–3*, 250
Choses de la vie, Les 211, 250
Chouchou 218, 250
Chouraqui, Élie 160, 187, 188, 189, 256
Christian-Jaque 58, 79, 241, 251, 259
Christophe 239, 240
Ciampi, Yves 66, 253
Ciboulette viii, 29–34, 250
Cinquième Empreinte, La 66, 250
Clair, René 2, 3, 4, 13, 14, 23, 36, 61, 175, 245, 247, 255, 257, 259
Clarika 228
Clément, Coralie 225
Clémenti, Pierre 186
Cléo de 5 à 7 162, 250
Clerc, Julien 206, 239
CloClo 236, *237*, 250
Clouzot, Henri-Georges 243, 257
Cocciante, Richard 225
Cocteau, Jean 167, 168, 170, 171, 235, 239, 245, 248, 258
Cœur de Lilas 58, 59, 250
Colin, Grégoire 239
Collard, Cyril 218, 249, 256
Colombier, Michel 169
Comar, Étienne 236, 251
Combret, Georges 103, 104, 255
Comencini, Luigi 249
Compagnons de la chanson, Les 64, 106
Comte Obligado viii, 29, 30, 250
Condé Marie-Sohna 226
Congrès s'amuse, Le viii, *19–21*
Constantine, Eddie 145, 146
Construire un feu 30, 250
Cookie Dingler 240
Copp, Oscar 230

Corbiau, Gérard 198, 199, 203, 252, 254, 258
Cordy, Annie 64
Corneau, Alain 198, 200, 201, 259
Cornillac, Clovis 243
Côte, Laurence 177
Cottençon, Fanny 182
Coulais, Bruno 234, 242
Crime au concert Mayol 104, *111*, 250
Crime de Monsieur Lange, Le 24, 243, 250
Crise est finie, La viii, 9, 13, 35, *36–42*, 134, 165, 250
Croisset (de), Francis 29
Cromwell, John 59, 247
Crosby, Bing 126, 146
Crustacés et coquillages 206, 218, 219
Cuny, Louis 115, 257
Curtis, Michael 254
Cyrano de Bergerac 200, 250

Dactylo 17, 251
Dagmar, Berthe 117, 253
Dahan, Olivier 236, 255
Dale, Grover 163
Dalida 206, 212, 213, 236, 240
Dalida 236, 237, 251
Dalleyrac, Joachim 199
Dames 13, 251
Damia 60, 61, 65, 116
Damnation de Faust, La 79, 87, 251
Daniel-Norman, Jacques 52, 115, 255, 259
Darrieux, Danielle 10, 23, 159, 163, 164, 169, 170, 210, 211, 212
Dassary, André 64, 105, 116
Dassin, Joe 226
Daumery, Jean 13, 255
Daviaud, Olivier 228
Davison, Tito 64, 255
Dean, James 150
Debout, Jean-Jacques 152
Début de soirée 240
Decoin, Henri 145, 148, 250, 252
Decouflé, Philippe 239
Dédé 29, *31–3*, 251
Delacour, Alfred 10
Delannoy, Jean 114, 169, 251, 252

Delmet, Paul   117
Delpech, Michel   219, 226, 240
Del Ruth, Roy   26, 252
Delyle, Lucienne   64
Dembélé, Habib   227
Demoiselles de Rochefort, Les   ix, 159, 160, *162–6*, 168, 172, 173, 174, 182, 183, 211, 219, 220, 221, 251
Demoiselles ont eu 25 ans, Les   160, 251
Demy, Jacques   x, 4, 8, 9, 11, 12, 30, 102, 157, *159–74*, 175, 176, 177, 178, 179, 181, 182, 183, 184, 185, 187, 188, 189, 205, 211, 214, 218, 219, 220, 221, 222, 223, 225, 228, 232, 245, 251, 256, 257, 260
Demy, Mathieu   218, 219
Deneuve, Catherine   x, 152, 159, 162, 165, 166, 168, 169, 187, 188, 210, 211, 212, 219, 220
Denicourt, Marianne   177
Denner, Charles   182, 183
Depardieu, Gérard   169, 200, 211, 240, 241
Depardieu, Julie   215, 216
Dernier Métro, Le   211, 251
Desireless   241
Destins   ix, 118, 119, 120, 122, 123, 124, *126–7*, 251
Détective   152, 251
Deux amours   9, 117, 118, *122–3*, 124, 125, 251
Dhéry, Robert   103, 104, 249
Diamant-Berger, Henri   75, 104, 130, 249, 259
Dieterle, William   13, 136, 252
Disparus de Saint-Agil, Les   241, 251
Distel, Sacha   102
Django   9, 67, 155, 156, 230, 236, *237–8*, 251
Doll, Dora   110
Dombasle, Arielle   236, 239, 256
Don César de Bazan   79, 251
Donen, Stanley   62, 146, 177, 253, 256, 258
Don Giovanni   251
Donnadieu, Bernard-Pierre   243
Doré, Gustave   193

Dorémi   115
Dorléac, Françoise   162
Dossier 1413   251
Doutey, Mélanie   215, 216, 224
D'où viens-tu, Johnny?   ix, 9, 11, 89, 150, *151–7*, 251
Dranem   206
Dreigroschenoper, Die   21, 22, 251
Drei von der Tankstelle, Die   15, 251
Dréville, Jean   241, 242, 249
Drôle de Félix   218, 251
Ducastel, Olivier   206, 214, 218, 222, 245, 251, 254
Ducis, Pierre-Jean   52, 248
Dullin, Charles   119
Dumont, Bruno   235, 236, 239, 244, 254
Dunne, Philip   153, 261
du Pont, Floyd   68
Dupuis, Claudine   111
Durand, Jean   117, 253
Duraton, Les   108, 251, 252
Duris, Romain   229
Dussollier, André   205
Dutronc, Jacques   186, 206, 226
Duty, Claude   223, 224, 252
Duvivier, Julien   58, 243, 248, 257

Eaubonne (d'), Jean   15
Ein Walzertraum   15, 25, 261
Ellis, Warren   238
Elloy, Max   90, 91, 93, 100
Enfants du paradis, Les   165, 241, 243, 251
Enfer des anges, L'   251
Énigme aux Folies-Bergère   251
Enrico, Robert   162, 249
Enright, Ray   13, 251
Entraîneuse, L'   58, 251
Envoi de fleurs   115, 117, 118, 251
Enzo Enzo   177
Estrougo, Audrey   223, 226, 227, 259
Éternel Retour, L'   169, 251
Étienne, Pauline   228
Étiévant, Henri   68, 259
Étoile sans lumière   viii, 60, 62–3, 252
Étrange Madame X, L'   28, 252
Être et avoir   241, 252

Europa di notte   103, 252
Eustache, Jean   66, 186, 220, 254
Évein, Bernard   159, 169, 170, 174
Evreïnoff, Nicolas   29, 257

Fabian, Françoise   171
Fagot, Georges   79, 252
Falk, Henry   90
Famille Bélier, La   233–4
Famille Duraton, La   108, 252
Fandango   138, 141, 252
Fantasia   87, 252
Farinelli   ix, 198, *201–3*, 235, 252
Fashions of 1934   252
Faubourg 36   *243–4*, 245, 252
Faust (1910)   79, 252
Faust (1922)   79, 252
Feldman, François   241
Femme d'à côté, La   211, 252
Femmes de Paris   104, *110–11*, 112, 252
Fernandel   149
Ferré, Léo   206
Ferrier, Paul   10
Feux de joie   viii, 90, 91, *94–5*, 96, 100, 101, 116, 252
Fièvres   114, 118, 119, *125*, 252
Filles perdues, cheveux gras   *223–4*, 225, 252
Fin de Don Juan, La   79, 252
Flaming Star   152, 252
Flers (de), Robert   29
Florelle   23, 24, 60, 243
Florey, Robert   2, 7, 258
Foïs, Marina   215, 223, 224
Folies-Bergère (1935, aka *L'Homme des Folies-Bergère*)   26, 252
Folies-Bergère (1957)   ix, *145–9*, 252
Folies-Bergère de Paris   26, 252
Footlight Parade   36, 252
Forestier, Frédéric   240, 259
Forman, Miloš   200, 219, 247
Forst, Willi   16, 115, 250
Forster, Rudolf   24
Fortuny, Jean   104, 249
Fosse, Bob   176
Fra Diavolo   79, 252
Francis, Joe   68, 251

Franck, Paul   58
François, Jacqueline   64
Franz   238, 252
Frauen von Folies Bergères, Die   68, 251
Frédérica   74, 75, 252
Freed, Arthur   130
Fréhel   10, *57–60*, 61, 63, 65, 68, 237
French Cancan   viii, 64, 65, 66, 252
Frères Jacques, Les   110, 237
Fresnay, Pierre   15, 87
Friedland, Georges   60, 256
Fritsch, Willy   21
Fuller, Lester   255
Funès (de), Louis   102, 104, 110, 142, 159

Gabin, Jean   9, 57, 58, 59, 63, 65, 68, 243
Gabutti, Raymond   15
Gadjo Dilo   *229–30*, 231, 252
Gaillard, Jimmy   94
Gainsbourg (vie héroïque)   *236–7*, 238, 252
Gall, France   186, 206, 237
Gance, Abel   9, *79–87*, 88, 191, 193, 195, 196, 203, 253, 254, 255, 258, 260
Gangsters du château d'If, Les   viii, 53, 54, 55, 56, 252
Garat, Henri   8, 10, 16, 18, 19, 21, 25, 28, 34, 206
Garçonne, La   *60–1*, 252
Gardian, Le   117, 154, 253
Garrel, Louis   218, 219
Garvarentz, Georges   152
Gasté, Louis   115
Gatlif, Tony   223, 228, 229, 230, 231, 252, 254, 259
Gautherin, Pierre   248
Gavault, René   80, 255
Gay, John   22
Gazon maudit   218, 253
Genée, Richard   10
Genès, Henri   90, 91, 92, 93, 109, 110
Genet, Jean   109, 110
Genina, Augusto   255
Gentelet, Hugues   240
Gentlemen Prefer Blondes   9, 163, 253
Giannoli, Xavier   236, 257
Gigolette   58, 253

Giovinezza   75, 253
Girault, Jean   102, 257
Give a Girl a Break   177, 253
Godard, Claude   111
Godard, Jean-Luc   11, 111, 152, 160, 175, 176, 177, 178, 193, 220, 245, 248, 251, 257, 260
Godet, Danielle   108
Gohou, Michel   227
Gold   241
Golden Eighties   ix, 9, 160, *181–5*, 219, 224, 253
Gold Diggers of 1933   viii, 13, 37, 38, 41, 42, 165, 183, 253
Gold Diggers of 1935   13, 253
Gold Diggers of 1937   13, 253
Goretta, Claude   195, 256
Gotainer, Richard   187
Grand Refrain, Le   7, 253
Grangier, Gilles   9, 115, 130, 131, 247, 249, 254, 260
Grémillon, Jean   viii, 27, 28, 252, 257, 261
Gréville, Edmond T.,   68, 257
Greystoke: The Legend of Tarzan, Lord of the Apes   188, 253
Grousset, Didier   160, 187, 258
Guerre des valses, La   15, 253
Guétary, Georges   ix, 10, 16, 56, 64, 102, 106, 107, 113, 115, 116, 127, *129–37*, 139, 140, 141, 143, 148, 154, 241, 244
Guiraud, Ernest   96
Guissart, René   6, 9, 29, 35, 89, 247, 251, 257, 259
Guitry, Sacha   58, 64, 65, 257, 258
Gut, Jacques   15
Guy-Blaché, Alice   79, 252, 255

Haddon, Dayle   187
Haffner, Karl   10
Hagen, Jean   62
Hahn, Reynaldo   29
Halévy, Ludovic   10
Hallyday, Johnny   ix, 11, 89, *149–56*, 183, 186, 206, 237, 239, 240
Hand, David   259
Handel, Georg Friedrich   125, 201, 202, 203

Hans Christian Andersen   146, 253
Hardt-Warden, Bruno   29
Hardy, Françoise   150, 151, 212
Hardy, Oliver   39
Hartl, Karl   136, 248
Harvey, Lilian   15, 19
Haut bas fragile   160, *176–8*, 253
Hawks, Howard   152, 163, 253, 254
Hélian, Jacques   89, 103, 109
Hepburn, Audrey   90, 98
Hérain (de), Pierre   255
Hérouet, Marc   181
Hesme, Clotilde   218
Hess, Johnny   74, 132
Heymann, Claude   15, 247
Heymann, Werner R.,   115
Hiroshima mon amour   205, 253
Holiday Inn   126, 253
Homme des Folies-Bergère, L' (aka *Folies-Bergère*)   26, 252
Homme du train, L'   152, 253
Honoré, Christophe   9, 137, 149, 206, 214, 218, 219, 220, 221, 222, 232, 245, 249
Hornez, André   92
Houssin, Jacques   252
Howard, Noël   9, 11, 89, 111, 150, 152, 153, 155, 163, 251, 253, 254
Hudson, Hugh   188, 253
Hugon, André   2, 7, 58, 114, 137, 249, 258, 260
Huillet, Danièle   192, 255, 261
Hunnebelle, André   249
Huppert, Isabelle   210
Huster, Francis   170
Hylton, Jack   89

Ich bei Tag und du bei Nacht   15, 253
Idoles, Les   155, 160, *185–6*, 253
Iglesias, Julio   240
Igorrr (aka Gautier Serre)   239
Île d'amour, L' (1928)   117, 253
Île d'amour (1944)   117, 241, 253
Il est charmant   viii, 9, 29, 31, 32, *34–5*, 43, 53, 98, 253
Images   241
Innocent, L'   58, 253
Ito, Keïko   170

Jacquot, Benoît   84, 160, 191, 192, 195, 196, 253, 259
Jacquot de Nantes   160, 253
Jade, Claude   221
Jaoui, Agnès   205
Jarman, Derek   248
Jasset, Victorin   79, 251, 252
Jeanmaire, Zizi   ix, 143, 145, 148
Jeanne   236, 254
Jeanne Dielman, 23 quai du Commerce   181, 254
Jeanne et le garçon formidable   206, 218–20, 221, 222, 254
Jeannette, l'enfance de Jeanne d'Arc   236, 238–9, 254
Jean-Philippe   236, 239–40, 242, 254
Jeanson, Henri   254
Je chante   74, 75, 254
Je n'aime que toi   139, 141, 254
JoeyStarr   215, 216
Jo la romance   131, 254
Jolson, Al   60
Journey, The   126, 152, 254
Jozelon, Xavier   227
Jugnot, Gérard   241, 242, 243, 255, 258
Juliette Gréco   64, 106, 107, 109, 237

Kaefer, Olivier   240
Karina, Anna   175, 177, 221
Karlson, Phil   153
Kaye, Danny   146
Kelly, Gene   62, 129, 133, 146, 163, 176, 183, 256, 258
Kérien, Jean-Pierre   111
Keroul, Maurice   29, 255
Kidd, Michael   147
Kid Galahad   153, 254
Kiepura, Jan   75
King Creole   152, 254
King of Jazz   67, 254
King of Kings   152, 254
König, Hans   130
Königswalzer   25, 27, 28, 254
Koshetz, Nina   59
Kosma, Joseph   75, 114

Labro, Maurice   130, 258
La Cava, Gregory   75, 183, 249, 254

Lacombe, Georges   9, 60, 255
Lady in the Lake, The   120, 254
Lady Paname   254
Laforêt, Marie   212
Lagiscarde, Jeanne   142
Lahaye, Jean-Luc   225, 241
Lalo, Édouard   123
Lama, Serge   206
Lambert, Christophe   187
Lamy, Alexandra   224
Lancret, Bernard   91
Land of the Pharaohs   152, 254
Lang, Michel   160, 187, 247, 259
Langmann, Thomas   240, 241, 259
Latcho Drom   x, 229, 230, 231, 254
La Tour (de), Georges   200
Laurent, Jacqueline   243
Laurent et Safi   223, 227, 234, 254
Laviron, Jean   104, 259
Lavoine, Marc   241
Lawrence of Arabia   152, 254
Lean, David   152, 254
Léaud, Jean-Pierre   183, 221
Lebon, Yvette   120
Leconte, Patrice   152, 253
Ledoux, Fernand   166
Ledoyen, Virginie   210, 218
Lefèbvre, René   10, 16, 18, 91
Legrand, Michel   159, 161, 162, 164, 165, 166, 168, 169, 172, 174, 175, 188
Legrand, Raymond   89, 115
Léhar, Franz   25, 136
Lellouche, Gilles   224
Lemaire, Philippe   99
Léonard, Herbert   225
Léopold Nord et Vous   241
Leplée, Louis   61, 236
LeRoy, Mervyn   13, 37, 253, 258
Lesœur, Marius   111
Lespert, Jalil   208
Letessier, Dorothée   183
Lewis, Robert   146, 247
Liebe ist ja nur ein Märchen   131, 254
Limur (de), Jean   42, 60, 248, 252
Lio   182, 219, 241
Liszt, Franz   119
Litvak, Anatole   58, 59, 152, 250, 254
Living in a Big Way   183, 254

López, Albert   193, 249
Lopez, Francis   113, 130, 137, 138
Losey, Joseph   251
Loubignac, Jean   80, 104, 247, 248
Louise   viii, ix, 79, *84–7*, 177, 191, 193, 195, 196, 197, 198, 203, 210, 211, 214, 254
Love in the Afternoon   152, 254
Love Me Tonight   13, 254
Loysel, Jean   125
Lubitsch, Ernst   9, 15, 25, 254, 255, 256, 259, 261
Lucchesi, Roger   115
Luchini, Fabrice   239, 240
Lully, Jean-Baptiste   200, 203, 204
Lumières de Paris   118, 254

Macbeth   194, 254
MacDonald, Jeanette   14, 25
Madame Butterfly   192, *193–4*, 254
Mademoiselle s'amuse   viii, 90, 91, 92, 94, 96–7, 100, 254
Mademoiselle Swing   89, 96, 100, 254
Maen, Norman   164
Magne, Grégory   240, 247
Mahler, Gustav   199
Maisch, Herbert   27, 28, 254
Maison du Maltais, La   58, 254
Maître de musique, Le   *198–200*, 254
Malet, Laurent   171
Malick, Terrence   231
Mallas-Godlewska, Ewa   202
Malle, Louis   241, 248
Mallory, Michael   212
Maman et la putain, La   66, 220, 254
Mamoulian, Rouben   13, 254
Manon Lescaut   79, 255
Manson, Marylin   9, 187
Marais, Jean   142, 159, 166, 167, 168, 169, 170, 171, 173, 200
Marais, Marin   198
Marchand, Léopold   13, 15
Marguenat (de), Jean   253
Mariage de Figaro, Le   80, 255
Mariano, Luis   ix, 10, 52, 56, 64, 102, 105, 113, 115, 116, 117, 118, 119, 127, 129, 130, 131, 133, 135, 136, *137–43*, 145, 151, 154, 236, 237

Marinella   9, 115, 117, 118, *120*, 122, 255
Marker, Chris   174
Marlène   117, 255
Marseille mes amours   52, 255
Martineau, Jacques   206, 214, 218, 219, 221, 222, 245, 251, 254
Martinet, Henri   119, 126
Mas, Jeanne   241
Masque d'Hollywood, Le   13, 255
Massenet, Jules   84
Mastroianni, Chiara   x, 219, 220
Mathot, Léon   29, 42, 250, 256
Mattes, Willy   115
Mauban, Maria   121
Maurel, Annie   159
Maury, Jacques   16
Max, Zappy   108
Max et les ferrailleurs   211, 255
May, Claude   44, 48
May, Mathilda   171
Meerson, Lazare   68
Meilhac, Henri   10, 25
Méliès, Georges   30, 79, 248, 251
Mercanton, Louis   9, 29, 253
Méré, Pierre   250
Merkès, Marcel   56, 149
Mérimée, Prosper   193
Merry Widow, The   25, 255, 261
Mesnier, Paul   115, 260
Meyer, Jean   80, 255
Micheyl, Mick   64, 106, 111
Mignon (1906)   79, 255
Mignon (1912)   79, 255
Million, Le   viii, 2, 3, 4, 36, 111, 255
Milton, Georges   8, 10, 29, 30, 42
Minnelli, Vincente   145, 146, 162, 247, 248
Mirande, Yves   7, 53, 89, 247, 253
Mireille   59, 80, 255
Misérables, Les   255
Misraki, Paul   115
Miss Helyett   29, 255
Mistinguett   58, 129, 147, 149
Mitchell, Eddie   150, 151, 152
Mitry, Jean   3, 4, 104, 111, 251
Mitterrand, Frédéric   191, 192, 193, 235, 254
Moix, Yann   236, 257

Molière 3, 186, 200, 203, 204, 235
Môme, La 59, 68, 235, 236, 237, 255
Mon amour est près de toi 114, 118, 255
Monca, Georges 29, 255
Mondo di notte, Il 255
Monroe, Marilyn 162, 166, 172
Monsieur Batignole 241, 255
Montagné, Gilbert 225, 241
Montand, Yves 64, 105, 113, 171
Montazel, Pierre 9, 64, 104, 115, 130, 254, 256, 257
Monte Carlo 25, 255
Monte Carlo Baby 90, 255
Montgomery, Robert 120, 254
Montmartre-sur-Seine 9, *61–2*, 255
Moreau, Jeanne 109
Moreno, Dario 149, 183
Morgan, Michèle 243
Moross, Jerome 153
Morte a Venezia 255
Moses und Aaron 255
Mouloudji, Marcel 64
Mozart, Wolfgang Amadeus 118, 200, 233
Murger, Henri 79
Muriel ou le temps d'un retour 162, 255
Musica de siempre 64, 255
Musique en tête 103, 104, 255
Musso, Jeff 58, 257
Mussorgsky, Modeste 84, 194

Nalpas, Mario 68, 259
Nanty, Isabelle 208
Naples au baiser de feu 117, 255
Napoléon vu par Abel Gance 255
Nelly et Monsieur Arnaud 211, 256
Nerval, Michel 160, 189, 258
Neuf garçons, un cœur 60, 256
Nicoletta 212
Nissoti, Arys 68
Noé, Yvan 58, 75, 249, 253
Noël-Noël 108
Nohain, Jean 106, 107
Nous irons à Deauville 102, 256
Nous irons à Monte-Carlo ix, 90, 91, *92–3*, 94, 98, 99, 256
Nous irons à Paris ix, 9, 90, 91, 93, 94, *98–102*, 256

Novarro, Ramón 139, 142
Nu comme un ver 42, 256
Nuits de Paris, Les 104, 256
Nuits fauves, Les 218, 256
Nyssen, Jean-Jacques 228

Obal, Max 68, 251
Offenbach, Jacques 10, 29, 68, 79, 87, 88
Ogier, Bulle 186
Oh! Qué mambo 149, 183, 256
On connaît la chanson ix, 9, *205–8*, 209, 225, 235, 256
On the Town 146, 163, 256
On va s'aimer x, 223, *224–5*, 226, 235, 241, 256
Opéra de quat'sous viii, *22–5*, 256
Opium 235, 236, *239*, 256
Orfeo 195, 256
Orval, Claude 58, 59, 103, 104, 255, 260
Otello 256
Otero, Carlos 111
Ouvrard, Gaston 206
Ozep, Fedor 58, 247
Ozon, François 205, 206, 210, 211, 212, 213, 215, 216, 222, 224, 247

Pabst, Georg Wilhelm 21, 22, 23, 24, 251, 256
Pagliero, Marcello 104, 110, 258
Pagnol, Marcel 51, 56, 125, 126, 249
Pallu, Georges 29, 257
Panique au music-hall 104, *111–12*, 256
Parade d'amour 25, 256
Parapluies de Cherbourg, Les x, 8, 9, 11, 157, 159, 160, *161–2*, 163, 166, 169, 170, 172, 173, 176, 182, 220, 221, 256
Parély, Mila 62
Paris chante toujours viii, ix, 9, *64*, 104, *105–6*, 107, 113, 116, 130, 152, 256
Parisian Life 256, 261
Parisiennes, Les 151, 152, 256
Parking ix, 160, 168, *170–1*, 173, 178, 189, 256
Paroles et musique ix, 160, *187–9*, 256
Parsifal 257
Pascal, Gisèle 91

Pas de week-end pour notre amour   141, 257
Pasquali, Fred   99
Passe ton bac d'abord   231, 257
Pas sur la bouche (1931)   29, *33–4*, 257
Pas sur la bouche (2003)   x, 206, *208–10*, 214, 222, 257
Pastina, Giorgio   75, 253
Pattes blanches   28, 257
Peau d'âne   ix, 30, 160, *166–9*, 170, 171, 173, 174, 257
Pédale douce   218, 257
Péguy, Charles   53, 239, 248
Péguy, Robert   248
Pépé le Moko   58–9, 257
Perles de la couronne, Les   65, 257
Perrault, Charles   166
Perret, Léonce   29, 248
Perrey, Mireille   59
Perrin, Jacques   159, 163, 166, 188
Peter et Sloane   241
Peters Sisters, The   100, 101, 102
Petit, Roland   145, 146, 147, 148
Petit Café, Le   15, 257
Petit Louis   116
Philibert, Nicolas   241, 252
Philipe, Gérard   110, 142
Phi-Phi   29, 257
Piaf, Édith   viii, 10, 11, 57, 59, *60–6*, 106, 113, 127, 137, 146, 151, 206, 236, 245
Pialat, Maurice   231, 257, 261
Piccoli, Michel   159, 163, 169
Pierreux, Jacqueline   133
Pietri, Julie   241
Pigalle-Saint-Germain-des-Prés   89, 104, *109–10*, 257
Pills, Jacques   10, 11, 16, 30, 35, 43, 44, 45, 47, 49, 51, 53, 55, 64, 65, 74, 116, 129, 146
Pingault, Claude   115
Piollet, Serge   151, 248
Placard, Le   218, 257
Playboy of Paris   15, 257
Ploquin, Raoul   15, 251, 253
Plume au vent   ix, 115, 130, 131, *132–5*, 257
Podium   236, 239, 240, 257

Poelvoorde, Benoît   239
Poitrenaud, Jacques   151, 256
Polanski, Roman   168, 258
Pollet, Jean-Daniel   151, 260
Polo   228
Ponnelle, Jean-Pierre   191
Potter, Dennis   206
Pottier, Richard   89, 102, 114, 115, 250, 251, 254, 255, 258, 261
Pouic-Pouic   102, 257
Pouponnière, La   7, 257
Préjean, Albert   2, 10, 23, 24, 33, 42, 68
Prends la route   viii, 16, 35, *44–5, 48–50*, 257
Prénom Carmen   193, 257
Presley, Elvis   152, 153
Prévert, Jacques   29, 75, 109, 110
Prévert, Pierre   29, 75, 109, 110, 247
Prévost, Daniel   208
Prince de Minuit   6, 257
Princesse Tam-Tam   viii, 68, *71–4*, 257
Printemps, Yvonne   15, 87
Printemps à Paris   75, 104, 257
Puccini, Giacomo   80, 192
Pujol, René   9, 32, 52, 53, 252, 259, 260

Quai des orfèvres   257
Quand j'étais chanteur   236, *240*, 241, 257
Quatorze juillet, Le   2, 23, 257
Quatre jours à Paris   115, 141, 257
Quitte ou double   104, *108*, 258

Rabenalt, Arthur Maria   115, 136, 248, 254, 260
Radiguet, Raymond   235, 239
Raft, George   102
Ragin, Derek Lee   202
Rameau, Jean-Philippe   242
Rampling, Charlotte   215, 216
Rappeneau, Jean-Paul   200, 250
Ray, Nicholas   150, 152, 254, 258
Raynaud, Fernand   56
Rebel Without a Cause   258
Rech, Lou   230
Red, Axelle   225
Reinert, Emil-Edwin   252
Reinhardt, David   238
Reinhardt, Django   67, 230, 238, 243

Renaud, Line   64, 106
Rendez-vous à Grenade   115, 137, 141, 258
Rendez-vous au tas de sable   ix, 160, *187*, 189, 258
Renoir, Jean   24, 64, 65, 235, 243, 250, 252
Repulsion   168, 258
Resnais, Alain   9, 29, 162, 168, 174, 205, 206, 207, 208, 209, 212, 222, 225, 247, 253, 255, 256, 257, 261
Rêves d'amour   79, 258
Reynolds, Debbie   62
Richard, Firmine   210
Richard, Nathalie   177
Riedmann, Gerhard   136
Rigaud, Francis   102, 256
Rigoletto   79, 258
Rimsky, Nicolas   29, 208, 257
Rimsky-Korsakov, Nikolaï   84
Rivers, Fernand   58, 249, 258
Rivette, Jacques   11, 160, 175, 176, 177, 178, 184, 249, 253
Robbins, Jerome   164, 261
Robert, Yves   110
Robin, Muriel   215, 216
Roddam, Franc   248
Rode, Alfred   104, 152, 249, 251
Roeg, Nicolas   248
Rogers, Ginger   37
Roi danse, Le   198, *203–4*, 235, 258
Roi des galéjeurs, Le   52, 258
Rojo, Tatiana   227
Rolland, Romain   80
Romance, Viviane   117
Romance de Paris   74, 75, 77, 97, 258
Roman d'un tricheur, Le   58, 258
Roman Holiday   90, 258
Ronde des heures, La   123, 258
Rose rouge, La (cabaret)   109, 110
Rose rouge, La (film)   104, *110*
Rosi, Francesco   249
Rossi, Tino   10, 52, 56, 64, 66, 75, 91, 102, 106, *113–27*, 129, 130, 131, 132, 136, 137, 138, 139, 140, 141, 143, 151, 154, 237, 241, 244
Roue, La   80, 258
Route du Bonheur, La   130

Route enchantée, La   7, 74, 75, *76–7*, 258
Roy, Jean-Claude   75, 104, 257
Rozier, Jacques   155, 162, 247
Rue sans joie, La   58, 258
Rue sans nom, La   58, 258
Ruiz, Olivia   228
Russell, Jane   162, 166, 248
Russell, Ken   248
Ruttman, Walter   17, 251
Ryder, Alexandre   123, 258

Saad, Margit   136
Sablon, Jean   106
Sabrina   241
Sagnier, Ludivine   210, 218
Saint-Cyr, Renée   28
Saint-Saëns, Camille   96
Salieri, Antonio   200
Salkin, Pascale   182
Salvador, Henri   92, 100, 101
Sanda, Dominique   169
Sandrich, Marc   126, 172, 253, 259
Sandy   160, 189, 258
Sang d'un poète, Le   168, 258
Santillan, Antonio   256
Sardou, Michel   206, 233
Sartre, Jean-Paul   109, 110
Sautet, Claude   104, 211, 249, 250, 255, 256, 260
Savall, Jordi   200
Schmitt, Tchavolo   230
Schneider, Paul   219
Schneider, Romy   211
Schönberg, Arnold   192
Schubert, Franz   79, 119, 120, 125, 126
Schüfftan, Eugen   15, 41
Scotese, Giuseppe Maria   103, 247
Scout toujours   241, 258
Sérénade   79, 258
Sérénade aux nuages   ix, 117, 118, 120, 122, 241, 258
Sérénade au Texas   115, 141, 258
Serrault, Michel   102
Servaës, Ernest   80, 255
Sevilla, Carmen   131, 133, 141
Sexe faible, Le   36, 258
Seyrig, Delphine   166, 168, 181, 182, 185
Sfar, Joann   236, 252

Shaffer, Peter   200
Sheila   150, 151, 212, 239
Show Girl in Hollywood   13, 258
Siegel, Don   152, 252
Siksou, Benjamin   225
Simon, René   129
Simone (de la), Albin   228
Simonelli, Giorgio   130, 258
Simons, Moïse   44
Sinatra, Frank   137, 237
Sinfonie der Grosstadt, Die   251
Sins of the Fathers   15, 258
Siodmak, Robert   9, 13, 29, 35, 36, 37, 42, 250, 256, 258, 261
Sirène des tropiques, La   68, 259
Sirène du Mississippi, La   211, 259
Siri, Florent-Emilio   236, 250
Si tu veux   7, 55, 258
Si Versailles m'était conté   64, 65, 258
Smiling Lieutenant, The   25, 259
Snow White and the Seven Dwarfs   9, 166, 167, 259
Soirs de Paris   104, 259
Solidor, Suzy   61
Solomon and Sheba   152, 259
Some Like It Hot   172, 259
Son dernier Noël   115, 117, 119, 259
Sous les toits de Paris   2, 3, 5, 14, 23, 32, 36, 57, 259
Souza Barros (de), Carlos Alberto   103, 247
Spillane, Mickey   147
Stars 80   240–1, 259
Stars 80, la suite   241, 259
Steinhoff, Hans   29, 32, 249
Stelli, Jean   115, 251, 260
Stengel, Christian   74, 79, 108, 252, 254, 258
Stiller, Mauritz   15, 259
Straub, Jean-Marie   192, 255, 261
Straus, Oscar   15, 25
Strauss, Johann   10, 15, 115, 129, 131, 133, 136
Street of Sin   15, 259
Sturridge, Charles   248
Sullivan, Ed   130, 137
Sur quel pied danser   223, 228, 259

Swing   229–31, 259
Syberberg, Hans-Jürgen   257
Symphonie fantastique, La   viii, 79, 87, 88, 235, 259

Tabet, Georges   16, 30, 35, 43, 44, 45, 47, 49, 51, 53, 55, 64, 74, 116, 129
Tarkovsky, Andrei   247
Tautou, Audrey   208
Tchao Pantin   188, 259
Teeyah   227
Temple, Julien   248
Testud, Kostia   223, 259
Thiele, Wilhelm   9, 14, 17, 19, 250, 251
Thill, Georges   85, 193
Thomas, Frank   243
Timsit, Patrick   240
Titin des Martigues   viii, 52, 54, 259
Toi, c'est moi   viii, 9, 43–8, 208, 259
Toi, moi, les autres   x, 223, 225–7, 234, 235, 259
Top Hat   172, 259
Tosca   ix, 84, 93, 192, 195–7, 259
Toscan du Plantier, Daniel   191, 192
Tourbillon de Paris   90, 91, 94, 96, 259
Tourments   115, 117, 259
Tournée des grands-ducs, La   104, 259
Tourneur, Maurice   261
Tous les matins du monde   198, 200, 201, 203, 235, 259
Tous vedettes!   160, 259
Tout le monde il est beau, tout le monde il est gentil   186, 259
Tout va très bien Madame la Marquise   90, 260
Tragédie de Carmen, La   260
Traviata, La   260
Trenet, Charles   7, 67, 68, 69, 71, 73, 74–7, 89, 96, 103, 106, 107, 113, 127, 146, 236
Trente et quarante   130, 241, 260
Trois de la Canebière   56, 149, 260
Trois de la marine   51, 53, 56, 149, 260
Trois Masques, Les   2, 260
Trois places pour le 26   ix, 160, 171–2, 173, 260
Trois Valses, Les   15, 29, 260

Trollflöjten 260
Tronc, Nicolas 182
Truffaut, François 136, 145, 182, 183, 211, 221, 248, 251, 252, 259
Tuel, Laurent 236, 254
Tzarévitch, Le 260

Ulmer, Georges 64, 106
Un clair de lune à Maubeuge 151, 260
Un cœur en hiver 260
Un de la Canebière viii, 9, 51, *52–3*, 55–6, 260
Une balle au cœur 151, 260
Une chambre en ville 160, *169–70*, 171, 173, 219, 220, 228, 260
Une chante, l'autre pas, L' ix, 160, *178–81*, 260
Une femme est une femme ix, 160, *175–6*, 177, 221, 260
Une fille sur la route 115, 130, 131, *132*, 260
Une histoire simple 211, 260
Une java 58, *59*, 61, 62, 260
Une nuit aux Baléares 115, 131, 260
Un grand amour de Beethoven viii, 9, 79, *80–4*, 85, 87, 235, 260
Univers de Jacques Demy, L' 160, 260

Vadim, Roger 151, 168, 250
Vagabond King, The 15, 261
Vajda, Ladislas 115, 248
Valentin, Albert 58, 79, 249, 251
Valentino, Rudolph 116, 139, 142
Vallin, Ninon 129
Valse de Paris, La 25, 79, *87–8*, 235, 261
Valse royale viii, 25, *27–8*, 261
Van Gogh 261
Van Parys, Georges 44, 75
Vanzi, Luigi 103, 255
Varda, Agnès 11, 160, 162, 174, 178, 179, 180, 250, 251, 253, 260
Varda, Rosalie 159
Vartan, Eddie 152, 154
Vartan, Sylvie 150, 151, 152, 154, 155, 206, 212, 213, 240

Vassil, Anton 223, 234, 254
Vaucorbeil (de), Max 250
Veber, Francis 218, 257
Ventura, Ray 67, *89–102*, 103, 110, 116, 149, 252
Verdi, Giuseppe 194
Vergez, Gérard 238, 248
Vergiß wenn Du Kannst 130
Vernay, Robert 104, 115, 247, 258
Vernon, Howard 111
Veuve joyeuse, La 9, *25–6*, 261
Vian, Boris 109, 110
Viard, Karin 215, 216, 233
Viard, Stéphane 240, 247
Vidor, Charles 146, 253
Vidor, King 152, 259
Vie de bohème, La 79, 261
Vie en rose, La 66, 255, 261
Vie est un roman, La 205
Vie parisienne, La 29, 261
Vigny, Benno 74, 248
Vigo, Jean 241, 261
Vincy, Raymond 52, 53, 126, 138
Violettes impériales 115, 131, 137, 141, 261
Visconti, Luchino 199, 255
Voie lactée, La 168, 261
Volpone 261
von Aschenbach, Gustav 199
Von heute auf morgen 192, 261

Wagner, Reinhardt 243
Wagner, Richard 243
Wakhevitch, Georges 84
Walbrook, Anton 136
Waltzerkrieg 15, 261
Weigl, Petr 191
Weill, Kurt 21, 22, 23
West Side Story 163, 164, 261
Wilder, Billy 66, 152, 172, 254, 259, 261
Wilder, Victor 10
Wild in the Country 153, 261
Wild Ones, The 150, 261
Willemetz, Albert 15, 29, 34, 47
Wilson, Lambert 205, 208

Wise, Robert   261
Wolff, Hans   16, 115, 250
Woman from Moscow, The   15, 261
Wonder Bar   13, 261
Wulschleger, Henri   260
Wyler, William   90, 153, 249, 258

Xanrof, Léon   25

Yanne, Jean   160, 186, 250, 259
Yvain, Maurice   29, 114, 208
Yvan Audouard   155

Zazie   226
Zeffirelli, Franco   256, 260
Zelnick, Frederic   136, 248
Zéro de conduite   241, 261
Zouzou   viii, *68–71*, 261
Żuławski, Andrzej   85, 191, 194, 249

www.ingramcontent.com/pod-product-compliance
Lightning Source LLC
Chambersburg PA
CBHW041730300426
44115CB00021B/2965